CW01471693

SURVEY OF LONDON

MONOGRAPH 18

CHARTER
79 HOUSE.
Gainsborough 1748.

SURVEY OF LONDON

GENERAL EDITOR: ANDREW SAINT

MONOGRAPH 18

The Charterhouse

Philip Temple

Published for English Heritage, 2010
by Yale University Press, New Haven and London
on behalf of the Paul Mellon Centre for Studies in British Art, London

First published 2010 by
YALE UNIVERSITY PRESS
302 Temple Street, New Haven CT06511
47 Bedford Square, London WC1B 3DP
for
ENGLISH HERITAGE

Library of Congress Cataloging-in-Publication Data
Temple, Philip, 1957–
The Charterhouse / Philip Temple.
p. cm. -- (Survey of London)
Includes bibliographical references and index.
ISBN 978–0–300–16722–1 (alk. paper)
1. Charterhouse (Smithfield, London, England) 2. Smithfield
(London, England)–Buildings, structures, etc. 3. Historic
buildings--England–London. 4. Architecture–England–London.
5. London (England)–Buildings, structures, etc. I. Title.
DA687.C4T46 2010
942.1′2--DC22
2010027780

Designed by Sophie Kullmann
Printed in China through World Print

Preface

This account of the Charterhouse—throughout its long and august history successively monastery, mansion and almshouse—completes the Survey of London's work on the Clerkenwell area. It complements the two 'parish' volumes published in 2008 (*South and East Clerkenwell* and *Northern Clerkenwell and Pentonville*). The history of the Charterhouse's site and the complexity of its buildings indicated a different approach in scale and treatment to these. For that reason it appears in the Survey's monograph series—only the third such volume to appear since the war.

It had to be asked whether there was enough to add to existing knowledge to justify such a study in the first place. Much has been written over the centuries about the Charterhouse and its buildings, some of it by eminent scholars and archaeologists. In the late 1940s, the archaeological investigations made possible by the impending reinstatement of the buildings (burned in the Second World War) led to a significant reassessment of the monastery layout, and gave some impetus to unravelling the post-Dissolution history of the site. But it was soon apparent that many things were still unresolved. The post-war work itself, moreover, had become of interest, not least for its idiosyncratic approach to restoration. Nineteenth-century additions and alterations, often ignored or derided by past writers, could now be given fair consideration. Another incentive was the abundance of archive material relating to Sutton's Hospital, which had only been catalogued after the war and still not yet been made much use of. Here was an exceptionally detailed record of the buildings and governing institution over four hundred years. All these factors suggested that a comprehensive new study was worthwhile.

Though the format is identical to that of the parish volumes, the content is in parts more expansive, archaeological, and speculative, reflecting the complexity of the subject and the often fragmentary nature of the fabric, and of the documentary evidence for the period before Sutton's Hospital was founded in 1611–14. The historical and architectural range is wide, from the fourteenth-century Carthusian monks' cells to the most recent accommodation for Brothers of the hospital, completed at the start of the twenty-first century. There is new material on aspects of the site which have eluded or been underplayed by past historians, including details of the occupation by the office of the King's Tents in the 1540s and the subsequent development of the mansion known as Howard House—after Thomas Howard, fourth Duke of Norfolk. As well as Sutton's Hospital itself, which now occupies less than half the monastery site, the book describes the development of the less well-known buildings and institutions at the Charterhouse: a second, long-demolished mansion, Rutland House; Merchant Taylors' School (in occupation from the 1870s to the 1930s); and the Medical College of St Bartholomew's Hospital.

The project has involved several staff over a number of years. Research, investigation and drafting of text were carried out by Stephen Porter, initially with the assistance of the late Catherine Steeves, and by Harriet Richardson, under John Greenacombe as General Editor of the Survey. Following Dr Porter's retirement from the Survey, additional research and reappraisal, particularly on the post-suppression period, Howard House and the historiography of the Charterhouse, was undertaken by Philip Temple, who has written and edited the present text and made the inventory transcripts. The drawings have mainly been prepared by George Wilson and Helen Jones, with additional work by Malcolm Dickson and Andrew Donald. All of the specially commissioned photography is by Derek Kendall, and the photo-rectification for the interior view of the Norfolk Cloister is by David Andrews. Many of the images were prepared for publication by Charles Walker. Copy editing was carried out by Hester Higton, and the book was designed by Sophie Kullmann.

Baroness Andrews obe
Chair
English Heritage

Acknowledgements

Many institutions and individuals have helped in various ways with the preparation of this volume. Their help is gratefully acknowledged. Special gratitude is above all due to the governors and staff of Sutton's Hospital in Charterhouse, without whose support and cooperation over a number of years the project could not have been completed, and particularly the successive Masters of Charterhouse during that time: Mr Eric Harrison, Professor James Spencer Malpas and Dr James P. S. Thomson. Thanks are also due to the following institutions and individuals, and others cited in the references at the end of the book:

Arundel Castle Archives (the Duke of Norfolk's Archives); Bodleian Library; British Architectural Library, Royal Institute of British Architects; British Library; British Museum; Cambridge University Library; Carlisle Record Office; Charterhouse School; Chetham's Library; College of Arms; Guildhall Library, Corporation of London; Institute of Historical Research; Islington Local History Centre; Lambeth Palace Library; London Library; London Metropolitan Archives, Corporation of London; Medical College of St Bartholomew's Hospital Trust; Merchant Taylors' Company; Merchant Taylors' School; Museum of London; Museum of London Archaeology Service (now Museum of London Archaeology); The National Archives; National Monuments Record Centre, English Heritage; Norfolk Record Office; Queen Mary and Westfield College, University of London; Royal College of Physicians Library; St Bartholomew's Hospital Archives; Society for the Protection of Ancient Buildings; Spencer Research Library, University of Kansas; Staffordshire Record Office; Surrey History Centre.

Jeremy Ashbee; Geoffrey Brown; Karen Cook; Susan Foister; Nick Davie; Claire Gapper; Mark Girouard; Ken Griffiths; Tara Hamling; Maurice Howard; Michael Kerney; Stephen Little; Pam Ovenden; Stephen Porter; Susan Powell; John Martin Robinson; William G. Streitberger; Heather Warne; Adam Webster; Adrian White; Steve Wiles; Richard Williams; Thomas Woodcock.

Owners of photographs and other illustrations reproduced in this volume are acknowledged in the List of Illustrations.

Contents

List of Illustrations

Illustrations are copyright of English Heritage except where otherwise indicated. NMR denotes images held at the National Monuments Record Centre, Swindon

Frontispiece. 'The Charterhouse' by Thomas Gainsborough. © Coram in the care of the Foundling Museum, London/The Bridgeman Art Library

SURVEY OF LONDON

MONOGRAPH 18

Introduction

Founded in 1370–1, the London Charterhouse was one of a handful of Carthusian monasteries in medieval England, out of several hundred throughout Europe. Of those few it was the biggest and best endowed, and, while its architecture, in the Carthusian tradition, was unspectacular, the site was one of the top prizes of the Dissolution in the London area. The religious community was disbanded in 1538, three years after its charismatic prior John Houghton was hanged, drawn and quartered at Tyburn, and in 1545 the former priory passed into the ownership of Sir Edward North, later Baron North, one of the key players in the dispersal of monastic properties throughout the country. What North created from it was, under its later name of Howard House, one of the political power-houses of Tudor and early Stuart England and, for a time in the 1570s–80s, a centre of London Catholicism. Then, in 1611, this private palace was sold to the aged and fabulously wealthy Thomas Sutton, who had plans for something very different.

A lifetime after they had closed behind the last monks, the gates opened to admit eighty old men and half as many young boys to what was now a richly endowed almshouse and school of surpassing magnificence. This was Protestant charity on a scale almost to suggest atonement for the suppression, though in another reading it was the brainchild of a man intent on keeping his fortune out of his relations' hands. There remains something mysterious about Sutton's real intentions. So patently unsuitable were the buildings for their new purpose that the greater part of the living accommodation had to be converted at great expense from stables and other outbuildings, leaving the mansion house itself relatively unaltered and under-used. Was this what Sutton planned, or had he intended literally to house the poor in a palace? Barely had a start been made when he died, leaving others to see the project through.

Perceptions have long been coloured by the coincidence of an almshouse for men having been founded on the site of a dissolved monastery, for the parallel between the priory with its cowled brethren and the almshouse with its gowned Poor Brothers is such that it is easy to overlook the three-quarters of a century separating the two institutions and the absence of any other than superficial similarity. To Archdeacon William Hale, Preacher in the 1830s and later Master, Sutton's Hospital was a 'Monastery without moroseness'.[1] Thackeray, an old boy of the school, played up to the conceit in the 1850s, with Colonel Newcome 'in the habit of a Poor Brother of Grey Friars', that 'ancient foundation of the time of James I'.[2] A commemorative plaque put up much later in the Chapel lists the Carthusian priors side by side with the Masters of Sutton's Hospital. As late as the 1920s, it was possible for the then Master, the Rev. Gerald S. Davies, to imagine that stools and tables in the Library were relics of the priory, as if the upheavals and changes of ownership in the sixteenth century had never happened.[3] Even today, it is probably true to say that the Charterhouse is more often thought of as a former monastery than as the great courtier's house which for many years it was.

Architecturally, a great house is what it remains. Loosely planned around a series of courtyards, such a house is not to be judged on external magnificence (of which there is little), still less as an exercise in architectural style or composition. While containing a Great Hall, Great Chamber and suites of

1. The Charterhouse and environs in 1999, looking north. At the west of the site is the Admiral Ashmore Building, under construction

grand rooms, it is also to be understood as a caravanserai for periodic occupation, with various sets of 'lodgings' and extensive ancillary buildings. Parts of this house already existed when North took over, having been built as the guest-house, lay brothers' quarters and service ranges of the priory, together with detached stabling, stores and workshops. The rest, as with many houses converted from monasteries,[4] had no claim to architectural originality or innovation. In addition to this main house, there is now much that has been added by Sutton's foundation, including the separate nineteenth-century ranges of Pensioners' and Preacher's Courts. Each phase of the complex building history of the site has its own significance and claim to attention.

* * *

Much has been written about the Charterhouse since one of the expelled monks, Dom Maurice Chauncy, compiled the first version of his history of the last years of the priory in the late 1540s. Most of this writing has been concerned chiefly with the priory, or with Sutton's Hospital from an essentially institutional angle. Conversely, Howard House has received little attention, and most of that has focused on the fourth Duke of Norfolk and his involvement in the plot against Elizabeth I apparently fomented by the Italian banker Roberto di Ridolfi. The actual buildings, monastic and later, were slow to attract serious scholarly attention—perhaps a reflection of their retired location and public unfamiliarity with them. Early architectural investigations were mainly the work of staff members or ex-pupils. Consequently, when half of Norfolk's garden gallery or 'cloister', including the remains of two monk's cells, was demolished in the early 1870s the event was hardly noticed outside the Charterhouse itself. That changed as the growing movement for recording and preserving historic buildings began to take off. In 1880, the Society for Photographing Relics of Old London published a dozen views of the buildings, and a few years later the Charterhouse found itself at the centre of a heated preservationist campaign, when collapsing revenues led the governors to try to sell off most of the site for redevelopment. The threat to the Charterhouse was averted. But many aspects of the buildings had still to be fully investigated and recorded when fire destroyed most of the interior in 1941.

The Charterhouse before the fire was a remarkable survival, but it was no untouched time capsule. Considerable historic fabric existing when Sutton's Hospital was founded had gone, as had a number of buildings and interiors created for the foundation itself in the seventeenth century, including one building on which Sir Christopher Wren had advised. What survived had been subject to the gradual attrition which often affects institutional complexes. All the old buildings to the north and west of the house itself had been demolished, and there were no fine interiors left intact from the Howard House period apart from the Great Hall and Great Chamber, though some panelling and ornate chimneypieces survived. When serious study of the buildings began to be made in the late nineteenth century, attention naturally focused on the oldest remains, and it was mistakenly thought that most of the house was in fact of monastic origin, overturning an earlier understanding that most of it was post-suppression. This may have been due to reluctance, perhaps unconscious, to accept the Charterhouse as essentially a secular house of the sixteenth century rather than a medieval priory. If so, it doubtless had something to do both with the romanticized appeal of the monastic past and with the moral crisis faced by Sutton's Hospital in the mid-century, when its character was brought under hostile scrutiny. That scrutiny, occasioned by a piece in Dickens's *Household Words*, resulted in a characteristically Victorian reinvention of the institution and a new reverence for its origins and traditions, which favoured the suggestion of continuity from monastic times.

2. Sutton's Hospital. Entrance Court front to Master's Court, looking east in 2003

To Robert Smythe in the early nineteenth century, one of the first authors to consider the buildings archaeologically, the remains of the monastery were fragmentary. Wash-house Court was the most substantial relic, but he pointed to other possible remnants, including traces of the Great Cloister and 'some parts of the basement of the Chapel'.[5] Similarly, in the 1830s the antiquarian Archdeacon Hale found no reason to doubt that large parts of the buildings, including Master's Court and the Great Hall, had been built by Lord North.[6] They did not look monastic. Wash-house Court was a different matter: 'the sign of a cross worked in brickwork, and an I.H.S.,[a] denote the ecclesiastical character of the building, and favours [sic] the conjecture of its being a part of the ancient monastery'.[7] He went further than Smythe, however, concluding that the Chapel itself had been part of the priory church, in his opinion the nave. Hale's analysis of the buildings was broadly similar to other early Victorian writers on the Charterhouse, with a consensus that North had done extensive building, including the Great Hall. In the 1840s, William Roper held up to scorn the belief (put about by the porter on guided tours) that the Upper Hall (now the Library) 'was formerly the refectory for the lay-brothers', though he conceded its 'gloomy and monastic air'.[8]

By the late 1860s, Hale's view had undergone a remarkable shift. He was now sure that Master's Court and the Hall were monastic, erected in the mid-fifteenth century for accommodating 'strangers'. The thick walls of these buildings, he explained, 'are rarely cut into for the purpose of alteration or repair without pieces of wrought masonry being brought to light, mullions, and transoms, pieces of pillars, and fragments of monuments, so numerous as to indicate that some important building had been destroyed'. Possibly, he thought, they had been built with stones from the Hospitaller priory of St John, in Clerkenwell, sacked by the Poll Tax rebels in 1381, 'supposing them to have been lying waste'.[9]

Hale's belief that the old buildings were almost entirely monastic took hold, notwithstanding this trickle of physical evidence that they were extensively built from the wreckage of the Carthusian priory itself. It received support in the 1880s from William Morris's associate George Wardle, who saw North firmly as an adaptor of the priory rather than a builder, even to the extent of identifying the Great Chamber as having been the prior's reception room.[10] In the same decade, the monastic interpretation was taken further, and given wider currency, by the architect R. H. Carpenter, an Old Carthusian with a particular interest in the buildings. Carpenter identified Master's Court as the monastic Little Cloister, with a guest-house on its west side and a 'guesten hall' on its north. This interpretation was enshrined in his plan drawn in 1888 for the historical account by Dom Lawrence Hendriks, *The London Charterhouse*. Based on Francis Carter's 1613 plan of Sutton's Hospital, it shows the core buildings to be monastic, with only minor additions by Lord North or the Duke of Norfolk.[11]

Carpenter accepted the traditional identification of Sutton's Hospital Chapel with the church, though, unlike Hale, he took the view that it was the choir not the nave, and therefore that the north aisle was the site of the medieval sacristy. This last could be deduced from a source long known to historians: a plan of the priory and its water-supply system, drawn up in the fifteenth century (Ills 12, 13).[b] He explained the ante-chapel at the west end as having been the lay brothers' choir, and identified the blocked door on the south side of the Chapel as the lay brothers' entrance to the church.

Carpenter's interpretation was largely endorsed by the architect George Patrick, honorary secretary of the British Archaeological Association, in a paper read at the Charterhouse in 1896.[13] A refinement of Carpenter's thinking was put forward in 1902 by another architect and Old Carthusian, Basil Champneys.[14] He suggested that Master's Court had replaced the Little Cloister in the early sixteenth century, in order to provide a guest hall, guest chambers and 'Prior's lodgings', together with a buttery

[a] There is no evidence that an 'S' ever existed (see pages 121–2).

[b] The plan was examined at a meeting of the Society of Antiquaries in 1746. It was apparently given to Nicholas Mann, Master of Sutton's Hospital in 1737–53, from whose executors it passed to a later Master, the Rev. Samuel Salter, who gave it to the hospital, where it remains.[12]

and offices; in the same period, the lay brothers who had lodged around the Little Cloister moved to new accommodation in Wash-house Court. In effect, the whole of the buildings around Wash-house and Master's Courts had comprised a lay zone, reflecting the increasing importance of outsiders in the latter years of the priory. As for the Chapel, Champneys had no reason to doubt its provenance, and explained the ante-chapel as having been for the use of guests attending services.

William F. Taylor, in *The Charterhouse of London* (1912), accepted the by now conventional notion that the post-suppression owners had merely 'adapted the old monastic buildings to the secular dwelling', without going into any detail, though repeating Hale's theory about stones from St John's priory.[15] As yet, any understanding of the buildings was informed by very little documentary evidence, with the notable exception of the water-supply plan. Hendriks had published transcripts of some documents, including a post-suppression account of the dispersal and allocation of the priory's contents and buildings. This was the statement of William Dale, keeper of the dissolved priory, an important enough document. But there was still little on which to base a secure building history. This was to change with the coming to light of a short history or chronicle of the priory compiled by one of the monks in the late fifteenth century.[16]

Even as Taylor wrote, Davies, the then Master, was working on his history of the Charterhouse marking the tercentenary of Sutton's foundation, and his interim pamphlet took Taylor by surprise on the eve of his own book's appearance.[17] Publication having been delayed by the First World War, Davies's *Charterhouse in London* came out in 1921. It was the first fully balanced account of the Charterhouse, giving due weight to each main historical phase and attempting an analysis of the buildings. Replete with information, it was based on extensive research (though remarkably little from the early records of Sutton's Hospital), a lifetime's familiarity with the site and a good deal of lively conjecture. It has never been entirely superseded, though, as the historian Dom David Knowles put it in the 1950s, 'some of his judgments and opinions … were hazardous even when made, and have been rendered entirely meaningless by the documentary and architectural evidence that has come to light in recent years'.[18] Nevertheless, Davies's appreciation of the essentially post-monastic nature of the Master's Court ranges (though he excepted the Great Hall) marked a step forward in understanding the history of the buildings.

An amateur himself, Davies received some help from Sir William St John Hope, a monastic historian and archaeologist then of the highest repute, who had studied the medieval chronicle and had published in 1902 a detailed account and facsimile of the water-supply plan.[19] Hope, who was working on his own history of the Charterhouse and its buildings, died in 1919, leaving what might have been a great work of scholarship unfinished. The completed portion, edited by A. Hamilton Thompson, appeared in 1925 as *The History of the London Charterhouse from its Foundation until the Suppression of the Monastery*. It included a transcript and translation of much of the chronicle. In the same year, Alfred Clapham's account of the buildings in the West London inventory of the Royal Commission on Historical Monuments went further in elucidating the buildings than Davies had been able to do. Clapham confirmed the extensive nature of the sixteenth-century reconstruction. Unlike Davies and the late-Victorian historians, he was sure that the Great Hall was entirely post-monastic, and therefore neither Carpenter's guesten hall nor the monks' refectory, as Davies thought. He too had no qualms about the Chapel. No further work of importance was to be done on the buildings for many years, although the Charterhouse was to figure prominently in E. Margaret Thompson's study, *The Carthusians in England* (1930), which made use of the hitherto unexploited priory accounts at the Public Record Office.

The Second World War left most of the sometime Howard House a burned-out shell (Ills 3–6). Reconstruction, protracted by materials and labour shortages and the building-licence system, gave ample opportunity to pick over the site. Only then did doubts emerge about the Chapel. The train of discovery was set off by an attack of dry rot which necessitated digging up the floor of the Great Hall.[20] From the

THE DAMAGED BUILDINGS IN 1942:

3. Master's Court east range, looking north.
The walls show how extensively the sixteenth-century stone structure had been reconstructed in later centuries
4. The Great Hall under its temporary roof.
Leaning against the wall is the 1657 portrait of Thomas Sutton in the frame ornamented by Edward Blore in the early 1840s
5. The Library and Great Chamber under their temporary roof
6. Chapel Court, looking north-west

remains uncovered there,[c] it began to look as if the south walk of the Great Cloister had lain well south of its long-presumed position, and that the Chapel had originated as the comparatively narrow chapter-house at the north-east corner of the choir (as shown on the water-supply plan), which had been destroyed along with the rest of the church. Then a hidden squint was found in the Treasury over the ante-chapel, seemingly placed to have overlooked the high altar in the church. Confirmation came with the subsequent pinpointing of the altar site in Chapel Court, and the disinterment in May 1947 of the remains of the priory's founder Sir Walter Manny, where he had been buried at the foot of the altar step in 1372.

Thus far, the process of discovery and re-evaluation had been led by the architects commissioned to reinstate Sutton's Hospital, Paul Paget and the Hon. John Seely (from 1947, Lord Mottistone), on their own initiative. With the discovery of Manny's tomb, things were put on a more professional footing. In November 1947, with no immediate prospect of rebuilding, W. F. Grimes of the London Museum was invited to make further excavations.[22] The upshot was firm evidence for the footprints of the priory church and Little Cloister, and a radical revision of the accepted layout of the priory had to be made. In itself, this was something of a sensation, but it also demonstrated how the evidence offered by the water-supply plan had been misinterpreted in the past. Hope had brushed the plan aside as plain wrong where it conflicted with his preconceptions about the buildings' layout. But the reconstruction plan in Taylor's study had also set aside the evidence of the water plan, placing Cell A (the prior's cell) to the north of the frater instead of to the south. Taylor did not address the anomaly, remarking evasively that the prior's cell and frater were 'at the corner' of the cloister.[23]

More excavation was undertaken by Grimes in 1951. The findings from the excavations and new documentary research were celebrated in 1954 in a short book by David Knowles, with drawings and an account of the excavation by Grimes, *Charterhouse: The Medieval Foundation in the Light of Recent Discoveries*. In the restored buildings, the new-found outlines of the medieval structures were marked out on the floors and courtyards. It was now clear that the long-accepted identification of the Library with the site of the monks' (not lay brothers') frater was correct, though it had been based on false reasoning. Cell A had indeed stood on the south side of the frater. Clapham's dating of the Great Hall also seemed to be confirmed, because it was clearly built on the site of Cell A. Stripped of render, it was in any case revealed to have been built using stone from the demolished church and other priory buildings. Having largely established the true monastic plan, Knowles and Grimes went further, speculating on the whereabouts of extra cells dating from the last years of the priory, using hitherto unknown documentary evidence. Here, however, their conclusion now looks wrong.

As with Hope's work, the post-war study was curtailed. The book as it appeared was only a fragment of what might have been a full reassessment of the buildings. Knowles, who had been brought in at the suggestion of (Sir) Robert Birley, headmaster of Charterhouse School, was ill at ease with this sort of building history, acknowledging that 'all the best suggestions' had come from Seely and Paget, and that they were best qualified for the task. He was 'appalled' by the prospect of taking the story further, down to Edward Blore's alterations in the mid-nineteenth century, beyond his specialist field. Accordingly, John Summerson was approached but, although he undertook to research the early seventeenth-century history, the project petered out, chiefly because of the cost and the long time that it was taking to

[c] The salient finds were the foundations of the outer south-west corner of the Great Cloister and the east wall of the first cell in the west side of the cloister, Cell A. Further proof then emerged in the form of a monastic doorway in the wall of the Great Staircase compartment, standing across the supposed south cloister walk—clearly an anomaly. Knowles's comments about the significance of a 'watercourse' also found under the Great Hall, however, make no sense. According to his account, this watercourse was identified as the pipe shown on the medieval water-plan running obliquely from near the south-west corner of the Great Cloister to the south side of Cell A. In fact, it could not have been this pipe, being in the wrong place altogether: cutting through Cell A (on the site of the Great Hall), not running alongside it as on the plan. Nothing therefore could be inferred from it.[20]

catalogue the foundation's archives.[24] Consequently, the post-Sutton development of the buildings remained almost entirely obscure for many years. It was not until the late 1950s, when the architectural writer Arthur Oswald was given access to the records, that Francis Carter was identified as having been the architect of the conversion of Howard House into Sutton's Hospital in 1613–14. Thirty years later, some additional information appeared in a short pamphlet written by the then Master, Eric Harrison, and more valuable detail was given in Anthony Quick's history of Charterhouse School (1990).[25]

Since the work of Lawrence Hendriks and subsequently that of Thompson and Knowles, scholarly writing about English Carthusianism has become more dispassionate, and less concerned with the glory of the Carthusian martyrs. The most important recent work to focus specifically on the London Carthusians is by Andrew Wines, whose doctoral thesis 'The London Charterhouse in the Later Middle Ages: An Institutional History' (University of Cambridge, 1998) examines previously neglected material and has new insights into the priory's foundation, economics and character, including its ambivalent relationship with secular society. Recently, too, excavation by the Museum of London Archaeology Service has, among other things, brought more light to bear on the monastic layout, revealing evidence of successive buildings at the western edge of the precinct, probably including temporary structures from the early days of the priory, and has supplied a more detailed understanding of the design and construction of the cells in the Great Cloister. The findings are contained in a detailed monograph published in 2002.[26]

* * *

A complex building history: a history of change and attrition; a disastrous fire. What is left? Restoration by Seely and Paget began in the late 1940s. It was far from complete when Nikolaus Pevsner in the new *Buildings of England* series asserted that 'Most of the architectural damage can be repaired'. Restored, the Charterhouse did indeed 'again convey a vivid impression of a large rambling C16 mansion as they must have existed all round London'.[27] But many features had gone, along with the patina and eccentricities acquired over several centuries. Literal restoration, even with unlimited resources, would have been impossible. In the event, Seely and Paget not only restored and reinstated but also altered and reconfigured the damaged buildings in ways which may now seem capricious and misguided. Not surprisingly for the time, little respect was shown to the nineteenth-century alterations and embellishments. But the separate nineteenth-century ranges, unaffected by the fire, were also treated with disdain and partly demolished to supply building materials.

One of their main achievements involved something of a rediscovery of the buildings themselves. Before the war, Master's Court had presented an unromantic appearance, the Great Hall coated in cement render and the rest faced in plain Georgian brickwork. Now the underlying patchwork of masonry, most of it reused from the demolished priory buildings, was revealed. This was only one of the most startling aspects of a complete transformation of the buildings, inside and out. Delight at the restoration and the rediscovery of the monastic plan was unreserved. It was even suggested that the fire had not been an unmitigated disaster, and 'one can almost view the calamity as a blessing'—Oswald's verdict of 1959, endorsed more than 30 years later by Eric Harrison.[28] That seems Panglossian today, but, amid the shabbiness of post-war London, the effect must have been stunning. Within a few years, the critic Ian Nairn was to pronounce the restoration phoney: 'instant picturesqueness rather like one of those deep-frozen American dinners'.[29] Nairn's complaint may still ring true for the purist, but the effect is real enough, as Anthony Powell found on a visit in 1985: 'I went under an arch, entering a complex of utterly deserted quadrangles. It was like moving into the Fourth Dimension, several centuries back in Time, everything round about completely still, like a dream'.[30]

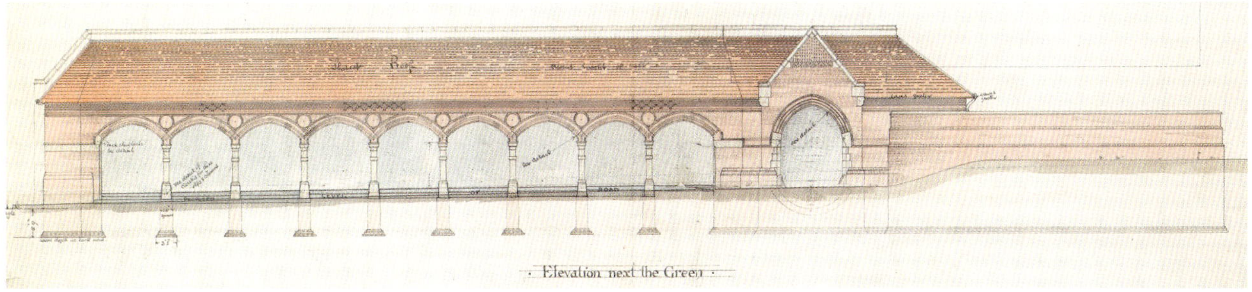

Though the monastic cloisters were destroyed after the closure of the priory in 1538, the cloister or arcaded walk has recurred at the site ever since, and was transplanted to the new Charterhouse School at Godalming in the 1870s. Most recently, the Admiral Ashmore Building, completed in 2000, incorporates a simplified arcade along its front

7. (*far left*) Norfolk Cloister. Built for the fourth Duke of Norfolk, *c.*1571, on the site of the monastic cloister, for recreation or meetings and access to the real-tennis court

8. (*left*) Chapel Cloister. Francis Carter, architect, 1613–14. For access to the Chapel from the main buildings; the arcade was open to Chapel Court until 1847

9. (*below left*) Preacher's Court. Redmond Pilkington, architect, late 1820s. For recreation and covered access to main hospital building

10. (*above*) Cloister at Merchant Taylors' School, providing covered access to main school building from north entrance lodge. Edward I'Anson, architect, 1873–5. *Demolished*

11. (*below*) Cloister beside the sunken garden, Medical College of St Bartholomew's Hospital. Easton and Robertson, architects, 1961–3. The cloister gives access to an earlier service tunnel crossing the college green

For all its faults, the restoration was a remarkable achievement in the circumstances, and did more than Pevsner had anticipated. The Charterhouse remains one of the major historic sites in London, both in the general sense that he described and for its associations: but also for several exceptional individual buildings and interiors, including the Chapel and the monastic Treasury, both undamaged by the fire; the restored Great Hall and Great Chamber; and the battered remnant of the Norfolk Cloister, a rare survival of a great Elizabethan garden gallery.

* * *

The aim of this monograph is to set out the history of the Charterhouse from the fourteenth century to the present, and, more particularly, to describe and explain the principal buildings. The first three chapters are designed to give a coherent account of the history of the site through its principal phases of institutional or private occupation, dealing with its changing character, the broader picture of development, building use and adaptation, and some individual demolished structures. Chapters IV to IX focus on specific parts of the fabric of Sutton's Hospital. In each case, the approach and level of detail varies, according to historical or architectural significance, completeness, and the nature of the documentary and physical evidence. Had the core buildings escaped the Second World War unscathed, a somewhat different approach might have been appropriate. As it is, there seems little point in trying to describe, let alone bring under scrutiny, all the documented alterations to buildings or interiors which no longer exist. The final three chapters are concerned with parts of the Charterhouse separated from the main site.

The account of the priory is partly a summary of what has long been a well-established story.[31] But it also offers some revision of earlier accounts, placing greater emphasis on the ancillary and lay buildings which made up such an important part of the complex. It also sets out new discoveries about the priory buildings, and offers a new solution to the problem of the 'extra' cells. Some familiar material is rehearsed in the account of the immediate post-suppression years, but the picture given of the occupation by the King's Tents office is very different from that in earlier studies, which have dismissed this phase as insignificant. Far from being a mere store, it is clear that the Charterhouse was a major works depot for making and repairing tents and timber houses, particularly for Henry VIII's Boulogne campaign in 1544.

Howard House must be central to a study of the buildings. The account here draws on a range of previously untapped sources. They include the household and estate accounts of the fourth Duke of Norfolk and his son Philip, the thirteenth Earl of Arundel, and state papers relating to Arundel's prosecution and attainder, among them the Howard House inventory of 1588. Transcripts of this and earlier inventories are printed as appendices. Much about the history and appearance of Howard House is still unclear, but it has been possible to give a fuller account of its occupancy and building history than hitherto. Without doubt, there is further documentary evidence to be unearthed.

Just as the investigations of the late 1940s brought about a revision of the priory plan, the new investigations for this monograph supply important revisions to the plan of Howard House. In particular, it is evident that the present Chapel was already attached to the main body of the house when Sutton acquired the property, and that Francis Carter's extension of it was not completely new but an adaptation of part of Lord North's bowling-alley range on the south side of the Great Cloister. It is also evident that there is at least one more figure to join North and Norfolk as creators of the house acquired by Sutton: Norfolk's son Thomas, first Earl of Suffolk.

The story of Sutton's hospital and school is a large subject and, with some gaps, well documented. Consequently, in focusing quite narrowly on the buildings, this volume has had to ignore much of the contextual history of the institution and the social, political and other seams running through it.[32] The accounts of the buildings, while dealing in most detail with the historic core, bring the story of their development up to date. The nineteenth-century ranges are described much more fully than in any earlier account, and the most recent additions, completed in 2000, are also described.

Finally, there are the accounts of other sites and buildings which were or still are part of the Charterhouse proper: Rutland House, a long-demolished mansion on the south-east part of the priory site; Merchant Taylors' School, built following the departure of Charterhouse School to Godalming in the 1870s, now largely demolished; and the Medical College of St Bartholomew's Hospital, which took over the school site after Merchant Taylors' School itself departed, to Northwood in the 1930s.

For 'the Charterhouse', it must be stressed, is not synonymous with Sutton's Hospital. That is more correctly known as 'Sutton's Hospital in Charterhouse'. The term Charterhouse originally referred to the entire site defined by the precinct walls of the priory. Charterhouse Churchyard, later called Charterhouse Yard and now Charterhouse Square, refers to the ground south of the priory, originally set aside for public burials at the time of the Black Death and partly developed with houses from the fifteenth century. In the sixteenth century, houses in the churchyard were often loosely described as being 'in the Charterhouse'.

Rutland House was part of the Charterhouse proper, its site reflecting a division within the priory dating back to the immediate post-suppression period, when several buildings were separately let. The redeveloped site is now partly subsumed into Charterhouse Square, while the eastern part now belongs to Aldersgate Street and Goswell Road, and Glasshouse Yard behind. Earlier paring away of the Charterhouse occurred in the late sixteenth or early seventeenth century, when the area at the south-west corner, now partly occupied by Charterhouse Mews, was separated from Howard House.

In the nineteenth century, ground at the north end of Sutton's Hospital was taken by the Metropolitan Board of Works for the construction of Clerkenwell Road. In connection with the new road's development, part of the land acquired by the Merchant Taylors was sold for commercial building soon afterwards. All these sites, now peripheral to the Charterhouse, are described in the Survey of London, vol. XLVI, *South and East Clerkenwell* (2008).

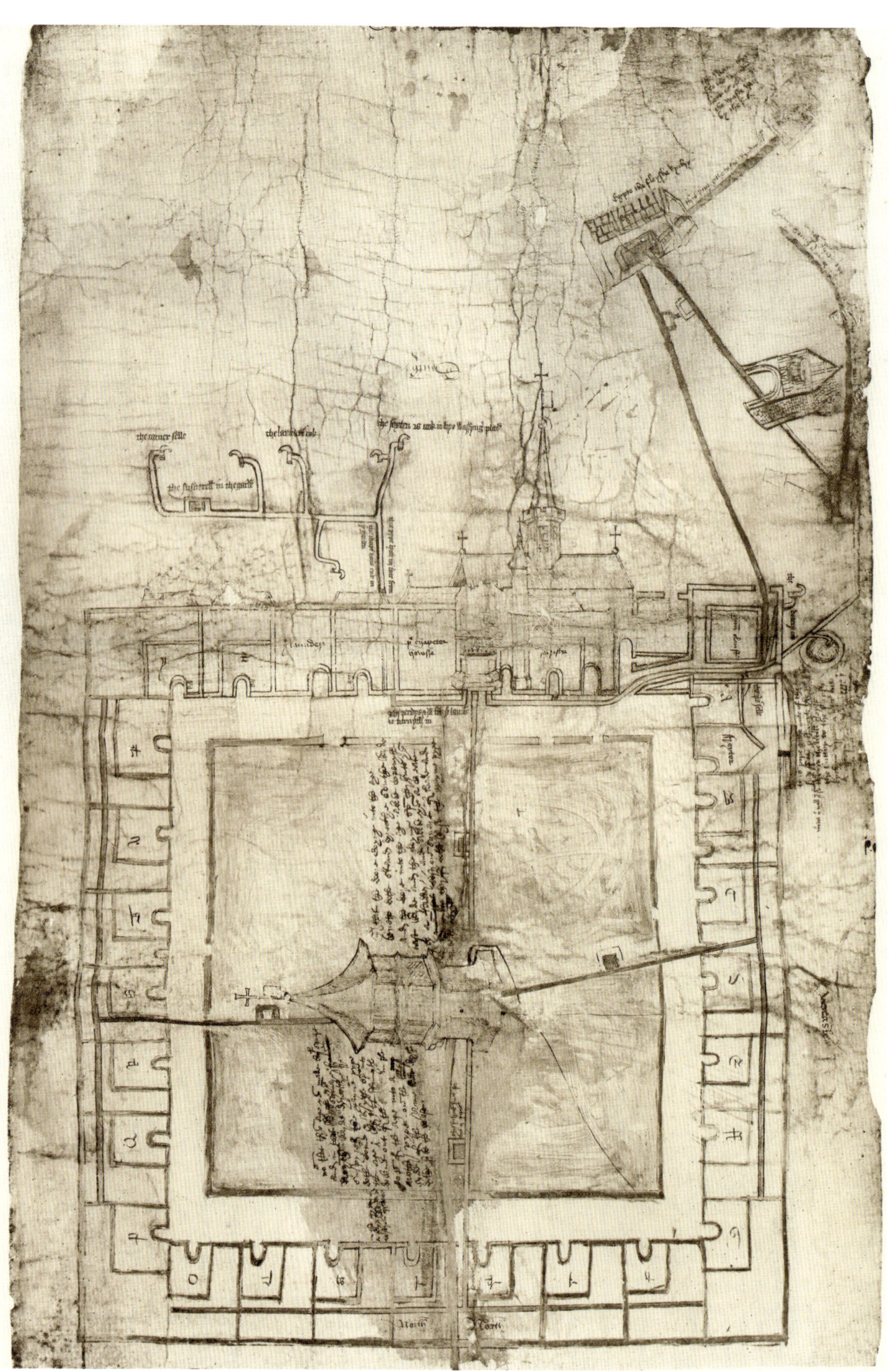

12. Water-supply plan of *c.*1450. Detail showing main priory buildings

CHAPTER I

The London Charterhouse

Charterhouse is the name given to a monastery of the Carthusian order, an Anglicization of Chartreuse, after Grande Chartreuse in the French Alps, the mother house founded by St Bruno in 1084. The London Charterhouse was the fourth of only nine Charterhouses in medieval England, between Beauvale in Nottinghamshire (1343) and Kingston-upon-Hull (1377), and it was the largest and the best endowed of them all. If its early development was hesitant, by the sixteenth century its reputation and influence were assured, and membership carried considerable cachet. On the evidence of one of the last monks, Maurice Chauncy, men gave up great expectations merely to work there as lay brothers.[1] Lasting fame was secured by the steadfastness of Prior Houghton and a number of the monks in the face of Henry VIII's demands for recognition of royal supremacy over the Church, resulting in their deaths.

Unusually for a London monastic site, much of the priory's footprint is stamped indelibly on the topography, and substantial fragments of the complex are still standing. Other parts have been the subject of archaeological digs. As it is also comparatively well documented, a relatively full picture has been formed of its history and architectural character. But there are gaps, particularly regarding new buildings and changes of use in the last thirty to forty years of its existence.

Useful documentation for this period is uneven. Though several account rolls have survived, the most informative deals only with the 1490s. Other promising documents are too ambiguous to bring the buildings fully into focus, notably the post-suppression inventory of 1539 and the statement of William Dale, keeper or co-keeper of the site after its closure.[2] Studies of the Charterhouse have therefore relied most heavily on the priory's own chronicle compiled towards the end of the fifteenth century and, above all, on the earlier water-supply plan. However, the chronicle is far from comprehensive and not without its own problems of interpretation; while, as recent archaeological investigators conclude, the plan's very survival 'has contributed to a view of the London Charterhouse as a rather static institution, whereas … the complex underwent considerable changes throughout its history'.[3]

If the plan has led to a static view of the buildings, the saga of the suppression has also had its effect. Successive writers have tended to play down or excuse the degree of worldly involvement and material prosperity at the Charterhouse, anxious to stress the piety and austerity of the monks. As well as allowing a false impression of their living conditions to be formed, this has to some extent diverted attention from the complexity of the priory as an institution and from the many ancillary buildings needed for it to function. This tendency can be traced back to Hendriks, and an exaggerated impression of the hardship of the monks' life has been passed on by successive writers.[4]

In the 1920s, E. Margaret Thompson felt it necessary to justify the church fittings recorded in 1539 with the claim that the monks were probably 'almost forced to accept these ecclesiastical luxuries as gifts from rich benefactors and other devout persons who could not understand the plain simplicity, the stark abnegation of the Carthusian life both out of church and in church'.[5] In the 1950s, David Knowles acknowledged that the church interior would have had 'a warm and rich appearance … on a level with the neighbouring parish churches', and had to concede that 'here, as in some other respects, the monks of London had to pay a price for the support and endowment they received'.[6] In fact, there is nothing in the documentary record or the remains of the buildings to demonstrate any 'stark abnegation' in the everyday life of the Charterhouse. Luxury items may have been few compared to other monastic houses, but it is, for instance, impossible to be certain, as Thompson claimed, that such items as a set of leather-covered feather cushions in the parlour were exclusively for use by guests.[7]

From quite early days, the priory had drawn criticism from the Order for too-casual relations with the lay community, particularly in admitting women to the church. Perhaps this was, as the priory claimed, for fear of upsetting the populace. But a relaxed attitude is implicit in the complaint in 1424 that the prior and procurator had been accompanied outside the gates by servants in fashionable parti-coloured clothes.[8] Willingly or not, the priory was bound to outside society and dependent on close relations with wealthy and powerful individuals, lay and ecclesiastical.

Carthusianism is among the most ascetic of the Christian monastic orders, demanding a high degree of solitude, silence and simplicity. But this can be misinterpreted. As Nikolaus Pevsner remarked, apropos the Carthusian house of Mount Grace in North Yorkshire, 'What hardship silence imposed, this amount of space must have compensated any monk. Space to oneself was a very rare comfort in the Middle Ages'.[9] As with silence and space, so with other things. Carthusian austerity was ritualized and selective. (The regime at London was probably not exceptional: as a recent guide to Mount Grace explains, despite the monks' life 'of remarkable physical harshness, their required poverty was not necessarily reflected in the buildings and the contents'.[10]) Each monk occupied his own two-storey cottage 'cell'. He had his own secluded garden and covered walk for exercise, his own latrine, fire, candles, fresh water on tap, and meals delivered to his door. Physical labour was confined to absorbing handicrafts, such as writing and illumination, bookbinding, carpentry or weaving—as perhaps in the case of Thomas Golwyne, a monk whose goods, listed on his transfer from London to Mount Grace in 1520, included a loom.[11] Others might study medicine, for instance, such as the famous Andrew Boorde, who obtained a dispensation from some of the discipline of Carthusian life from Prior Batmanson, and finally left the Charterhouse by permission of Thomas Cromwell, for a career as a physician, traveller and writer.[12]

Golwyne's possessions show a more comfortable existence than that imagined by Thompson, disproving the notion that the monks owned nothing in their own right and were barred from accepting gifts.[13] Besides habits and hoods, his clothing included a lined coat, fur gowns, mantles, caps, shirts, socks, hose, cork-soled shoes and double-soled shoes, felt boots and lined slippers 'for matins'. He had pillows as well as blankets, a cushion for kneeling, various pots and pans including chafing-dishes and a butter dish, and a still for alcohol. His collection of books included the popular works *Aesop's Fables* and the *Golden Legend*.

Tasks such as baking, brewing and laundering were done by permanent lay brothers (*conversi*), lay or clerical brothers who might become full monks (*redditi*), and paid servants (*donati*). Numbers varied, but by *c.*1500 there were fifteen or more servants, and by the suppression perhaps as many as 18 lay brothers.[14] Day-labourers were also employed. If monastic discipline embraced celibacy, fasting, hair shirts and five-hour sessions in church on winter nights,[15] it was endured in an atmosphere of calm, cleanliness and security unattainable by the mass of the population. But the monks were not drawn from that mass, most of them being educated men from wealthy and privileged backgrounds. Visitors, too, were likely to be from the upper social echelons. In the accounts from the early 1490s, foodstuffs bought by the priory included such luxuries and exotica as claret, spices, dates and raisins, prunes, almonds, rice and sugar. Much of this may have been exclusively for guests. This level of sophistication was fully reflected in the buildings, which were not only well built but well appointed and well furnished. They were also extensive, with a multiplicity of structures in addition to the main communal buildings off the Great Cloister.

The following account of the priory begins with an outline of its origins and development, based largely on the main published histories. This is followed by a discussion of the buildings, including particular demolished buildings and aspects of the priory plan which remain uncertain, and a summary of what remains of the priory today. Fuller descriptions of the surviving buildings, which have been greatly altered and adapted over several centuries, are to be found in subsequent chapters. Finally, there is an account of the site between the suppression and its acquisition by Sir Edward (later Lord) North in 1545.

History to 1537

The London Charterhouse was founded in 1370–1, but its origins go back to the arrival in England of the Black Death in 1348. In that year, the Bishop of London, Ralph Stratford, set up a cemetery for the plague dead in an area of south Clerkenwell called Nomansland. Following Stratford's lead, Sir Walter Manny set up his own, larger cemetery on ground adjoining to the south, called Spitalcroft after its previous owner, St Bartholomew's Hospital. Manny, a native of Hainault in what is now Belgium, who became one of Edward III's top military commanders, built a chapel there in 1349, intending for it a college of twelve priests. It was begun on the same day that Stratford dedicated the cemetery—the feast of the Annunciation, which provided the subject of his sermon that day, and more than twenty years later was to suggest the name of the priory: the House of the Salutation of the Mother of God.

Authority for Manny's college was obtained through a papal bull in 1351. Three years on, the college had failed to materialize but a hermitage had been built near the chapel for two anchorites to pray for the souls of the departed.[16] How many of these there were remains unknown, but claims of tens of thousands of burials, made in the bull and on a stone cross in the old graveyard seen by the historian John Stow, are implausible. London's entire population probably numbered under a hundred thousand.[17] However many there were, it is probable that burials in Manny's ground were restricted to the southern portion, the greater part of which is now Charterhouse Square. Robert Smythe mentioned in 1808 that many human remains had been found during foundation-digging in the square.[18]

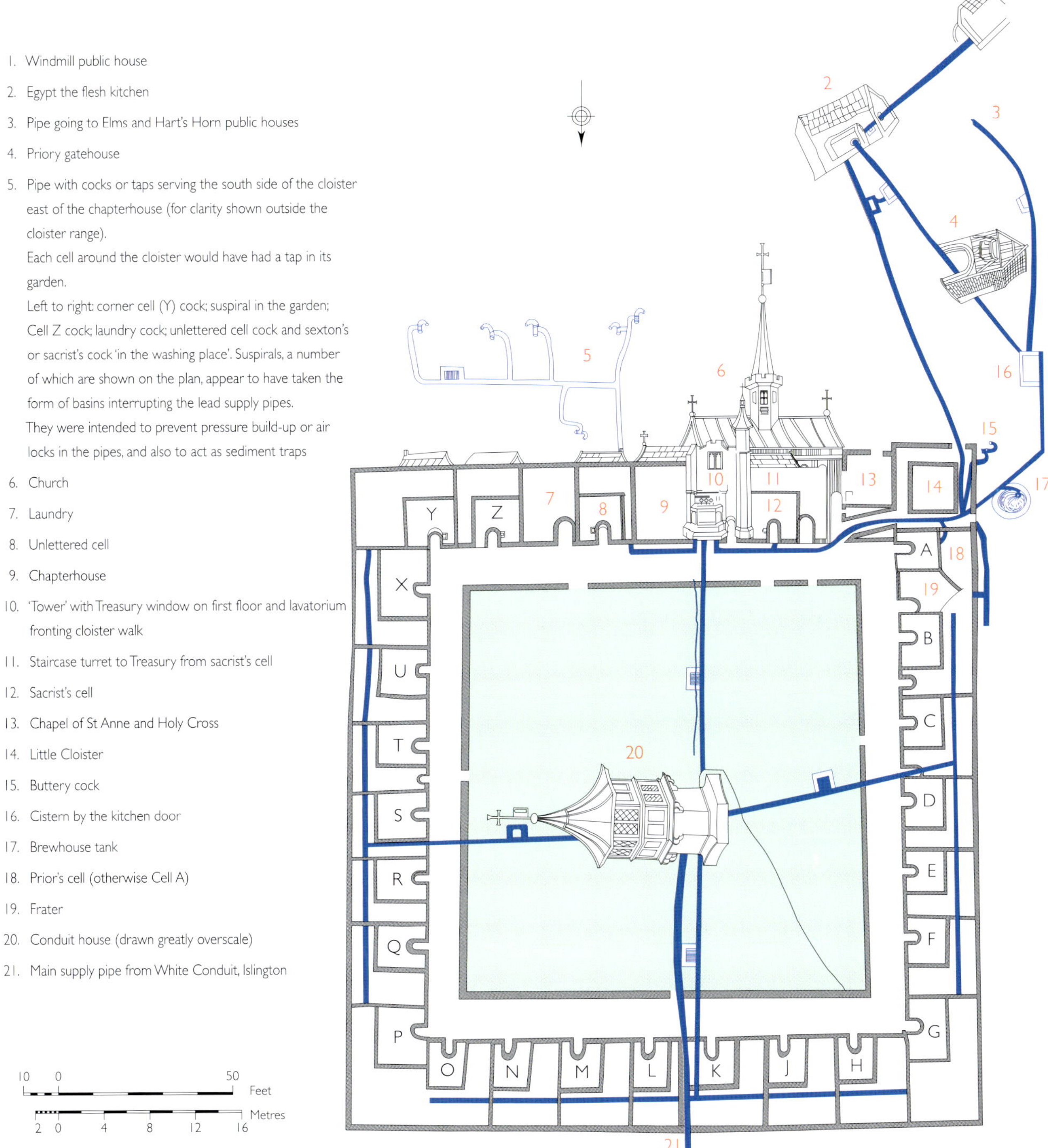

13. Plan of main priory buildings. Redrawn from the medieval water-supply plan

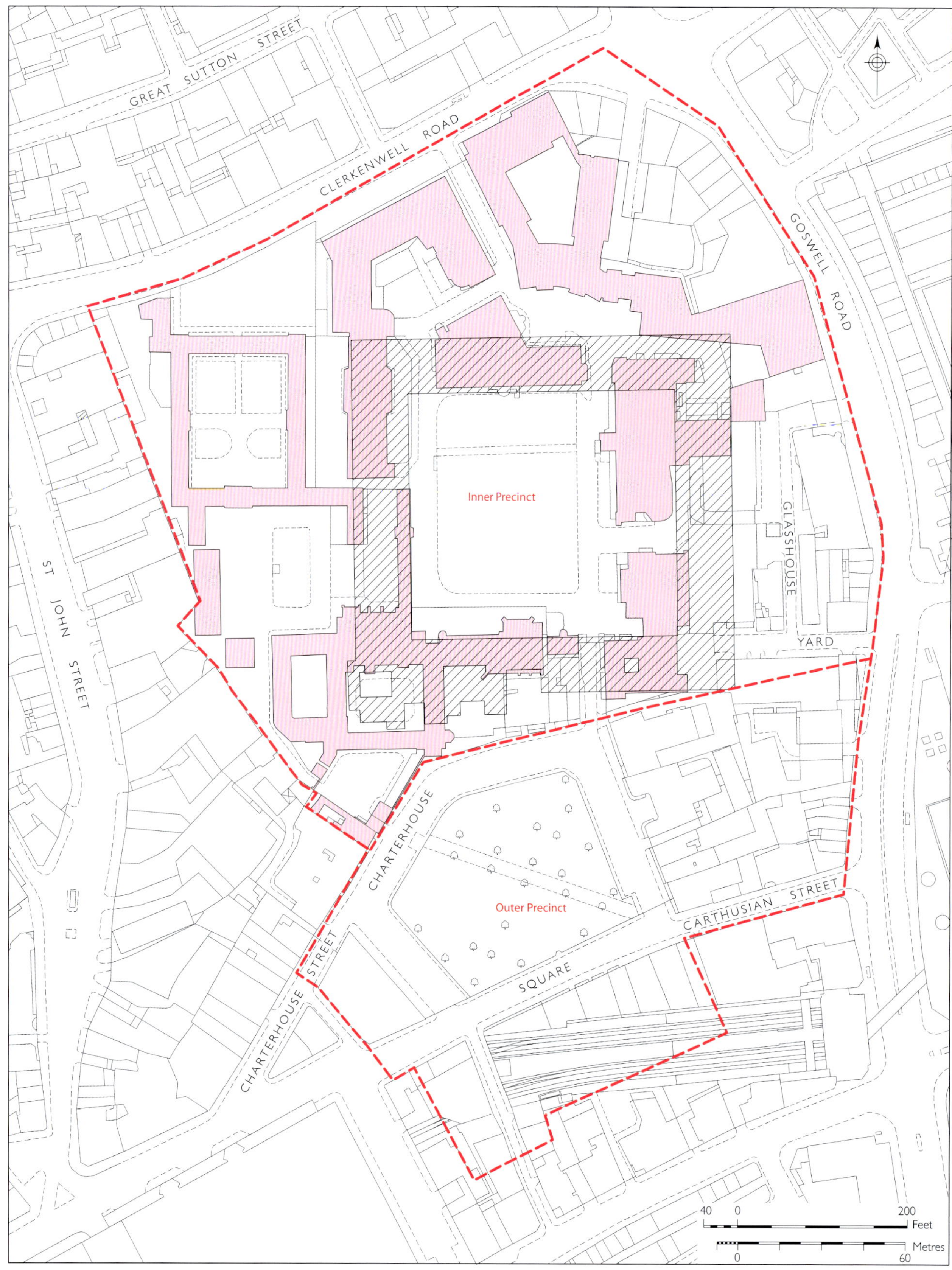

14. Simplified outline of priory precinct and Great Cloister, superimposed on modern street-plan

Sir Walter's 13¼-acre graveyard may have proved an overreaction to the epidemic, but Stratford's successor as bishop, Michael Northburgh, persuaded him to make use of the site by setting up a full-scale monastery, giving him 1,000 marks towards it. That it was to be a Carthusian monastery was also due to Northburgh, who knew and admired the Charterhouse of Paris.[19] Not only was the cemetery the seedbed of the priory but this history led to a particularly close association with the lay community. The circumstance of a religious house founded in a plague cemetery was in itself highly unusual: with the exception of St Mary Graces, a Cistercian house, at East Smithfield in 1350, possibly unique.[20]

Less unusual was the founding of a Carthusian house so near London, however much this might seem to conflict with the order's original pursuit of isolation; over the previous century continental Charterhouses had increasingly been set up close to cities and towns. The site was at the very edge of the City, adjoining St John Street: a main road into London and drovers' route to Smithfield market.

Northburgh died in 1361, leaving property and money for the foundation, but this may never have been received and it was probably only due to the determination of John Luscote, the newly elected prior of Hinton Charterhouse near Bath, that the project came to fruition. He was to become the first prior. Not until March 1371 were all necessary formalities dealt with and the charter of foundation obtained.[21] Manny, who died a year later, left property, and money owed him by the king and Black Prince. Other legacies and gifts of property and valuables followed. A number of benefactors funded the building of individual cells, including the City merchants Sir William Walworth, Adam Fraunceys and indirectly—through the initiative of his executor, Walworth—John Lovekyn, who died several years earlier. Recent research suggests that the roles of Luscote and these secular patrons may outweigh those of both Northburgh and the titular founder, Manny.[22] Not all the promised wealth was forthcoming, and the more distant properties proved hard to manage. Before the end of the century the house found itself in difficulties. In 1403 its affairs were taken over by the king and put into administration. Such a close connection with the monarch was not uncommon among English Carthusian houses. How long this situation lasted is unclear.

Meanwhile, the process of building had more or less come to a halt. By the time Luscote died in 1398, much remained to be done, including the building of several cells, the chapterhouse, frater, infirmary and parlour. Following the royal rescue, further building took place, including the chapel of St Anne and Holy Cross at the west end of the church, the Little Cloister, the south boundary wall and the gatehouse. By about 1420 the priory was more or less complete, with the construction of the chapterhouse (1414) and probably the last cells in the Great Cloister soon afterwards.

The priory was a 'double' house, accommodating two dozen monks besides the prior (a standard Charterhouse having only twelve). It was laid out on a spacious plan, devised by the mason-architect Henry Yevele. Manny and Luscote entered into agreement with Yevele for building the first cell and starting the Great Cloister in May 1371. Unless there was some later change of plan, Yevele's scheme called for additional ground and was probably drawn up on the understanding that this was available. Accordingly, four acres on the east side of Spitalcroft were acquired in 1377 from the nearby Hospitallers' priory of St John, enough and to spare for gardens to the cells on that side, and for the cells on the south side east of the church. The decision to place the cloister so far east may be explained by one or more factors. The line of the south side was dictated by the position of Manny's chapel, which would have to serve as the priory church, and by the need to avoid disturbing ground already used for burials. There were also reasons for avoiding the west side of the site. Not only was this near to busy St John Street but the ground there fell away towards the road, in a natural valley where there may once have been a stream. This sloping ground was gradually made up, and is now more or less level. It has also been suggested that the layout may have been determined in part by old gravel workings.[23]

More land was acquired to the north of Spitalcroft, in stages between 1370 and 1392: this covered the area bounded today by St John Street, Clerkenwell Road, Goswell Road and Dallington Street, including Bishop Stratford's cemetery, known as Pardon Churchyard. This area was never part of the priory precinct, and seems to have passed out of the priory's hands before the suppression, most of it apparently reverting to its former owner, St John's priory. But after the suppression it was acquired by Sir Edward North and remained thereafter in the same ownership as the core of the Charterhouse, until sold by Sutton's Hospital in 1995.[24]

The priory may have been mostly complete by about 1420 but it was not until the early 1430s that it secured a plentiful water supply, piped from a source on the high ground over Clerkenwell at what was to become White Conduit Fields. The source itself and ground to lay pipes were granted in 1430 by John and Margery Feriby, and agreement was reached with St John's priory and the neighbouring nunnery of St Mary to lay pipes through their land also, and for branches to supply them both. Construction of the aqueduct or conduit was paid for by William Symmes, a grocer, and Anne Tatersale, and Symmes also made an endowment for its repair and maintenance. Within the precinct, the water fed into a lead cistern in a conduit house about 30ft north-west of the centre of the Great Cloister.[25] From there pipes distributed water to each side of the cloister. On the south side a second cistern was necessary, to supply not only the laundry and cells on that side but also the buttery and brew-house off the Little Cloister, and the building called Egypt beyond the priory gates. The cistern, built into the sacrist's tower adjoining the chapterhouse (the present Chapel Tower), presumably also served as a laver for ritual washing.[26] There was another large cistern in Egypt, from which a pipe served public houses called the Windmill and the White Hart in the area of Charterhouse Lane. Another branch led off from 'the cisterne by the kychen doore', near the south-west corner of the Little Cloister, to two more public houses, the Elms and the Hart's Horn. The cistern may have been on, or close to, the site of the conduit house built in the early seventeenth century near to the south side of Wash-house Court (page 125).[27]

Though the details of the water-supply system are interesting in themselves, its great importance as regards the history of the Charterhouse is that it generated such a detailed plan, showing the priory buildings as well as the pipes (Ills 12, 13). This document is the single most valuable source of information about the priory's layout and appearance. Sir William St John Hope's conclusion from internal and external evidence was that it dated from 1442 or shortly thereafter, and before the original source, having failed, was superseded in 1457, requiring the redrawing of the first portion of the plan. There seems no reason to revise this view.[28]

The priory's financial position remained uncertain throughout most of the fifteenth century, and by 1482 the buildings were dilapidated.[29] There was some mismanagement, and it was not until the 1490s, under the procurator Philip Underwood, that the debt was cleared and a comfortable annual surplus achieved.[30] Underwood's accounts show not only his zeal in obtaining funds but practical measures against waste and pilfering, such as putting up 'hangings' in the flesh-kitchen roof to keep the beef and bacon safe from rats, and partitioning the wood-store between the cook and the baker so that their respective consumption could be monitored.[31]

Under the leadership of William Tynbygh, prior from 1500 until 1529, the Charterhouse probably reached a high point in its religious life and reputation, and this success may have been reflected in material prosperity and new building. Little of Tynbygh's building works can be identified with confidence. The vaults in the present antechapel, and in the Treasury above, date from his period of office. But the expansive view of his activities put forward by Gerald Davies, attributing to him the building of the Great Hall, has had to be revised in the light of the post-war discoveries and recent scientific dating. Improvements went on under John Houghton, prior from 1531, with the completion or partial rebuilding of Wash-house Court, and the priory experienced a surge in membership, with up to thirty professed monks and about as many other residents. But falling donations, rising prices or increased consumption put the finances under strain. According to Thomas Cromwell's agent Jasper Fyloll, the house had become too big, and too much was spent in 'dainty fare', and on food and ale doled out to strangers and vagabonds.[32]

In 1534, Henry VIII's commissioners had difficulty in obtaining the oaths required from the monks under the first Act of Succession, and Houghton and the procurator were briefly imprisoned in the Tower. In 1535, the mandatory acknowledgement of Henry's supremacy over the Church in England was something that Houghton and others could not make. After his execution in May that year the priory lingered on, depleted and demoralized. Fifteen more monks were executed or left to starve to death in prison, the last in 1540. There was co-operation by some monks with the government, and eventual acceptance of the royal supremacy. In 1536, William Trafford became the thirteenth and last prior, and in 1537 he formally surrendered the Charterhouse to the king.

The priory buildings and their layout

Following the usual layout of Carthusian houses, the priory consisted principally of a Great Cloister, around which were the individual cells of the monks, together with the church, chapterhouse and frater. Of these buildings, only the chapterhouse survives, much altered and enlarged, as the chapel of Sutton's Hospital. Its history is given in Chapter IV.

The individual cells were lettered alphabetically, each letter being the initial of a specially chosen verse on the front. Though there were only 25 cells in the Great Cloister, because one letter served for both I and J and one for U, V and W, there was some repetition: three cells bore the letter S, one in sequence and the others on the south side of the cloister, one of them the sacrist's.[33]

In contrast to the spacious formality of the cloister, the west and south parts of the priory filled up with buildings rather more haphazardly—an accretive process, influenced by the confines of the site. Here were an unknown number of buildings, comprising storehouses, service rooms, counting-house, infirmary, sheds, workshops, stabling, living quarters for lay brothers and *redditi*, guest rooms, extra cells for resident or visiting monks, and a variety of other structures. These may have included

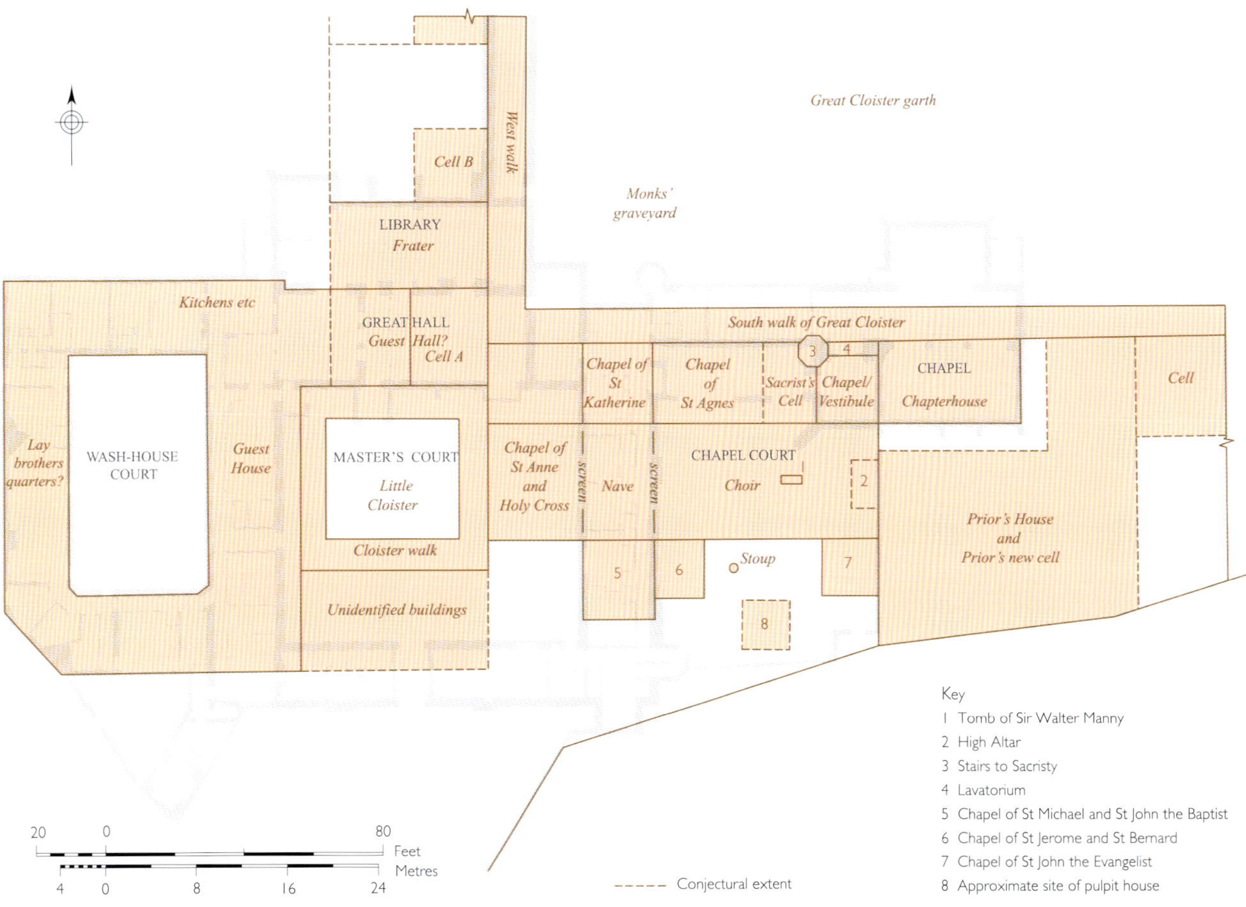

15. Schematic plan of buildings at south-west corner of Great Cloister, showing correspondence with present-day buildings

servants' quarters; the suggestion that the houses in Charterhouse Square were intended for servants is questionable (the few houses there seem generally to have been large), but some priory servants lived in St John Street, eleven being listed there in 1525.[34]

South and east of the church, on the site of what was to become Rutland House, the buildings have disappeared without trace. The more coherent pattern of building around the Little Cloister and Wash-house Court informed the layout of the core of Howard House, Wash-house Court itself surviving largely intact. More buildings were ranged along the west boundary and a wall extending north-east from the kink in the west boundary just north of Wash-house Court. The line of this wall continued to inform the layout of new buildings until the nineteenth century but is now obliterated. There may have been other buildings in the gardens and orchard north and east of the Great Cloister, but probably none of much size or permanence.

While stone of various kinds was used for the walls of the cells, church, chapterhouse and gateway, the buildings as a whole were varied, brick and timber-framing also being employed, and some outbuildings were probably entirely of timber. The chief monastic brickwork surviving today is in Wash-house Court, where it dates from the early 1530s, and the precinct wall and inner gateway in the same area, which may be of about the same date. Brick was used earlier to some extent. Accounts for 1515–16 show £6 8*s* 2*d* spent on bricks and tiles, and in 1504 the priory was bequeathed 10,000 bricks by John Bramston, apparently a brickmaker in Whitechapel, who left the same quantity to St Bartholomew's Hospital. Choice of building material may have been contingent on such windfalls as much as on taste or cost. This argues against a simplistic explanation such as that of Basil Champneys, who suggested that the stone building at Wash-house Court and the Little Cloister/Master's Court should be attributed to Prior Tynbygh's time and the brickwork to the later Prior Houghton.[35]

The shed or summer-house described below with other accommodation for guests was one of several wooden structures at the priory. At the time it was erected, repairs were also made to two sheds in the infirmary garden, and mention is made of the construction of a large, long 'house' for sawing timber frames and storing timber. The very existence of such a building points to the amount of timber-building at the priory, almost all of which has vanished. The only remnants today are in the north-west part of Wash-house Court, including the slype there (Ill. 51), and at the back of the gatehouse, where the archway is framed in timber.

New thinking on the plan and buildings

The chief revisions made after the Second World War to the hitherto accepted priory plan stemmed from the identification of Sutton's Hospital chapel as the priory chapterhouse. They were prompted and proved by excavation. As it happened, they also demonstrated the reliability of the water-supply plan, which had shown the real layout all along. But the attempt to fix the location of cells thought to have existed beyond the south side of the Great Cloister, the joint effort of Knowles, Grimes, Seely and Paget, and their researcher Mabel Mills, was wide of the mark. The reconstruction eventually published, although superficially plausible, fails to stand up to analysis and could in fact never have existed.[36] Another apparent discovery has also proved illusory. This was the identification of the conduit house beside the inner gateway of Entrance Court as part of the priory.[37] It was, in fact, part of Francis Carter's work for Sutton's Hospital (page 125), though it may have replaced a cistern on or near the site.

More recent archaeological work, particularly that in Preacher's Court in 1998, has added little to our understanding of the late development of the monastery. The only discovery of relevance was a stone-built range of uncertain extent standing against the west boundary, dating, on the evidence of pottery, from the very late fifteenth or early sixteenth century.[38] This range, which may have had a lighter, timber-framed or brick upper storey, has been tentatively identified as a barn or granary, partly on the analogy of surviving buildings at Mount Grace. Direct archaeological evidence, in the form of a few charred grains and seeds, seems weak. The monastic granary may have been the later granary by the entrance to the Charterhouse, described in the 1590 survey (page 54) as a brick building of 74ft by 28ft. The rediscovered building might perhaps be identifiable as the mill-house also listed in the 1565 inventory (Appendix I).

Several new findings and possibilities are put forward in the following accounts of individual parts of the priory. The most significant is the identification of the Bishop of Lincoln's house, built in the late fifteenth century. Since this house seems to be identical with (or latterly incorporated) the 'prior's new cell' referred to after the suppression, an important element in the final layout can be put in place. Evidence for the additional cells is tied up with the post-suppression occupation of the priory and is discussed later, in that context.

Some buildings or rooms remain completely obscure. There must, for instance, have been a library (the priory probably held the Order's head library in England), but there is no definite clue to its whereabouts. It might have been the sacristy strong-room, now called the Treasury, where several books remained in 1539.[39] One building whose function and location are alike unknown is the 'green cell' (*viridis cella*) listed in Underwood's summary of improvements of the 1490s. It contained cupboards and aumbries, chests, bedsteads and hangings, for which a Master Thomas Thomas was paid the sum of £3 6*s* 8*d*.[40] These furnishings suggest accommodation for guests, or perhaps a storehouse for fitting up guest rooms.

It is certain that many changes were made to the southern part of the priory, including the buildings fronting the Great Cloister, between the drawing of the water-supply plan and the suppression. The parlour came and went; new chapels were added to the church; the sacristy was encroached on; and the laundry probably moved to the new court, known after the suppression as Laundry (now Wash-house) Court. Somewhere east of the Bishop of Lincoln's house (or Prior's House, as it became), new cells were built. More cells, so called, for the use of laymen or visiting monks, may have been built in the vicinity of the Little Cloister.

The Great Cloister and cells

The Great Cloister was a nearly square rectangle, 340ft from east to west and 300ft from north to south, the covered way around the sides being, on the evidence of the excavation of the north and east walks in 1949, about 9ft wide, and nearer 8ft on the south.[41] The east side was about 4ft below the west and much of the south, and there was also a north–south fall, these changes in level presumably being dealt with by steps.

Completion of the cloister was spread over many years, only two cells, A and B, being built in the first year of the priory's existence. Most of the cells were finished before the close of the fourteenth century, and the last two were probably completed before 1420. The date of 1436 for Cells X and Y given by Knowles and Grimes is improbable. In the case of X it is based on Hope's insecure dating of the Little Cloister (discussed below), the same donor having funded both.[42] Y probably dated from soon after its donor's reception into the Charterhouse 'brotherhood' in 1418; there is no reason to assume that it was built at the same time as X adjoining.[43]

While the names of the donors are known, the precise date of construction in most cases is not, though it is apparent that the cells were not built in strict sequence. Four (B, C, T and the sacrist's) are shown on the water-supply plan to have had a second door to the cloister, giving access to their gardens. The reason for such extra doors is not obvious, unless to admit lay brothers, perhaps to do gardening. The plan also shows the cells on the south side with pitched, tiled roofs parallel to the cloister walk, and a chimney at one end. These were no doubt representative of the rest.

The cells were stone-built, using chalk, flint, ragstone and Reigate stone, and there is some suggestion of decorative flintwork. They were finished internally with plaster or wainscot: fragments of plaster with colouring and black-letter inscriptions have been recovered, and the removal of wainscoting from the cells is referred to in the statement of the keeper William Dale.[44] A presumably covered passage led along one side of the garden to a latrine built against the outside of the back garden wall. A wider covered passage, or cloister in miniature, behind the front wall provided a place for exercise out of the weather. Excavation has revealed coloured Flemish tiles on the floors of these mini-cloisters, laid chequerwise, and evidence of cement or joisted timber floors inside the cells.[45] The entrances to Cells B and S also retain coloured floor tiles.

Descriptions of Carthusian cells vary, but those at London were of the two-storey type and would have contained three or four rooms.[46] A typical cell was about 25ft square externally, taking up about a quarter of the walled enclosure. They varied slightly in size and shape. Downstairs, the rooms were buffered from the cloister walk by twin lobbies, the one offset from the cloister door probably containing stairs or a ladder to the first floor or loft, as well as giving access to the mini-cloister. Meals and letters and messages were placed in a serving-hatch with a flap beside the front door, a few of which are indicated on the water-supply plan. How the room uses were allocated is not certain.[47] Davies, who had visited 60 Charterhouses, describes the usual arrangement as comprising an entrance lobby giving on to a small workshop, the rest of the cell containing an oratory or prayer room, a sleeping room, a living room and a wood-store.[48] The cells at Mount Grace, which were of similar size to those at London, are described by Thompson as consisting of three ground-floor rooms besides the entrance lobby: a living room, a bedroom-cum-oratory, and a little study. On the first floor was a single room for manual work. That is the arrangement in a cell reconstructed there in the early 1900s, and now fitted up as it might once have been.[49] Lawrence Hendriks, a late-Victorian monk of St Hugh's Charterhouse, Parkminster, describes the typical cell as having 'workshops' at ground level, the upper floor being divided into an ante-room and just one more room: the 'cell' proper, for eating, sleeping, prayer and study.[50] At London, no evidence exists as to which rooms were on which floor.[51]

16. Former entrance to Cell B in 2000

There is no record of the appearance of the Great Cloister alley, though the keeper Dale refers to there having been four great painted 'tables', probably boards with religious texts or imagery, one in each corner.[52] Remains of the south walk, uncovered after the Second World War, consisted of diagonally laid tiling interspersed with memorial slabs.[53] Some impression of the cloister walk is preserved by the Norfolk Cloister, and what seem to be filled-in sockets for beams or the sites of corbels in the wall there suggest that the monastic roof was not high.

The church

Manny's chapel, however it may have been altered or enlarged, became the church of the new priory. A stone-built, rectangular building of some 97ft by 38ft externally, it compared closely in scale with the churches at Hinton Charterhouse (96ft by 26ft internally) and Mount Grace (initially 88ft by 25ft internally).[54] Its height, on the evidence of buttresses incorporated into the walls of the present chapel and tower, was over 33ft. The building's original plainness may be assumed, but by the time of the suppression it had been embellished and enlarged by the addition of at least six chapels, the earliest—the chapel of St Anne and Holy Cross (1405)—being a full-width extension of the nave. The church is shown in some detail on the water-supply plan, with a steep-pitched roof and polygonal bell-turret with battlements and a spire. St Anne's chapel, however, is shown in plan only, as if it were a separate building and of different status.

From the start, the church had a dual role as the place of worship for priory and laity. Lay men and women, often benefactors, were buried in the church or cloister throughout the priory's existence. After the chapel of St Anne came those dedicated to St John the Evangelist (1437), SS Michael and John the Baptist and SS Jerome and Bernard (both 1453), all on the south side. The last two of these were built and endowed by the soldier and courtier Sir John Popham. Fragments of the chapel of SS Michael and John the Baptist, where Popham was interred, survive in the front wall of the east range of Master's Court. On the north side were the chapels of St Agnes (1475) and St Catherine (1517). The latter was endowed by Sir Robert Rede, a judge, who was buried there in 1519, having provided money for a secular priest to sing daily masses there for himself and his family.[55] It was through these chapels and chantries, which promised financial security for the house, that the monks found themselves increasingly distracted from their lives of contemplation and seclusion.

In the middle of the choir was Manny's monument, almost certainly designed by Yevele, who did considerable

17. Fragment from tomb of Sir Walter Manny, now displayed in Chapel Cloister

business as a monumental mason. In his will, Manny specified an alabaster tomb with his effigy, citing as a model that of Sir John Beauchamp (d. 1360) by Yevele in St Paul's Cathedral. This was a chest tomb with side panels ornamented with Beauchamp's arms.[56] Fragments of Manny's tomb have been discovered: one substantial piece, part of an arched niche with his arms in the spandrel, possibly from a canopy rather than the chest itself, was found in the 1890s during restoration of the south front of the former long gallery.[57]

As suggested above, the inventory of 1539 dispels any suggestion of bareness internally. What was listed was perhaps only part of the whole, for there are hints that other items had already been removed or spoiled and so were not recorded. In the 'midst' of the west end was a timber screen with iron spikes, which presumably separated the chapel of St Anne from the short nave. Partitioning and panelling is much in evidence, and there was a good deal of carved or painted imagery. Vying for attention with Manny's tomb was a bone or ivory reredos at the high altar, 'wrought wyth smalle Imagys Curyouslie' to show the story of the Passion, with three tabernacles above and images of SS John the Baptist and Peter at either side. The alabaster back of the altar was carved with the Trinity and other images, and at the sides were an aumbry and a cupboard with a picture of Christ.[58]

In the yard south of the church there was an ornamental well or stoup for disposing of holy water, the remains of which were discovered after the Second World War, and a small building called the pulpit house (see page 35). The present boundary wall closing the east side of Chapel Court incorporates part of the east wall of the church, but all trace of the high altar, and of a little chapel at the east end mentioned after the suppression and probably built in connection with the adjacent Prior's House rather than the church itself (page 35), has long been obliterated. The high altar site, however, is marked by a stone slab and a mural tablet commemorating the Carthusian martyrs, designed by John Seely and erected in 1958.[59]

The frater and other communal buildings

The frater, or refectory, used for communal meals on Sundays and feast days, was apparently built sometime after Prior Luscote's death in 1398. It appears on the water-supply plan between Cells A (the prior's) and B, on what had formerly been part of A's garden. Unsatisfactory as this arrangement might seem, it was like that at Mount Grace in placing the frater near the prior's cell, and was presumably worked out as part of a general reorganization of this part of the priory in the early fifteenth century, which included the building of the Little Cloister and the chapel of St Anne. There may be some significance in the fact that the labelling of 'the prior cell' on the plan is in a different hand to that of the frater and other buildings around the cloister, and is written across the garden, not the cell itself. Possibly, therefore, Cell A had not always been the prior's cell. Davies went further, deducing that the prior's cell was a separate building at the back of Cell A and the frater, a theory not taken up by later writers.[60] Nor was his further theory that the frater was replaced by what became the Great Hall in the early sixteenth century.

Two more buildings whose position is recorded on the plan are the sacristy and laundry. Like the chapterhouse, they were on the south side of the Great Cloister, the laundry occupying a site identical to one of the cell plots. The sacristy evidently consisted of the sacristan's cell and garden alongside the choir of the church, and the first-floor Treasury in what is now Chapel Tower adjoining.

Among buildings not shown is the infirmary, although it would presumably have needed a water supply. Like the chapterhouse and frater, it was only built after Luscote's death. It is mentioned in the accounts of the 1490s, when it was repaired and decorated with limewash and red ochre. Mention is also made of the reconstruction of a 'greete dovshousse on the ffermory', and of sheds in the infirmary garden, one for seeds and tools, the other for making vinegar and alegar.[61]

The Little Cloister

According to the priory chronicle, the Little Cloister (*parvum claustrum*) was built in 1406 with money from John Clyderhow, a Chancery clerk between 1399 and 1414. The oft-stated date of 1436 arose because its building is related out of sequence in what is otherwise a chronological account of the priory, between the provision of the water supply in 1431 and the dedication of St John the Evangelist's chapel in 1437. Hope evidently assumed that a transcription error had been made, m°ccccvj (1406) being written instead of m°ccccxxxvj (1436).[62] This assumption has no stronger basis than the possibility that the writer accidentally missed out the Little Cloister in its proper place. Whatever the case, the date 1406 was repeated in the summary history of the Charterhouse, deriving from the chronicle, inserted into the cartulary of St Bartholomew's Hospital.[63] There are reasons for accepting 1406 as correct. First, the cloister's form was partly dictated by (and perhaps therefore conceived at the same time as) the west wall of the chapel of St Anne. Secondly, the route of the water pipes, following two sides of the Little Cloister, suggests that it had already been built when they were laid. There is also no evidence that Clyderhow lived into the 1430s, while the phrase 'de bonis Johannis Clyderhow' may imply that he gave the money during his lifetime, not in his will. The same term is used to describe William Symmes's gift providing for the water conduit, which was during Symmes's lifetime.[64]

The Little Cloister was 41ft east to west and 35½ft north to south, with a walk of about 6ft to 7ft wide, probably under a pentice roof. W. F. Grimes concluded, from the foundations he uncovered, that the west side was filled by timber-framed buildings oversailing the walk. He was probably correct about the timber-framing, but the rest of his thinking has been discredited by recent analysis.[65] This range (the supposed 'guest-house') must have been rebuilt by North. On the north side was Cell A (in the fifteenth century, though perhaps not at the suppression), and on the south buildings of uncertain function, probably more guest rooms or cells, again apparently timber-framed.

As shown on the water-supply plan, access between the north-east corner of the Little Cloister and the Great Cloister was by a covered way crossing a yard between the Great Cloister and St Anne's chapel and leading to a door on the south walk of the Great Cloister. The question of how many keys to this cloister door had been issued to lay people was of great interest to the king's investigators in 1535, seeming to disprove the solitariness of the monks' lives.[66]

The Bishop of Lincoln's house

In 1490, the Carthusian general chapter approved the building of a house within the Charterhouse for its benefactor John Russell, Bishop of Lincoln and conservator of the Order in England, with strict injunctions against it ever being occupied by a married man or a woman.[67] By then about 60 and perhaps in failing health, Russell had spent most of his career in the service of the Crown, chiefly as an administrator, which latterly kept him in London much of the time. He died in 1494, and in 1500 his house was leased by a lay benefactor of the priory, Sir Thomas Thwaites, a mercer, the lease running for his lifetime plus one year. Thwaites, who died in 1503, left the 'jewels and stuff' from his own chapel—possibly at the back of this house—to be used in the chapel of St Jerome, where he was buried.[68]

Thwaites's lease describes the house as adjacent to the laundry, and there can be little doubt that it was the dwelling-house, near the laundry site, called the Prior's House when it was occupied by the Italian musician Alvise Bassano after the suppression.[69] If so, it would appear to have been the building earlier referred to by the keeper Dale as the 'pryor sell', and by Henry VIII's commissioners as the 'priours Newe Celle'. Whether it was taken for the prior's use soon after its reversion following Thwaites's death, or later, is not known. But, as the original water-supply plan still shows Cell A as the prior's cell, a later date is more likely: probably after 1511, the date given of what must have been a late annotation, though not necessarily the last, made on the plan before it was superseded by a revised copy. Further, there is a likelihood that Thwaites's house was later occupied by another ecclesiastic, Robert Langton, who died in 1524, leaving to the priory the contents of 'my house here in Charterhouse'. This may mean that he was living within the priory on a similar life-lease to Thwaites's, and that their houses were one and the same. But 'in Charterhouse' might merely mean in Charterhouse Churchyard.[70]

Though Dale's statement makes no link between the prior's cell and the house let to Sir Arthur Darcy and a succession of others, they must again be the same place. Confusion about the identity of this house has arisen in the past because Darcy later had the reversion of another, larger house adjoining the Charterhouse at the north-east corner of Charterhouse Yard. This house, formerly occupied by the Bishop of Pershore, had been leased by Prior Houghton in 1529 to Sir John Neville, later Lord Latimer. As the priory estate rental of 1538–9 shows, it was then still in Latimer's occupation.[71]

The Prior's House is shown on the 'Agas' map and other maps deriving from the lost 'Copperplate' map as an oblong building with a gable to the churchyard. Its true extent is uncertain, but on the west side it must have abutted the chapel of St John the Evangelist, because Bassano had access from the upper floor to the chapel roof.[72] It is also said to have abutted, and had a door into, the Great Cloister. That would have been essential for the prior, and could only have been achieved by taking in part of the site of the unlettered (or extra 'S') cell adjoining the chapterhouse. It cannot have been part of the original arrangement of the house, given its occupancy, and possibly therefore the 'prior's new cell' was an extension rather than the house itself. Corroboration for the identity of the house is supplied by Dale, who records that the buyer of a table from the frater carried it out through the Earl of Angus's house, as the Prior's House briefly was: this would have been impossible had Angus's been the house at the corner of the churchyard, as it would have had no access from the cloister, where the frater was.

The Prior's House is discussed further below, in connection with Bassano's tenancy and the 'new' cells, and with Rutland House, of which it was the nucleus (Chapter X).

Accommodation for guests

As the principal reception room for meetings with outsiders, the parlour occupied a special position in the priory. We first hear of it as having formerly been on the site where St Agnes's chapel was built in 1475, on the north side of the church. Hope took this to mean that the parlour replaced the sacrist's cell in that position, and that a replacement cell had had to be built elsewhere. Knowles and Grimes concluded that it must have been built over the sacrist's garden, in the same way that the frater was built over the garden of Cell A. It seems odd that this would have been done when adjoining the garden was the presumably vacant site taken in 1517 for St Catherine's chapel, a fair size at 27ft across and 20ft front to back. A possible explanation might be that the assumed positions of the two chapels should be transposed. However, the chapel listed under 'North syde of the Qwere' in the 1539 inventory can only be that of St Agnes; St Catherine's (Rede's) chapel is separately listed and therefore must have been the chapel on the north side of the short nave, excavated after the Second World War. Possibly both sites were taken up by the sometime parlour, or else St Catherine's chapel itself displaced some other structure. Whatever the case, the water-supply plan seems to confirm that the sacrist's cell lost its garden, for it shows a water-pipe running into the cell itself; in all other cases the pipes run through the gardens. Loss of the garden may also explain the note about a tap near the laundry and chapterhouse: 'the sexton's [sacrist's] cock in his washing-place', as if a new place had been assigned the sacrist in lieu of his garden.

The 1539 inventory lists the contents of both a 'drinking parlour', probably the room described by Dale as the drinking buttery, and 'the prior's parlour', probably the same as the 'parlour' itself. Round tables in each suggest that they served much the same function.[73] The parlour at this time would no doubt have been in the Prior's House, but where it was in the intervening period after 1475 is unknown.

Among the improvements of the 1490s was the construction of a shed ('shade') in the cook's garden. It was not what this description calls to mind, but for 'the recreacion of greete especiall frendes and there to be secrete with our lerned counceill in matiers of charge and weight'. It had a boarded floor, ceiled roof and latticed windows. As Thompson commented, it must have been a summer-house, an alternative to the perhaps inconvenient parlour in fine weather.[74] Although unidentifiable in the 1565 inventory, if the building survived that long it may have been the 'summer parlour' listed in 1588 and described in the survey of 1590. If so, its dimensions of 110ft by 16ft (one end then taken up by a still-house) may point to an early form of garden gallery.[75]

The summer parlour of the 1580s seems to have stood against a masonry wall defining the north side of the privy garden, which may well have been the priory cook's garden, being immediately north of the kitchens. The line of the wall survived in the layout of the site until the creation of Pensioners' and Preacher's Courts in the 1820s, and part of the structure itself, dated loosely to *c.*1400, has been excavated.[76] This would have been a private, sunny spot.

Board and lodging for guests demanded a hall and bedrooms, and Dale confirms their existence, referring to a hall, 'certen lodgyns' and 'all the beddys in the gest chamberes'. Whether they can simply be equated with the guest-house (*hospitium*) of the chronicle is another matter: probably not. According to the chronicle, the Little Cloister was built between the guest-house and the church in 1406, when an altar was also dedicated there, so it was probably newly built at that time.[77] This seems to place the guest-house on the west side of the Little Cloister, a view generally accepted since it was introduced by R. H. Carpenter in the 1880s.[78] More precisely, Carpenter put it south of the kitchen and pastry shown on Francis Carter's plan (Ill. 30), but he also interpreted the Great Hall of Sutton's Hospital as having been the priory 'guesten hall' (as did Hope, though he preferred to call it the Prior's Hall).[79] As far as Davies was concerned, however, there had been no guest hall, and guests would have had their meals 'in large upper rooms' in their quarters, basing this conclusion on his knowledge of other Charterhouses. In his view, the Great Hall was the monks' refectory or frater, and built in the early sixteenth century by Prior Tynbygh to replace the frater shown on the water-supply plan. In fact, it is clear from Dale's statement that the hall and frater were different buildings, and it is possible that the hall formed the basis for the present Great Hall (see page 133), and was part of a more extensive 'guest-house' than a few rooms on the west side of the Little Cloister. Such an arrangement seems to be implied by the statement in the chronicle that Prior Luscote's grave was 'opposite the cloister door by which one goes from the cloister to the guest-house, at a distance of 30 feet from the said door'.[80] The door can only have been the one on the south side of the Great Cloister, leading to the Little Cloister, as the west side was taken up by cells and the frater. Why would the writer have seen this as specifically a door to the guest-house rather than to the Little Cloister in general, if the guest-house was confined to the west side of the Little Cloister? Corroboration that there were guest rooms around the Little Cloister is given by Sir Thomas Thwaites's lease of Bishop Russell's house south of the chapterhouse, in which he gave up any claim to a 'cell' and unspecified rooms adjoining 'in parvo claustro', where he must previously have lodged. (He also relinquished a 'mansion' over the west gate of the churchyard, occupied by one Richard Crook.)[81] Probably, by 1538, the accommodation for guests was considerable, taking up perhaps most of the west and south sides of the Little Cloister as well as including a hall on the north side. This is much as Basil Champneys conjectured in 1902 (page 6). It is also possible that the later Physician's house, built partly over the priory gate, had its origins in lodgings for guests.

The term 'guest' may be extended to an unknown number of residents who, like Russell and Crook, were neither monks nor lay brothers, and who evidently occupied private houses technically within the priory. Another such property was the 'little house', a lodge and garden within the precinct, taken on a 40-year lease in 1534 from Prior Houghton by John Whalley, a fishmonger. Did Whalley live there with his wife Eleanor? The place cannot be identified, but was possibly the house west of the gatehouse later occupied by John Sinclair, the keeper of Howard House.[82]

Egypt, le Garneter and other ancillary buildings

Egypt was the name of a somewhat mysterious building shown on the water-supply plan apparently outside the priory gates (Ills 12, 13). It is labelled both 'Egipt' and 'Egipte the fleyshe kychyn', but there was more to it than that one use. As shown, and as described in a note on the plan, it was an oblong building containing a cistern 'on a lofte', fed by branch pipes running from Cell B and the brew-house in the area of Wash-house Court. From the cistern, an outlet pipe supplied water to the Windmill and White Hart taverns. The annotation describing this seems to distinguish between Egypt itself and the flesh kitchen, and Procurator Underwood's statement in the 1490s has separate headings for each. The contents of 'Egyptum' included tools and materials for making candles and deed-boxes, as well as for softening dried fish, something that might seem more appropriate to the separately listed fish kitchen. In another account, one entry is for combined spending on the parlour, Egypt and the laundering of tablecloths: costs relating to the entertainment of guests.[83]

Archdeacon Hale may have been the first to make the link between the name and the flesh-pots of Egypt in Exodus 16: 3.[84] But the distinction between Egypt and the flesh-kitchen makes it as likely that the name refers to the building's location in the world outside the priory, from which the monks were barred after the building of the south precinct wall and gatehouse. The flesh-kitchen was probably just a part of the building. After the suppression, the house called 'Egipt and Fleshall' was granted on a life-lease to the Clerk Comptroller of the King's Tents, John Barnard, along with an adjoining house called le Garneter and a small kitchen garden.[85] These were described as being within and upon the walls of the Charterhouse, but the lines of the pipes on the water-supply plan can only mean that Egypt was physically outside the gates, though very likely close to le Garneter, which must be the granary next to the gatehouse mentioned in the 1590 survey (page 24). The site of Egypt was possibly the 105ft by 32ft plot on the west side of the churchyard leased in 1580 by John Sinclair from Philip Howard (page 48). R. H. Carpenter, however, placed it within the precinct, on the other side of the gatehouse.[86]

The chapel in Charterhouse Yard

The chapel in the churchyard (otherwise Charterhouse Yard) shown on sixteenth-century maps is said in the chronicle to have been built in 1481. This may be incorrect, as the chronicler goes on to say that it was dedicated in the same year to the Virgin Mary and All Saints in a compromise between the wishes of the founder, Robert Hulett, and the then prior, Dan Edmund. The prior in 1481, however, was John Walsyngham, who succeeded Edmund Storer in 1477. It seems to have stood in the northern part of the churchyard, though excavation following a geophysical survey in 1997 failed to find any trace of it.[87]

Whether the chapel was intended primarily for funerals or for lay people not admitted to the priory church is unknown. It appears to have been a brick building of oblong plan with a tiled roof and small bellcote. Two organs were provided for it in the 1490s.[88] After the suppression it evidently remained in use and was kept in good repair, judging by its contents and the perfect condition of the glazing in 1561, when Lord North allowed it to be used rent-free by Thomas Cotton as a school. It was then furnished with pews, reading-desks and other seats, and was divided by a wooden screen with double doors into choir and nave.[89]

Use as a school appears to have continued for, in 1584, William Smithers was accused of keeping an unlicensed 'common scole' there.[90] The fourth Duke of Norfolk undertook not only to allow the inhabitants of the churchyard area to continue to worship there and maintain the building but not to demolish it or convert it to any other use.[91] It is recorded in the Charterhouse survey of 1590, and although not mentioned by Stow appears to have stood until 1615 or 1616, when the accounts of Sutton's Hospital record payments for 'pulling downe and carrying in the old Chappell' and levelling the ground and causeway in the churchyard.[92]

The remains of the priory

What survives of the priory today includes much of the general layout, a few more-or-less intact buildings and various fragments, some left in place, others being detached archaeological artefacts. Most obviously, the Great Cloister garth remains an open space, while the west, south and north boundaries of the precinct remain recognizable. On the east side, building along Aldersgate Street on the priory orchard site has destroyed any sense of the monastic enclosure from the road itself. However, the approaches to the gatehouse from both Charterhouse Lane and Carthusian Street still preserve a sense of entering an outer enclosure to the walled priory precinct itself.

Of the more substantial survivals above ground the most important are the gatehouse, sections of the precinct wall, the inner gateway in Entrance Court (partly rebuilt after being hit by a lorry during the post-war building

18. Chapel Court, looking east towards the site of the high altar of the priory church. Ecumenical commemoration of the Carthusian martyrs, 2009

works), the chapterhouse and sacristy 'tower' (the present Chapel and Chapel Tower), much of Wash-house Court, and the cell-front wall of half the west side of the Great Cloister, including the complete entrance and serving-hatch to Cell B. More fragmentary are the remains of the entrances to Cells S and T (wrongly identified by Hope and by Knowles and Grimes as T and V) on the east side of the cloister, where a substantial section of stone wall (in continuation of the north cell-front wall) has also been uncovered recently.[93] Both entrances are preserved *in situ*, respectively in the boundary wall between the former Medical College of St Bartholomew's Hospital and Glasshouse Yard and in the college's Rotblat Building. The entrance to Cell S retains its hatch too, but both entrances are in poor condition, in contrast to the well-preserved entrance to B. Within Sutton's Hospital, some of the tiling of the west cloister walk is preserved beneath the floor of the present Library.

These remnants cover the whole period of the priory's existence, from 1371 (B entrance) to Houghton's priorate in the 1530s (the west front of Wash-house Court). A number of stone doorways in the north range of Master's Court, their spandrels variously carved with shields, foliage or other decoration, may have belonged to the monastic buildings. Otherwise, they must date from Lord North's building operations, either as new pieces or salvage from elsewhere. None of the distinctively narrow cell doorways from the Great Cloister survive reused inside the buildings.

Much depends on whether the Great Hall originated as the 'hall' mentioned in the immediate post-suppression years. If it did, the plinth and the ground-floor doorways, including those in the screens passage, could be late-period monastic work. The first-floor doorways to the Great Chamber, side gallery of the Great Hall and Terrace walk, and those on the east side of the Great Staircase, may also be of monastic origin, but not for certain. Several of these doorways show damage to the carving, which might be deliberate post-suppression mutilation.

The surviving monastic buildings have been much altered internally and externally. The former chapter-house retains something of its original external appearance on the south and east sides, including an intact early fifteenth-century doorway, but, having been extended to the north and completely re-roofed, it is otherwise unrecognizable as a medieval structure. Inside, a stone aumbry (or more probably, piscina) survives at the east end. Chapel Tower adjoining contains the only recognizably intact monastic room on the site, the Treasury, which retains its vaulting, windows and floor tiles, as well as the squint

19. Late fifteenth-century statue of St Catherine of Alexandria, discovered during post-war reconstruction in Master's Court and identified by the archaeologist E. Clive Rouse. The figure being trodden underfoot is the pagan Roman emperor Maxentius, who ordered Catherine's death. The statue, which was probably London-made, has traces of gilding and blue paint, applied over gesso on a red base. It has been hacked for reuse as building stone[96]

which gave a view of the high altar. Under the Treasury, the ante-chapel retains its vaulted ceiling of 1512 and the archway from it into the Chapel is also essentially monastic; otherwise, the space is completely remodelled.

It is probable that the present cellar beneath the Library derives from an undercroft to the frater, as the outer or cell-side cloister wall (in the Norfolk Cloister) goes down to this level, but apart from that there is nothing identifiably medieval in the fabric. No other cellars from the priory seem to have been retained.

Two niches in the wall of what is now the Manciple's office below the west end of the Great Chamber may be of monastic origin, but if so must have been removed from elsewhere, as the wall itself is of post-suppression date.

Wash-house Court from several viewpoints gives vivid impressions of the priory, but all require some imaginative adjustment. The west front, in particular, is misleading, for the dominance of the chimneys is a post-suppression feature, and the blocked opening traditionally described as a 'dole-hatch' is probably nothing of the sort but of post-suppression date too. Allowance has also to be made for an appreciable rise in ground level. But the complete ensemble, including the path and boundary wall alongside, and the slype leading off towards the north end, gives an essentially monastic picture. Others are the view from the main gate towards the inner gate, and the gateway itself from Charterhouse Square, with its traceried wooden doors and the chequer-work boundary wall adjoining.

Apart from pieces of Manny's tomb (Ill. 17), the smaller detached relics include a headless statue of St Catherine from Sir Robert Rede's chapel, retaining traces of gilding and blue paint, retrieved from a wall in Master's Court after the Second World War (Ill. 19).[94] More remarkably, in 1848 it was discovered that the slab and brass covering a tomb in St Laurence's Church, Reading were reused from the tomb of Sir John Popham in the chapel of SS Jerome and Bernard. The tomb was that of Walter Barton, gentleman, who died in 1538, the year the Charterhouse was closed.[95] Recent finds on site, together with excavated portions of the monastic buildings, are described in the MoLAS monograph of 2002.

After the suppression

On 10 June 1537, Prior Trafford surrendered the Charterhouse and its properties to Henry VIII. But it was not until 15 November 1538, when the remaining monks and lay brothers were turned out, that the priory finally closed. The Charterhouse now entered upon a period of secularization, during which the buildings were stripped of their fittings and adapted as storehouses, workshops and lodgings for the king's servants. The most important use for which evidence exists was as a storage and works depot for the King's Tents. This mixed occupation continued until the acquisition of the entire site by Sir Edward North in 1545, and its conversion into his private mansion.

Two documents already referred to are particularly informative on the immediate post-suppression period. First is the statement by William Dale, keeper of the greater part of the Charterhouse for at least a year and a half after November 1538.[97] Dale describes the stripping of the buildings of their panelling and glass, lead piping and cisterns, furniture and fittings and other contents down to the 'kitchen stuff' and stock of vinegar and malt. He describes the sale of the great clock from the belfry, the beds from the guest rooms, the wall-hangings and a map of the world. He records the grounds cleared of trees and plants; carp taken from the ponds, birds from their cotes, and stocks of stone and timber carried away. He deals too with the tenancies of various cells and other buildings. The second document is the inventory and account made in March 1539 by the king's commissioners responsible for the Charterhouse, which names many of the buildings and some individual rooms.[98]

Both were discussed by Hope and Davies, with their own transcripts, in the early part of the twentieth century; Davies's modernized transcript of Dale's statement appears to be largely copied from that published earlier by Hendriks.[99] Hope realized that Dale's account raised questions about the number and location of the cells, and it was on this subject that fresh speculation about the priory layout was made after the Second World War. The result was the reconstruction mentioned above, postulating three garden cells outside the Great Cloister, at the south-east corner of the site.[100] This speculation was fuelled by the discovery of a third document, about the buildings occupied in the early 1540s by the Bassano brothers, a group of Italian woodwind players at court.

The presence of the musicians gives a rather different impression to the picture of the closed priory given by the monk Maurice Chauncy, an account so lurid that Davies was reluctant to accept 'the extreme of all his details', on the grounds that he was probably relying on hearsay.[101] Chauncy's description of the post-suppression priory varied from version to version of his account of the Charterhouse story, but he was right about the royal tents stored in the church, and his overall picture of thieves and prostitutes in the cloister and cells, wrestling, dicing on the altars and the smashing with axes of holy imagery may be accurate; though probably there was a more disciplined atmosphere after the Tents officers took over the site, and the carved imagery in the ceilings of what are now the ante-chapel and Treasury was not damaged (it was not, of course, in the way, unlike altars and monuments in the church). Protecting such a large and rambling site would have been impossible without full-time watchmen, and the keepers, their wages kept in arrears, were not necessarily models of probity or diligence. Dale's self-justifying account gives its own hints. He mentions the fear of glass being stolen, the theft of wainscot by one 'lyttyl sir Wyllyam', its recovery by Dale and a colleague, and their sale of it when they were in prison for some unspecified offence.[d] He stands up for another keeper and 'hys folkes' against the charge of stripping two cells out of the twenty which he has just claimed were specifically in his own keeping. He is strenuous in denying that he ever had charge of the church and adjoining cells, presumably because there had been some complaint about them.

Management of the site seems to have been confused. More or less immediately after the suppression, Dale (initially in collaboration with John Groves) was appointed keeper for the king's commissioners, who had formal responsibility, but parts of the site were put into other hands. According to Dale, the church was in the keeping of Francis Cave, one of the commissioners, while the Prior's House and five cells adjoining were the responsibility of Jerome Haydon, one of the priory servants, who with Richard Billingsley, one of the lay brothers, acted as bailiff and collector of the former priory's estates. One cell was in the keeping of Master Talbot from the suppression. Meanwhile, another lay brother, Thomas Owen, was employed as keeper of the orchards, gardens and cells, implying some overlap of responsibility: Dale names Master Cawton as keeper of the orchard, and of the two cells mentioned above as having been despoiled. Later, in 1546, Anthony Stringer was appointed bailiff and collector.[103]

Occupation of the Prior's House passed, together with that of the five cells, to a succession of short-term tenants: first Sir Arthur Darcy, a protégé of Thomas Cromwell; and then Archibald Douglas, sixth Earl of Angus and Henry VIII's former brother-in-law, who was in exile from Scotland and may have been staying here when attending court.[104] He was followed by Sir Marmaduke Constable, a soldier and knight of the body who had taken part in several Scottish campaigns, who was in occupation when part of Dale's account was written, in February 1539.

At some point in the very early 1540s, the Bassanos took over Constable's old house and several adjoining cells, surviving as sitting tenants when the Charterhouse was granted to officers of the King's Tents in 1542. Their occupation is considered below, together with the evidence that it throws up concerning the cells outside the Great Cloister. This discussion is followed by an account of how the remainder of the site was used from 1542 in connection with the Tents, and its subsequent acquisition by North.

[d] Davies, with no evident justification, identifies little Sir William as Sir William Parr, Katherine's brother. In fact, he is more likely to have been the 'Sir Wylliam Ibry' listed as one of the priory servants, 'Sir' presumably being used here as the title of a non-graduate priest; Ibry received the same 40*s* compensation as the monks, much more than the other servants and the lay brothers.[102] His relatively low status (in comparison with Parr's) might explain why Dale and his colleague dared to take back the wainscot he had purloined.

Maurice Chauncy's evidence

Maurice Chauncy wrote a series of accounts of the Carthusian martyrs between 1546 and 1570. The earliest survives in a manuscript copy in the Guildhall Library, while the best-known version was first published in Mainz in 1550 and has been reprinted in various editions since, including one published in London and Montreux in 1888 and an English translation published two years later. Two more early versions, one now in the Hague and one in Vienna, and a late version, the 'Passio Minor' of 1564, now in the Vatican, were published in the late nineteenth and early twentieth centuries. The final version, the 'Short Narration', was written and published in 1570 and reprinted, with an English translation in parallel with the original Latin and an introduction by E. Margaret Thompson, in 1935.[105]

Chauncy does not have a great deal to say about the post-suppression priory but, besides giving a general impression of what occurred, has two particular comments of interest. His 1570 description of North's activities vividly conveys the necessarily destructive process of making a house from a monastery: 'confounding sacred and profane, pulling down and building up, interchanging squares and circles, he erected a splendid mansion to suit his habits, his taste and his whims'.[106] The phrase about changing squares into circles was one he had used in the first version of the history, and (being in exile after 1547) he did not update the description to take account of the changes that had occurred since the 1540s. In the revision published in 1550 he is matter-of-fact: 'our House, cleansed from this filth, was given to a certain Sir Edward North, who built himself a palace there, and made a banqueting hall of the church, and almost entirely overthrew the cloister [*propemodum totum claustrum evertit*]'.[107] The remark about the church, not included in any of the other versions, has given rise to some conjecture (see page 133). In the Vienna version, which omits the details of sacrilege, he mentions the disinterment of Prior Batmanson's body during North's building work, an unambiguous and useful piece of evidence about the new house (page 110).

The Bassano brothers and the extra cells

The Bassanos' connection with Henry VIII's court went back some years to when, in the late 1530s, they moved permanently from Venice at Henry's invitation, forming a royal recorder consort. At least some of them were in England in 1537, and Anthony was employed as an instrument maker by Henry the following year. In April 1540, Alvise, John, Anthony, Jasper and Baptist were appointed court musicians, back-paid to the previous Michaelmas. It was probably about this time that they took up residence in the Charterhouse with their families (Alvise had four sons by 1545, and Jasper one).[108] They were later employed in the household of Henry's sixth queen, Katherine Parr, who before her royal marriage in 1543 had lived in Charterhouse Churchyard as the wife of John Neville, third Lord Latimer. The Latimer house adjoined the very part of the Charterhouse where the Bassanos lived, and the Parr connection went further, for Katherine's brother William (from 1547 Marquess of Northampton) was also their patron. He was living in a house in Charterhouse Yard in 1545, when the house was acquired, together with the Charterhouse, by Sir Edward North.[109] In 1542, when the Charterhouse was granted to Bridges and Hale of the Tents office, William was one of those appointed by Henry VIII to settle the division between their holding and that of the Bassanos.[110] This seems to have put the Bassanos on a firm footing, and when North acquired the Charterhouse in 1545 his grant included clauses safeguarding the brothers' tenancies while they remained in the king's service. With Henry's death, their security of tenure died too, and they were probably lucky to have held on as long as they did, perhaps as late as 1552. North accused them of spoiling the property by taking away wainscot and other materials, but they claimed to have spent £300 on the buildings.[111] The extent of the Bassanos' tenancy is of some importance in elucidating the priory buildings at the time of the suppression, in particular the questions of how many cells there may have been in addition to those on the water-supply plan, and where they were. The Bassanos also supply evidence about the bowling alley and gallery built by Lord North on the south walk of the Great Cloister (see page 39).

Questions about additional cells arise because, although it had been a 'double house' of two dozen monks under the prior, the Charterhouse had up to thirty monks shortly before the suppression, including the prior. This is stated categorically by Chauncy, and is corroborated by records of the monks' oaths and surrenders. (As Knowles pointed out, two of the latter-day monks were probably members of other houses, 'but as they were residing at the Charterhouse they would occupy cells'.[112]) There are also references in the keeper Dale's and the dissolution commissioners' statements to one or more new cells. Hope was unable to suggest a convincing explanation, but Knowles and his colleagues came up with a theory, discussed below, which has been accepted hitherto, with some reservation.[113]

According to a survey of their holdings in March 1545, the Bassanos occupied more or less the entire south-east corner of the Charterhouse east of the chapterhouse.[114]

Alvise was living in the Prior's House, which had its own yard, garden and door to Charterhouse Yard. From the 'high chamber' he could go out and take the air on the flat roofs of the chapels on the south side of the church. His workshop (like Anthony he was an instrument maker) was on the first floor of a small building west of the Prior's House called the pulpit house, separated from the church by a yard, which probably dated from when the monks had preached to congregations in the churchyard (a practice forbidden them in 1405).[115] He also had use of a little old stone chapel built against the east end of the church, which, as Knowles suggested, may have been the prior's private chapel.[116] In the Great Cloister, he had two cells clearly identifiable as S and T. For a while he had also occupied another 'chapel' north of the little chapel, but it had been taken from him by Bridges. This must have been the chapterhouse.

Between the Prior's House and Alvise's cells in the east cloister were seven cells jointly occupied by Anthony, Jasper, John and Baptist Bassano. However, here the description becomes confusing, because the Prior's House is earlier said to have abutted a cell in the tenure of Anthony Bassano, evidently the unlettered cell adjoining the chapterhouse on the water-supply plan. Five of the seven cells opened on to the south side of the cloister. The fifth also had a door into the orchard on the east side of the Great Cloister, and must therefore have been Cell Y. Alvise wanted to get hold of the northern three cells on the east side (P, Q and R) for himself, and to let his brothers have T. This would have given the Bassanos a continuous run of buildings from the chapterhouse to the north-east corner of the cloister: continuous, it would appear, but for the laundry shown west of Z on the water-supply plan. It is hardly likely that they would have made no attempt to get hold of the laundry too, supposing it still existed, thus consolidating their holding. It is likely, therefore, that it no longer existed, or that it was classed as a cell by William Hamton, who made the survey. If it had been in someone else's occupation, he would have had to mention the fact.[e]

The theory put forward by Knowles was based on the assumption that, since the fifth cell was Y, and only Z and the laundry apparently lay between it and Anthony's cell, there must have been three more cells here not actually abutting the cloister walk. The architect John Seely tried to fit these three cells on the tapering scrap of ground east of the prior's new cell (Prior's House), but there was clearly insufficient room. Knowles himself seems to have realized that there would have been room for the cells if the laundry had moved, but Grimes then came up with the idea that the cells had been on the site of 10 and 11 Charterhouse Square.[118] The published reconstruction (drawn by Grimes) was possibly influenced by the layout of Mount Grace, and shows three garden cells more or less identical to those in the Great Cloister itself.[119] The problem raised by the impossibility of their having opened on to the cloister walk, as Hamton's survey specifically said they did, was not addressed. There was, in any case, nothing to support Grimes's reconstruction, beyond a hunch about the existing property boundaries being ancient, and the theory cannot hold water because the site was occupied by Lord Latimer's house (page 28).

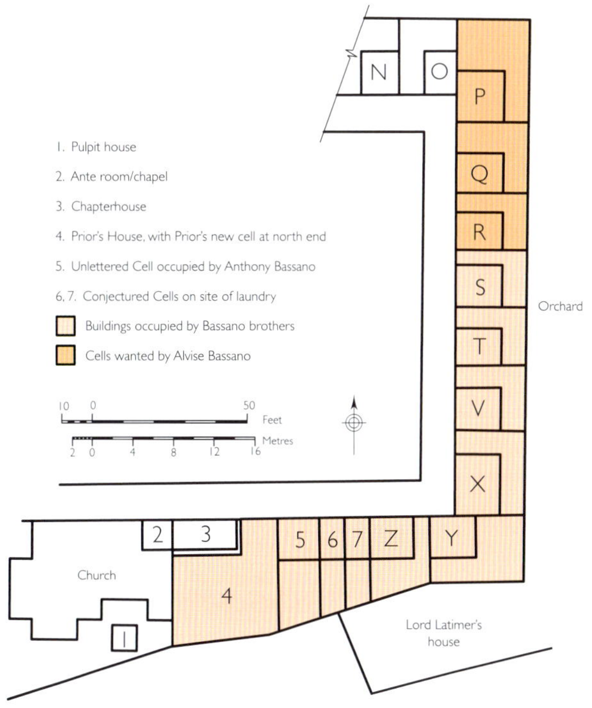

20. Sketch plan showing conjectural arrangement of cells by 1538. Outlines of lettered cells based on the medieval water-supply plan

[e] The 1539 inventory lists the laundry between the 'prior's new cell' and the brewhouse, which is followed by other ancillary rooms identifiable as what is now Wash-house Court – a sequence which could mean either that the laundry was still in the cloister or that it had indeed been replaced by the eponymous wash-house.[117]

A close reading of Hamton's survey points to Anthony's cell as having actually been one of the seven jointly occupied cells, and it is therefore only necessary to account for two extra cells, not three. One may really have been the laundry, but if the laundry had moved, two small cells may have taken its place (Ill. 20). Further, Hamton states that the Prior's House abutted the cloister, which could only be the case if it was built over part of the garden of the unlettered cell. The resultant arrangement would account for the 'thre small celles adionyng' Darcy's house (the Prior's House) mentioned by Dale: presumably the same as the 'iij celles in the kepyng of Syr Marmaduke Cunstabyll', another tenant of the Prior's House. There is nowhere else that these three little cells can have been, because on the other side of the Prior's House were the pulpit house and yard.

This new explanation does not account for all the assumed 30 cells. It brings the total to 27, assuming Cell A to have been replaced by the Prior's House and its site taken for the guest hall (page 133), or 28 if A survived. Any more cells must have been elsewhere, perhaps south of the Little Cloister, and they too may have been small or with very small gardens, if any. Foundations excavated on the south side of the Little Cloister, shown on Grimes's reconstruction plan, follow what may be a cellular arrangement.[120] They were not necessarily new or specifically for monks, as 'cell' was used more widely for lodgings and small dwellings.[121] As mentioned above, in 1500 Sir Thomas Thwaites had relinquished his claim on a 'cell' and adjoining rooms in the Little Cloister, and the accounts for 1493–4 mention the 'cells of the Visitors'.[122]

The King's Tents

In June 1542, John Bridges and Thomas Hale were granted possession of the Charterhouse by Henry VIII's letters patent, for the purpose of storing the portable buildings known as the king's tents, hales and pavilions.[123] These were the structures used in the field for military campaigns, royal progresses, diplomatic events, tournaments, banquets and masques, providing temporary lodgings, function rooms, workshops, offices and stores. They ranged from simple canvas or hide shelters to two-storey timber structures of considerable size and elaboration. The timber buildings were modular in construction, covered inside and out with leather and cloth, and painted externally in imitation of brick or stone.[124] As Yeoman and Groom respectively of the Tents office, Bridges and Hale were executives in a small hierarchy of officers under the Sergeant of the Tents, John Travers, and his successor (more grandly styled Master of the Tents), Sir Thomas Cawarden. Bridges and Cawarden occupied corresponding positions in the Revels, an office long associated with the Tents and, under Cawarden's direction, brought even closer to it.[125]

In their dispute with North, the Bassano brothers stated that Bridges and Hale had got their grant 'secretly', without the Bassanos' knowledge, and that when they complained to Henry he had ordered Sir Edward North, as head of the Court of Augmentations, to make out new letters patent, dividing the site between them and Bridges and Hale. The division was arbitrated by the Marquess of Northampton,[f] Sir Philip Hoby, Sir Thomas Cardew and Sir Henry Knyvett, but no record of it has survived.[127] In their corner, the Bassanos carried on with their work, while the remainder of the site, or a significant part of it, became the headquarters of the Tents office and its principal depot, not merely for storage and maintenance but also for manufacture. The Charterhouse gave the Tents a large site all its own, its storage facilities having been shared for many years previously with those of the Revels at Warwick Inn, in Warwick Lane.[128]

In contrast to Maurice Chauncy's picture of anarchy and debauchery in the post-suppression priory, the records retained by Cawarden show an apparently sophisticated and disciplined organization at work, with as many as several hundred men employed at any one time. These records relate largely to 1544 and 1545, when there was intense activity in connection with the Boulogne campaign, and just how the Charterhouse was used in the previous two years remains obscure. It is not even clear whether the tents themselves had yet been moved to the Charterhouse when they were inventoried in December 1542, before Henry and Emperor Charles V had agreed to invade France. If there were significant changes to the buildings during their occupation by the Tents, however, they were most probably made during that earlier period.[129]

Among the works done at the Charterhouse in 1544 was the making of a new timber lodging or tent for the king's own use. It is almost certain that this was an addition to the timber lodging 'For the warres' made at Whitefriars during the spring and summer of 1543, which replaced an unserviceable canvas lodging used by Henry at Tournai

[f] So described by the Bassanos. William Parr became Marquess of Northampton in February 1547, the month after Henry's death, and the arbitration was presumably made several years earlier, when Parr would have been Lord Parr of Kendal and, from December 1543, Earl of Essex.[126]

many years earlier (where he had also had a timber tent).[130] This seems to be confirmed by an incomplete record of payments made concerning the 'Kyngs newe Tent of Tymbre' which covers the period from July 1543 to the following March, implying that the Whitefriars and Charterhouse timber tents were consecutive parts of the same project.[131] Accounts for March to June 1544 show activity at the Charterhouse rising to a peak as Henry's departure for France became imminent. In the four weeks from 16 March, there were 76 tailors (including Hale and Bridges themselves), 2 carpenters, 4 cordwainers and 2 winders of thread at work. In the next few weeks, the workforce grew to 364 tailors, 8 cordwainers, 13 thread-winders and overseers, and 39 carpenters, plus 5 joiners and 12 sawyers making staves for the walls of Henry's lodging or cutting masts. Most of the men were making canvas tents for Boulogne, but in May to June ten tailors were cutting cloth specifically for the timber lodging, and a couple of joiners were still making staves for it.[132] In addition, John Luke and his company of twenty joiners spent two days and a night setting up the new lodging in the church, burning 12lb of great candles and six links or torches in the process. Given that the internal width of the church was only about 32ft, excluding the various chapels on either side, this must have been only the Charterhouse-made part of the 'newe Tent of Tymbre', for the whole structure comprised many rooms: 'on a small scale, a Tudor palace in timber'.[133]

Henry sailed back from France on 30 September, and by late November the timber house and other tents had returned to the Charterhouse for storage in the church, some in a chapel on the south side. An inventory of them records 200 individual 'houses', variously described as 'hales' or halls, round-houses and guard-houses, and distinguishes between seventeen tents comprising the king's 'fyrst lodging' and fourteen comprising his 'laste lodging'. There were also 40 'bare hides' laid up 'over the Sowth syde of the Church'.[134]

How the Charterhouse looked during this period can be imagined, though there is nothing to show whether the workmen were living on site. There was probably room for many of them, in the stripped-out cells or elsewhere, but many of the buildings were needed as stores and workshops. Presumably the kitchens were put to use, but these domestic arrangements would probably have been a matter for Bridges and Hale as tenants, and are not revealed in the official accounts. Chauncy appears to have been correct about 'implements of war' (other than tents) being stored at the Charterhouse, for an armoury is mentioned (and weaponry was certainly kept at Whitefriars during its occupation by the Tents office in 1543).[135]

Carpenters and joiners had their own workshops, while sawpits would have been dug in the Great Cloister or other open ground. The orchard was used for parking wagons.[136] A reference to the armoury and 'the door next the same' suggests the use of the old cells, while the existence of 'twoo cupboords in the churche to putt thred in' may indicate that the church was normally used by the tailors, or the thread-winders-cum-overseers.[137]

The fitting of locks may indicate the adaptation of hitherto unused or little-used buildings as stores or workshops, where good security was necessary. A porter controlled the 'great gate', and the periodic presence of the king's marshal's servant may have been, as at the Tents depot at Whitefriars, to search out any skiving workmen and have them jailed.[138] It is mainly through payments for locks or keys that the names of individual buildings or rooms are known, but few can be identified with much confidence. The 'hall' was no doubt the monastic guest hall, probably later rebuilt as the Great Hall of North's house, while the 'storehouse', if it was a main storehouse distinct from the collective storehouses mentioned, may have been the chapterhouse, the granary or the supposed priory barn on the west side of the site. (A large key excavated in a post-suppression make-up dump on the site of one of the western outbuildings is as likely to be from the Tents occupation as from the priory period.[139]) The counting-house, where a clock was installed, may have been the old monastic counting-house mentioned in the 1490s accounts.[140] The only substantial building work mentioned took place in April to May 1544, when lime, sand and 4,000 bricks were delivered, and a bricklayer was employed in 'the stopping and mending of certeyn wyndowes and holes aboute the storehouses'.[141]

In addition to the small army of men working with fabrics, leather and wood, there was a succession of craftsmen and suppliers bringing tools and materials or coming to carry out specialist tasks in the making or maintenance of the tents: blacksmiths with iron fittings for woodwork; a turner with ball finials for round-house tops; a roper with cord for tackling or guys; merchants with canvas, buckram, thread and trimmings; tailors with batches of Birmingham-made shears, plaster of Paris to make pounce for treating fabric, red ochre for marking-out and paste for paper patterns; cordwainers with wax, ox-hides, calf-skins, and ox-wombs for making button-holes for tackling; women with coloured tapes; a joiner with boards for cutting out cloth on; and a basketmaker with wicker hampers. The deliveries of timber were on a large scale: over four weeks from April to May 1544, 49 masts, 364 spars and 99 poles were brought by ship from Hull dockyard to St Katherine's Pool, whence they were taken by lighter to Puddle Dock and then on by road to the Charterhouse.[142]

All this time, Cawarden, who had been involved with the Tents office since 1542 and had been knighted by Henry at Boulogne, was in charge. But it was not until March 1545 that he officially became Master of the Tents, back-dated by one year.[143] John Barnard was similarly made Clerk Comptroller of the Tents on the same day, receiving a life grant of Egypt and Flesh Hall, together with le Garneter adjoining and the Charterhouse kitchen garden.[144] However, the Charterhouse was soon to be redundant, with the establishment of Blackfriars (where Cawarden set up home and acquired considerable property interests), as the new Tents headquarters. Cawarden's interests were no doubt the driving force, but Blackfriars had the advantage over the Charterhouse of being on the riverside. That April, Sir Edward North obtained the reversion of the Charterhouse from Henry VIII, and shortly afterwards bought out Hale and Bridges with an annuity of £10.[145] Over the course of a year to the beginning of March 1546, the tents and pavilions at the Charterhouse were taken to Blackfriars in 128 cartloads. The king's new lodging alone took at least six joiners and two labourers five ten-hour days to dismantle and load into carts.[146]

CHAPTER II

Howard House

Lord North at the Charterhouse, 1545–64

The acquisition of the Charterhouse by Sir Edward North, as he then was, brought to an end the makeshift use of the old buildings, but it took several years to get rid of the Bassanos. Following their appeal to Henry VIII, he accepted that they could stay while still in the king's service (a dilution of Henry's instructions, they claimed). But they failed to go when Henry died, and a three-year extension of their tenancy seems to have been agreed. It is not clear when they were finally forced to leave. According to one source, they had gone by June 1552, but they were still trying to regain full possession of their premises more than a year later, vainly petitioning the new queen, Mary.[1] It was an important delay, for it perpetuated the long-standing division of the site, the relatively small area they occupied forming the nucleus of what was much later to become Rutland House.

The Bassanos claimed that within two years of Henry's death North began to undermine their foundations, and made a gallery 'on that part of a cloister' which had been assigned to them, telling them that they could use the 'nether part' of the cloister. Having finished this gallery, North blocked up their gate into the cloister, and pulled down a wall dividing their part from his. In short, they said, he had taken away their piece of cloister and converted it into a bowling alley.[2] The bowling alley and the gallery above are listed in the 1565 inventory and parts of the structure still survive, notably the remnant of the portion adapted as the north aisle of Sutton's Hospital Chapel in 1613–14 (see page 112).

North appears to have set out the main lines of his great mansion as it exists today, incorporating some of the monastic structures more or less unchanged but destroying the two elements vital to its original use: the church and most of the cells, together with the cloister walk (Ill. 15). It is presumably to this destruction that the chronicler of Grey Friars refers when he notes that the Charterhouse was pulled down in September 1545.[3] Most of the ancillary buildings comprising Wash-house Court, some of which was less than fifteen years old, were left intact, but the eastern range was reconstructed to form the west side of an enlarged Little Cloister (now Master's Court). This enlargement was done partly at the expense of the entrance court inside the gate from the churchyard. The gateway itself and the dwelling house over it were left standing, as were ancillary buildings along the western boundary of the site.

The south range of Master's Court, with a long gallery on the first floor, can confidently be attributed to North, and the gallery is clearly there in the 1565 inventory. But the north side is more problematic. The double-pile plan, with the Great Hall and present-day Library on the ground floor, most probably perpetuates a late-monastic arrangement of guest hall and frater, and probably incorporates some of the monastic fabric *in situ*, if only foundations, though North must have enlarged these rooms by extending them over the cloister walk. He certainly built the Great Chamber over the Library, as well as the short addition on the north side which now separates the Great Chamber ante-room from the upper terrace of the Norfolk Cloister.

21. Early twentieth-century view of disused fireplaces in the former pastry kitchen on the west side of Master's Court, thought to be part of Lord North's work in the 1540s. Beyond the post and rails there was by this time a way through to the slype between Master's and Wash-house Courts (see Ill. 37). *Destroyed 1941*

22. South range of Master's Court, from Entrance Court, undated late nineteenth-century view. This was the main front of Howard House. Far left: part of Registrar's house. Right: Master's Lodge; 10 & 11 Charterhouse Square in distance

On the east side of Master's Court, the chapel of St Anne and Holy Cross at the west end of the church was completely demolished and a new range built with its front wall on the foundations of the original west wall of the church and its continuation as the sides of the chapels to north and south. Behind this eastern range of Master's Court, the choir of the church, the chapels and other additions were all demolished, leaving just the chapter-house and adjoining treasury. The greater part of the church site remained open, and perhaps at this time the ground immediately south (including the site of the pulpit house) was built up with a range fronting Charterhouse Churchyard, joining the new mansion to the former Prior's House.

At the back of North's new house, the Great Cloister garth also remained open, bordered by the ruins of the cells. His destruction of the cells was neither systematic nor total, probably for the simple reason that complete demolition would have been expensive and the stone not needed for his own buildings difficult to dispose of.[g] On the south side, the site of the cloister walk was largely taken for his bowling alley and gallery range, and on the other sides the cell-front walls continued to define the edges of the former cloister garth. Cell G at least, at the north-west corner, seems to have survived more or less intact and may have been used as a garden pavilion or served some more workaday purpose. On the east side, the cell-front wall was to become the boundary between Howard House and the grounds of the future Rutland House, while that on the north served to divide the garth—which took on the character of a formal garden—from the ground to the north. This was mainly garden and orchard, and was to become a more-or-less wooded belt buffering Howard House from the building development on Whitwellbeach and Pardon Churchyard. But, as late as 1590, the site of the razed north cells was 'vacant ground', suggesting that it remained no more than a demolition site. Both the north and east cloister walls were obscured by banks of earth, or demolition spoil, forming terraces around the main garden, and there was probably some other earthworking to level the ground. At some point the northern cell-front wall was extended eastwards, forming a division between what were to become Howard House and Rutland House. Part of the wall, incorporating a blocked gateway more than 9ft wide, survives.[5] The west wall probably remained fully exposed, screening the garden from the stables and other outbuildings to the west, with the doorway to Cell B perhaps serving for through access.

When North acquired the Charterhouse he had been knighted only three years earlier, and his career had some way to go. After Edward VI's accession, he was appointed to the Privy Council by Lord Protector Somerset. His resignation as Chancellor of the Court of Augmentations in 1548 was apparently under pressure from Somerset, with whom he had fallen out, and accordingly he supported the *coup d'état* by John Dudley, then Earl of Warwick, in 1549. He sold the Charterhouse to Dudley (by then Duke of Northumberland) in May 1553. But his subsequent support for the bid to secure the crown for Dudley's daughter-in-law Lady Jane Grey was brief. Queen Mary rewarded him with the return of the Charterhouse in October, and in April the following year made him Baron North.[6]

Gerald Davies's suggestion that Northumberland wanted the Charterhouse for his son Guildford and Lady Jane Grey is a possibility, although at that stage there was no prospect of Jane becoming queen. The sale took place on 4 May, and the marriage of Guildford and Jane on the 21st. It was not until after this, perhaps well into June, that Edward VI's illness prompted him to amend his 'devise for the succession', naming Jane as heir to the throne. The duke never seems to have used the buildings. Though the Charterhouse is included in a list of his houses made on his attainder, the inventories of his properties made for the Crown make no mention of it. He did have some items at the former St John's priory near by, but it is not apparent on what Davies based his claim that Northumberland stored furniture there that was intended for the Charterhouse.[7]

Possibly it was only after its reacquisition by North that the house took on the stately character that made it a fit place for Elizabeth to visit at her accession in 1558 and again in 1561. A century later, Dudley, third Lord North wrote of his great-grandfather:

> The bravery of his mind may best be judged of, by his delight to live in an equipage rather above than under his condition or degree ... and by his magnificence in other kinds, but especially by his buildings, which were very noble for materials and workmanship, as may appear by the two houses which he set up at *Kirtling* and *Charterhouse*.[8]

Kirtling Castle in Cambridgeshire, which (as plain Edward North) the first Baron had bought in 1533, was rebuilt by him as Kirtling Hall, probably from 1537, but,

[g] There was a lot of such material from dissolved monasteries. Stow records the difficulty that Sir Thomas Audley had some years earlier in disposing of the church at Holy Trinity Priory in Aldgate, there being almost no market for stone since houses were mostly built of brick and timber.[4]

as at the Charterhouse little is known of the chronology. A recent account suggests two building phases, one before 1549, one in 1556–8: a pattern perhaps paralleling works at the Charterhouse. Extensive earthworks were involved. All that remains of the great mansion is the three-storey gatehouse, a building in architectural contrast to the Charterhouse.[9] In the first place, it is built mainly in local red brick, whereas at the Charterhouse North was working mostly with salvaged stone, of which there was plenty to hand. The tall, turreted gatehouse form, well established by this date, was used to effect at Kirtling but eschewed at the Charterhouse, where the monastic gateway was left unaltered. Cost may have played its part here, though the different status of town and country houses was perhaps another factor. While the Kirtling battlements and plain mullioned windows had their counterparts at the Charterhouse, there was nothing there to match the fashionable bowed oriel over the entrance at Kirtling. North did raise a tower at the Charterhouse (Chapel Tower), but it was a very plain affair. If Kirtling Hall was a place for architectural show, North's London house depended on its location and range of accommodation to impress.

The site being so large, North never incorporated the Bassanos' portion into the main house. Instead, he seems to have preserved the Prior's House as a separate dwelling, perhaps enlarging it, and to have built another house east of it, with extensive gardens between the east side of the Great Cloister and Aldersgate Street. These houses were later enlarged and united, eventually becoming known as Rutland House (see Chapter X).

Besides the Charterhouse itself, North had interests in Charterhouse Yard, where the priory had had a number of houses. North's sister Joan and her husband William Wilkinson, a mercer, were living in one of these well before North acquired the Charterhouse, their house standing on the east side (roughly on the site of present-day Florin Court), south of Lord Latimer's house. By 1543, the antiquary John Leland (North's old schoolfellow) was living next door to the Wilkinsons in another house, perhaps hived off from theirs.[10]

After Wilkinson's death, North bought the two houses from Joan, and in 1555 sold or mortgaged the property for £560 to an official at the Exchequer. It was described then as a single house converted from the earlier two, but also as 'late new buylded' and so may have been another building project by North. The site evidently extended to Aldersgate Street, for it included tenements 'standyng upon the wall at the farder ende of the orchard next to the high waye'. A schedule of fittings suggests a substantial but not necessarily extensive building, with a great hall, great and little parlours, and upstairs a great chamber directly over the great parlour, and a gallery.[11]

Howard House under the Duke of Norfolk

North died at the Charterhouse on the last day of 1564, the day before it was to have been sold to Thomas Howard, fourth Duke of Norfolk; the deal went ahead in accord with a deathbed codicil to his will, which stipulated that part of the proceeds be used to settle the debts of his heir, his eldest son, Roger. The purchase price of £2,200 was payable in nine instalments, the last due on 1 May 1569.[12] Included in the sale were the gates to the Charterhouse in Charterhouse Lane and what is now Carthusian Street, and the water-supply system from Islington, but not the future Rutland House. In a separate transaction the following month with the new Lord North, Norfolk paid £320 for Whitwellbeach and Pardon Churchyard north of the Charterhouse.[13] This was part of a large area acquired by Sir Edward North between what are now Goswell Road and St John Street, extending to the Hermitage at their junction.[14] Finally, in the following year Norfolk rounded off his acquisition by purchasing from Hale, the former groom of the King's Tents, the annuity with which North had bought out his interest in the Charterhouse granted by Henry VIII. The other annuitant, Bridges, was already dead.[15]

Norfolk's purchase of North House is easy enough to understand. In 1558–9 he had sold his ancestral London seat, Norfolk House in Lambeth, close to the parish church, where the Howard Chapel had been built by the second duke in 1522. That residence, low-lying and flanked by two inns, sold, together with more than 40 acres of marsh and other ground, for only £400.[16] The sale followed Norfolk's marriage in November 1558 to Thomas, Lord Audley's daughter Margaret, the widowed Lady Dudley. This brought him the house in Aldgate built by her father out of the former Augustinian priory of Holy Trinity or Christchurch, otherwise called Creechurch. Before Audley's death in 1544, the priory had been partly rebuilt as a mansion. It has been suggested that Norfolk may have carried out work there, including the creation of the Ivy Chamber, its grandest room, formed in the crossing of the church at first-floor level. But there is no proof. Under Norfolk's occupation, the building became known as Duke's Place. Queen Elizabeth visited in January 1559, just before her coronation, and may have come again in 1561. Duke's Place, however, was no match for the Charterhouse. There was no garden on the scale of the Great Cloister, and the site had been partly developed with comparatively lowly tenements from the 1540s; a surviving deed of 1562 records the sale of houses and shops there by the duke and duchess to a bowyer.[17]

The duchess died in the Howard palace at Norwich in January 1564, after which Norfolk left court to live with his children in the country, where he seems to have remained until late summer.[18] The purchase of the mansion at the Charterhouse therefore coincided with his return to the world of court in-fighting. His standing must have been in the forefront of his mind. In September, when negotiation for the purchase would have been imminent or in progress, his rival Lord Robert Dudley was made Earl of Leicester. And in December, Norfolk, Leicester and Lord Darnley were suggested by Elizabeth I as possible candidates for the hand of Mary, Queen of Scots. Norfolk was again proposed as Mary's husband the following year (by her secretary, William Maitland of Lethington). Marriage to Mary was to become Norfolk's fatal obsession. But not yet. In 1565, 'he undoubtedly looked on such a match … as tantamount to political suicide'.[19]

Not only did the new house have huge potential, it was away from the river's damp air, unlike Norfolk House and so many of the great royal and aristocratic strongholds in or near London. Lord Latimer, living in Charterhouse Yard in the 1530s, had wanted his house there 'because it stands in good air out of the press of the city',[20] and the same held true for the Charterhouse 30 years later. In November 1558, Elizabeth I had found the Charterhouse the most suitable place to stay when she made her way to London from Hatfield to claim the throne. She was in no hurry to show herself in London or Westminster, and therefore the Charterhouse was the ideal place to establish herself in government without doing so. For the duke, based for much of the year at Kenninghall in south Norfolk, a house accessible from the north without entering London itself had obvious attractions too, on grounds of both convenience and health.[21] Nor is it too fanciful to see the edge-of-town location as reflecting his aloof character and disdain for life at court. More than today, the Charterhouse was cut off from the ordinary townspeople. The churchyard was part of the Howard House freehold and effectively policed by the duke's men. Access from Aldersgate Street was controlled by means of the gate in Carthusian Street, and from Charterhouse Lane by a chain and posts. It was recorded in 1590 that the duke's and later Philip Howard's bailiff was able to 'make Arests and serve all the Queenes processe within the Church yard there and none other to enter and meddell within the same place to do the same'.[22]

Norfolk's occupation and improvement of this exceptional property were to be closely tied up with his own extraordinary status and political ambition. He was then England's only duke, and therefore the highest-ranking peer; he was of royal descent, and was also second cousin to Queen Elizabeth (Anne Boleyn's mother having been the sister of his grandfather, the third duke). He had vast estates, particularly in Norfolk and elsewhere in East Anglia, where he enjoyed great loyalty and popular support, making him one of England's most powerful magnates as well as perhaps its richest man. As hereditary Earl Marshal he had an important role in state ceremony and the control of patronage, and he took his duties seriously, carrying out a reform of the College of Arms. When he bought North's house he was a widower twice over, and in early 1567 he married again: to Elizabeth Dacre, widow of the fourth Baron Dacre of Walden and the mother of four children closely matched in age to his own. In September, Elizabeth died in childbirth, and Norfolk sank into a state of depression and physical illness from which he did not recover for many months. But Elizabeth's death left the way open for a fourth marriage, and two years later he was planning to marry the Catholic Mary, Queen of Scots. The match held the prospect of his becoming not only king of Scotland but, if the English succession could be resolved in Mary's favour, of England too. This plan had a definite appeal to conservative, Catholic factions, though Norfolk himself was a Protestant and always remained so. Dynastic ambition apart, 1569 was a year in which Norfolk was particularly concerned with expanding the wealth and power of his family, and the aggrandisement of Howard House was a natural corollary. In May his six-year-old ward and stepson, George Dacre, was crushed to death trying to adjust a vaulting-horse in a gallery at the duke's Thetford house. Norfolk had intended George to marry his daughter Margaret. Now George's three sisters became substantial heiresses, and Norfolk took steps to marry them in due course to his own three sons. Philip and William did marry their stepsisters, but not Thomas, the other Dacre girl dying young (see Ill. 24).[23]

It is likely that the duke carried out some improvements to the property early on. He was out of London in Norfolk for sixteen months from late 1566, returning in May 1568. Unusually, he remained there through that summer, when normally he would have been home in Norfolk. In July, there was a visit from Elizabeth I; among the business transacted at Howard House was the formal submission before the queen and Privy Council of the Irish rebel, the fourteenth Earl of Desmond, a prisoner in the Tower since the previous year.[24] In October, the duke was in York for the conference or tribunal to resolve the problem of Mary—accused of the murder of her husband Lord Darnley and forced to abdicate in favour of her young son, James (with her half-brother, the Earl of Moray, as regent), and her possible restoration to the throne.

The 1568 tribunal failed to resolve the problem, although the 'casket letters' produced there were an effective character assassination, seeming to prove her guilty of complicity in her husband's murder and of adultery. As yet, however, Norfolk still had no thought of marrying her himself: his advisor Lawrence Bannister (or Banastre) recalled how, in May 1569, Norfolk had talked to him in the garden at Howard House of how he was being pressed by friends to marry Mary, but was inclined to think his brother Henry a more suitable husband for her.[25] But that summer Norfolk changed his mind, and by early September news of the proposed marriage was out: 'the most sensational news of the year'.[26] In the event, he bungled the scheme as badly as he could possibly have done, failing to seek Elizabeth I's support for it, or even to raise the matter with her, despite being given repeated opportunities by her to do so. Having given every impression of harbouring treasonable intentions, he then failed to make a stand against her, when he might conceivably have exploited his own popularity in East Anglia and the support of the Catholic nobility in the north country. Instead, later that September, he simply fled, from the court to Howard House and thence to Kenninghall. Summoned by Elizabeth a few days later, he was placed under arrest in the charge of Sir Henry Neville and taken to the Tower.

Norfolk's eventual transfer in August 1570 to house arrest at Howard House, with Neville as gaoler, was ostensibly on the grounds of his failing health and an outbreak of plague in the Tower Hamlets. In the meantime, the political situation had changed, with the suppression of attempted risings in Norfolk and the crushing of the Catholic-led Northern Rebellion. But these were followed immediately by the opening moves in the improbable plot which was to bring about Norfolk's death. Roberto di Ridolfi, with whom he had had financial dealings for some time, called in the week of his return and the first of their meetings out of Neville's way was arranged by Norfolk's secretary William Barker. Six months later Ridolfi was back, and Norfolk became drawn inextricably into the plot, which seemed to offer his only means of salvation. Elizabeth was to be overthrown, Catholicism restored, and Norfolk and Mary Stuart set up as king and queen. He may only then have begun to embellish and improve Howard House on a grand scale. The Great Hall screen, Norfolk Cloister and perhaps alterations to the Great Chamber ceiling date from this time. Building was still in progress when, on 6 September 1571, as the uncovering of the plot proceeded, he was returned to the Tower. On 16 January 1572 he was found guilty of treason at Westminster Hall, and on 2 June was beheaded on Tower Hill.

The duke's improvements

In his 'last defence', written from the Tower in February 1572, Norfolk referred to the supposed consequences to London had the Ridolfi plot succeeded in overthrowing Elizabeth:

> I was also charged, as though I should be privy that there was a certain meaning against this city. God knoweth I have never heard words of any such matter, and I think any reasonable man will purge me thereof, if he do but look into my doings in this city in building Howard House, in purchasing the reversion of Arundel House[h] (I speak not of Christchurch) that this were no token that I meant to harbour conquerors there, whereby nobody shall be sure to keep his own: so myself and mine to lose both my purchase and costs in building.[28]

This gives some insight into how Norfolk saw his building activities, but it is far from clear how much building he did at Howard House. The most important evidence for his work is in a series of accounts of successive receiver-generals of his and his son Philip's estates, in inventories, and in the Crown survey made in 1590 after Philip's attainder.[29i] Evidence gathered by the state in the course of investigating the Ridolfi plot touches on the building work going on at that time.

Only the building of the Norfolk Cloister (half of which survives in carcase) and the installation of some stained glass in the Great Chamber is reliably documented. Nothing survives of the tennis court adjoining the Norfolk Cloister, but this too must have been the work of the duke, a keen player, who granted the keeping of it to one of his servants. In the Great Hall, the screen has been scientifically dated to Norfolk's day, and in any case it carries the initials TN for Thomas Norfolk and the date 1571. In one of the arch spandrels of the oriel at the high end of the hall, the words 'Thynke and Thanke' may be a punning reference to the same version of the duke's name, and a pointer to his having built or embellished the oriel.[30] In the Great Chamber, the ceiling carries the Howard arms with the ducal crown, though these may be replacements for other motifs. The chimneypiece in the same room (one of a pair, the other now destroyed) is probably of Norfolk's day, on stylistic grounds. But it is impossible to point to any substantial building by him apart from the Norfolk Cloister, and the destruction of so much fabric in 1941

[h] As part of the marriage settlement of Philip Howard, heir to the Earldom of Arundel through his mother, Mary Fitzalan. Arundel House was the great Fitzalan house in the Strand.[27]

i Philip Howard, known as the Earl of Surrey until 1580, when he became Earl of Arundel, is referred to throughout as Philip Howard.

23. Great Chamber range in 2003, looking south from the former privy garden. Norfolk Cloister is on the left

means that the question 'North or Norfolk?', posed by Gerald Davies, remains to some extent open. The two men's main contributions are indicated in Illustration 25.

Norfolk's artistic patronage has been summed up as 'the last and not the least distinguished flicker of the early sixteenth-century English Renaissance'.[31] This is not clearly borne out by his work at the Charterhouse, because what remains is either too fragmentary or its attribution too uncertain. On the basis of his decorative work in the Great Chamber, he was perhaps more interested in genealogy, heraldry and general display of wealth and power than artistic refinement. However, such display was appropriate to the function of the room and his taste may be more reliably reflected by the up-to-date decoration of the monument to his first two wives in Framlingham church.[32] The Great Hall screen at the Charterhouse, too, is relatively advanced in its Renaissance detailing. The Norfolk Cloister is difficult to assess because the upper parts, the original windows and all the interior decoration have gone. There is a marked difference between the two fronts, the west being distinctly unsophisticated; it is a later addition and may date from after Norfolk's death. The east front, however, hints at a more avant-garde taste, which would be in keeping with a tendency then and later in great houses for architectural fashion to be most strongly manifest in garden fronts, or garden buildings themselves.

Such might be expected from the son of the poet Henry Howard, Earl of Surrey, whose mid-1540s house overlooking Norwich has long been seen as a great lost work of art. In fact, Mount Surrey has been mythologized and, though the myth continues to be repeated, detailed architectural evidence is lacking. It is not known on what, if anything, Surrey's early nineteenth-century biographer G. F. Nott based his extraordinary claim that it was 'purely Greek' and the first building in the kingdom 'formed correctly on ancient models'. Speculation that it was the work of Italian designers is no more than that, and, while Surrey overstretched himself in furnishing it, both the magnificence of the contents (inventoried at Surrey's fall) and the grandeur of the building have been exaggerated.[33] In any case, the driving force at Mount Surrey was probably not simply aesthetic but dynastic, and this was more certainly the case at Howard House, where Norfolk's embellishment of the Great Chamber echoes his father's treasonable use of the royal arms at Norwich, for which he was executed (see page 148).

Expenditure on building

Norfolk's accounts, while lacking much specific detail, give some impression of the scale of his building works. In the period from 1 February 1571 to 19 March 1572, the very large sum of £1,485 9*s* 11*d* was paid to the keeper, John Sinclair, for building works and repairs at Howard House. It is impossible to say when the works began or whether this sum represents the bulk of the money spent on new works. It cannot amount to the whole, for several years later the bricklayers Drewe and Arden were paid the last £80 owing for the building of the Norfolk Cloister. The rest of their £560 contract may have been subsumed in the £1,485 paid to Sinclair, but it may not: the £39 paid to Drewe the previous year for unspecified work may also relate to the cloister, while other payments may have been made before 1571. This and other instances make clear that payments to individual craftsmen do not necessarily appear under the category of 'building and repairs' to the various Howard properties. Only occasionally can these other payments be tied to particular works and properties. The £12 paid to Henry Deacon, a plumber, in 1576–7, was for work at Howard House. So too may have been the sums paid out to a whole range of craftsmen—among them the plasterer Henry Watson; Curwen of London, freemason; Stephen Rowley of London and William Bacheram, painters; Michael Hosier and Ralph or Radolphus Botte, arras-makers; David Vynes and William Mambie, carpenters; and a man recorded only as 'The Duche Joyner'.[34]

The Norfolk Cloister is likely to have been the biggest single undertaking, and must have cost much more than Drewe and Arden's £560, whether or not this included all their materials and whether or not it included the adjoining tennis court. There would in addition have been appreciable bills for paving and other stonework, carpentry, iron- and leadwork, glazing, plastering and painting. It may have cost something like £1,000, not far off half the sum Norfolk had paid to acquire the house in the first place.

Work on the improvements may have continued after the duke's return to the Tower in September 1571, but the Norfolk Cloister gives reason to think that the intended work was eventually curtailed. It is not possible to say how the money was spent in detail, but one of the biggest items was probably the continuing construction of the cloister. By the end of that November, £200 was still owed to the workmen at Howard House.[35] In the fifteen months after March 1572, £124 5*s* was paid to Sinclair for building, perhaps representing more or less the completion of the works begun by the duke. The next eight months' accounts show a payment of £48 10*s* 3*d*. Repairs or other building works in the following years were yet smaller (£13 13*s* 4*d* in 1574–5, £4 19*s* 2*d* in 1575–6, £25 18*s* 8*d* in 1576–7), and may represent comparatively trifling repairs or alterations only. As before, other payments on building and repairs may not have been recorded as such. But even under that specific heading, outlay at Howard House during the 1570s greatly exceeded that at other Howard houses in that period. Apart from Howard House, only the Norwich and Kenninghall palaces appear regularly in the accounts. Annual payments ranged from just £1 10*s* 10*d* at Norwich in 1572–3 to as much as £120 12*s* 6*d* at Kenninghall in 1577–8, the two houses averaging annually about £30 and £43 respectively.

The Ridolfi plot evidence

Howard House was the backdrop against which some of the more theatrical scenes of the Ridolfi affair were played out: the secret meeting or meetings with Ridolfi, smuggled in under the very nose of the duke's gaoler, Sir Henry Neville; William Barker, the treacherous secretary, lurking nearby as Ridolfi and the duke conversed in the long gallery; incriminating letters and ciphers hidden under mats or more cunningly concealed in the roof. In the evidence variously accumulated or fabricated by Lord Burghley and his men, we find fleeting and tantalizing glimpses of the house and the work being done. Neville Williams remarks in *A Tudor Tragedy* that the toing and froing of so many workmen made it difficult for Sir Henry to keep tabs on Norfolk's visitors and correspondence.[36] In fact, it is as likely that slack security was part of a deliberate policy, as Gerald Davies suggested.[37] This view of the plot, with the suggestion that Ridolfi himself may have been a double agent or an agent provocateur, was developed in detail by Francis Edwards in *The Marvellous Chance* in the 1960s, after Williams's biography of Norfolk had appeared. Recent scholarship has not brought about a consensus on this conspiracy-theory interpretation, and the truth about the Ridolfi plot remains unknown. The likelihood, however, is that the plot was indeed a government set-up. There is good reason to think that Ridolfi was 'turned' on his release from imprisonment in 1569–70 on suspicion of fund-raising for Mary, Queen of Scots.[38] Equally, there is reason to think that some of the evidence against Norfolk was planted. But, whatever Ridolfi's role, Norfolk acted so recklessly during his imprisonment that a convincing charge of treason could probably have been brought in any case. His commissioning of a new pedigree with Mary Stuart's arms prominently displayed as well as his own, the Scottish thistles in the ceiling of the Great Chamber alcove and his blatant display of his own royal heritage in the windows (page 148), were little short of madness in the circumstances.

The first point of interest is the handing over to Barker of the bag of gold for Mary, Queen of Scots which was to lead to the unravelling of the plot when the carrier's suspicions were roused. Davies understood that this incident took place in the chapel at Howard House. In fact it took place in the chapel of the ambassador's house.[39] There was no doubt a chapel at Howard House, as there had been in North's day, but evidence for it remains elusive. Then there is the staircase, referred to by Barker in describing how he had brought Ridolfi into Howard House to meet the duke in the Gallery (on the south side of what is now Master's Court), by the duke's bedchamber:[40] 'up on the Back Side by the long Workhouse at the furder end of the Lavendry Cort. So up a new Payer of Stayers that goeth up to the old Wardrobe and so thoroughe the chamber where my Lady Lestrange used to dine and suppe'.[41] Davies thought their route was through the western slype of Wash-house Court, across Master's Court to the north-east corner where a door 'opened on to the Great Staircase, newly built'.[42] The long workhouse he identified as part of the west range of Wash-house Court, 'now divided up into smaller workshops'. But there was no doorway from Master's Court as he describes, and the Great Staircase itself did not yet exist. While the staircase does seem to have replaced a smaller one in the same area, that would not have been new in 1571; nor would Barker have referred to stairs serving the Great Chamber in such an obscure way. In any case, 'pair of stairs' did not necessarily mean two flights, as Davies thought. Without knowing where the old Wardrobe and Lady L'Estrange's chamber were, Barker's route cannot be established. However, it is just possible that the Ridolfi staircase was the now-disused staircase, off the western slype of Wash-house Court (Ill. 51). It is certainly an insertion, cutting through the floor beams, and ideal for covert entry from the back of the house. For Ridolfi's second secret meeting, Barker brought him in by way of the stairs to the entry to Sir Henry Neville's chamber. Davies seems to have identified these as Preacher's Stairs, on the north side of the house between the Great Staircase and Brooke Hall;[43] there is, in fact, nothing to suggest their location.

Equally irresolvable is the riddle of the missing cipher-key for letters between Norfolk and Mary. In the early stages of the exposure of the plot, under interrogation in the Tower, one of Norfolk's secretaries, William Higford or Hickforth, had revealed that this document 'was left undre the Matte, hard by the Wyndowes Syde, in the Entrye towards my Lord's Bed-chamber, wheare the Mappe of *England* doth hang'.[44] (The room was probably Lord North's old bedchamber, over the pastry on the west side of present-day Master's Court.) It was not to be found when Burghley's men arrived at Howard House, post-haste. The idea that 'Norfolk had got to it' first[45] would seem to be mistaken, for in its place was discovered a yet more incriminating document, a letter to him from Mary. Norfolk was to claim that he had understood this letter to have been burned on his orders a year earlier.[46] Other secret papers, including letters and cipher-keys, were allegedly found hidden in the duke's bible and other books in the Howard House library.[47] As for the key to the letters said to have been under the mat, this was finally traced to the roof of the house. It was apparently the duke who first revealed this hiding place to his interrogators. The precise place was eventually disclosed by Higford, whose illness had led Norfolk to recall from retirement the older Barker, who, like Higford, was to crack under threat of the rack. The episode was recounted to Burghley in September 1571:[48]

> charging [Norfolk] that he had the Cifer which we missed, and which should lie under the Matte, he cast out a word, and said that Higforth's memory might fail; yt had been, and might lie betwixte tiles. We called Higforth before us. At the first he said that was before the House was full buylded, now it was ceeled there, and toke it to be under the Matte. Yet after a night he remembered himself but he could not demonstrate it that any man might fyend it. If he went by himself he doubted not to fyend it if it were there. Whereupon I, Dr Wilson, went this day with hym and one of the Tower his keper to Haward House and founde it indede betwixt two tiles in the Roof so hid as it had not been possible to have founde it otherwise than by unrypping all the Tiles except one had been well acquainte with the Place.[49]

The implication here is that major building work had been going on, but the precision with which the location of the mat had been described by Higford was strangely not matched when it came to the roof. There is no clue to where this roof was or how the space was accessed after it was ceiled. The story, indeed, may have been to a greater or lesser extent fiction.

Something at least is to be gleaned from another enigmatic part of the evidence concerning more papers, trinkets and other gifts sent by Mary to Norfolk. Barker told how, about Midsummer 1570, he had, on the duke's order, given a bag of documents, including letters from her, to a carpenter named William Tailor, to be buried in the ground until called for.[50] Tailor, who lived locally at the White Lion in Aldersgate Street, turns up elsewhere in the story of the plot, for another participant, John Cuthbert, secretary to Mary's ambassador the Bishop of Ross, spent several nights hiding in Tailor's house.[51] Barker's bag of documents was seemingly not buried but hidden in some sort of box nailed under a bed at Tailor's, together with the trinkets. Francis Edwards concluded that Tailor was a government agent deputed to keep these incriminating items, intercepted or recovered from Howard House, until the time for exposure of the plot. But this scheme, he reasoned, was abandoned in favour of the more convincing ploy involving the mats and tiles at Howard House, places where the duke might plausibly hide these things. Consequently, no mention of the finds under the bed was made at the duke's trial. It is indeed odd that there seems to be no record of Tailor himself having been interrogated. But he was certainly one of the men working at Howard House, if he was the William Tailor of London, carpenter, whose bill for £39 *6s* 7½*d* was among Philip Howard's debts in 1585. If so, he was probably associated with Howard House for many years. In light of this, Barker's claim that he gave the papers to Tailor on the duke's orders seems more credible. Tailor would have been a trusted figure, routinely coming and going with tools and materials, and able to construct a suitable hiding place. Whatever the truth about the secret papers, the story identifies one of Norfolk's craftsmen at Howard House.[52]

John Sinclair

The man responsible for arranging and overseeing building work at Howard House was John Sinclair, keeper under a grant made on 12 August 1569, a few weeks before Norfolk's downfall. The duke was then with the queen at Loseley in Surrey, but had recently returned from a visit to Howard House and it was no doubt then that instructions for the grant were given. This may mark the start of his main campaign of improvements, which is generally thought to have been concentrated in the period of his house arrest, from August 1570. Davies's assertion that, having acquired the Charterhouse in 1565, 'he seems at once to have set about the changes which were to make it perhaps the finest palace in London' seems to be no more than an assumption.[53]

Sinclair, 'a Scottis mane borne' said to be 'in great credit' with Norfolk, was an important member of the staff.[54] Davies refers to him as 'John Syncleer, alias Gardener, he being the gardener of Howard House', and relates how, after his interrogation over the Ridolfi plot, he was held prisoner in the Tower for a while before being sent 'back to his vegetables'. He otherwise refers to him as 'caretaker' of Howard House and the tennis court, but the tennis court never seems to have been his responsibility. Williams mused that Sinclair was perhaps 'the first of the long line of Scots that have beautified the gardens of English noblemen'.[55] As suggested by his interrogators' view of his testimony ('alehowse babbling such as is common with such raskalls'),[56] he was probably a working man, unlike most of Norfolk's senior staff. His official position was keeper, not gardener, a position that had its counterparts at the duke's other houses and that seems to have involved much more than caretaking. He is Sinclair 'alias Gardener' in the estate accounts, and elsewhere 'John Gardiner the keper of howard house'; Burghley's men said that he was 'scarcely known' as Sinclair but 'called John Gardener'. At that time (1571) he had been with Norfolk for ten years and before that worked for seven or eight years for Sir Nicholas L'Estrange of Hunstanton Hall in Norfolk, the duke's chamberlain. Sinclair got into trouble with the authorities as a result of talking to a fellow Scot about the duke's plan to liberate Mary Stuart and boasting that 'there was nothing spoken in the court touching the Duke, but he knew of it every night before he went to bed' from L'Estrange.[57]

In 1580, Sinclair took out a 70-year lease, presumably a building lease, from Philip Howard, of a plot (105ft by 32ft) on the west side of Charterhouse Churchyard. In 1590, this was described as containing a tenement and a bowling alley, at the end of which Sinclair had set up dicing houses. These were kept open day and night and were blamed for attracting crime and disorder.[58] He is still named as keeper in the list of staff remaining at Howard House in 1585, after Philip Howard's imprisonment, appearing with his wife, six children, brother-in-law and two servants of his own. Subsequently his position was that of rent collector for Howard House, which presumably included responsibility for the properties north of the Charterhouse in Whitwellbeach and Pardon Churchyard. However, the accounts suggest that, from the early 1580s, he was no longer responsible for building work, and had become rent collector by about 1582. Davies records, without giving his source, that Sinclair gave up the keepership as late as 1593, when Edward Morris, gentleman, of London, was appointed in his place. But he is still named as collector of Howard House on an undated list of rents due to James I.[59]

Howard House after Norfolk's death

Norfolk placed Howard House, with Whitwellbeach and other properties, in the hands of his estate managers John Blennerhassett, William Dix, William Cantrell and Lawrence Bannister, as trustees for Philip Howard.[60] Despite his attainder, the trust was respected, and after the duke's execution Howard House continued as an important Howard base, while parts were let to various tenants. The duke had decided in 1571 that, in the event of his

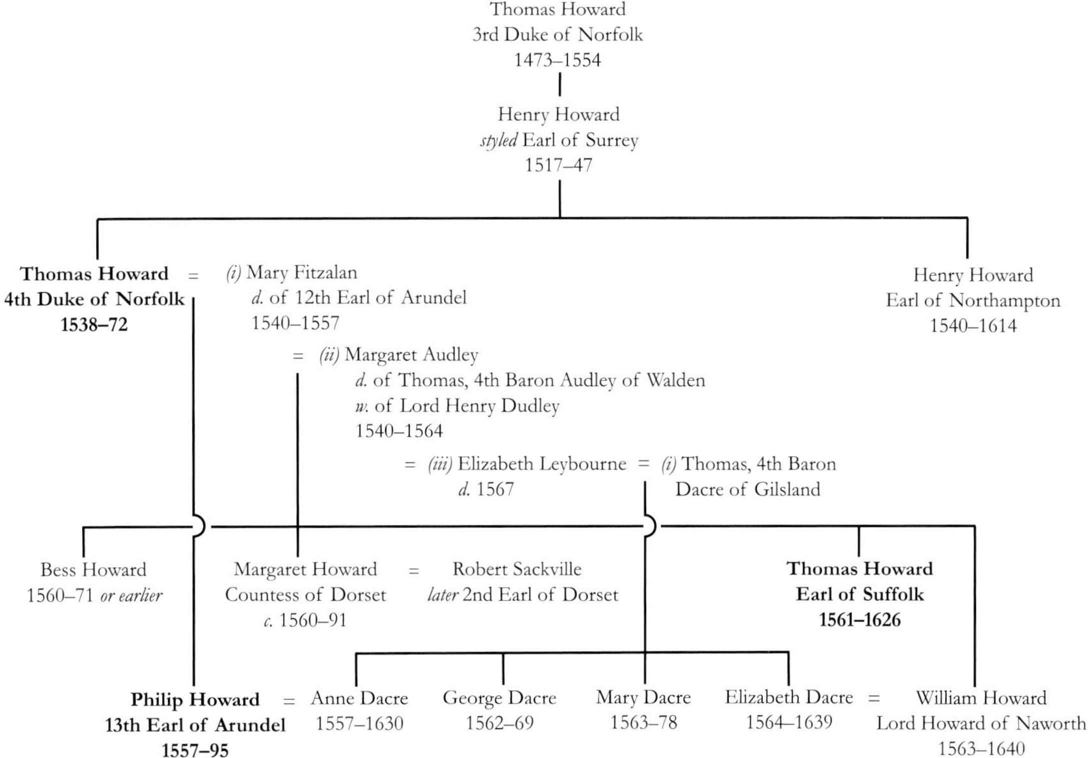

24. Simplified Howard genealogy, showing successive Howard owners of Howard House (bold type)

death, the children should be brought up at Framlingham Castle in Suffolk, the ancestral home of the Dukes of Norfolk; in the event they were sent, by orders of the Privy Council, to Audley End, the house of Norfolk's second son, Lord Thomas Howard.[61] Estate business was run from Howard House after Norfolk's death, and Dix and Bannister still had their own chambers there in 1588, as did their colleague Robert Buxton, the duke's solicitor; Blennerhassett was long dead.[62] But with Philip Howard's coming of age the house once again became a Howard family residence.

Philip Howard was a rather less attractive character than his father, described by recent writers as 'spendthrift and sycophantic' and 'a sexually promiscuous playboy'.[63] His early attempts to become an important player at court failed ignominiously, and his subsequent life might have been of little historical interest had it not been for his Catholicism, deeply held at a time of anti-Catholic paranoia on the part of the authorities. Under constant suspicion, and with his movements restricted by order of the queen, he finally found the situation intolerable and attempted to leave England for exile on the Continent. His eventual conviction for treason, made on worthless evidence extracted under torture from a fellow prisoner in the Tower, resulted in attainder and a death sentence in 1589. As with his father, Elizabeth was reluctant to see the sentence carried out, and he remained in the Tower until 1595, when he died, apparently of poison.[j]

Following his attainder in 1589, the house had been taken into Crown hands, put into repair and let. But in 1601 Philip's half-brother Thomas, by then Lord Howard de Walden, obtained possession. Visits by Elizabeth and James I, and stylish improvements to the fabric, restored Howard House to its old status as one of the most important addresses in London, a brief last flowering before the sale to Thomas Sutton in 1611.

[j] As one who had suffered for his faith, Howard was beatified in 1929, and canonized as St Philip Howard in 1970.

Determining who occupied the buildings after 1572 is not straightforward because the less specific name Charterhouse continued to be used along with that of Howard House, and might refer to the North family property adjoining (later Rutland House), or to houses elsewhere in Charterhouse Churchyard.[64] In any case, there was not a simple pattern of occupation. Parts of the buildings were let for short seasons or longer terms, and to think of the house as a single residence in sequential occupation is misleading. In the 1920s, Davies identified successive residents: the Portuguese ambassador Francisco Giraldi from 1573; the third Earl of Cumberland from 1593 or earlier to 1595; Lord Thomas Howard from 1595. As for the gap between Giraldi and Cumberland, he could find no occupant apart from Philip Howard's wife on occasional visits. He was categorical that Philip Howard never lived there.[65] The reality is more involved. Giraldi occupied part of the house only. The Countess of Arundel did stay, but Philip Howard also lived there, particularly in the late 1570s before he inherited Arundel House, and other occupants during the 1570s and 1580s are known. Cumberland's occupation, which fired Davies's imagination, does not seem to be well documented; there is no reason to think that he ever occupied the whole house. Thomas Howard may have been living there before his grant in 1601, but Davies was mistaken in thinking that this was an absolute grant and that Howard previously held the property in fee-farm. It was itself a grant in fee-farm only, specifying a large annual payment in perpetuity. He only obtained the property outright in 1604, from James I, together with Pardon Churchyard and Whitwellbeach, and much other old Howard property in East Anglia and elsewhere.[66]

Besides Giraldi's, there was at least one tenancy in the years immediately following the duke's death: that of Thomas, Lord Paget (*c.*1544–90) and his wife. Paget was the son of the statesman William, first Baron Paget. He succeeded to the barony in 1570 and about this time married Nazareth Southwell, the widow of Thomas Southwell of Woodrising in Norfolk. The Southwells were Catholics, and another member of the family, the priest Robert Southwell, was to become a strong influence on Philip Howard's religious outlook.[67] Stray household accounts show Paget living at Howard House in the early months of 1577,[68] and other records point to his periodic residence there over a long time. First is an inventory of 'household stuff' from the Paget archive, made in 1573 (Appendix II), which lists the Hall and Parlour, 'my Lords chamber', another unidentifiable chamber, a study, wardrobe and 'inner dining chamber'. This can probably be ascribed to Thomas Paget's tenancy. A list of hangings and bedding, dated 1580, again mentions the inner dining chamber and my lord's chamber. Some of the furnishings evidently came from the Southwells, for they included hangings with the family arms and a bed with Sir Richard Southwell's name on it.[69] The 1573 inventory is suggestive of a somewhat more spartan household than another Paget inventory, made in May 1583 (Appendix III), the study, and items such as swords and daggers, pointing to an essentially male set-up. In contrast, the later inventory includes many luxurious furnishings and a number of stools for women's use. It lists more rooms, too. As well as the Hall and Parlour, mention is made of the Great Chamber and a little chamber at one end, the Withdrawing Chamber, chambers for 'my lady' and a maid, and the wardrobe and buttery. No mention is made of Paget's own chamber, nor of the study or the inner dining chamber, which suggests that the apartments listed were for the occupation of his wife, from whom he was now separated. It was probably her death in London on 16 April 1583 that prompted the taking of the inventory.[70]

In the same year, Paget went into exile, where he died in 1590. He had been noted as having Catholic sympathies at the time of the Ridolfi plot, and by about 1580 seems to have become a committed Catholic. His brother Charles was a leading Catholic activist, working in Paris as an agent of Mary, Queen of Scots, and he was an accomplice of the plotter Francis Throckmorton. Paget fled to Paris to join Charles when the Throckmorton plot was uncovered, and his property was seized by the state; Burghley's order for an inventory to be made of his household goods 'in his hows at the charterhows' survives.[71]

Paget's fellow tenant at Howard House was the Portuguese ambassador. Giraldi appears to have been there from 1573 until April 1578 or later.[72] As the inventories show, Paget's rooms were mainly at the back of what is now Master's Court, while Giraldi's included the long gallery, at the front of the court. This was used by Giraldi as a chapel, much frequented by English Catholics, and in 1576 a fracas took place there when the Recorder of London came to investigate. Also present on that occasion was the Spanish ambassador.[73]

Another Catholic figure to be connected with Howard House is the plotter Charles Arundell, one of the authors (with others, probably including Paget) of the underground polemic *Leicester's Commonwealth*. Arundell was closely involved in the Catholic Throckmorton plot, and fled abroad at the same time as Paget. A glimpse of life at the Charterhouse in those days is given in a letter written some years later by Sir William Cornwallis, the friend of Ben Jonson, to Sir Robert Cecil. Recalling his acquaintance with Arundell, Cornwallis described waiting to fight a duel with him in Islington Fields, 'he and I having fallen out the night before at Charterhouse at cards, and he having, out of good claret and wine and sugar, given me evil words'. In the end, Arundell had apologized and they made up.[74]

Was this at Lord Paget's or at Philip Howard's? As mentioned above, Howard seems to have had a large household at Howard House from the late 1570s, before getting possession of Arundel House. This was possibly from around April 1578, when Giraldi had some cause to complain about the servants of the Earl of Surrey, as Howard then still styled himself ('Conte disore' in Giraldi's Italian).[75] He may have occupied part of Howard House earlier, soon after leaving Cambridge, where he became MA in November 1576. A recent writer mentions him living at Howard House while 'spending great sums in playing the part of a courtier'.[76] Meanwhile, the countess was left 'abandoned' in the country, though making use of lodgings at Howard House on occasional London visits.[77] But the Howard House staff list of 1585 suggests that Philip took up occupation about 1578. While a few had 'served long', many had served for just seven years, implying that they were all taken on together at that time.[78]

Some confirmation of the family's presence in Howard House comes from the statement in 1583 of George Law, the former groom of the chamber to the countess. Law claimed that she and her sister-in-law (and stepsister) Lady Margaret Sackville visited Howard House every Easter, when they would hear mass each morning in a secret chamber fitted up with an altar. This chamber had been Philip Howard's wardrobe, but was later used as a bedchamber by his half-brother William.[79] This account fits with the conclusion of Philip's biographers in 1919 that, once he had inherited Arundel House, Howard House seems 'to have been used chiefly for followers, servants and retainers'. But it may also have been used by him as an alternative, Catholic base, in tandem with his life at Arundel House. As a former priory, it had a special significance, and in a letter to his wife written from the Tower he asked her 'to let my son know when he comes to any years of discretion, that I was fully resolved to make *Howard-house* and *Norwich house* religious houses, and to restore all religious lands (if I had lived to see a Catholick time)'.[80] He attended mass there, and it was at Howard House that he was received into the Catholic Church by Father Weston in 1584, there that he came for correspondence with Cardinal Allen in Rome, and from there that he set off on his intended journey into exile in 1585.[81] Luke Bateman (or Baitman), his groom of the chamber, claimed under interrogation that Philip Howard 'wold verie often go from Arundell howse and once from Howard howse' to Blackfriars, where he would take a boat to the Tower to meet the Earl of Northumberland on the leads of the roof. A pro-Mary Stuart conspirator and probable crypto-Catholic, Northumberland had helped Thomas Paget and Charles Arundell to escape to France at the time of the Throckmorton plot, and he had been taken to the Tower early in 1584.[82] Howard House was evidently so notorious that, in October 1588, 'Martin Marprelate' claimed that 'poperie at the least' had been printed there by John Charlewood in 1587 for Philip Howard. Charlewood had described himself as working for him in 1581 and 1583, though by 1587 Howard was in the Tower and the house was in Crown hands, so if the claim had any truth the date at least was presumably wrong, or else another part of the Charterhouse was involved.[83]

The government's list of servants at Howard House in May 1585, when steps were taken by the Privy Council to discharge them, gives some idea of the establishment, though an unknown number had already gone. There were 47 individuals left, including 8 or 9 children of servants and 7 servants of servants. Almost all were male, as was usual with such establishments. They comprised: clerk comptroller; two gentlemen waiters and a yeoman waiter; yeoman and groom of the chamber; groom of the wardrobe; an unspecified servant of the wardrobe of the beds; barber; butler; yeoman of the bottles; cook; caterer; sculleryman; kitchen boy; porter; footman; gentleman of the horse; two coachmen and a groom of the stable; Sinclair the keeper, his family and servants; Ward, the keeper of the tennis court, and his family; and finally the laundress, her daughter and servant. Four—the yeoman of the chamber, cook, porter and one coachman—were described as poor men.[84] (By way of comparison, there were about 120 servants at Kenninghall palace when Norfolk's establishment there was broken up in 1571, and over 200 there before the fall of his father, the Earl of Surrey.[85]) The countess and their children went to live in part of Arundel House, and later in Spitalfields and Acton, though she also had a house at Romford, where it was proposed to send some of the servants and horses from Howard House.[86]

Howard House, or at least the greater part of it, was now in limbo, and still full of Philip Howard's things until at least 1588, when they were inventoried. Among the papers relating to Philip's attainder is a statement of unpaid rent of Howard House covering four years from Michaelmas 1588. This gives an annual rental figure of £67 9*s* 2*d*, of which only £1 was paid, for a little tenement in the backyard (rented by Luke Bateman). There is nothing to say who owed the remainder, or how many tenancies it represented, but it is probable that some of them had been in existence for several years. That would explain the apparent omission of certain buildings, such as the gatehouse and granary, from the 1588 inventory. The Crown's survey of Howard House and the ground to the north in April 1590 shows how the property was then divided, but without identifying tenants. This, together with the survey of dilapidations made earlier that year, must represent the start of the Crown's active management of the property, and new leases are recorded of parts of the Pardon Churchyard and Whitwellbeach property, which had belonged to Philip Howard along with Howard House.[87]

The chief tenancy was the main house, let (possibly to the Earl of Cumberland, see below) at the yearly rent of £58 6*s* 8*d*, together with the square garden on the site of the Great Cloister, the Terrace (Norfolk Cloister), tennis court and adjoining garden. The rest of the site was split into a series of small lets, some with outbuildings. The outer (entrance) court was one, and included buildings either side of the main gate. West of this was the granary yard, together with the brick-built granary and a small house adjoining: this was in the occupation of Robert Sackville (later second Earl of Dorset), who had married Philip Howard's half-sister Margaret in 1580.

The Sackville house or 'lodging' was previously occupied by John Sinclair, as a statement by 'Gardiner' among the papers of Arundel's servant Robert Buxton shows; it also reveals the muddled way that the property was managed. Sinclair/Gardiner claimed to have taken out a lease of the property from Arundel's 'lessees', Dix and Sir Roger Townsend, who had refused to grant 'any part of the Charterhouse' without the approval of Lady Margaret, despite the fact that she had 'no estate therein'. Sinclair was told to leave the property on Burghley's orders, and Lady Margaret had then sought the queen's permission to occupy it herself, in the meantime looking for lodgings in Southampton House and at a house in Holborn. Sackville then claimed he had an earlier lease than Sinclair's, and evidently emerged victorious from the dispute.[88]

North of this contentious holding was a walled garden called the granary garden. Going further north, where the site opens out beside and beyond Wash-house Court, was the back yard, a large area in two unequal parts which extended beyond the end of the Norfolk Cloister. The back yard contained stables and other buildings, partly ranged against the west boundary of the site, and at the north end of the larger part was a pond, probably a former fishpond of the priory. There was another pond on a separate plot somewhere near the north end of the Cloister. East of this was the plot along the north side of the site that was later planted as the Wilderness Garden. At this time it consisted of a garden or orchard, where a conduit house had been built to replace the monastic conduit house which had stood in the Great Cloister. South of this, a piece of vacant ground (mostly the site of the monks' cells H to P) stretched along the north side of the square garden and east to Aldersgate Street.

Building and repairs under Philip Howard

The sums recorded as having been spent on building at Howard House for several years after Norfolk's execution were small, but £96 17*s* in 1577–8 is high enough to suggest some substantial work. Significantly, for this year the accounts refer to Howard House as the house of the Earl of Surrey. Then aged 20 or 21, Philip Howard had not yet come into the title and estates of the Earl of Arundel, and it was natural for him to expand the establishment at Howard House for his own occupation. Besides money from the Howard estates he also had at this time a useful yearly allowance of £720, via trustees, from the Arundel estate.[89] Some improvements would doubtless have been desirable, though the amount does not necessarily indicate his habitual extravagance. (In the same year, William Dix worried whether the late duke's debts would ever be cleared, household spending by his son at Audley End having nearly tripled, and Philip also ran up huge debts entertaining the queen at Kenninghall and Mount Surrey.[90])

In the year from the end of February 1578, 'divers' repairs and building works at Howard House amounted to £34 5*s* 5½*d*. Subsequent accounts run from Michaelmas to Michaelmas. In 1580–1, building and repairs cost £32 14*s* 10*d*, and the next year only £2 11*s* 7*d*, though an additional £15 4*s* was spent on 'le Fountayne'. This may have been the fountain in the middle of the formal garden (mentioned in the 1590 survey and shown surmounted by a cross in a later illustration), or a marble fountain which stood in the privy garden in 1611; either of these may relate to the 'worke for a fountaine of allabaster gilt', stowed in the armoury in 1588.[91] The work was done under the supervision not of Sinclair but of Richard Radcliffe and Robert Buxton respectively, Buxton also overseeing works to the Howard house at Rushford, near Thetford and another at Ivy Bridge (in the Strand). With his succession to the Arundel earldom and estates in February 1580 (the title was not finally confirmed for more than a year),[92] Philip Howard now had his birthplace, Arundel House, as well as Howard House, but his life was increasingly dominated by his move towards his wife's Catholicism, leading to his reception into the old church and involvement with Catholic plotters against Elizabeth. This culminated in his final attempt to flee the country in April 1585 and his subsequent incarceration. The sum of £84 13*s* in 1581–2 may have been the last appreciable spending on repairs or building at Howard House for many years. In 1585–6, just £43 was divided between repairs at Howard House and Arundel House. This may include the £17 6*s* 8*d* owing to Sinclair for 'reparacions by hym done at Howard howse', recorded in a list of Philip Howard's debts made in 1585.[93]

The receiver-generals' accounts refute Gerald Davies's picture of 'a house not kept in repair from year to year, or month to month' in the years after Norfolk's death. Even after Howard's imprisonment, the buildings were evidently maintained in reasonable repair, as the survey of 1590 shows (see below). Arundel House, in contrast, was left 'in great neede of repaire'.[94]

The 1588 inventory and 1590 survey

Though not a full picture of the usual contents, the 1588 inventory (Appendix IV) gives some idea of how the house was furnished under Philip Howard and probably earlier. Many of the items may be presumed to date from Norfolk's day (and some had his monogram on them), and many room uses were no doubt unchanged since the early 1570s. Certain continuities and changes of use since 1565 are evident, but it is impossible to match many of the rooms with much confidence (Ill. 25). The Great Dining Chamber is clearly what is now (and was in North's day) called the Great Chamber, while the room opening off its west end, shown on Francis Carter's plan as the Withdrawing Chamber (Ill. 30), is here identifiable as the bedchamber at the end of the hall, for the inventory mentions a door between this room and the Great Dining Chamber. Particularly interesting is the reference to a room 'over the skrine at the east end of the hall', separated from the Great Dining Chamber by a 'great dore' with iron bolts and 'a great springe plate locke'. Possibly this ironmongery was to do with the letting of portions of the house in the recent past. The exact arrangement—in particular, the nature of the 'skrine', can only be guessed at. Presumably a screen, not a scrine (i.e., shrine) is meant. This screen may have been a version of the traditional canopy at the dais end of a hall. The description of the room implies a connection between it and the hall, which may be explained by a window here, looking down into the hall (see Ill. 105). This room over the screen occupied the site of the future Great Staircase, or rather shared it with a small staircase, the landing of which is mentioned in the 1565 inventory. The room itself contained a billiard table similar to a modern one in its dimensions, covered with green cloth and mounted on turned legs: a very early instance of a billiard room in England. Cues and balls for the game are listed among the contents of the wardrobe.

Where this capacious wardrobe was cannot be determined, but it was probably in Wash-house Court. It may not have been the 'old' wardrobe mentioned by Norfolk's secretary Barker as being up 'a new pair of stairs' in 1571, for the statement (page 51) by one of the Countess of Arundel's servants suggests that the wardrobe was moved again in the 1580s (when the 'high gallery' was taken over for the wardrobe of the beds, pages 114–15).

The 'lowe rome called the auditors hall' is identifiable as the later Library at the back of the Great Hall, directly beneath the Great Chamber, while the ladies' dining chamber on the first floor (over the pastry kitchen) appears to be the room, or part of the room, used by North (who mentions in his will the walnut bedstead there) and then by Norfolk as a bedchamber. As was normal practice at the time, this large apartment evidently served for business as much as for sleeping, for a deposition of 1573 mentions it as the place where a group of eight or more men gathered in 1569 for the signing and sealing of deeds by the duke.[95]

The 'great sealed [i.e., ceiled or panelled] chamber' under the chambers at the end of the gallery was probably the large room shown on Carter's plan (where it is partitioned into three) south of the Wash-house Court slype on the west side of what is now Master's Court, with a stair tower at the external angle. It cannot be identified with certainty in the 1565 inventory and may have been Norfolk's creation. The chamber between the 'great sealed chamber' and the 'gate' must refer to the room on the west side of the Master's Court entrance, again shown partitioned by Carter, which had large windows looking into the courtyard. These have since been walled up, but the brick arched heads are still in place. The two 'tower chambers' must be the upper rooms in the tower attached to the former chapterhouse. From its place in the list, the armoury may perhaps have been the chapterhouse itself (previously Lord North's chapel).

Under a chamber at the end of the 'tarris' (Norfolk Cloister) is mentioned a bathing house, which would have complemented the adjoining tennis court. The combination of baths and tennis court was probably not a new one, but this is an early and explicit reference to it.[96] The room contained a great metal cistern, perhaps for filling tubs rather than for bathing in. It may have been here or at Kenninghall (where there was a large, well-equipped bathroom) that a servant mentioned in the receiver-generals' accounts as the 'grome de le Bathhowse' attended.[97] The room above was probably some sort of banqueting room. Its contents in 1588 were no more than a fairly small cupboard and boards to go over the windows. But when in use it would no doubt have been supplied with seats or cushions, as well as the wall hangings—depicting fruits, roses and satyrs—specified for it in the wardrobe list. The tennis court itself is not mentioned in the inventory, because it was either empty or in the hands of a keeper. If the latter, the bathing house and chamber above cannot have been part of the facilities belonging to the court mentioned in the grant to Anthony Norton (page 160). Nor is the interior of the terrace building itself mentioned; it may already have been suffering from rainwater seepage, a problem described by the Crown commissioners in their survey a couple of years later, and so unsuitable to be furnished or used for storage.[98]

While no mention is made of a chapel, makeshift or otherwise, the 1588 inventory does hint at the religious character of the house in those days. In the long gallery were a portrait of the former Spanish ambassador Alvaro de la Quadra, Bishop of Aquila, and a small glass-work picture of the Virgin with Adam and Eve. Another glass picture, showing Christ triumphing over Death, the Devil and Hell was in the keeper's custody. (Also in the long gallery was a portrait of Bishop Stephen Gardiner, the third Duke of Norfolk's friend in whose household the future fourth duke briefly served as a page.) But the most important religious iconography must be the painting on the Great Chamber chimneypiece, with its depictions of the Annunciation, Last Supper and heads of the Apostles, if these date from this period (see page 152).

The apparent absence of a chapel is interesting, for there was one in Lord North's day as the 1565 inventory shows, distinct from the chapel in the churchyard where North had allowed a school to be kept in 1561 (page 30). Services may have been held in a room such as the Great Chamber or Great Hall. Continued absence of a chapel in Howard House itself in its later years may be suggested by the existence in 1615 of an 'old chapel' in contradistinction to the implicitly new chapel created by the enlargement of the one-time chapterhouse. It is clear from the 'carrying in' of the materials after its demolition that this old chapel was the chapel in the churchyard, part of the Howard House freehold but used as a chapel of ease by local people, as well as for a school.

The house had presumably been cleared and left in the hands of only a skeleton staff when, in February 1590, the queen's agents made a detailed report on repairs needed; Philip Howard's wife and son Thomas were living at Arundel House. This gives the names, locations and dimensions of several buildings, including the barn, granary, stables and summer parlour. If the buildings had generally been in poor repair it would have been much more informative. Evidently they were not. Disregarding a burned-out coal-store which was probably not worth repairing, the only major repairs needed were to the Terrace (Norfolk Cloister) and the buildings at either end to it (see pages 156–7). Further information as to the arrangement of the buildings at this time is given in a companion survey made a couple of months later, describing the main divisions of the Howard House site, and tenancies there and in Whitwellbeach and Pardon Churchyard to the north.[99]

The last years of Howard House

While Philip Howard neared his end in the Tower, Howard House is said to have been occupied by George Clifford, third Earl of Cumberland, with his wife and children. Cumberland was a sailor-adventurer in the classic Elizabethan mould, a naval commander and privateer. But he did not himself take part in the 'eighth voyage' he organized, in 1594, when two Spanish officers, captured with their ship, were brought back to England for ransom. Cumberland was 'then residinge with his Ladie and their familie within the Charterhouse', and it was there that the men were held for nine months before the ransoms were paid and they returned to Spain.[100]

On the evidence of unidentified letters, Gerald Davies thought that Cumberland lived at the Charterhouse from 1593 to 1595, and probably both earlier and later. He cites one from Clifford to Burghley of September 1594, pressing for Philip Howard's half-brother Lord Thomas Howard to be given an unnamed property of Philip's, which he identifies as Howard House. The two men knew each other well. Howard, too, was a naval man, and like Cumberland had served in the Armada campaign in 1588, later taking part in operations against the Azores fleet in 1591 and at Cadiz. In fact, the property was almost certainly not Howard House. While the 'Lord Tomas' may have been Howard, the only clue to the property is its low value. Granted in fee-farm only, 'it will not be worthe any thynge' and 'in grantynge the fee-simple she geveth but 120L. and 2 or 3 pound for the lyfe of my lord of Arundayll and his sunne'.[101]

More to the point, it is not known how much of Howard House was in Cumberland's occupation; perhaps none, as he may have been living elsewhere in the Charterhouse, in part of the North family property. Cumberland had some association with the Norths, being of great service to them in helping to quell an anti-North riot in Cambridge in 1598.[102] His daughter Anne, in her account of the lives of herself and her parents, makes no mention of the Charterhouse other than as the birthplace of her first husband, Richard Sackville, third Earl of Dorset (son of the Duke of Norfolk's sister Margaret). This seems an odd omission for someone who supposedly had been partly brought up there herself.[103]

The Cumberlands may have left the Charterhouse in 1596, for in that year Edward Morrice (doubtless the Edward Morris mentioned above as John Sinclair's successor) wrote to Burghley praying that his cottage and garden in the Charterhouse, and another tenement there, might be excluded from the lease of the Charterhouse now to pass to an unidentified 'my Lady'. And in that July, concerned about the Charterhouse changing hands, Robert Sackville wrote to Sir Robert Cecil in connection with the lease of 'my little tenement, parcel of Charterhouse' (i.e., the granary yard and house); he obtained a new thirteen-year lease of it in 1601, the year that Norfolk's second son, Thomas, obtained a grant of Howard House itself.[104] In October, Cumberland was writing 'from my house in Broad Street in London', but in December took a lease of a new house on Clerkenwell Green which his half-sister, Countess Dowager of Derby, had briefly occupied up to her death at the end of September 1596.[105]

Two years later, in December 1598, the College of Physicians considered buying a 'house in Charterhouse', where the college itself and its physic garden might be more conveniently situated. The college was then at Amen Corner in the City, while the garden (established some years earlier under John Gerard the herbalist) appears to have been elsewhere. A committee was set up to negotiate, but the college annals are silent as to what transpired. While a 'house in Charterhouse' might refer to various properties, Howard House itself offered an eminently suitable garden. There were Howard connections with the college, for Philip Howard's uncle by marriage, Lord Lumley, was the founder of the Lumley lectureship on surgery in 1582, and the annals record a favourable response to an appeal in 1600 by 'the most noble lady Howard' on behalf of Simon Read, who had been fined and imprisoned for practising medicine without a licence.[106]

It may have been in this mid-to-late 1590s period that the tenancy was first granted to Lord Thomas Howard, whose loyalty to Elizabeth had been amply demonstrated by his distinguished naval service. Howard, who was created Baron Howard de Walden in 1597, received a new grant of Howard House (together with Pardon Churchyard and Whitwellbeach) in 1601. The annual charge was £822, a very large sum and many times more than the rent cited in the 1580s.[107] The queen paid her final visit in January 1603, when she was 'entertained and feasted' by him.[108]

Shortly afterwards, Elizabeth died. As she herself had done, her successor began his reign with a visit to Howard House, staying three nights and creating 133 knights (presumably in the Great Chamber) before leaving on May 11. Howard laid on 'such abundance of provision of all manner of things, that greater could not be, both of rare and wild foules, many rare and extraordinary bankets, to the great liking of his Majestie, and contentment of the whole Trayne'. Two months later, James conferred on him the earldom of Suffolk, and in February 1604 confirmed Elizabeth's grant, not in fee-farm but absolutely, together with a share of the confiscated estates of the Duke of Norfolk.[109]

The other recipient of the confiscated estates was Suffolk's bachelor uncle Henry, Earl of Northampton, with whom he was closely associated as one of James's senior advisors. Northampton probably retained an apartment at Howard House, and his presence there may be guessed much earlier. He had been a correspondent of the Catholic plotter Charles Arundell (pages 50–1), and was a supporter of Mary, Queen of Scots and 'tangled up in plots against Elizabeth'.[110] He wrote from Howard House in 1605; after that time he had his own London mansion at Charing Cross—Northampton House, later called Northumberland House—and a house in Greenwich Park, of which he had been made keeper. The founder of three substantial almshouses himself (at Greenwich, Castle Rising in Norfolk and Clun in Shropshire), he was to return to Howard House as one of the early governors of Sutton's Hospital.[111] Another Charterhouse occupant before the founding of Sutton's Hospital was the naval officer Sir William Monson, the protégé of Lord and Lady Suffolk. He had once been a close associate of Cumberland's, until they fell out over a privateering voyage in the 1590s. Monson, who had his own estate near Reigate, had his London pied-à-terre at the Charterhouse, approached by its own gate 'hard by the westgate' at the end of Charterhouse Lane. Monson's 'lodgings' were probably in the old Sackville tenement (page 52), on the site of the present Malmaison hotel at 18–21 Charterhouse Square.[112]

Even at this date, there may still have been a strong association between the Charterhouse and Catholicism, for in 1607 a priest had been arrested coming away from a house in 'the Charterhouse' occupied by a Master Leake. This may not have been part of Howard House itself, but Northampton was a Catholic sympathizer and suspected of being a Catholic himself (he finally converted in 1614); he was instrumental in the rehabilitation after the Earl of Essex's rebellion of Roger Manners, the Catholic fifth Earl of Rutland, who took up residence at the old North property adjoining Howard House in 1602. Monson, too, was a crypto-Catholic, and in receipt of a secret annuity from the Spanish king.[113]

In May 1611, Suffolk sold Howard House to Thomas Sutton. The timing is not hard to explain. Suffolk was in the middle of rebuilding Audley End, an almost ruinously

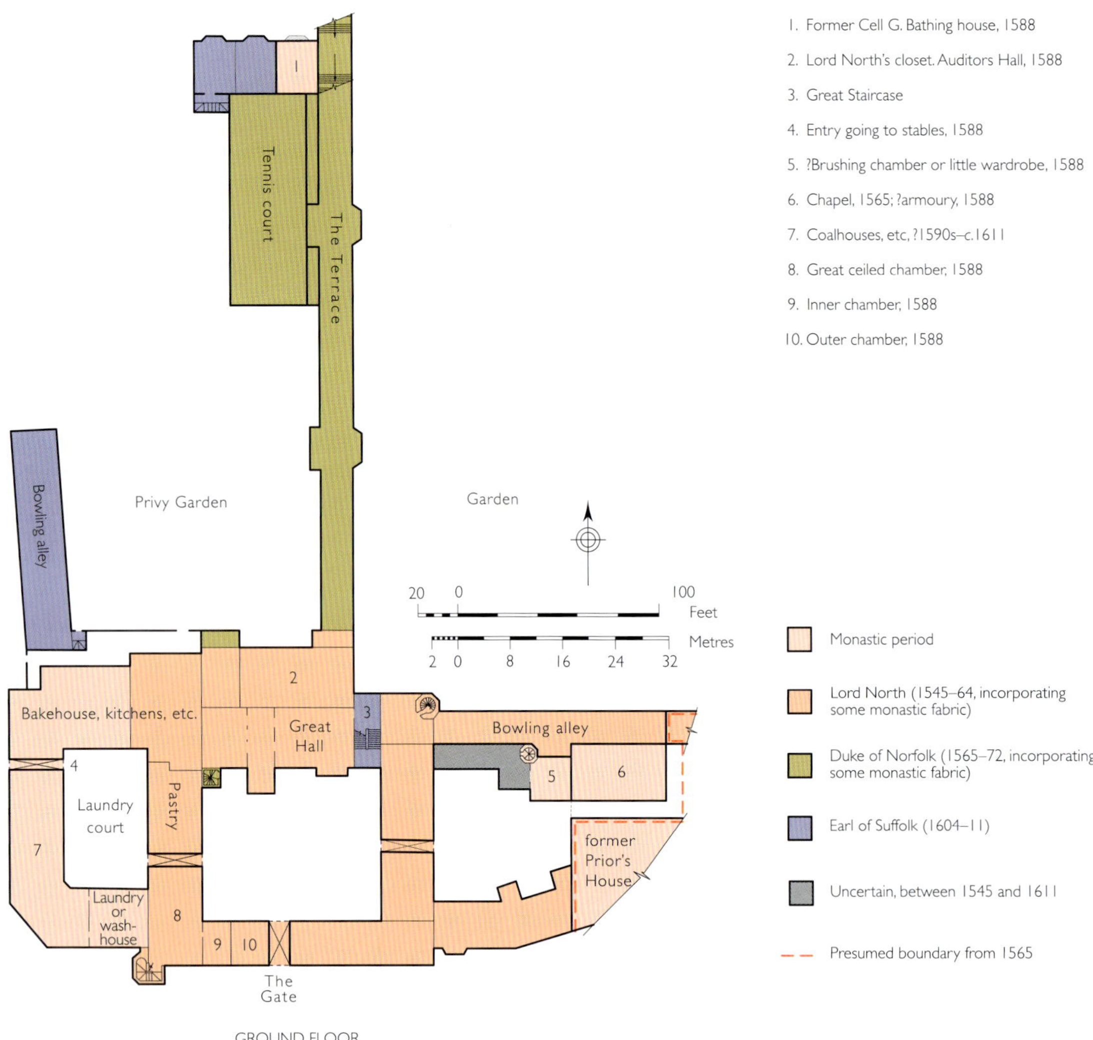

expensive undertaking, and in Northampton's new Charing Cross mansion he had a ready London base, which he duly inherited in 1614. The sale brought about the end of Howard House as a private palace. Although some preparatory work for Sutton's hospital and school began on site that summer, progress was interrupted by Sutton's death and the subsequent legal disputes as to the fairness and viability of his plans. In April 1612, the 200-strong entourage of the Duc de Bouillon lodged there while negotiations took place for the marriage of Princess Elizabeth to the Elector Palatine.[114] This may have been the last occupation of the buildings by a large household before their conversion into Sutton's Hospital.

Suffolk's improvements

Suffolk's period of ownership is apparently little documented, but there is evidence that during this time important changes were made to the fabric. He and the countess were great builders, responsible for work at Charlton Park in Wiltshire about 1607 besides the reconstruction of Audley End between 1605 and 1614. Suffolk's uncle Northampton played a supervisory role at Audley End, and his influence at the Charterhouse is probable. His Charing Cross house was designed by Bernard Janssen, also said to have designed Audley End.

At some point during Suffolk's ownership the Great Staircase must have been constructed, probably following

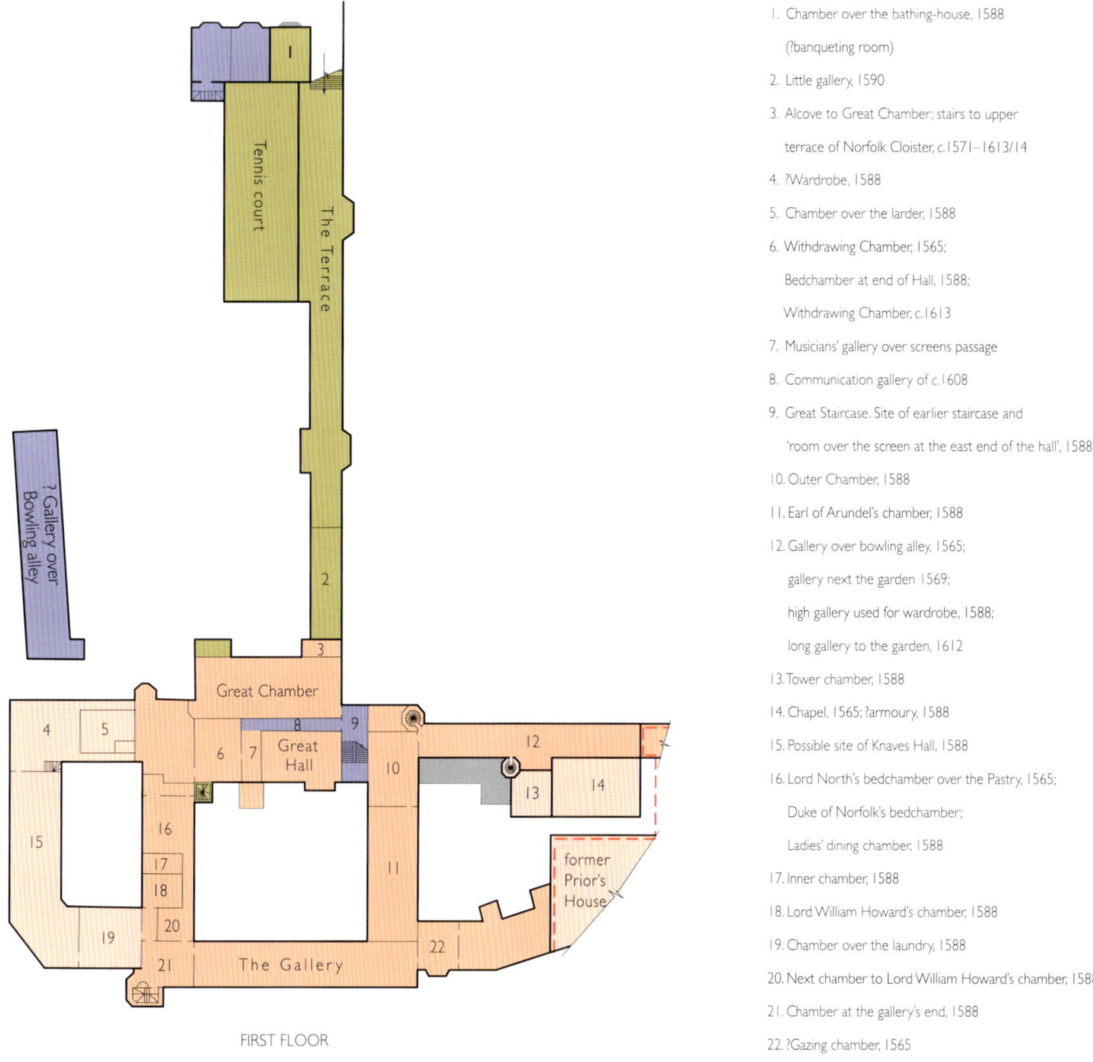

25. Howard (formerly North) House, *c.*1547–1611. Schematic plans of the principal ranges, showing main phases of construction or remodelling and names of rooms, etc.

James I's grant of the fee simple in February 1604. This improvement would have supplied a serious want in a house of such social and political importance. The staircase was destroyed in 1941 but is sufficiently well recorded for its Jacobean provenance to be certain (page 142). It was clearly related to the slightly later, and considerably grander, stairs at Hatfield House. The lion brackets over the main gate may also have been added by Suffolk (page 166). Minor modifications to the staircase were evidently carried out after Sutton's acquisition of Howard House in 1611, with new finials added and carvings with Sutton's greyhound crest let in. This may have been the work referred to in 1628, when 9*s* 10*d* was paid for timber, nails, glue and work done in altering Suffolk's arms somewhere in the buildings.[115] The access or communication gallery along the north side of the Great Hall was probably installed soon after the creation of the Great Staircase, by-passing the Great Chamber and so improving access between the east and west parts of the house. Dendrochronology has shown that it cannot be earlier than 1607, narrowing its construction to the last few years before Sutton's purchase.[116] It is very unlikely that it dates from later, as there is nothing in the Sutton's Hospital records to suggest that, and the ornamentation, having nothing to connote Sutton, points to Suffolk.

A feature of the staircase and gallery improvement is what appears to be a reused monastic doorway leading to the gallery. Its installation seems to have done away with a brick-arched opening, presumably a window, the surviving half of which was uncovered in the post-Second World War restoration (Ill. 105). Most likely the doorway was already in use in the vicinity, as there can have been little left of the priory at that time from which stonework could be directly salvaged. It possibly stood at the head of a stair replaced by the Great Staircase—the stairhead listed in the 1565 inventory, between the Hall and Great Chamber.

Extensive outbuildings were erected, too, involving the reconfiguration of the area north-west of Wash-house Court. These changes can be deduced from the 1590 survey, the record of work done in 1613–14 and archaeology. Excavation has revealed traces of successive buildings here, one find being a monastic wall, built conjointly with the western precinct wall, running north-east from the kink in the west boundary and then turning a little south before joining up with the back wall of the cell gardens on the west side of the cloister.[117] The line of this wall was central to the layout of the west part of the site until the creation of Pensioners' Court in the nineteenth century. By 1590, one, probably two, long ranges had been built on the south side of the wall: a block of stables and haylofts to the west, remains of which have also been found, with a 'shed', perhaps a lean-to, alongside on the north of the wall; and a narrower building comprising a summer parlour and a still-room, extending along the east part of the wall up to or nearly up to the side of the tennis court.[118] There was presumably a gate or gap between them for access into the back yard to the north. The origins of neither building can be determined. They may have been part of the works undertaken by North or Norfolk, or even of monastic origin; the summer parlour could have originated with the 'shade' built in the 1490s for important guests (page 29).

The presumed main changes made by Suffolk in this area were three. The old stables along the monks' wall were largely demolished, together with the lean-to. New stables were built, as well as a bowling alley (probably with a gallery on top, since the building was subsequently made into two floors of living accommodation for Sutton's pensioners). This ran north from Wash-house Court, closing off the privy garden from the stable yard. Just when this was done is not clear. Among the items in a list of repairs of December 1612 is some work to the guttering and tiling of the 'great stable', 'between the old and new stable'. There were two ranges of stabling, one along the west precinct wall and the other running off more or less at right angles at its north end. In the same list, repairs to the tiling were needed to the 'cock rooms' and the coach-house. These buildings appear to be the same as the 'new long stables, cock-house and barn' converted to pensioners' accommodation a year or so later. Illustration 29 shows what remained of the range alongside the precinct wall by the late eighteenth century; much of it had been destroyed by fire in 1671 (page 69). The porch was an old feature, and there had been a staircase adjoining it, removed as part of the conversion work in 1613–14.[119] The first mention of the bowling alley is in the building accounts of Sutton's Hospital in 1613–14, when it was converted to pensioners' rooms. Its position suggests that it was built about the same time as the long stables, as part of a general redevelopment of the west part of the site. This would have involved pulling down the stables and haylofts noted in 1590. The summer parlour was probably also demolished as part of this redevelopment. Some of the outbuildings, including the bowling alley and stables, before or after conversion to Sutton's pensioners' lodgings, can be seen in the plan held by Sutton in his posthumous portrait as engraved by John Faber the younger in 1754 (Ills 26–7).

Finally, Suffolk must also have been responsible for the enlargement of the bathing and banqueting house at the north end of the Norfolk Cloister, apparently based on the monastic Cell G. Extended to three times its original size, the building was subsequently used as accommodation for the Schoolmaster and Preacher of Sutton's Hospital.

CHAPTER III

Sutton's Hospital

Thomas Sutton and his foundation

Thomas Sutton, who was probably in his eightieth year when he died in December 1611, had all the qualifications for founding a great charitable institution. Essentially self-made, he was not only very rich and well-connected but lived frugally and apparently without much interest in the trappings of worldly success. Above all, there was no one to whom he wished to leave his money, for his wife was dead and he had long ago cut off support to his illegitimate only son, Roger. He brought to the founding of his hospital and school the thoroughness he had shown throughout his career, without which the scheme could well have failed.

Sutton's early employers may have included the fourth Duke of Norfolk. But it was his appointment as Master of the Ordnance in the North Parts, through his patron Ambrose Dudley, Master General of the Ordnance, that set him on the way to success, giving him the opportunity to prove himself in military service during the Northern Rebellion in 1569 and the subsequent campaign against Mary, Queen of Scots' supporters over the border. Thanks to the influence of Dudley's brother Robert, he was able to obtain a lease of coal mines formerly belonging to the Bishop of Durham, and in 1582 he married the wealthy widow of a distant cousin of the Dudleys. In time, Sutton was able to amass property and to lend money on a large scale on mortgages and more lucrative recognizances, lending £220,000 to individuals from a wide social spectrum in the last eighteen years of his life.[1]

As early as 1595, Sutton planned to leave extensive, mainly agricultural, property throughout the country for endowing a hospital, chapel and school at Little Hallingbury near Bishop's Stortford. In the years that followed, his plans matured, as he looked into comparable establishments, including the Earl of Leicester's old soldiers' almshouse at Warwick (the Lord Leycester Hospital), set up by the Dudleys, and the College of St George at Windsor, an almshouse for gentlemen who had seen military or other royal service.[2]

In 1610, he obtained an Act of Parliament for the creation of 'The Hospital of King James'. Still intended for Little Hallingbury, this was to be in the hands of governors drawn from the upper echelons of the Establishment, including the Archbishop of Canterbury, the Lord Chancellor and the Chief Justice of the Court of Common Pleas.[3] It cannot have been much later that he abandoned his plan for a purpose-built hospital in Essex and entered into negotiations with the Earl of Suffolk for the purchase of Howard House. The fact that Suffolk was then rebuilding Audley End, twelve miles from Little Hallingbury, may have had some bearing on how the deal came to be struck. Suffolk probably had the disposal of Howard House in mind for some time, as he had been prepared to grant only a very short lease (from Christmas 1610) of a house on the site, in case this hindered the sale of the whole property.[4]

The conversion of Howard House, Sutton doubtless saw, was no simple matter. But there were two probable attractions. Howard House was in London, and therefore easy of access for the proposed governors—so it would not have to be managed at a distance. It was also a place of the highest status, a palace in its own right, where successive monarchs had held court and which could match the dignity of the governors. In other respects it was ill-suited to the new purpose; and there was something shocking about what Sutton was proposing to do with it.

The sale of Howard House, together with Whitwellbeach and Pardon Churchyard, was concluded on 9 May 1611, the price being £13,000. Rather than seek another Act, Sutton obtained letters patent authorizing the establishment of 'The Hospital of King James, founded in Charterhouse within the County of Middlesex'.[5] Old though he was, he now flung himself into the business of turning the mansion into an almshouse and school, appointing Francis Carter as architect and John Sergeantson of Coventry as chief mason. At the time of his appointment, Carter, originally a carpenter, was clerk of works to Henry, Prince of Wales, under the surveyorship of Inigo Jones, and when Jones became Surveyor of the King's Works was made chief clerk.[6] By the second week in July, he was pleading pressure of work for not having completed his survey of the buildings, promising it soon. Meanwhile, the porter was set to work gathering up the stone lying about the site, and a quantity of Caen stone and brick was delivered. Throughout August, a team of up to fourteen masons, with several labourers, were at work under Sergeantson's direction, producing mullions,

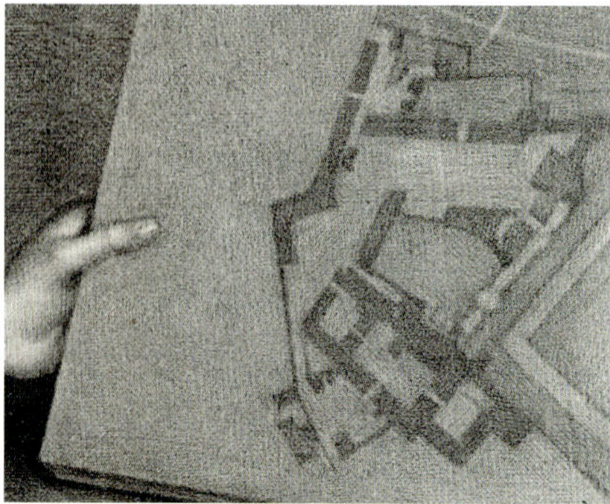

26. Thomas Sutton, mezzotint by John Faber the younger, 1754

This is a reversed copy of the posthumous portrait of Sutton believed to be that commissioned by the governors from an unknown artist in 1657. The painting was for the Great Chamber but has long hung in the Great Hall.[45] On the evidence of this and later copies, and of the painting itself, the painting appears to have been cut so as to bring the face into the centre of the composition. This has resulted in the loss of most of the plan held by Sutton, and of his arms and crest. The actual reduction of the painting is assumed to have been done subsequent to Faber's engraving (in which he appears to have cropped the image, though less severely, for the same reason) but before July 1817, when a line drawing of the painting was made by William Bone, senior.[46] Bone's drawing shows the plan as repainted (Ill. 28), bringing the buildings up to Sutton's thumb, without which the remaining portion would have been largely blank. The words 'Plan of the Charterhouse' weredoubtless included to explain the curtailed plan, now lacking the immediately recognizable square garden of the monastic cloister.The plan as shown by Faber is carefully delineated, its accuracy evident, for instance, in the positioning of slypes and porches, as well as in the general layout. It is the earliest known plan of the Charterhouse, apart from Francis Carter's floor-plans of the main house, since the medieval water-supply plan. The original from which the portrait plan was taken was possibly that drawn by Carter for Sutton in 1611 or a later revision showing the conversion of the whole Howard House property. Some features, such as buildings apparently adjoining the Norfolk Cloister, and the regularization of Chapel Court, may indicate intended alterations not carried out. The outline of the burial ground (see Ill. 31) seems to be shown, though this was apparently not part of Carter's original scheme, which was to set aside part of the former cloister garth as the 'churchyard' (see Ill. 30). The buildings on the south side of the burial ground are similar to those shown by Kip (Ill. 34), which include the pensioners' new lodgings built in 1671. That was well after the portrait is thought to have been painted, and suggests that the new buildings were built on the old foundations

27. Detail (reversed) of Faber's engraving
28. Detail of Sutton's portrait in the Great Hall, showing repainting of the mutilated plan

transoms, jambs, cills, quoins and 'principal pieces'.[7] Whether for repairs or alterations, presumably this was to some preliminary plan by Carter. On 12 December, Sutton died.

His will proved a great disappointment for his relations and some took legal action. Claims by his stepdaughter and her husband, Sir Francis Popham, and by another relation, Ambrose Upton, both failed. Roger Sutton, who had been left nothing, managed to obtain £300 and a £20 annuity. But the most high-profile action was that of Simon Baxter, son of Sutton's sister Dorothy. Baxter had been left a mere £300, and wanted the whole estate. In February 1612, he and his men came to Howard House, broke the locks off the gate and took over some of the buildings. Items were stolen, including a marble fountain and lead cistern from the privy garden and a 'portal' from one of the chambers. Dozens of fruit trees were uprooted in the orchard and privy garden.[8] Baxter's claim was investigated by the Privy Council, which ordered it to be heard in the courts, and he brought an action for trespass against Sutton's executors and the governors of the new charity.[9] The claim was dismissed in July 1613, but at a price. In the same month, Sutton's executors gave £10,000 to the king towards the cost of building the bridge at Berwick-upon-Tweed begun a couple of years earlier. This very large sum (two-thirds of the final cost) was half of a contingency fund set up by the will to be put towards the hospital or the poor, or some other purpose.[10]

The Baxter case is chiefly of interest for the critique produced for the Privy Council by the solicitor-general Sir Francis Bacon, who was acting for Baxter. He warned that the foundation would be exploited as others had been, and 'swiftly tumble down into a misemployment'. There was plenty of evidence about fraud, negligence and failure on the part of charity trustees and officers to support his thesis.[11] Besides, to use a building 'fit for a Prince's habitation, for an Hospital, is all one as if one should give in alms a rich embroidered cloak to a beggar'. In the end, such an institution would become the 'receptacle of the worst, idlest, and the most dissolute persons of every profession, and so become a cell of loiterers, cast serving men, and drunkards, with scandal rather than fruit to the commonwealth'.[12] Instead, Bacon argued, the legacy should go towards several smaller almshouses across the country, or—dispensing with Sutton's wishes altogether—to a 'colledge for controversies', a seminary for converts from Catholicism, or to endow preachers. But if the plan was to go ahead, given the scale of the endowment, it should provide for a superior class of pauper: 'maimed soldiers, decayed merchants and householders, aged and destitute churchmen, and the like; whose condition being of a better sort than loose people and beggars, deserveth both a more liberal stipend and allowance, and some proper place of relief not intermingled or coupled with the basest sort of poor'. Bacon was to express hostility to almshouses again in 1618, when he argued against Dulwich College on the grounds that 'hospitals abound, and beggars abound never a whit less'.[13] But if his arguments really reflected personal conviction, Sutton's Hospital as it took shape brought him round to a more appreciative viewpoint. He included the Charterhouse in a list of recent buildings tending to 'publique use and ornament' in a proclamation against new building drafted in 1615, and in 1619 became a governor himself.[14]

An idea of just what sort of institution Sutton planned is given by the ordinances drawn up in 1609 for Little Hallingbury. They proposed an initial intake of 80 men, with an allowance of 3*s* 4*d* a week, plus £2 annually for food and clothes. Another 60 were to be admitted once revenues permitted. As the Master, Archdeacon Hale, was at pains to make clear in the 1850s, the same schedule would have been applied at the Charterhouse (the property endowment being the same as for Hallingbury), had Sutton lived to see his plan through. The allowance, he concluded, was 'adapted to a class of society little above that of the common Pauper', and the Charterhouse would have become a mere 'Pauper Hospital', precisely Bacon's fear.[15]

As proposed for Hallingbury, most of the sixteen governors were divines or lawyers. The Archbishop of Canterbury, the Bishops of London and Ely, and the Deans of St Paul's and Westminster made up the clerical contingent, together with the first Master—appointed by Sutton himself, John Hutton, rector of Littlebury near Audley End. (According to a future Preacher of Sutton's Hospital, Percival Burrell, in his sermon read on the third anniversary of the Founder's death, Sutton had originally intended the Master's post for himself.[16]) The lawyers included Thomas Lord Ellesmere, Lord Chancellor; Sir Edward Coke, Chief Justice of Common Pleas; Sir Henry Hobart, Attorney General; and John Law, procurator in the Court of Arches and one of Sutton's two executors. Among the other governors were the second executor, Richard Sutton (unrelated to the Founder), Auditor of the Prest in the Exchequer,[k] and the Earl of Salisbury, the Lord High Treasurer. They held their first assembly on 30 June 1613, and in the following year tried to get an Act of Parliament to confirm the foundation. They were unsuccessful, and it was not until 1627 that a confirming Act was obtained.[18]

[k] Law, who had long acted as agent to Thomas Sutton, died in 1614 and was buried in the Charterhouse chapel, where he has a wall monument (see page 109). Sutton, who was knighted in 1619, died in 1634.[17]

Decisions as to size and administration were settled at that first meeting. The number of pensioners was set at 80, that of boys at 30—soon raised to 40.[19] Thirty-two officials were specified, including Preacher, Schoolmaster, Usher, Registrar, Receiver, Physician and Steward (later designated Manciple). Rules for admission were set out, and here Bacon's influence ensured a betrayal of Sutton's wish that the hospital should simply serve the 'poor, aged, maimed, needy and impotent'.[20] Pensioners, it was decided, would be unmarried men over 50 (40 if maimed), who had been servants of the king: 'either decrepit or old Captaynes either at Sea or Land', maimed or disabled soldiers, merchants fallen on hard times, or those ruined by shipwreck, fire or other calamity, or enslaved by the Turks. Disabilities apart, they had to be 'cleane and sound of body'. References as to good character and religious orthodoxy were required. These qualifications were further tweaked in the charity's 1627 statutes to specify 'gentlemen by descent and in poverty', poverty meaning those with an income no higher than £24 a year or an estate worth no more than £200. Qualifications for the boys were merely that they should be aged nine to fourteen and of poor parentage, but it was soon also decided that they must be 'well entered in learning' and own two suits of clothes.[21]

The first men were picked in late 1613, receiving an allowance until accommodation was ready, and the first boys had all been admitted a year later.[22] Here there was soon some further undermining of original intentions, for by 1630 the school was said to be attracting offers of money to secure a place.[23] As well as the resident 'gown-boys', up to 120 day boys were admitted from across London and the suburbs. Each governor might nominate one prospective pensioner or scholar, and the royal family were invited to make nominations too.[24] It became customary for two candidates to be nominated on behalf of the king, and one each in the names of the queen, the Prince of Wales and James's daughter, the Queen of Bohemia.

Set up in this way, Sutton's Hospital might seem to have been set to take on the rather high social status which is one of its distinguishing characteristics today. In fact, this is the result of nineteenth-century reform. What happened in the meantime is an involved story, but the hospital did eventually sink into squalor and indiscipline, though as a result of bad management and not admissions requirements. Essentially, these remained as set out in 1627 (with an interlude during the Civil War and Interregnum, when they were repudiated in favour of the more democratic spirit of the letters patent). As conditions at the hospital deteriorated, however, 'none but the meanest' sought admission.[25]

When changes did come, it was as a result of a considerable increase in funds, due principally to the higher rents made possible by rising agricultural prices. From 1771 to 1821, the country rents tripled, though there were substantial arrears.[26] From the 1820s major developments took place. All the buildings in the north-west of the site were razed to make way for new accommodation, and houses were built for the Schoolmaster, Scholars' Matron, Preacher and Manciple. The Master's Lodge was enlarged. The Great Hall and Great Chamber were renovated, and the Chapel was extended to hold the swelling ranks of schoolboys.

New regulations drawn up in 1872, with the departure of the school to Godalming, restricted potential Brothers to former army or naval officers, clergymen, merchants, or men in the professions, trade, agriculture or similar occupations, who had come into reduced circumstances by misfortune. This did not mean shop-workers and farm labourers. The new dispensation is suggested by Hubert von Herkomer in his 1889 painting *The Chapel of the Charterhouse*.[27] In the late twentieth century, the category of those 'engaged in public service' was added.[28]

From the start, men, boys and staff alike were disciplined or even expelled to preserve the character of the institution, but poor estate management and a series of incompetent or corrupt officials left the finances precarious in the early 1620s. It seemed that Bacon's predictions were already coming true. The Duke of Buckingham went so far as to propose the institution's closure. William Laud made a vigorous defence, but conceded that 'this Hospital is abused'. A similar view was expressed when the Bill for regulating the charity was debated in the Commons in 1626.[29] The very eminence of the governors was a contributory factor: they had more important responsibilities taking up their time.[30] However, with the help of advances from Sutton's estate, and better property management, finances recovered and in the 1630s there was sufficient surplus to buy more land.[31] The institution was to experience a number of such fluctuations in its fortunes, and these have been among the most obvious influences on the building history of the site.

The building works of 1613–16

The new governors took up more or less where Sutton had left off, though there was a transitional period in which only certain essential repairs and maintenance were carried out, on the order of Chancery, for which a schedule of December 1612 and an account of January 1613 survive. This was mainly to do with roofing and

29. Pensioners' lodgings in 1797. The only part of the outbuildings converted in 1613–14 to survive the fire of 1671. *Demolished*

guttering, and mention is also made of stone for the 'receipt house' door, presumably referring to the sixteenth-century conduit house at the north of the site. One major job was the rebuilding of the gable at one end of the Great Chamber, which had been blown down by the wind.[32]

Carter, who attended the first governors' meeting in 1613, was retained to make a plan showing the proposed conversion, making clear that the Great Chamber, the adjoining rooms and long gallery were to be for the governors' use.[33] For this he was paid £10. Though Sutton's appointee, he was not necessarily the automatic choice. A schedule of 'observations and instructions', probably written in 1613, merely notes that 'some skilful surveyor or contriver of buildings' should view the buildings and grounds and set out the best way they might be adapted, choosing also the most suitable places for a chapel and schoolhouse. Finally, the brief as set out at the governors' first meeting called for 'a convenient and stronge place to lay the Treasurie and Evidences' of the hospital. Carter's old associate, the architect Ralph Symonds (under whom he had worked as carpenter on the Great Hall at Trinity College, Cambridge in 1604–5), also attended the first meeting, and produced 'a plot of the house' for which he received £1. This was presumably an alternative scheme to Carter's.[34] The only suggestion of any input from the governors as regards the changes—no doubt much was not recorded—is the setting up that November of a committee to consider what rooms would be most suitable for the principal officers.[35]

Of Carter's drawings of the hospital, all that survive are ground and first-floor plans of the main house, comprising what are now Master's and Wash-house Courts, with their appendages (Ill. 30). The plans are not dated, and a marginal declaration on the ground plan is ambiguous as to whether it is Carter's original drawing (presumably of 1613) or a later copy: 'This plott was first drawen and set downe as yt is by Mr Francis Carter Surveyor of the workes and afterwards seene and viewed by Thomas Heyward esquire, Surveyor generall of the Land possessions etc of the Hospitall'. Purportedly a joint statement by Carter and Heyward (a lawyer, who was for some years registrar of the Charterhouse), it is in fact only signed by Carter. The plans evidently show the buildings as proposed to be altered, but beyond some obvious changes—such as the former bowling alley shown divided into small rooms—it is impossible to say just how far the room-plan of Howard House was modified. In some particulars, the drawing was not followed in the actual building operations, notably as regards the construction of Chapel Cloister and alterations to the Chapel Tower. More definite evidence for the works comes from the detailed but nevertheless sometimes unclear building accounts, upon which the following summary is largely based.[36]

Building began in July 1613, and was essentially completed by October the following year, when the men, boys and staff, or most of them, took up residence; additional work was carried out in 1615–16.[37] It was organized on a taskwork basis, the senior craftsmen contracting for the various aspects of the work. The teams, under Carter's overall direction, were headed by Edmund Kinsman (mason), Richard Brayman (bricklayer), Richard Hudson (carpenter), Jeremy Lawes (plumber) and Kelham Roades (plasterer). Jeremy Wincle provided turnery ranging from structural columns and balusters to the feet for settles, together with ornamental pieces in wood and stone for the Great Hall chimneypiece. James Leigh, the king's master plasterer, produced ornamental plasterwork and Ralph Treswell, senior, undertook the painting of doors, columns, staircases and other features. Many of the craftsmen were connected with the Office of Works or the Earl of Salisbury's building projects of this period; possibly some had earlier worked on the building for the Earl of Suffolk, given similarities between some of the late work at Howard House and that at Hatfield.[38]

Materials were variously supplied by individual craftsmen or other contractors: Kinsman, for instance, provided much of the stone himself, though more came from other sources, including William Southes, master mason

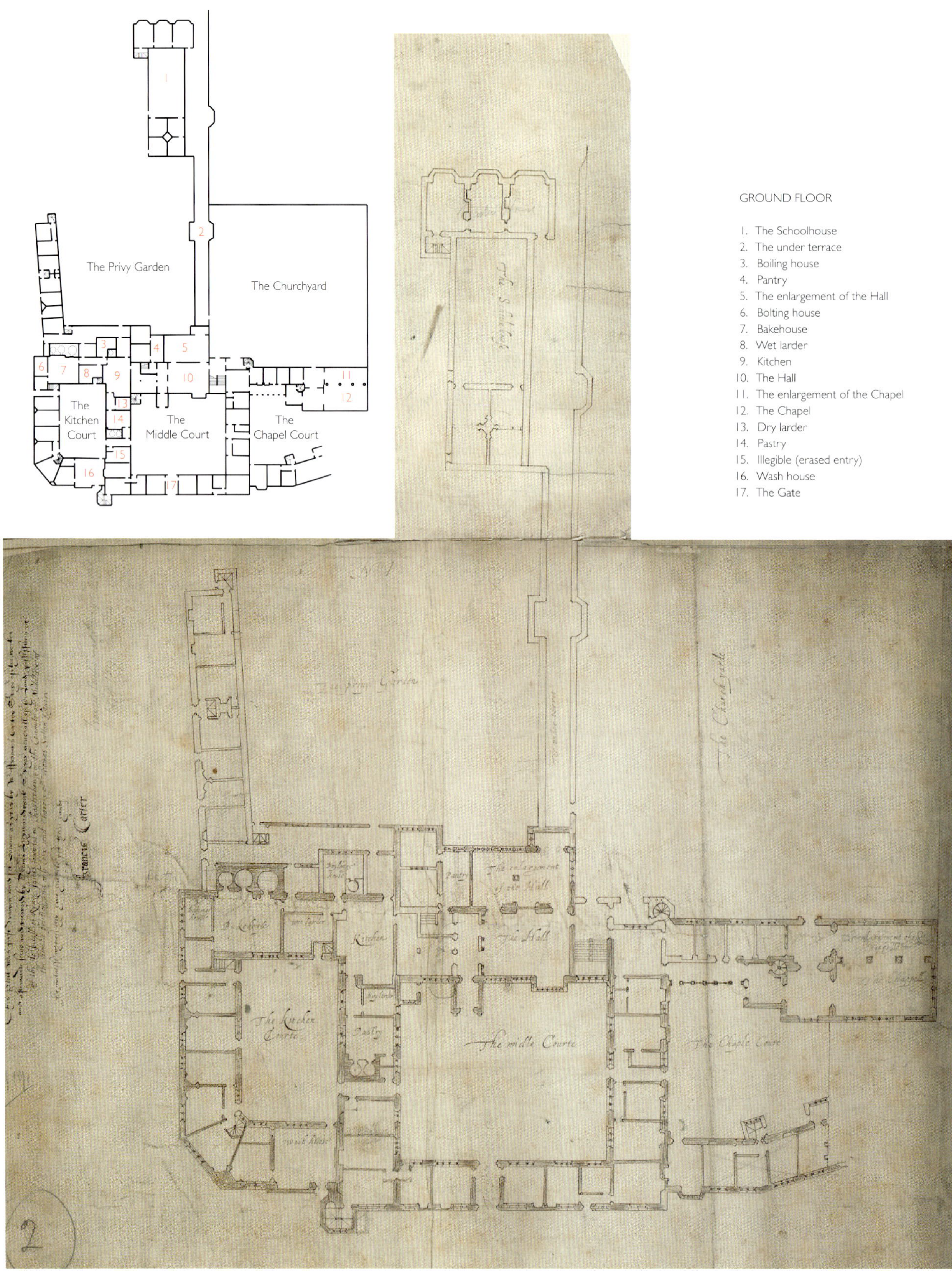
The Privy Garden
The Churchyard
The Kitchen Court
The Middle Court
The Chapel Court
GROUND FLOOR
1. The Schoolhouse
2. The under terrace
3. Boiling house
4. Pantry
5. The enlargement of the Hall
6. Bolting house
7. Bakehouse
8. Wet larder
9. Kitchen
10. The Hall
11. The enlargement of the Chapel
12. The Chapel
13. Dry larder
14. Pastry
15. Illegible (erased entry)
16. Wash house
17. The Gate

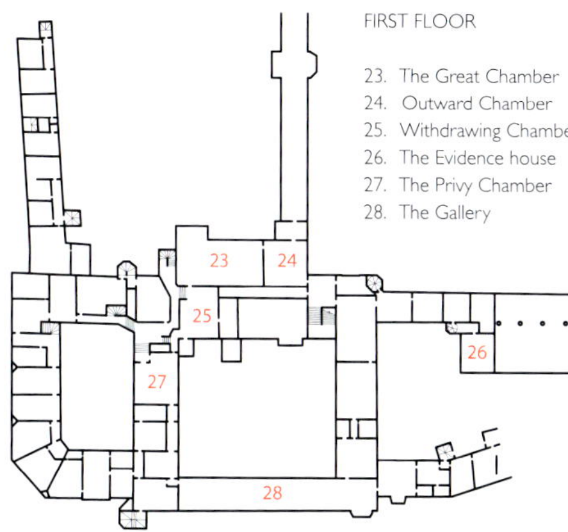

30. Francis Carter's plans for the conversion of the main ranges of Howard House, 1613. The original labelling is shown in the accompanying key plans (spelling and capitalization modernized)

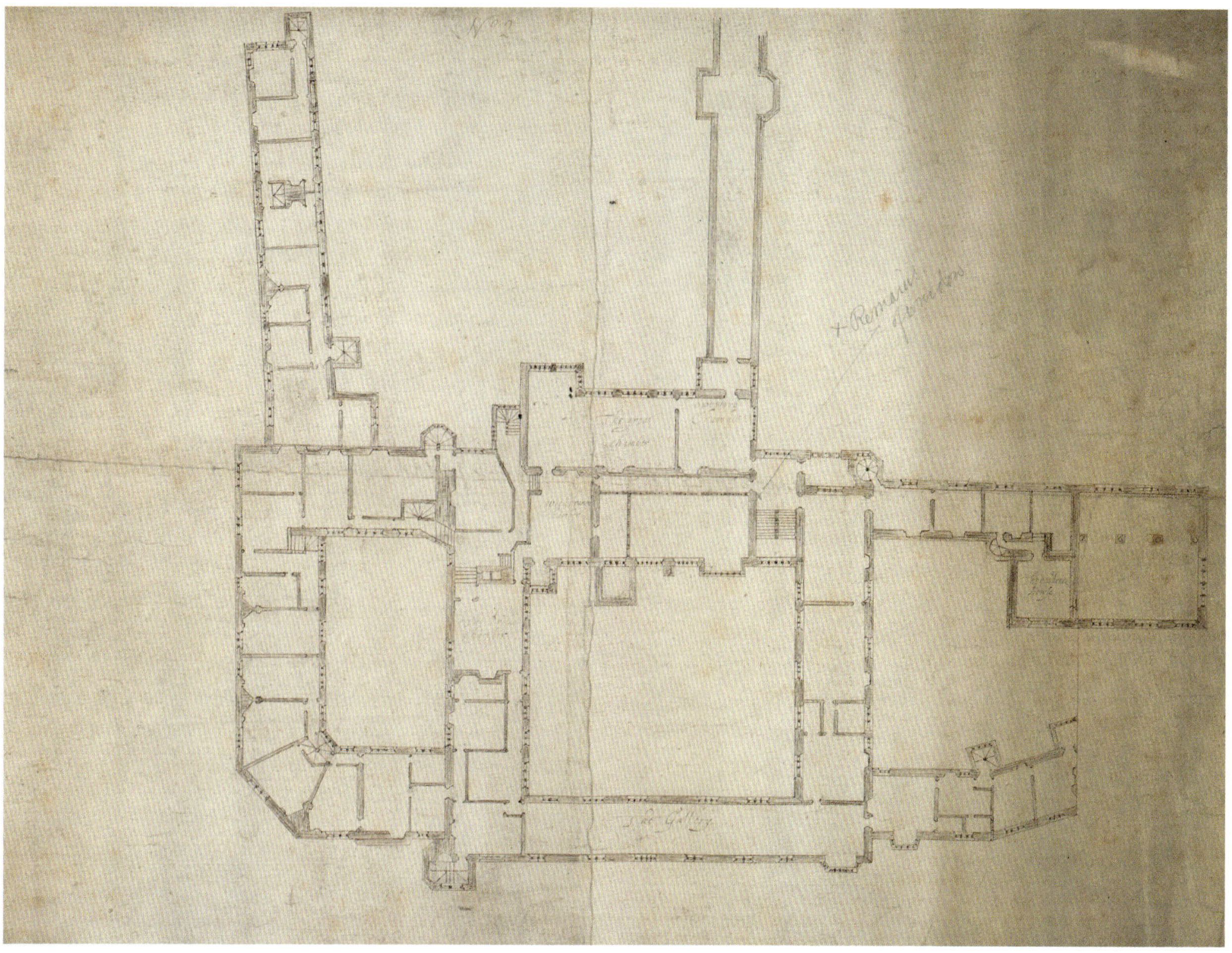

at Windsor Castle. Most was Caen stone, but costlier stone from Oxfordshire, and stone from King's Cliff in Northamptonshire and Beer in Devon, was also obtained. Purbeck and Reigate were used too, mainly for paving. Ironwork, decorative and otherwise, was supplied by William Shawe. Bricks totalling 611,000 were supplied by Adam Crisp. The tiles were from Anthony North and the decorative glass was supplied by Richard Butler of Southwark. In his role of architect, Carter worked 312 days from the start of building until late July 1614, for which he charged £104. In the autumn he was back, checking the painting and glazing.

The work was mainly conversion of existing structures, particularly for living accommodation, and so involved building chimneys by the dozen, stairs, partition walls, doorways, windows, floors and roofing. Just seven new chambers were partitioned in the Hall (Master's) Court, most of which was kept for the use of the governors and senior officers; the Master had a suite of first-floor rooms in the east range. A long, narrow range running from the north side of Wash-house Court, built as a bowling alley and probably gallery, was turned into two floors of rooms for pensioners. Seven new windows in the building were specified to match those already there; they were described as 'hannst' windows (that is, haunched or hanse-arched, the heads being three- or four-centred arches).[39]

More men's rooms were made in the 'further court' north-west of Wash-house Court, where the 'long new stables', cock-house and barn were. Racks, mangers and pens were removed and the spaces partitioned into rooms. At the back, a strip of ground was walled off in 1615 for burials: seemingly a change of plan, for Carter shows the greater part of the monastic cloister fenced off as the 'churchyard'. Twelve chambers in Wash-house Court were created in what had been (at least in part) coal-houses. The tennis-court walls were raised, roofed over and made into a school and dormitory, while the old bathing house was extended to make lodgings for the Preacher and Schoolmaster.

Of the grand rooms, the (long) Gallery appears to have been left essentially unaltered. What was done to the Great Chamber, which became the governors' meeting room, is less certain. It may already have been divided in two (as on Carter's plan), this change not being mentioned in the building accounts. But it needed work, particularly reinforcement of the ceiling, perhaps because of damage following the earlier fall of a gable. In the Great Hall—the main dining hall for officers and pensioners—a chimney was built in the north wall, with a great stone chimneypiece by Kinsman. Two large openings were made either side of the fireplace, with removable screens to allow the hall to be opened up to the former Auditors Hall behind, also used for meals. Here another chimney and fireplace, backing on to that in the Great Hall, was given a lesser chimneypiece by Kinsman, who also made the surround for the door into the Norfolk Cloister. New windows were put in the north wall, looking out to the privy garden. For the entrance to the burial ground towards the north-west of the site, Kinsman provided an imposing gateway, 11ft wide and 15½ft high, the pediment carved with memento mori and surmounted by funerary urns.[40]

With the exception of the new windows in the former bowling alley, there is little if any evidence that any of the new work was designed particularly to match the existing character of the buildings, Classically pedimented doorways and other additions in broadly 'mannerist' style being applied, with no sense of incongruity, to the largely Tudor structure. Carter's most advanced work stylistically was the arcade dividing the chapel from the north aisle, and the cloister joining the chapel to the main buildings of the Hall (Master's) Court. In the aisle was installed the magnificent monument over Sutton's tomb. The tower, too, was enlarged on plan, and given a bell and cupola.

The main gatehouse, though weak enough to need shoring up, was allowed to remain, and the west gate in Charterhouse Lane accommodated two matrons to look after the boys and sick pensioners. Little change was needed to the existing kitchen, scullery and larder, which must have been capable of providing feasts on some scale—the fireplace was said to be big enough to roast fifteen sirloins at once. However, a large window was inserted or replaced in the kitchen in 1613–14, and a new buttery was added in 1616–17.[41]

More work was required on improvements to the water and drainage systems, the water supply being augmented from additional springs. The most substantial item here was a new conduit house (page 125), on the right-hand side of the inner entrance going towards the back yard, replacing that in the garden to the north of the site.[42] In the gardens, work was mainly confined to gravelling and levelling, partly to rectify damage caused by laying pipes and drains. A house near the gardens was renovated for the gardener's use. If this was the same as the gardener's house in the early nineteenth century, it was close to the lodgings occupied by the Schoolmaster and Preacher at the north end of the Norfolk Cloister, and may originally have been the house occupied by the keeper of the tennis court in Elizabethan times.

In total, the works (including Sutton's tomb) cost slightly more than £8,000: the cost of building a decent-sized country house, and much above the £5,000 that Sutton had set aside for the purpose. By way of comparison,

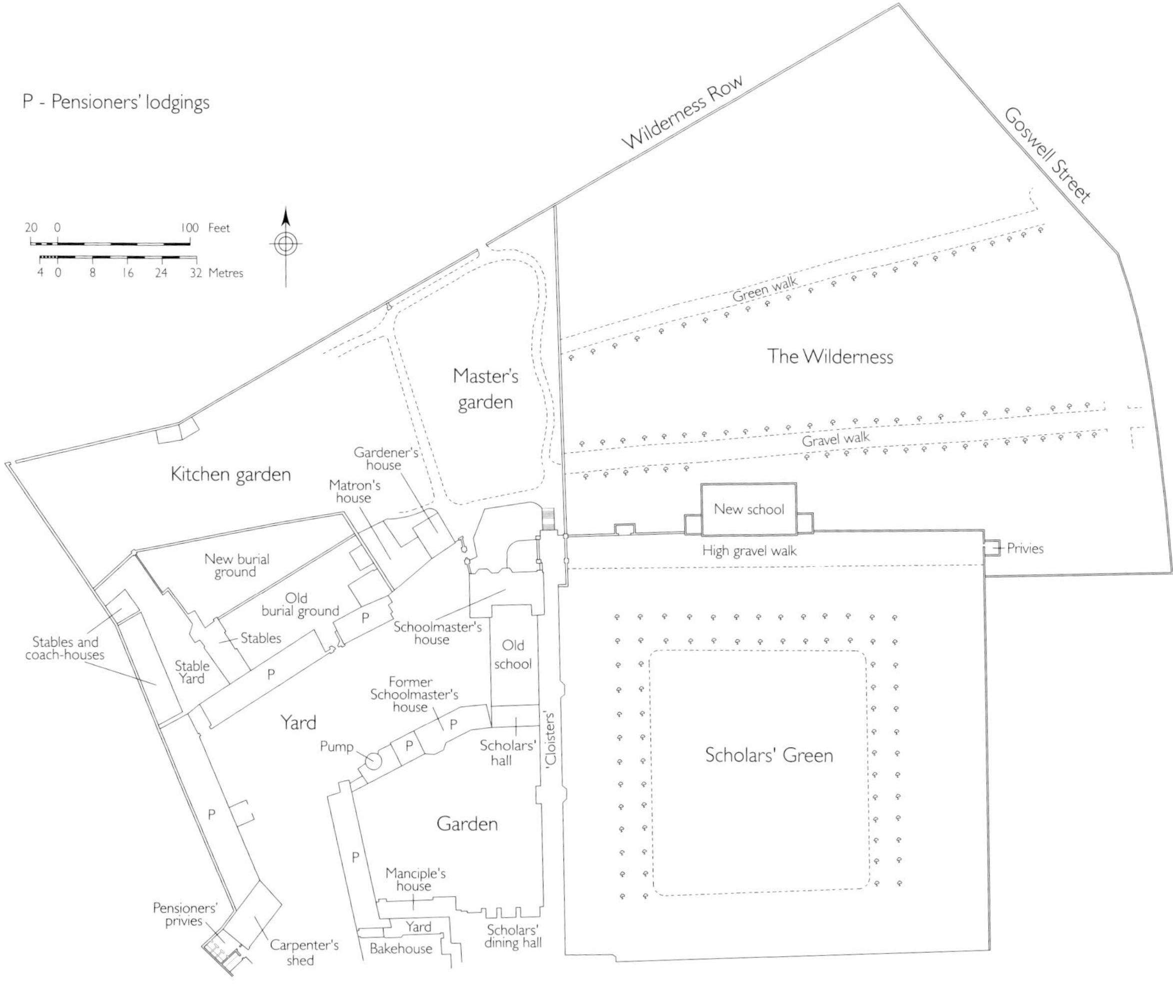

31. The northern part of Sutton's Hospital, early 1820s

Wadham College, Oxford, accommodating about the same number of people, cost a little under £11,000 to build in 1610–12.[43] While the governors did not stint themselves when it came to the decoration of the principal rooms, there was otherwise little that could be described as mere extravagance, given the character of Howard House. Quite lowly structures had been turned into residences rather than pulled down and rebuilt. But the alternative, to have turned state rooms into dormitories and schoolrooms, would have been almost unthinkable. As it was, the men's individual accommodation was modest. Each room was furnished with a bedstead, mattress, bedclothes and bolster, towels, two rugs, fire irons, table and chair, cup, spoon, candlestick and chamberpot.[44]

Architecturally, the original effect is now hard to judge, since nothing remains of the former stabling and bowling alley and there is little in the way of visual record. But the formal planning which has long characterized the design of almshouses was lacking here until the building of Pensioners' and Preacher's Courts. The simple conversion of the buildings perpetuated a loose, organic arrangement, partly inherited from the priory, and the converted out-buildings must have retained something of their original barnyard status.

CHANGES UP TO *c*.1825

For more than two centuries after the opening of Sutton's Hospital, the story of the buildings was one of piecemeal change. Some rebuilding was forced by exigencies of fire or decay, or else undertaken to improve staff accommodation or cope with expansion of the school roll. Many changes were minor, but over time there was much erosion of character, typical of institutional buildings over long periods, with plain brick additions or alterations. A particular loss was the gabled upper front of Chapel Cloister, when another storey was added to the Receiver's apartment in the mid-1770s.[48] Such alterations as this were unpicked by Seely and Paget in their post-1945 restoration.

A century before the changes to the Receiver's apartment, three buildings, now long demolished, had been built in the Great Court, the open area north and west of the old Privy Garden. These were houses for the Schoolmaster and Matron, built in the 1650s, and a block of pensioners' rooms for which Christopher Wren acted as consultant architect. Later, in 1716, the much-patched and altered house at the main gate was rebuilt, half the money for this coming from the prospective occupant, the Physician.

By this time, much of the fabric was deteriorating, and in 1736 it was reckoned that £400 a year ought to be allowed for repairs, the buildings 'growing now very Old'.[49] In the following year, the Preacher invoked Bacon's old complaint with the remark that 'whatever Embroidery there was in this rich Cloak, it is long since worn out'.[50] It was this perception, and frustration at the need for regular patching, that led to a most obtrusive—if only cosmetic—change. This was the re-fronting in brick of three sides of Master's Court in the 1750s: the work was well executed and can now be seen to have had some aesthetic value, indiscernible in the late nineteenth or twentieth centuries.[1]

During the eighteenth century, when the need or demand for more extensive senior staff accommodation became pressing, the response was a series of ad hoc improvements and makeshifts which gave the officials more complete physical dominance over the old Howard House. Space had originally been allocated with single men in mind and became too small when officers were allowed to marry and live on site with their families. This had already occurred in the mid-seventeenth century, when Edward Cressett became Master and opened up the Master's Lodge to his house outside the hospital at 15 Charterhouse Square. By the early 1680s, there were several married officers and servants, and an order went out that they must go within a year.[52] However, there was a social tide here which could not be swept back. Consequently, in the 1730s the Schoolmaster and then the Preacher also lived in Charterhouse Square, as did the Auditor from 1782.[53] The Schoolmaster's house and the apartments of the Registrar, Receiver, Preacher and Usher all had to be enlarged to make acceptable family residences.

From 1774, improvements were made to the old house at the end of the Norfolk Cloister so that the Preacher might live on site, but they failed to overcome the cold and damp of the north-facing situation.[54] In the case of the Registrar, whose apartment was in the south-west corner of Master's Court, enlargement in 1768 was made at the expense of the laundress's rooms and wash-house adjoining in Wash-house Court, and some pensioners' rooms on the west side of Master's Court too. A new house for the laundress and the displaced men was built on a plot adjoining the Matron's house in the Great Court.[55]

The building of a new schoolhouse in the early nineteenth century on the north side of the old formal garden, or bowling green as it had become, was a belated acknowledgement of the inadequacy of the original arrangement, with school and dormitories conjured up within the confine of the old tennis court. This can never have been very satisfactory, if only because of the absence of morning light and good ventilation to the schoolroom owing to the adjoining cloister. But the new schoolroom soon proved inadequate, as the result of irresponsible expansion of the school roll under the Rev. Dr John Russell. This increase in pupils forced various shifts to provide extra boarding accommodation. Some boys were lodged in houses in Charterhouse Square and Wilderness Row, a street of houses north of the Charterhouse, built in the eighteenth century and later incorporated into Clerkenwell Road.[56]

By the time the new school was built, there was a growing segregation of the site between pensioners, scholars and staff. In 1794, a passageway was made from the green into Rutland Court, off Charterhouse Square, and boarders were barred from using the main gate. The courtyards were also generally out of bounds to them.[57] Meanwhile, the pensioners were gradually pushed out of the historic core of the buildings as the officers'

[1] Gerald Davies, in the 1880s, described how the governors 'see opposite their windows a very ugly brick faced building and are not aware that the brick facing conceals the stone work of the other wing of the quadrangle of Howard House'.[51]

apartments were enlarged (although still taking meals in hall and of course attending chapel). They were thus increasingly concentrated in the Great Court. This left the eastern part of the site as the scholars' more-or-less exclusive patch, including the Norfolk Cloister which gave access to their own dining hall from the old schoolhouse.

The new school apart, Sutton's Hospital in the early nineteenth century was physically in a poor state. Robert Smythe found the buildings 'squalid and dilapidated … all of them, with two or three exceptions only, are far gone beyond the reach of substantial repair'. He urged 'a plan of general improvement—not a moment is to be lost'.[58] Change came in the 1820s–30s, with the redevelopment and reconfiguration of the Great Court and area to the north, and of part of the Rutland House site in and around Rutland Court. The irregular pattern of building and division in the Great Court area (Ill. 31), dating back in part to monastic times, was largely obliterated by two quadrangles conforming to the orthogonal grid deriving from the priory: Pensioners' Court and Preacher's Court. On the Rutland House site, the redevelopment provided new accommodation for the growing number of day boys.

Brief accounts are given here of the principal now-vanished buildings constructed up to that time, followed by a description of the changing character of the grounds during the same period. The surviving buildings are covered in later chapters.

Schoolmaster's and Matron's houses, 1654–6

Extra accommodation for staff was provided before the Civil War, notably in 1635, when another floor was added to the Steward's lodgings.[59] After the Civil War, new houses were built for the Schoolmaster and Matron, in 1654 and 1655–6. The Schoolmaster's new house stood near the south end of the schoolhouse, on the north side of the privy garden. It was designed and built by a bricklayer, William Jones, under the supervision of Mordechai Gifford.[60] About this time, it became the practice for the Schoolmaster to take some of the boys as boarders in his house. His former lodgings were added to the rooms occupied by the Preacher, at the end of the Norfolk Cloister.[61]

The Matron's house replaced the original accommodation for two matrons in the west gate, which was too far from the school. Her new house, of two storeys with attics, was built beside the burial ground gate, partly on the burial ground itself, facing the Great Court (Ills 34, 35). The house was probably not entirely new, as the records refer to its being an addition to existing buildings, and the aim was to provide the new accommodation as cheaply as possible. Her old rooms went to the porter at the west gate.[62] Later, the house was taken over for pensioners' rooms, and the Matron moved to an old house nearly next door.

New pensioners' rooms, 1671–2

In 1671 fire consumed a large part of the men's lodgings converted from outbuildings, some of which ran along the west boundary wall. Neighbouring properties in St John Street were also damaged.[63] What survived was about 80ft of the former stables: the quaint 'old houses' drawn in the late eighteenth century (Ill. 29). By the time the governors formally inspected the ruins with a view to rebuilding, they had procured 'a plot and design made by direction of Dr Wren'. Wren does not seem to have had any direct involvement with the hospital, but his late uncle Matthew, as Bishop of Ely, had been a governor for many years, before the Interregnum and after the Restoration. The actual work of measuring and drawing up the design was done by the surveyor Edward Woodroffe, who oversaw the building's construction by Abel Barton, bricklayer. Barton also built new stables at the back. Woodroffe, surveyor to the Dean and Chapter of Westminster from 1662, worked with Wren as Assistant Surveyor at St Paul's, and was one of the three surveyors appointed to rebuild the City churches after the Great Fire.[64]

Wren's contribution here was not necessarily very great, either in planning or detail. It appears from the plan in the posthumous portrait of Thomas Sutton (see Ills 26–8) that the rebuilding essentially followed the lines of the old buildings. It involved reconstructing the 60ft-long burned portion of the range along the west wall, and its continuation nearly at right angles to it, along the front of the burial ground.

Kip's view shows the eastern 'Wren' range in some detail, and Sutton Nicholls's shows the stable-yard entrance too (Ills 34, 35). There were only two front entrances, so the internal arrangement was presumably not of the collegiate or inns-of-court type with sets of rooms off common staircases, but made use of corridors. On the front of the range were Sutton's arms in Portland stone. Payment for this was made to 'Kath Marshall, stone cutter'. Catherine Marshall was the wife of the great statuary Joshua Marshall, whose workshop presumably undertook the work.[65] The building was demolished in the 1820s, along with that to the south, for the creation of Pensioners' Court.

32. View across Upper Green in 1844, with the new schoolhouse of 1803. The trees by the schoolhouse had been planted 'within the last few years'. On the left are the Norfolk Cloister and Schoolmaster's house, and in the distance are houses in Wilderness Row. From Radclyffe's *Memorials of Charterhouse* (1844)

The new school of 1803

Plans were drawn up by William Pilkington in the mid-1790s for new, Neoclassical-style school buildings on the north side of the green, a much better site than the old. They included a hall, schoolroom and dormitories; more dormitories were to be provided in a new storey on the existing schoolhouse.[66] The scheme must have been too expensive, and in 1802–3 a new schoolhouse was built to more modest plans by the same architect. The work was carried out by Samuel Remnant and Henry Munn, the in-house carpenter and bricklayer. Additional rooms for the Schoolmaster and Usher, added in short recessed side wings in 1805, were enlarged as classrooms in the late 1830s.[67]

Symmetrical and Classical, the building owed nothing to the prevailing architectural flavour of the Charterhouse. It was built of pale brick, with a rusticated stone frontispiece and stone cornice, suggesting pedagogic dignity, a quality emphasized by the inscription GRAMMATIKE over the entrance but perhaps undermined by the peculiar lantern-light sticking up behind. It failed to impress Robert Smythe, whose account of Sutton's Hospital was published soon after its completion. He saw no point in describing the exterior, 'as there appears to have been no design of making it ornamental'.[68] At all events, the site gave prominence to the building, which stood on a terrace a few feet above the green itself (Ill. 32).

Barring the little wings, the building originally comprised a single room, known as 'Big School'; in 1846 a much smaller room was built on at the back ('New School').[69] Big School underwent successive reorganizations as different teaching systems were tried. Illustration 33 shows the arrangement in 1844; an earlier view shows a comparatively bare room with forms and desks ranged round the walls, and a stove facing the master's desk immediately inside the entrance.[70]

The provision of the new building was one of two factors which made possible a great increase in the number of pupils under the new Schoolmaster appointed in 1811, Dr Russell. The other was Russell's adoption of the Madras or Bell's teaching method, with its use of monitors to relay lessons to a multitude of pupils. This increase—from about 140 to more than 500, many of them boarding outside the Charterhouse—was not sustained, and by 1832 had been entirely dissipated.[71]

33. Radclyffe's 1844 view of the 1803 schoolroom. By then the room had been variously reorganized for a succession of teaching systems, and the view shows it as 'it exists at the present, the "Horseshoes" of the original arrangement being restored. The canopies, curtains and chairs of the Masters' seats are modern additions'

The building was demolished following the move of Charterhouse School to Godalming in 1872, where some of the external stonework—which, in the tradition of the old schoolhouse, had been carved with the names of Old Carthusians—was reinstalled.[72]

The grounds, 1620s–1820s

Along with the buildings, significant changes were made from time to time to the grounds. The gardens were said to have been considerably improved during Sir Robert Dallington's time as Master (1624–38). Bay trees were planted, and in 1629 Rowland Buckett was paid for colouring ten seats in the Wilderness. In 1662, William Schellinks found 'a very fine, pleasant garden with attractive walks'.[73] But by 1668 the Wilderness (the area north of what was then the bowling green) had been ruined, the paths overgrown, trees felled and the cleared areas used by neighbours for drying clothes or misappropriated by the gardener for a private sideline in growing vegetables. Horses had been allowed to graze there too. The governors ordered its restoration to its 'former order & beauty', and access to outsiders was forthwith restricted to 'civil persons' wishing to stroll there. But whether the order was ever fully complied with is uncertain, since it had to be repeated in 1670. Succeeding decades saw a good deal of tree-planting, particularly of ash and lime, in the Wilderness, the bowling green and elsewhere. Pear trees were also planted.[74]

Visual evidence for the layout of the garden areas is sometimes conflicting, and some artistic licence can be assumed. Hollar's view of 1666 shows the formal garden or bowling green in the former Great Cloister as extending right up to Goswell Street, which is certainly wrong, and crossed by two paths, which may also be wrong. Another source shows the Wilderness as divided into rectangular plots.[75] On Ogilby and Morgan's map of 1676, the intersecting paths lie in a fully wooded Wilderness, and there is building development between the bowling green and Goswell Road, on part of the Rutland House grounds. The green itself is shown with two parallel paths or other features around its edge. In the privy garden is a conventional pattern of paths vaguely suggesting a

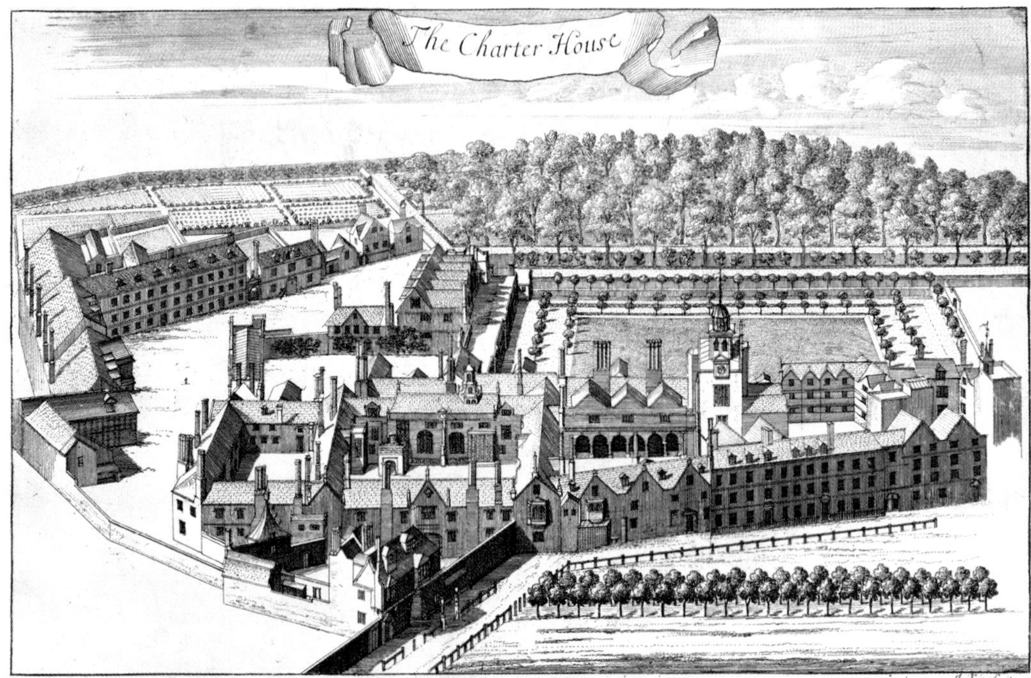

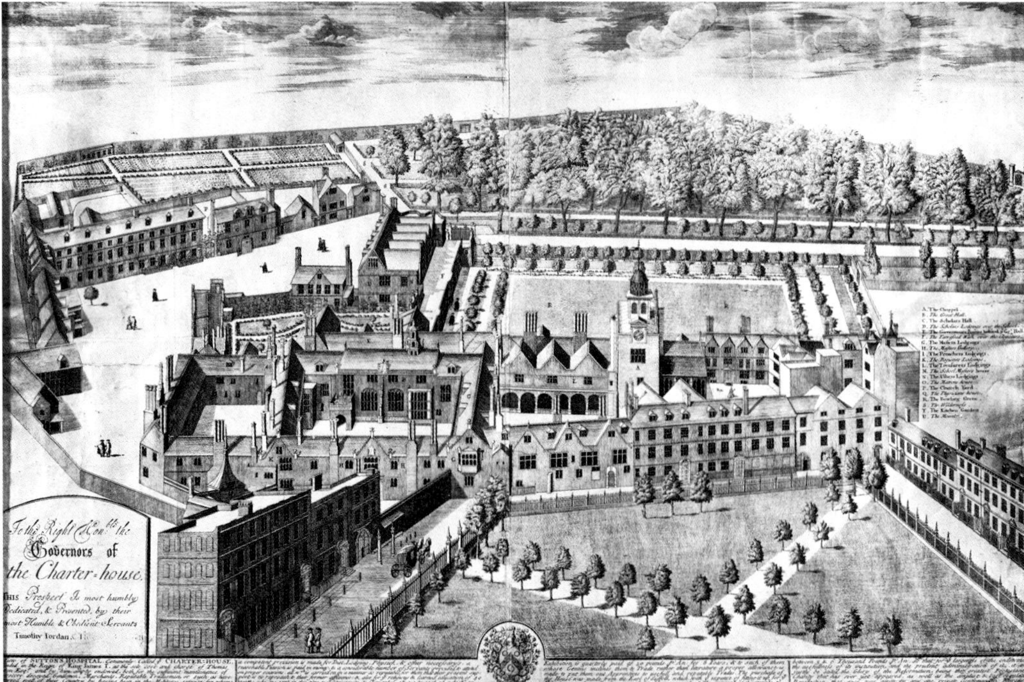

34. (*above*) View of the Charterhouse by Johannes Kip, prepared for the fifth (John Strype's) edition of Stow's *Survey of London* (1720)

Kip shows the posts in the square outside the gatehouse of Sutton's Hospital, set up in 1710. The house over and beside the gate is the old one, which was replaced in 1716 with the present 17 Charterhouse Square.[47] The view gives some impression of the buildings making up the western part of Rutland House., although these had by then been split up and partly replaced by terrace houses facing the square

35. View of the Charterhouse by Sutton Nicholls, engraved for the sixth edition of Stow's *Survey of London* (1755)

Based on the earlier view by Kip, it shows subsequent changes such as the building of 17 Charterhouse Square

spider's web, with a central circle. It was intended in 1658 to use this as a physic garden, but the scheme foundered and a renewed attempt was made ten years later.[76]

Johannes Kip's view, drawn in the 1710s, shows the bowling green surrounded by ranks of standard trees with a tree-lined terrace at the north end, accessible from a gateway at the end of the upper walk of the Norfolk Cloister; the Wilderness, full of mature trees, is crossed by parallel walks. Also shown are the kitchen gardens west of the Wilderness, and a small walled plot north of the burial ground. Espaliers are suggested on the south-facing walls within the privy garden, though the ground here is bare, as in the Great Court.

This view served as the basis for Sutton Nicholls's perspective published in 1755, which itself was apparently the basis (at least in part) of an excessively stretched-out view said to have been painted in 1756 for the Master, Philip Bearcroft.[77] Nicholls's view, which retains Kip's spatial distortions, details various elaborations and refinements in the appearance of the grounds. The privy garden is shown laid out with paths and shrubs, the north boundary wall is lined with espaliers, and a solitary tree casts a little shade in the Great Court. He also shows a walled-off plantation ('The Mount') south of the Wilderness, entered through a doorway in what must be the Carthusian cell-front wall on the east side of the bowling green. Kip depicts the entrance too, but no separate plot of ground behind. The Mount was a long-standing feature, however, as a deed of 1631 refers to 'a little walk or Mount' here.[78]

The kitchen garden produced vegetables and herbs, including some for medicinal use, though by the 1730s the gardener was complaining that its productivity was badly affected by smoke from nearby brewing, distilling and pipe-making works. Nevertheless, it remained in use throughout the century.[79]

The decline of the kitchen garden was matched by that of the Wilderness, which deteriorated into a 'gloomy grove' of smoke-blackened trees. A summer-house which stood here, repaired in 1769, eventually disappeared, and in 1821 the trees were felled, the ground was levelled and the wall separating the Wilderness from the former bowling green demolished. The bowling green had already been taken over by the school for games: football, cricket, hoop-racing.[m] In 1804, a fives court was made in the south-east corner.[81] The two areas, separated by the rise where the school stood ('Hill'), became known as Under Green and Upper Green (otherwise Scholars' Green). Under Green was the high ground, Upper Green the low, the names deriving from the respective seniority of the boys who used them.[82] Football as played on Upper Green was one of the variants from which modern football developed. The game had been played at Charterhouse throughout the eighteenth century, and in 1861 the rules were regularized. By 1867, the school was a member of the Football Association, which adopted the offside rule observed at the Charterhouse.[83]

As part of the 1821 changes, Under Green was bounded on the west side by a new wall continuing the line of the Norfolk Cloister up to the north boundary wall and cutting off a part of the Wilderness site.[84] West of the wall, this piece of the Wilderness was merged with a large portion of the kitchen-garden site as the Master's Garden (Ill. 31).

Later History

By the mid-1820s, Sutton's Hospital was badly in need of reform and reconstruction; thanks to improved revenues and the efforts of Archdeacon Hale, Preacher from 1823 to 1842 and then Master until his death in 1870, essential improvements to the buildings and administration were made. The effect of these developments was unquestionably great, bringing about a transformation in the lives of the Poor Brothers through improved living accommodation, diet and standard of nursing care, and, so far as can be judged, raising the morale of the whole institution.

As regards building, the chief event was the redevelopment of the north-west part of the site with what were to become known as Pensioners' Court and Preacher's Court (described, with the background to their construction, in Chapter IX). At the same time, the Schoolmaster, Dr Russell, was the prime mover in the redevelopment of property adjoining the hospital, in Rutland Court (discussed separately in the next section). The development of Pensioners' and Preacher's Courts was to end badly, in an ill-tempered dispute with the architect, Redmond Pilkington. With the more compliant Edward Blore, Hale also helped bring about a stylistic makeover of the by then much worn, altered and added-to buildings, disguising some of their heterogeneity but also restoring some obscured features. Hale's improvements and administrative reforms were insufficient to deflect criticism, however, and in 1852 a controversy was sparked in Dickens's *Household Words*, following bad reports from his friend William Moncrieff, a dramatist and one of the pensioners. In an article on 'The Poor Brothers', Henry Morley attacked the hospital for stinting the men while senior officers enjoyed large salaries and lavish living accommodation.[85]

At the centre of the storm was Hale himself, whose account of the Charterhouse, published in 1854, was

[m] The word CROWN, on the wall alongside Glasshouse Yard to the north of the Rotblat Building on the medical college site (page 189), is a relic of the hoop races. Said to have originally been painted by Lord Ellenborough while at the school, and representing a pub sign, it served as the winning-post.[80]

36. Sutton's Hospital in 1865

intended to set the record straight.[86] An inquiry by the Charity Commission found no grave cause for complaint, and there is no doubt that Hale was justified in taking credit for raising the pensioners' standard of living. Whether the remuneration and housing enjoyed by him and others were as justified is another matter. The affair harked back to the original dichotomy between the actual requirements of an almshouse and the architectural fact of a palace. Then, in 1853–5, a new work by Thackeray, an Old Carthusian, fixed in the public mind an image of the Charterhouse as a place of mellow buildings and touching memories. But where the author's depiction of Colonel Newcome and 'Grey Friars' was at least mildly ironic, public perception was only sentimental. Nevertheless, the romantic mantle cast over the Charterhouse by *The Newcomes* was to play its part in saving the hospital and its buildings.

From a high point in the early part of the century, the school had long been in decline (and firmly hemmed in by industry and commerce) when it came under the scrutiny of the Clarendon Commission on public schools, appointed in 1861.[87] The commission came down in favour of removal to the country, to be funded largely by sale of the old site, a plan opposed by Hale but supported by many Old Carthusians and above all the then headmaster, William Haig Brown. In 1866, it was decided to go. Within weeks, the Merchant Taylors' Company's offer of £90,000 for the 5½-acre school site was accepted.[88] The Merchant Taylors proposed redevelopment with their own school (Chapter XI), and commercial building along the frontages to Goswell Road and Wilderness Row, where Clerkenwell Road was already in the planning stage.[n]

Hale's death, in November 1870, gave opportunity to take stock in the face of a difficult financial situation. Under the reorganization of the charity to hive off the school, the estates income was split between it and the hospital, apart from a common 'general fund' for certain expenses. The school kept its takings from fees, leaving the hospital as the poor relation, with no equivalent means of boosting its income. It was proposed by the Archbishop of York that the hospital be done away with in favour of a system of 'out-pensions' and a small country residence for those with no one to take them in; the hard figures were larded with some nonsense about the moral degeneration of elderly men thrown into a 'quasi-monastic' lifestyle.[89] In the event, no drastic step was taken but the fall in agricultural prices, on which the bulk of the estates income ultimately depended, brought the hospital to a low pass. Rising rents from the Clerkenwell estate in and around Great Sutton Street[90] made up the income deficit for some years, but from the mid-1880s there was a steady decline in revenue, and vacancies among the pensioners were left open.[91] A financial review was called for by the Charity Commissioners, and it became clear that economies and the reduction in pensioners would not suffice. With farm prices low, the only solution seemed to be to sell off part of the Charterhouse itself.[92]

In 1882, the surveyors Cluttons had produced a scheme whereby an historic core consisting of the Great Hall, Great Chamber, Library, Chapel and Master's Lodge would be retained, and the rest of the site developed, with a new street connecting Charterhouse Square and Clerkenwell Road. No action was taken until 1885, when, with the agricultural depression worsening, it was decided to abolish the hospital and sell most of the site on building leases, 'subject to any question which might arise as to the preservation of objects of archaeological interest'.[93] This proviso was slightly naive. There was a ferocious outcry, orchestrated in part by Gerald Davies, then one of the masters at Godalming, who alerted the Society for the Protection of Ancient Buildings (SPAB) and was instrumental in getting 'inflammatory paragraphs' into the press.[94]

Opposition to the governors' Bill seeking statutory powers culminated in a public meeting in May 1886, organized jointly by the SPAB and the Commons Preservation Society.[95] In the House of Commons, the governors were accused 'of Philistinism, and of barbarism, and of Vandalism', and John Talbot, one of the abolitionist governors, complained that 'if *The Newcomes* had never been written there would not have been the present manifestation of feeling'. That was possibly true, and it was perhaps due to *The Newcomes* that American tourists had the Charterhouse on their itineraries.[96] The Bill was withdrawn. A revised version of the development plan was produced, but ultimately came to nothing.

The number of pensioners was now reduced to 48 and, as the income from country properties continued to fall, various shifts had to be made, such as letting office space and selling wine stocks. By 1893, conditions had improved sufficiently to allow a complement of 60 Brothers, and a repairs programme, including renovation of the Howard House front facing Entrance Court, was begun.[97] It was a brief respite. With the country estates becoming uneconomic, they were sold from 1913 and the proceeds reinvested more profitably, offsetting rising food and fuel prices.[98] By 1919, less than a sixteenth of the acreage was left. Strict economies were still made and new sources

[n] For this development, see *Survey of London*, vol. XLVI, pp.386–92

of income sought, including car-parking charges in Charterhouse Square (shared with the Square's trustees) and the sale of rare books.[99] Having limped on into wartime, the hospital soon had to confront once again the question of whether it could survive in its old form and on the same site.

On the night of Saturday 10 to Sunday 11 May 1941, in one of the heaviest raids of the Blitz, incendiaries began a fire in the roof next to the Chapel. Fanned by a north-east wind, the fire spread, largely away from the Chapel. As it was being brought under control that morning, the water supply failed and the fire continued unchecked for some hours. The buildings around Master's Court and Wash-house Court were almost entirely gutted, though the Chapel escaped.[100] The extensive nineteenth-century ranges, with the Brothers' own rooms, were unscathed. But with the kitchen and other service areas destroyed, emergency plans for evacuation were put into effect. For ten years, the buildings stood empty but for storage, the Great Hall and Great Chamber protected by temporary roofs (Ills 3–6).

Day Boys' Lodge and Rutland Place

In 1794 the governors bought the freehold of the house at the north end of Rutland Court, abutting the east end of the Chapel. A remnant of Rutland House, partly dating at least from the 1540s (when Sir Edward North had built his bowling alley and gallery over the south cloister walk of the old priory), this had remained a narrow building (the same width as the north aisle of the Chapel). The Surveyor, William Pilkington, saw to the construction of a passage through the house, alongside the Chapel, allowing direct access between Rutland Court and Scholars' or Upper Green (see Ill. 79), and the house itself was let to Matthew Raine, the Schoolmaster. Raine's successor, the Rev. Dr Russell, who had taken over the lease, obtained a new 21-year lease in 1820.[102]

Russell was already involved in property speculation here, having acquired 13 and 14 Charterhouse Square, to the west of Rutland Court, and turned them into boarding-houses for the scholars, whose numbers he was driving up to unsustainable levels through use of the Madras teaching system (page 70).[103] When in 1825 a large part of the Rutland House site came up for sale, Russell managed to acquire the property to the east, including the greater part of Rutland Court, part of which already belonged to Sutton's Hospital, with an eye to complete redevelopment. An agreement was reached with the governors by which he was to replace the house acquired in 1794 with a ground-floor 'lodge' for the day boys, on an 80-year building lease. Rutland Court was to be replaced with a spacious, regular court a little to the east, closed at the north end by a 'passage room' giving access from the new Day Boys' Lodge to the playground.[104]

As well as Day Boys' Lodge, Russell built two houses on the east side of Rutland Place, as the new court became known, and some years later a third house, on the other side (12A Charterhouse Square). In 1838, the first two houses, 1 and 2 Rutland Place, were leased by Sutton's Hospital with agreement for the purchase of the freehold in 1844, and altered and enlarged as a residence for the Usher and living accommodation for about 25 boys[105] ('Verites', after Oliver Walford, the Usher—known as 'Old Ver', one of four 'houses' into which the school was latterly divided).[o] Day Boys' Lodge, remodelled in 1863–4 to provide one long room and a dining room, survives as the core of Edward I'Anson's turreted entrance lodge built for Merchant Taylors' School (Chapter XI).[106] The Rutland Place houses were replaced in 1894 by a new house for the headmaster of Merchant Taylors' School.

Russell's activities ended badly, with the bursting of the bubble he had blown. In 1832, he had to seek 50 per cent abatement on the ground rent of Day Boys' Lodge, which had become 'a depressing burden' to him, and resigned his post.[107]

Restoration by Seely and Paget

It was perhaps as much for reasons of sentiment as uncertainty over the extent to which the War Damage Commission would pay for new buildings elsewhere that the governors decided in 1944 to retain the hospital on its old site. The choice of architects was made on the recommendation of one of their number, Sir Charles Peers, who had produced a preliminary report on how the buildings might be dealt with.[108] An architect and archaeologist, Peers had developed the dogmatically clinical approach to the display of ancient sites for ever to be associated with the Ministry of Works, in which he served as Chief Inspector. The damaged historic core was to be treated like one of his monuments, stripped of accretions in the interest of historic or stylistic purity. One of his original proposals was to pull down the undamaged Pensioners' and Preacher's Courts, and this was prompted at least as much by architectural taste as their supposedly 'very inconvenient and uneconomical character'. They were to have been replaced by something 'in keeping' with the

[o] The others were Gownboys (the old schoolhouse); Saunderites (in the Schoolmaster's house adjoining Gownboys); and Dickenites, in the Reader's apartment over Brooke Hall.

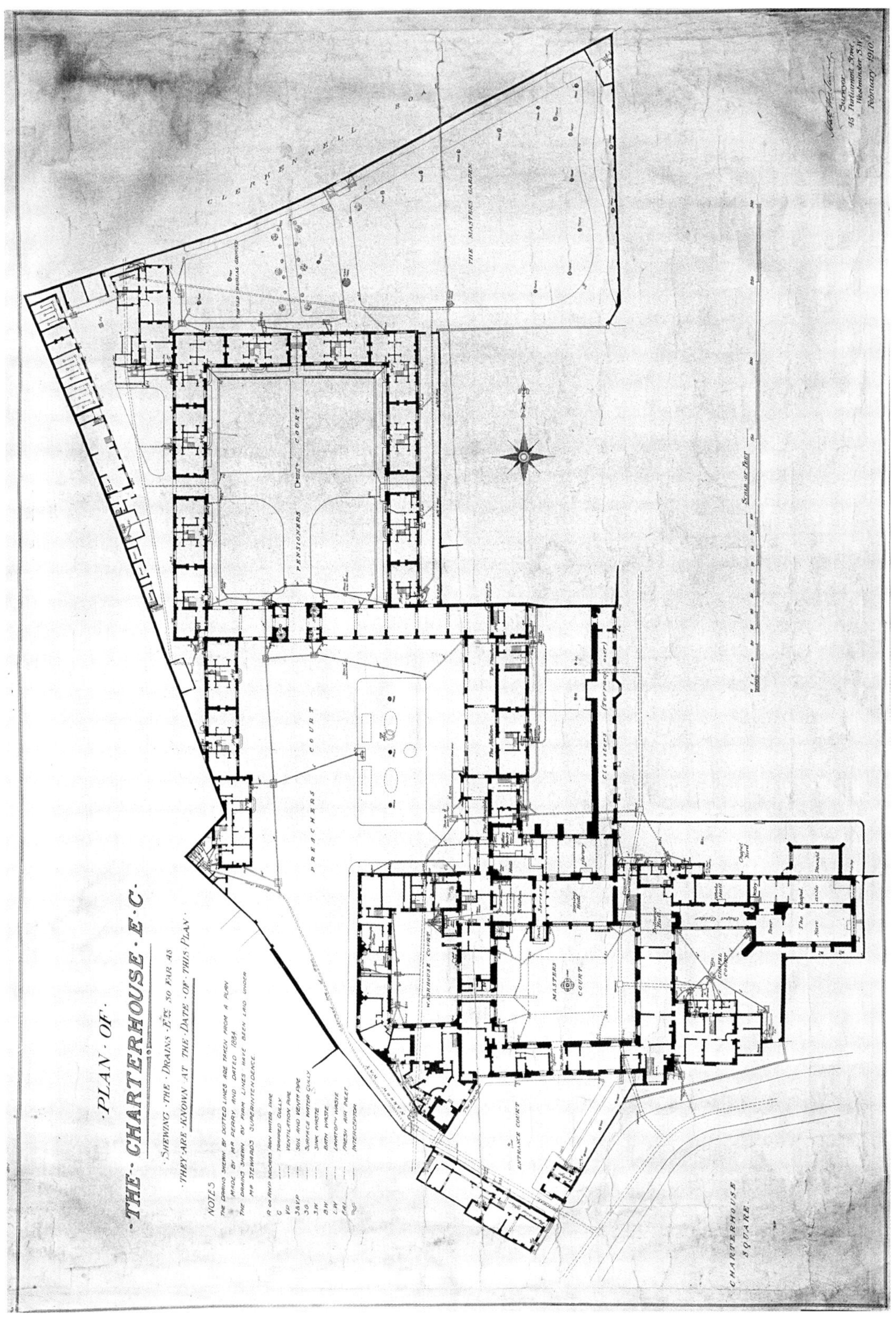

37. Sutton's Hospital in 1910

38. Undated view from Charterhouse Square, showing the gatehouse and 17 Charterhouse Square, the medieval precinct wall, and the south end of Master's Lodge

39. Master's Court and the Great Hall in 1938

40. Wash-house Court in 1940, looking north

character of Howard House—neo-Tudor of the twentieth century instead of neo-Tudor of the nineteenth.

The architects John Seely and Paul Paget were to find much employment restoring or reconstructing war-damaged historic buildings, including Lambeth Palace and the churches of All Hallows by the Tower, St Andrew Holborn, St Bartholomew the Less and St John, Clerkenwell. But the Charterhouse was to be a particularly big project, and one in which they were to take a close personal interest (partly because their home and offices were in Cloth Fair, which allowed very frequent visits). At the time of their first involvement, their most obviously relevant experience was their work in the mid-1930s at Eltham Palace for Stephen and Virginia Courtauld, though they also had the advantage of having worked at Charterhouse School, where they had remodelled the original chapel as a music school. At Eltham (where Peers had acted as consultant) they had been concerned not only with the restoration of the great hall of the largely ruined medieval palace but also with the construction of an almost entirely new house and with blending the whole into the landscape setting. The task at the Charterhouse was more complicated, partly because of the multi-layered history of the buildings, partly because of their essentially institutional character, and not least because of the financial and other constraints. There was little opportunity or motivation for, and no attempt at, a bold statement in the style of the day, inside or out. At the Charterhouse, what at first seemed in most respects an exemplary restoration now looks in some respects questionable, but without the compensation of really creative new work.

Following Peers's report, Seely and Paget's initial design in May 1944 included a new building on the site of Preacher's Court, with an entrance drive from Clerkenwell Road crossing the site of Pensioners' Court. This was to provide much of the Brothers' accommodation, the rest being in Wash-house Court, the west side of Master's Court and a first-floor addition to the Norfolk Cloister. Hopes that such ambitious reconstruction could be achieved were buoyed by the accumulation of a large cash surplus, partly the result of the drop in the number of pensioners, from 63 in the late 1930s to 18 in 1949. Standing at £62,700 in 1948, this surplus already accounted for well over a quarter of the estimated cost of restoration and new building.[109] But it was thought likely that it would be ten years or longer before enough might be saved to allow the reconstruction to take place. In the event, pressure from the Charity Commission and the prospect of timely assistance from the War Damage Commission forced the pace.[110] There were delays nevertheless, caused by shortages of labour and of materials, particularly steel and softwood, and by the system of building licences operated by the Ministry of Works, not finally abolished until 1954. Seely and Paget opted for a series of relatively small licences, with the risk of disruption if one or more were delayed, and in all 30 were issued, the largest being for £71,500 in 1949.[111] There were further delays while authorization for the release of materials was sought, and because of this oak trusses instead of steel were eventually used in the restoration of the Great Hall and Great Chamber. In contrast, steel rather than timber shuttering had to be used in Wash-house Court, where shortages also dictated the use of wood-slab rather than stud partitions, and oak roof trusses were again used, this time instead of softwood. Dealing with the bureaucracy of the licensing system was itself a continual source of frustration, made more protracted by the need to distinguish precisely between the elements of replacement and 'improvement' in the works proposed, involving costings for lost features which were not actually to be replaced (such as the chimneypieces in the Master's Lodge).[112] All this was played out against a background of inflation, which pushed up the estimated total by nearly three-quarters between 1944 and 1950, and actual building costs during 1949–56 by nearly half.[113]

On the other hand, the restraints imposed by the historic status of the buildings were far fewer and less onerous than would be the case today, though the main complex, including 17 Charterhouse Square but not Pensioners' Court and Stable Court, was scheduled as an ancient monument in 1950. One consequence of the involvement of the Ancient Monuments Branch of the Ministry of Works was the adoption of the now-discredited hard pointing used by the ministry on the structures in its care (though similar pointing had been used years earlier at the Charterhouse, notably on the Chapel).

Work got under way in 1946–7, with the replacement of the Great Hall floor and structural work to the Chapel Tower (weakened by the destruction of the Brooke Hall range adjoining), including the rebuilding of the monastic stair turret there. Further progress was delayed until the granting of an initial licence for the restoration of Wash-house Court in 1949. The kitchen area west of the Great Hall and Library was restored at the same time as Wash-house Court, where work was completed in 1951, allowing the thirteen surviving Brothers to return from their exile in Godalming (initially at Charterhouse School, then in private houses acquired for the purpose). Attention then turned to the north range of Master's Court, including the Great Hall, Library and Great Chamber. The rest of Master's Court was reinstated in 1953–6, together with the Brooke Hall range and Chapel Cloister. By the end of 1956, the greater part of the restoration, including refurbishment of the Chapel, was

41. Entrance Court: the Registrar's house (*demolished*) and inner gateway. Undated view

42. Chapel Court, looking north-west in the early twentieth century, showing Chapel Cloister and the Reader's apartment above

43. View south from the terrace walk of the Norfolk Cloister. Undated view

44. Entrance lobby to Reader's apartment in Brooke Hall range. Undated view

45. Brothers' common room, undated view. This room – part of the bedchamber of Lord North and later the Duke of Norfolk – was fitted up as a library in 1858 and burned out in 1941. It was at the north end of the west range of Master's Court, the window being over the scullery in Wash-house Court (see Ill. 87)[101]

SUTTON'S HOSPITAL PRE-1941 INTERIORS

complete. The Norfolk Cloister, undamaged by the fire but long neglected, was restored in 1957, leading to the reopening of the entrance to Cell B and the remains of the hatches to C and D. Removal of the stucco from the Charterhouse Square front of the gatehouse revealed yet more monastic stonework. Some work was still outstanding in February 1958, when the buildings were formally re-opened by Queen Elizabeth II and the Duke of Edinburgh, and in 1960 the restoration of the Havelock or Military Memorial in Chapel Cloister effectively brought the whole programme to a close.

As work progressed, it became clear that complete redevelopment of Pensioners' Court and Preacher's Court was financially out of the question. Even had the capital cost been managed, the consequence would have been too great a reduction in the number of Brothers who could be

46. (*right*) Great Hall in 1940, looking west

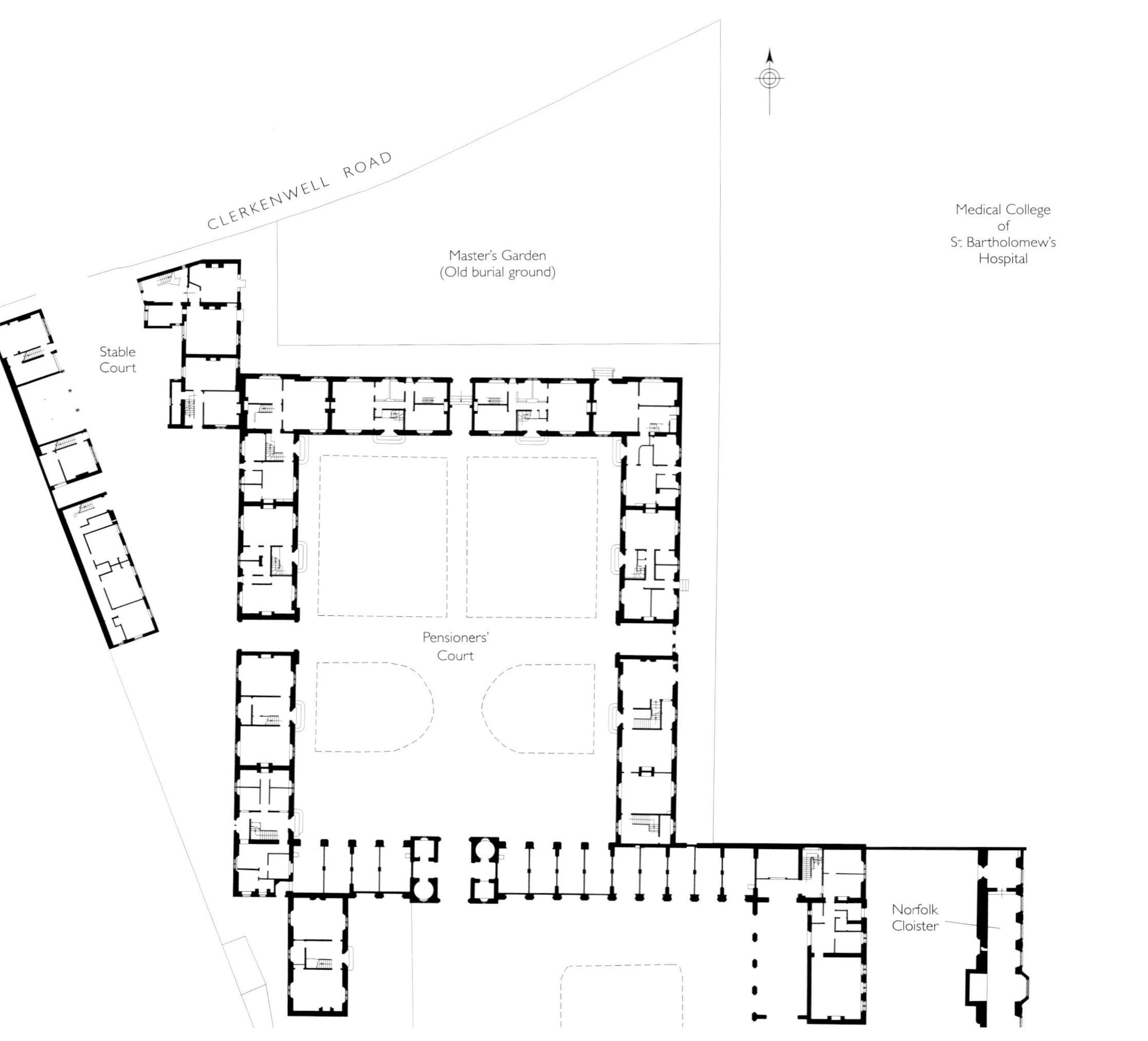
CLERKENWELL ROAD
Master's Garden
(Old burial ground)
Medical College
of
St Bartholomew's
Hospital
Stable
Court
Pensioners'
Court
Norfolk
Cloister

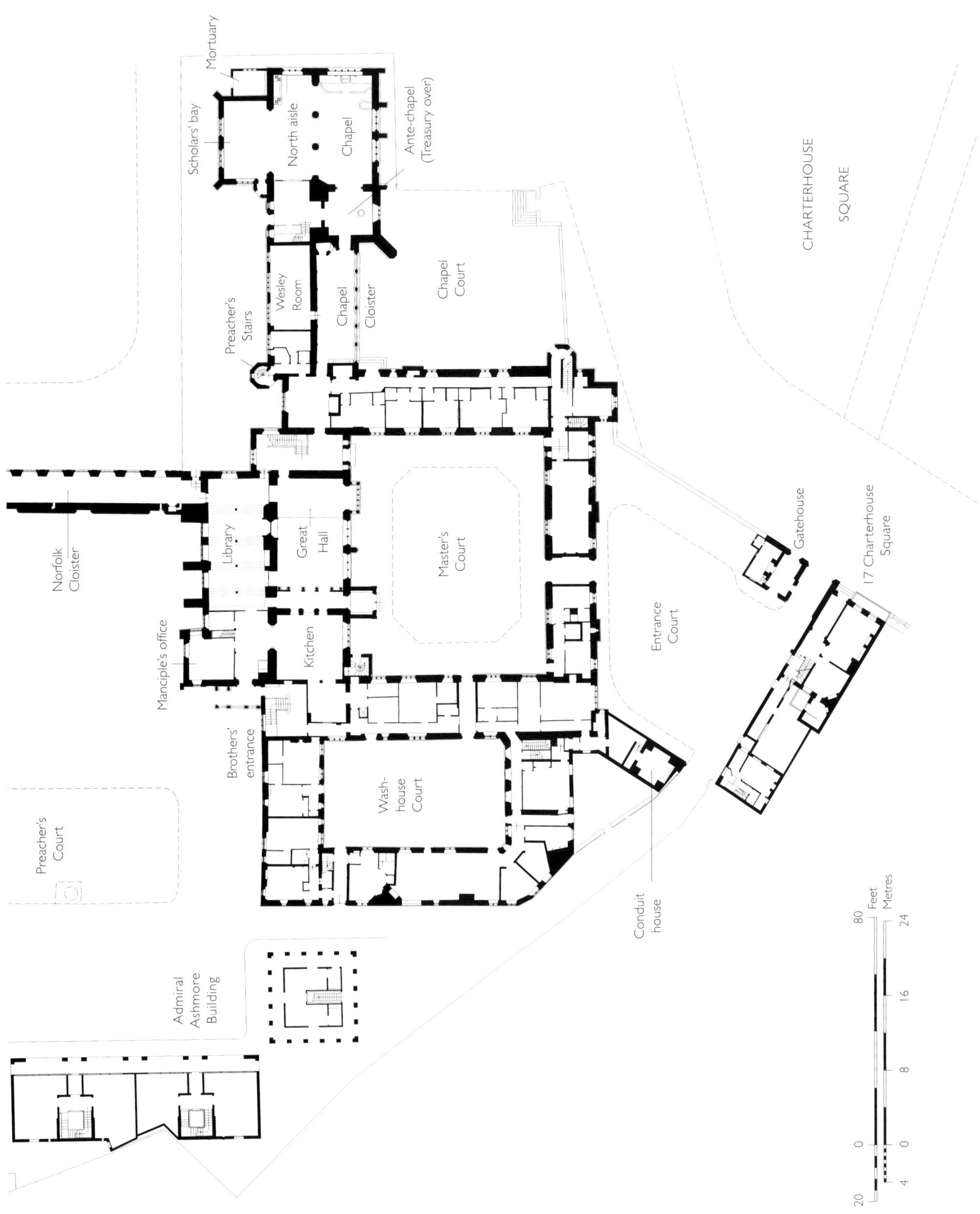

47. Sutton's Hospital *c.*2000

48. Staircase of *c.*1955 in new entrance hall, Master's Court, replacing the Jacobean Great Staircase

49. Main staircase of *c.*1950 in Wash-house Court

50. Timberwork of *c.*1950 on west side of Master's Court, attic floor

RESTORATION BY SEELY AND PAGET INTERIORS IN 1996

51. Wash-house Court, looking west on the first floor of the west range, showing original timber framework. The stairs (with modern balustrade) are those opening off the north side of the slype. The door is one salvaged or copied from the demolished nineteenth-century buildings

supported. As it was, only 32 were accommodated when the restoration was complete, as opposed to the target of 60 in 1950, and the number had barely risen by the mid-1970s.[114] Nevertheless, there was a strong feeling that as many as possible should live in the Howard House ranges rather than the nineteenth-century buildings. The proposed demolition of these was eventually to cause some friction between the governors and the architects, whose attitude is shown by their dismissal of the Manciple's house on the east side of Preacher's Court as 'a Blore building of no use or interest'. The Manciple's house came down, as did Blore's building on the west side of Preacher's Court, providing valuable salvage, but further demolition was checked. Proposals for part-redevelopment of the Clerkenwell Road end of Pensioners' Court with a building for the National College of Food Technology or flats and shops were briefly mooted. Plans to convert Pensioners' Court as commercial offices or staff accommodation had to be abandoned, and it was eventually turned into flats.[115]

Different pressures led to revision of the plan to reinstate the Master's Lodge in the east and south ranges of Master's Court, as set out in Peers's original proposals. There was an echo here of the *Household Words* controversy a century before. The Charity Commission found the intended accommodation, with five bedrooms and rooms for several servants, unacceptably grand and suggested that more rooms be made available for the Brothers in this area. The excessive scale of the proposed Master's Lodge also struck the Ministry of Works, and the governors found their collective arm being twisted. They and the then Master, the Rev. Dr E. Schomberg, had tried to justify it on the grounds of the Master's social duties as well as family requirements, but after his death in 1952 the plans were reassessed and the Physician's house at 17 Charterhouse Square became the new Master's Lodge.[116]

Seely and Paget's work was informed by detailed investigation of the historic fabric, including the archaeological excavations, backed by documentary research and knowledge of other historic buildings. But, on occasion, personal taste and perceived practical requirements trumped the claims of authenticity and even the historic fabric itself. Nineteenth-century work was generally treated with no respect. This is seen, for instance, in the destruction of Blore's work. Demolition of his Manciple's house allowed fuller restoration of the adjoining Great Chamber than would otherwise have been possible, but was far from necessary.

The question of authentic restoration raised difficult problems. It was no doubt right to rebuild the floor over Chapel Cloister in a convincing pastiche of the long-lost original by Francis Carter, and the use of the same style for the new Brothers' entrance from Preacher's Court was a reasonable enough choice. But, where the seventeenth-century appearance was not so aesthetically pleasing, every effort was made to avoid restoring it, notably in the case of the Great Hall ceiling. The ceiling before the fire was the original seventeenth-century work or a replacement on identical lines, with added decorative work by Blore. It was not restored, simply because it was thought unattractive. This pursuit of prettiness underlies the unsatisfying 'instant picturesqueness' complained of by Ian Nairn (page 11). In this light, even the use of such high-quality materials as handmade roof tiles and handmade two-inch facing bricks (made by the Gatwick Brick Company) was not necessarily advantageous.[117] Internally, the 'antiquing' of exposed timbers with an adze was little more than tea-shop fakery. The introduction of architectural salvage from elsewhere, though very limited, was equally unnecessary.

There was less justification for the treatment of the Great Staircase compartment than for that of the Great Hall ceiling. The stairs themselves had been destroyed but, even if a fully carved replica was out of the question, there was every reason to replace the staircase with a plain one of the same size and alignment. The arrangement adopted, with a smaller, realigned staircase and new door on to Master's Court, gave some easing of access but carried no overriding advantage, besides requiring ancient doorways to be moved and making redundant the historic entrance to the Great Hall through the Master's Court porch. In several other instances, ill-considered alterations were made to the historic fabric, such as the anachronistic lowering of the floor of the Norfolk Cloister to the level of the monastic cloister walk, and the changes to what had been the main front of Howard House, in Entrance Court. The Library fared particularly badly, losing its idiosyncratic spatial relationship with the Great Hall as well as the Jacobean woodwork, much of which had survived the fire. Half a century on, Seely and Paget's restoration can no longer be seen as favourably as when it was new. Nevertheless, in extraordinarily difficult circumstances, the preservation of the complex as a major monument in itself (as opposed to the preservation merely of certain remnants) was a great feat. The restoration, and an increasingly educated and eclectic taste in architecture on the part of the public, have fixed the diverse buildings of Sutton's Hospital as an historic ensemble. They have been added to, with the construction of the Admiral Ashmore Building in 1999–2000, but the demolition and remodelling of the 1950s now seem almost as remote as Lord North's four hundred years earlier.

CHAPTER IV

The Chapel and Chapel Cloister Range

As the post-Second World War investigations revealed, the Chapel of the Charterhouse originated not from part of the monastic church but from the adjoining chapterhouse (page 10). With hindsight, it is perhaps surprising that the correct identification was not made earlier, on the basis of what is shown on the water-supply plan and the physical evidence. But Sir William St John Hope had dismissed the plan as wrong, where it conflicted with tradition or preconceptions based on other Carthusian houses.[1] An important clue was the squint in the Treasury, the discovery of which was presented after the war as a matter of chance.[2] In fact it had always been visible externally, and when Alfred Clapham, Walter Godfrey and others inspected the Charterhouse for the Royal Commission on Historical Monuments in 1915, they noted the 'square stone pierced with a circular opening' under the Treasury window.[3] There was other evidence, too, including the remains of the buttressing of the church at its junction with the later chapterhouse, and the unsuitability of the ante-chapel and tower for their presumed role as the central portion of the priory church.

All this fell into place after the war. But there were implications, too, for understanding the plan of Howard House and the conversion of the buildings into Sutton's Hospital. These implications were overlooked, or ignored as relating merely to the post-monastic buildings, and are discussed here for the first time. They throw light on the origins of the north aisle of the Chapel, and correct the misapprehension that the chapterhouse stood more or less in isolation between the demolition of the priory church and the building works of 1613–14.[4]

This chapter deals first with the history and appearance of the Chapel and Chapel Tower, from their monastic origins up to the present. It concludes with an account of the range linking the Chapel with Master's Court, including Chapel Cloister. Evidence is presented to show that this range originated with Lord North and formerly extended for the whole length of the monastic south cloister walk, including part of the site later occupied by Rutland House, now incorporated into the Charterhouse Square campus of Barts and The London School of Medicine and Dentistry (the former Medical College of St Bartholomew's Hospital).

The chapterhouse

In 1394, John Blakeneye, fishmonger, left £30 towards the building of a chapterhouse. But as the priory register (see page 7) records, it had yet to be built when the first prior, John Luscote, died in 1398. Probably some temporary structure served until the completion of the permanent building, the date of which is evident from the dedication of the altar there to St Michael and All Angels in 1414. Two altars in the small chapel outside the door (in the base of the tower) were dedicated at the same time.[5] As today, the ante-chapel served as a vestibule, giving access to church and chapterhouse from the Great Cloister. Though there is no further record of money left specifically for the chapterhouse, it is possible that improvements made in 1512 were funded in part with the priory's £40 legacy from Henry VII, most of his bequests being paid out within three years of his death in 1509.[6]

The water-supply plan, probably drawn within 40 years of the chapterhouse being completed, shows it with a pitched roof, slated or tiled, and a cross over the gabled east end; the west end abuts the tower, which is about the same height (Ills 12, 13). What survives of the original building today is largely confined to the south, east and west walls and comprises coursed rubble-work in ragstone, with some banding or panelling of flint. There are patches, too, in dressed stone, which may be later sixteenth-century repairs done with material salvaged from demolished buildings. A chamfered plinth runs along the outside of the east and south walls, stopping at the tower because the tower's south side was not originally external but part of the north wall of the church. Apart from the windows, two monastic features are a blocked-up doorway in the south wall (Ill. 53) and a shelved recess in the east wall, discovered during alterations in 1842[7] and now concealed behind a hinged section of panelling. Though there is now no trace of a drain, this recess is probably a piscina used in conjunction with the altar dedicated in 1414. Such altars are a usual feature of Carthusian chapterhouses, but the existence of the piscina may have reinforced the old supposition that this was the east end of the priory church. The doorway, thought before the Second World War to have been the lay brothers' entrance to the church, is of

52. The Chapel and Chapel Tower from the south-west in 1915, showing the blocked squint over the ground-floor window, and use of demolition rubble for the upper stage of the tower. On the left is part of the Reader's apartment above Chapel Cloister. In the background are the roof of the gate lodge of Merchant Taylors' School, and the Headmaster's house

53. Early twentieth-century view of the chapel, showing the blocked-up doorway and partly blocked windows on the south side

Reigate stone, the head cut from a single block. On one side is an iron staple set in lead, possibly fixed for a padlock before the entrance was walled up.

On the south side, the three buttresses are part of the monastic structure but not original to the wall itself. Only the inner two are true buttresses; the one at the end is the remnant of a wall, probably the garden wall of the cell between chapterhouse and laundry. The buttresses may have been cut down when the upper part of the south wall was refaced in brick, probably in the eighteenth century. They are likely to have been added when taller windows were installed and the walls raised in height, changes perhaps desirable to improve natural lighting after the building in the 1490s of the Bishop of Lincoln's house to the south (page 28). The original roof seems to have been lower and of shallower pitch, going by marks on the east face of the tower inside the roof space and by the continuance there of the coping which once marked the top of the tower (see below).

The windows cannot be dated with accuracy. With their uncusped tracery and super-mullions they are similar, for instance, to the west windows of St Helen Bishopsgate, thought to be from the 1470s.[8] The Royal Commission investigators in 1915, probably influenced by the 1512 date of the vaulting in the tower, concluded that they were early sixteenth century, while in the 1950s those involved with the restoration of the Charterhouse thought they 'might well coincide' with the building of the chapterhouse, a point which supported the new thinking on the chapel's origins.[9] If they are not the 1414 originals, the fact that the priory finances seem to have picked up after the 1490s, and the silence of the priory register about them, make an early sixteenth-century date (i.e., after the register ends) plausible. They have been much shortened, and are now so restored as to give no impression of antiquity apart from where the decayed mullions and cills (of Reigate stone) remain in their blocked-up portions. From the use of stone rubble rather than brick for infilling towards the bottoms of the south windows, it is probable that this shortening was done in the sixteenth century rather than by Carter. Nor is there any mention of alterations to these windows in the records of the Howard House conversion. In 1726, as part of an improvement scheme, they were made 'as conformable as may be' to those on the north side, though what that means is open to question.[10]

A third south window once existed at the east end. Carter's plan shows one, and Sutton Nicholls's view shows one too (Ills 30, 35), but these are probably misleading. The window was most likely blocked up before Carter, for, as with those adjoining, the lower part of the opening is filled mainly with stone. The upper area is almost entirely brick, part of the refacing of the whole upper portion of the wall. But there are a few stones there, presumably bonders left in place when the brickwork was laid. This stonework looks like post-suppression infill; if it is, the end window on Carter's plan was a proposed reinstatement, meant to match the north wall, where he shows a group of three windows (the end one there being omitted when it was decided to erect Sutton's monument alongside).[11] Nicholls's end window may therefore be an error, over-correcting the omission of any windows in the earlier view by Kip. This detail is repeated in an anonymous and very inaccurate 1756 painting, derived from Nicholls's view (page 73).

The chapterhouse after the suppression

The history of the chapterhouse between the suppression and the creation of Sutton's Hospital is only partly known. Keeper Dale does not refer to it immediately after the closure of the priory, at least not by name. The king's musician Alvise Bassano seems to have had possession for a time, but lost it to the officers of the King's Tents when they moved into the Charterhouse in 1542. As noted above, a probable early alteration after the suppression was the shortening of the windows, which must reflect the new use of the building, and probably the destruction or removal of the glass. The blocking up of the lower parts may have been done by Bassano, the Tents officers or later on by North or Norfolk. However, the blocking up of the doorway may relate to Bassano's eviction, if this was his way in from the Prior's House a few feet away, where he was living (page 35). The work is done very neatly with large pieces of dressed stone, unlike the post-suppression stone-walling at the Charterhouse generally.

From the room sequence of the 1565 inventory the chapterhouse seems to have been converted into North's household chapel, the contents of which were listed (pages 222–3). No chapel is mentioned in the 1588 inventory, either because it contained nothing to be inventoried or because it had returned to secular use—if so, perhaps as the armoury of Howard House, which is listed in proximity to the tower in that inventory. It was finally converted, or reverted, to use for worship under Sutton's Hospital, having been enlarged under Carter's direction in 1613–14. Further enlargement of the building took place in 1825, when the projecting north 'transept' or scholars' bay was built for the increased number of boys attending Charterhouse School.

The tower

The tower is no longer easy to discern on the water-supply plan, but as the facsimile reproduced by Hope in 1902 shows (Ill. 12), it must have been of two storeys and had a two-light window high up in the north wall under a gable with battlements, chimneys or other features. The drawing also shows the monks' entrance from the cloister walk between the stair turret and a cistern built against the north side of the tower. The stair turret is shown hard up against the entrance, rising beyond the upper room, with a tall conical roof and lantern or belfry on top.

The cistern is described as a lavatorium on the water-supply plan, and was probably used for ritual washing. But its size and the pipe layout show that it also served as a holding tank for supplying this side of the priory. Above the taps are a quatrefoil frieze and small latticed windows or decorative panels in the tower wall (or an addition to it). The whole structure would have been under cover of the cloister-walk roof, not shown in the plan.

The turret, which gave access to the sacrist's store-room or treasury, survives partly embedded in the later extension of the tower, though it was almost completely rebuilt in the 1940s (see below). It was originally entered from the sacrist's cell to its west, and though it seems that the sacrist subsequently moved (probably to the cell east of the chapterhouse), to make way for the monks' parlour,[12] the upper room remained part of the sacristy, as a letter of 1534 shows. This concerns items of plate belonging to the Bishop of Bangor which had been deposited for safe-keeping in a chest in 'your tresure howse above your lytyll turnynge steyer yn your Sextrey [sacristy] in the Cloyster'.[13] The 1539 inventory of the priory's goods records two chests, a cupboard and books in this 'Sexten Chamber'.[14]

To a fair extent, the original two stages of the tower survive intact. The water-supply plan shows the north face, which is now hidden behind the later extension of the building. Two features still left are the two-light window on the first floor and, a short way above, a moulded, flat-topped cornice or coping, possibly added when the vaults over the present ante-chapel and Treasury were built in 1512. The window, now fitted with iron bars, has ogee-headed lights (Ill. 54). As for the coping, this may indicate that the gabled roof on the plan had been replaced by a parapet roof. A length of the same coping survives on the east face of the tower, in the roof space.

54. The original north window of the Treasury, redundant since Francis Carter's extension of Chapel Tower. Photographed in 1997. On the left of the void is Edward Blore's replacement north wall

55. Chamber at top of Chapel Tower, showing original fire-surround and extent of original, splayed window opening in south wall

On the west wall, which has been heavily patched and reconstructed, there survive another two-light window to the Treasury, with cusped heads, and, incorporated into the wall, a buttress of the church. The window was revealed after the Second World War, having long been covered by later building. On ground-floor level beneath the present window is a change in the stonework where the entrance to the church was blocked after the suppression. At the side of the window, the infill has since been replaced in brick. Above the window is the squint which gave a sight of the high altar (Ill. 52). Built against the east wall is another buttress belonging to the church.

The third stage of the building must, from its construction, have been added after the suppression, doubtless for Lord North, justifying its designation in the 1565 inventory as the 'Tower'. It was roughly built of demolition rubble used at random. Much of this has been subsequently replaced with brick, where alterations have been made or the masonry had decayed, and parts of the stonework have also been reconstructed. As with the filling in of the chapterhouse window noted above, several large bond-stones remain in areas mainly of brick. The 'Agas' map shows the new roof to have been pitched, with gables to north and south. What the third stage was for is uncertain, but while access involved quite a climb it was of some status, evidenced by the fireplace and large south window opening (Ill. 55). The window is shown (with mullions and transom) by Kip, and its reduction on Nicholls's view points to this change having been made in the very late seventeenth or early eighteenth century (Ills 34, 35).

The third stage comprised two rooms, a chamber at the front and a closet to the north, mentioned by William Hale in 1839 as two chambers over the Treasury, 'the fireplaces of which are of an ancient character'.[15] These rooms must have been knocked into one when the north part of the tower was demolished a few years later by Blore: there is

56. The ante-chapel in 1996, showing the vaulted ceiling of 1512 and the pulpit of 1843

only one room and one fireplace now (the hearth and flue rebuilt). Given the room's later obscurity, the finely moulded stone fire-surround is probably North's. The large chamber might have been a counting-house, being over the room where records and valuables could safely have been kept. Or it could have been his chaplain's room, as the 'Parson of Molton's chamber' comes immediately before the tower in the 1565 inventory.[p] But the heading 'In the Tower' (page 243) may well comprise both the Treasury and the upper floor, just as in the 1588 inventory the contents of the 'ij tower chambers' were lumped together (with the closet listed separately). The tower in 1565 contained a number of items for accounting and safe storage, including a counter table, chests, settles with locks, large hampers and a press, as well as a stock of iron bars. The contents in 1588 were meagre (page 291), as might be expected following Philip Howard's imprisonment. Deeds and records would no doubt have been seized early on. The six-foot wide 'fotstep' under the window suggests the upper room rather than the Treasury with its small windows, while the broken stool in the closet hints at disuse.

Unlike this chamber, the Treasury and ante-chapel below retain much of their old character, including their stone vaults, which have moulded ribs springing from angel corbels. That in the ante-chamber is dated 1512, and the one above is probably of the same date (Ills 56, 57). In the Treasury, the bosses are carved with foliage, the centre boss having a rose and IHS. As well as the squint, the windows and floor tiles there are monastic; some of the tiles, which have been relaid, have incised geometric patterns and traces of colouring. In the ante-chapel, the

[p] Molton is Moulton in Suffolk, where the North family held the advowson, just over the county border near Kirtling.

bosses are carved with an angel (the central boss) and the instruments of the Passion: scourges, spear and hammer, nails, bunches of hyssop. But, apart from the archway leading into the Chapel, the openings in the walls are post-monastic. The archway itself is offset from the axis of the chapterhouse. Here was an indication that the building was not the priory church for, had it been, the arch would probably have been wider and centrally aligned. The south window is a replacement probably made during Edward Blore's early 1840s alterations and subsequently restored; the present stained glass is dated 1853. On the north side, the monastic doorway from the Great Cloister was obliterated by Carter's work in extending the tower's footprint to match that of the enlarged Chapel. The archway partly infilling Carter's arch, one of Blore's alterations, gives on to a vestibule leading to the vestry and stairs to the Treasury, organ gallery and former scholars' gallery. On the west side, leading from Chapel Cloister, the entrance cut through the monastic wall may predate Carter's work in 1613–14, though the door surround (moved in the nineteenth century to make a small lobby or double entrance) is of this time.

Sutton's Hospital Chapel

Whether or not the chapterhouse had been the chapel of Howard House, it was chosen to be that of Sutton's Hospital, and Carter's plan shows that he intended the former cloister garth to be the burial ground or 'churchyard' (Ill. 30). But the building was too small to serve the new community of more than 150 pensioners, scholars and staff who had to attend chapel daily. There was no room for enlargement to the south and east, where it was close up to the boundary with the future Rutland House, and a western extension was out of the question because of the intervening tower and the overly long, narrow building that would have resulted. Retaining the roof intact, Carter therefore opened up the north wall with an arcade, and extended the chapel by adapting the existing structure there, part of what had been Lord North's bowling alley on the site of the south walk of the Great Cloister (pages 110–4). The enlargement added a north aisle to the existing 'nave' or south aisle. To the west, the new aisle continued across the base of the tower, which was extended at the same time, beyond which a small vestry was built. A gallery was put in over the west end of the new aisle.[16]

Internally, the most important architectural feature was the stone arcade of Tuscan columns separating the south and north aisles, its three round arches carved with strapwork and Sutton's arms. Carter was to design a similar feature a few years later for the Earl of Salisbury's chapel at Hatfield church. The Charterhouse arcade is an early use of the style in England, but not without precedents. These include the Tuscan columns respectively in St Wilfrid's church, Standish, in Lancashire (1582–4); between the nave and Morison chapel (1597) in St Mary's, Watford; and in the nave of St Wilfrid's, Metheringham, Lincolnshire (after a fire of 1599).[17]

The approach to the Chapel was by an open cloister walk from Master's Court, with an imposing stone doorway at the end, the work of Edmund Kinsman, leading into the vaulted space at the foot of the tower (Ill. 82). Like the extension of the tower on the north side, this space was awkwardly annexed by Carter as a part of the chapel proper; it is now divided off as the ante-chapel.

As built, the two north windows were individually wider than the three that Carter's plan shows. They had Caen stone tracery resembling that of the south windows (Ill. 79).[18] Because of the adjoining building, it was not possible to have a window in the wall at the east end of the north aisle, where Sutton's monument may originally have been intended to stand. There the monument would have been seen to some advantage, lit by the intended third window in the north wall and closing the view along the aisle. Instead it ended up 'lost in darkness and obscurity'.[19]

Two carpenters, William Wood and Tobias Williams, contracted for panelling ('ceiling') the Chapel. The nave retained its monastic open timber roof, but how the north aisle roof was finished is not clear. The only hint of ornamentation to either roof at this time is the payment to a joiner, John Brown, for 'glewing of roses for the roofe of the Chappell'.[20]

Enlargement of the tower

Carter's plan shows that he had not originally intended to extend the tower northwards, to match the enlargement of the Chapel itself. But in December 1613 the governors decided that he should provide somewhere for a 'great bell' and clock. The tower was the obvious place and, to take the weight, early in 1614 the north wall was reinforced on the ground floor with an 8½ft-thick brick arch and, on its east side, a massive pier rising through the upper stages of the tower. This pier cuts off the corner of the nave at an angle (a peculiarity omitted by Herkomer in his 1889 painting of Brothers assembling in Chapel).[21] It was probably this that decided Carter to extend the tower, so that the belfry could be placed symmetrically.

57. The Treasury in 1996. Under the window in the south wall is the squint which overlooked the high altar in the priory church

The bell, by Daniel Winch of Houndsditch, weighed almost 12cwt. At the same time, a smaller chapel bell (of under five stone) was acquired from Isaac Symes, also of Houndsditch. A clock supplied by Robert Harvey in 1614 was probably the one shown by Kip and Sutton Nicholls mounted on the south face of the tower (Ills 34, 35). It is not clear how the tower roof was originally adapted for the bell: Carter's accounts include merely a frame for the bell, but in 1617–18 a new 'roof' was fitted 'where the great bell hangs', perhaps meaning the bell-chamber and cupola shown by Kip. Winch's bell was recast or replaced in 1631 by Thomas Bartlett, and this is the bell still in place.[22]

At first-floor level, the gallery seems to have been used mainly by 'strangers'. In 1654, it was ordered that the gallery should be reserved for governors and their families, or, in their absence, for other 'persons of quality'. But in the following year the gallery was ordered to be divided to provide one space for governors and their families and another for the poor scholars, the Schoolmaster and the Usher.[23]

Carter's reinforcement of the tower evidently proved insufficient, for in 1615–16 the present brick buttress was built at the south-west corner, restoring the support originally given by the church. Even with this, the building was still to give trouble. Iron braces were fitted in 1726, and in 1780 the bulging of the Treasury wall caused part of the vaulting to fall.[24] Structural problems were to recur in the nineteenth century, and following the destruction of the Brooke Hall range in 1941.

On the first stage of the tower, Carter retained the former treasury as a strong-room for documents, blocking up the chimney and fitting iron bars at the window. On the third stage, the enlargement provided another small room, which in 1754 was added to the Receiver's (later the Reader's) accommodation above Brooke Hall. It no longer exists, since the remodelling of the tower by Edward Blore (see below).[25]

The organ gallery of 1626

No musical instrument is recorded among the contents of the Chapel listed *c.*1617, and it was not until 1626 that an organ was installed.[26] Under Carter's direction, a gallery was built at the west end of the nave, centred on the aisle and east window rather than on the arch behind the gallery. The joinery was by Robert Linton, Master of the Joiners' Company in 1627,[27] and the carving by John James. James's panels, now attached to the present organ loft in the north aisle, are charmingly carved with musical instruments, martial trophies and a range of weaponry and accoutrements (Ills 62–4). Linton and James were paid £29 9*s* 10*d* for the gallery and Thomas Hamlyn, organist, received £40 5*s* for supplying and installing the organ, which was decorated with gilding by Rowland Buckett. The composer Benjamin Cosyn, formerly organist of Dulwich College, was appointed organist, remaining in post until the Parliamentary ban on music in worship in the 1640s.[28]

Changes under William Laud

In the mid-1630s, the chapel was embellished and reordered under the influence of William Laud, who had become a governor in 1628 and, as the new Archbishop of Canterbury, chairman in 1633. It may be that the communion table was already at the east end, this being the arrangement favoured by the Chapel Royal and increasingly at Oxford colleges.[29] In 1635, a sanctuary was created by raising the table on two steps, tiled in black and white marble, and enclosing it with wooden rails. The following year John Colt, who had done the stonework for the sanctuary, supplied an ornate reredos, in the form of the Ten Commandments with figures of Moses and Aaron (see below). Two new pews, one of them for the Master, were fitted on either side of the sanctuary.[30] Other changes were probably made during this period, though all that can be identified today is an alteration to the railings and setting of Sutton's monument (described below).

The Civil War and after

The abolition of the organist Cosyn's post in 1644 was one of several liturgical and other changes to the chapel brought about by the Civil War. Both the organ and the reredos were complained about, and the redundant organ was disposed of in the mid-1640s. In 1651, the king's arms were taken down and those of the Commonwealth put up in their place, the process being reversed following the Restoration.[31] There is no direct record of the sanctuary being dismantled, but the presence in the Housekeeper's lodgings in 1663 of a 'parcell of Wanescoate belonging to the Chappell to Inclose Moses & Aaron' is suggestive.[32] (By the early eighteenth century, painted panels in gilt frames, with the Commandments, Lord's Prayer and Creed, were in position over the altar.) On the whole, the building escaped lightly from the hands of the Puritans and, while certain 'superstitious' inscriptions on the roof, probably relics of the monastic decoration, were destroyed in 1659, nothing was done to disfigure the monastic imagery on the ante-chapel vault.[33]

Organ music was restored in 1662 with the appointment of an organist, Nicholas Love, and the installation of an instrument 'of 6 sets of pipes'. Acquired from John Hingeston for £100 and installed by John Pease, this was probably the organ from the Chapel Royal in Whitehall, replaced by Hingeston the same year.[34] Under John Patrick, Preacher from 1671 to 1695, music flourished, and his psalter 'for the use of the Charter-House', published in 1679, was drawn on by Henry Purcell for psalm settings. Purcell's *Blessed is the Man that Feareth the Lord* was probably first performed as an anthem for the Founder's Day service in 1687, and was sung annually thereafter.[35]

In the mid-1720s, extensive repairs and improvements were made to the Chapel. The work began in 1724–5 with an overhaul of the by now decrepit organ and some reglazing of the windows, and in 1726 a fuller programme was carried out, under the supervision of the then Surveyor, Westby Gill. What was at first intended to be a fairly superficial refurbishment became a major project, though little of what was done is recorded in any detail.[36] Work on the bell-turret and cupola may have amounted to reconstruction, and it was at this time that the sides of the cupola were filled in and given their circular openings. The clock was repaired or replaced, and mounted on a diamond-shaped dial board. The windows of the chapel were reglazed with 'white' glass, and various improvements were made inside, including repaving with diagonally laid flagstones. The sanctuary paving and much of the woodwork was repaired and refurbished. The east window and the panel with the Commandments were restored, with the direction that they should be 'beautified with proper ornaments'.[37] Repairs and embellishments were made to the wooden fittings and furnishings by Tobias Priest. He also supplied a new communion table and railings and a carved cartouche and brackets. Of Priest's work only the cartouche seems to survive, and the communion table now in use is the Jacobean original. The cartouche, with a lion above and Sutton's arms, and cherubs below, was apparently made for the organ gallery (Ill. 59), and transferred with the panels by John James to the present organ gallery as part of Edward Blore's refit. Whether the carver of this baroque piece (Ill. 62) was Priest himself, described merely as a joiner, is not clear.

The upper part of the south wall may have been rebuilt or refaced at about this time, in brick. Work carried out on the nave and north aisle roofs is rather vaguely recorded, though it did not involve complete replacement of both. Payments to a carpenter named Thomas Woodward included money for timber for the Chapel roof; Thomas Spicer, whose name and the date 1726 are chiselled into one of the remaining old trusses over the nave, must have been one of Woodward's men.[38]

The organ was finally replaced in 1755 by one bought from John Snetzler, a German-Swiss émigré who was to become organ-maker to the king.[39]

Enlargement and improvements from 1805

No further major alterations were made to the Chapel until the first half of the nineteenth century, since which time the building has been little changed. A heating system was installed in 1805, using underfloor ducts to transfer warm air from two stoves, one between the antechapel and the north aisle, the other against the north aisle wall, to a radiator between the columns of the arcade. Smoke was extracted by a flue between the hot-air ducts, with removable stone covers for cleaning. The engineer was D. Chenu, French-stove manufacturer of Great Queen Street. His system was replaced by gas stoves in the 1850s.[40]

Repairs costing about £1,000 were made in 1811, including replacement of most of the external plaster with Parker's cement.[41] In 1825, the north transept or scholars' bay was added by Redmond Pilkington. With his more-or-less enforced resignation (pages 171–2), the task of further altering the building fell to Edward Blore, who in 1842 rearranged the interior, put in a second east window and cut away the upper portion of Carter's enlargement of the tower, producing the asymmetric arrangement of tower and cupola that remains today.

Behind the 1825 enlargement was the increase of scholars to nearly 500, the fruit of Dr Russell's introduction of the Madras system of teaching (page 70). Much of the cost of the extension (a little over £2,000) was raised by subscription from the boys. The only space available being on the north side, Pilkington took down the wall between the Founder's tomb and the tower, spanning the opening with a shallow arch giving onto a galleried brick extension, with windows on two levels and a burial vault beneath (Ill. 80). Access to the gallery was from a wooden stair against the east wall (removed by Blore). This work was followed by a general refurbishment of the seating, reading-desk and pulpit, with much use made of red and purple cloth. Russell's expansion of the school roll was short-lived, and by 1832 the scholars' bay was no longer needed.[42]

In 1841, following his decorative work in the Great Hall, Blore drew up a scheme for repairs and improvements to the Chapel, and this was mainly carried out in the summer of 1842, while services were held in the Great Hall.[43] Blore's challenge was the eccentricity of the plan, which without radical reconstruction precluded a liturgically satisfactory arrangement with the east end fully visible to all. The result was a compromise, but he was

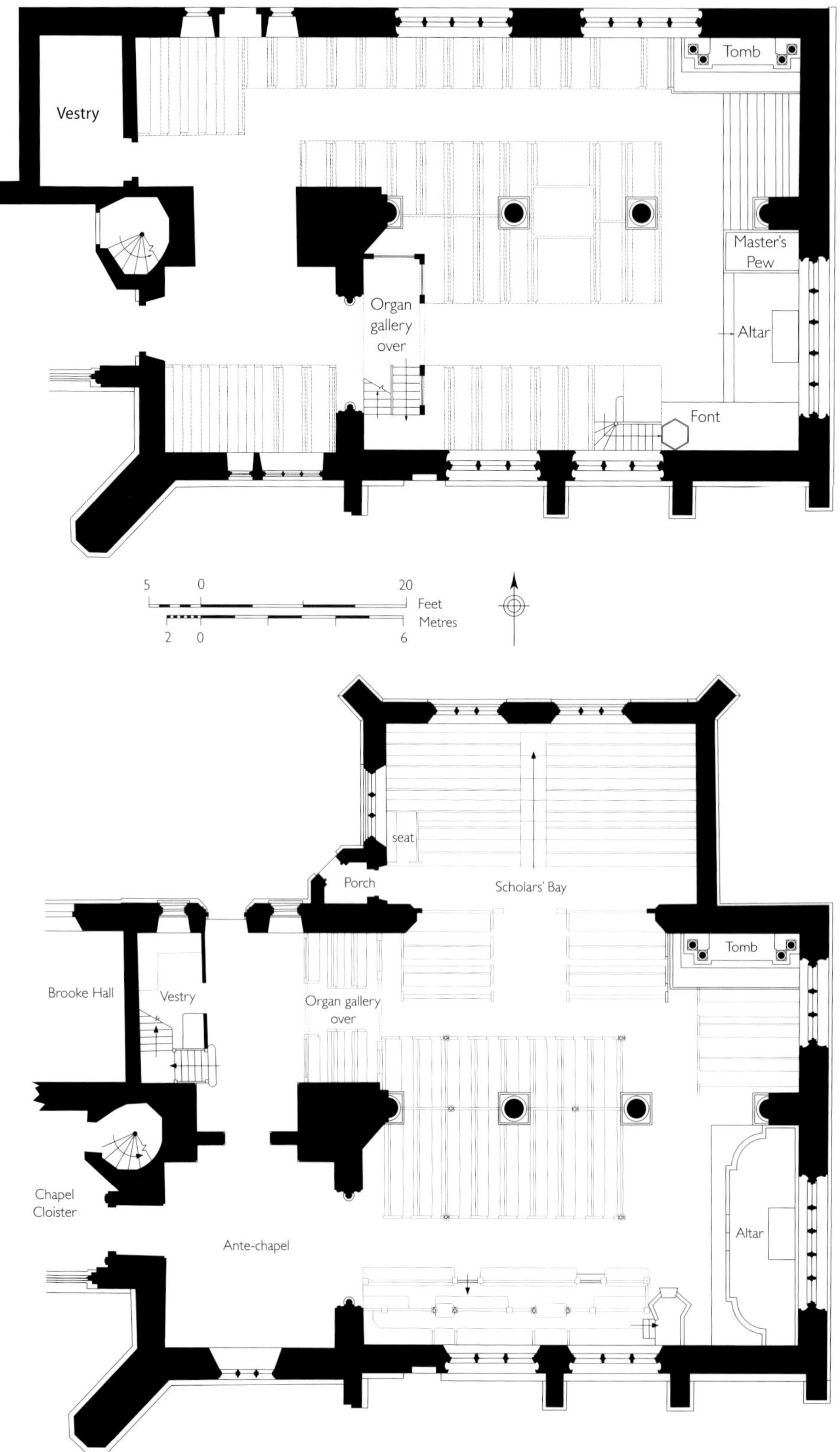

58. Plans of the Chapel, in 1805 (*top*) and following alterations of 1842 by Edward Blore

fairly successful in pulling the space together and imposing a greater sense of order. Adding some new seating and other fittings and Jacobean-style plaster ceilings, and moving many of the memorials, he was also able to achieve some aesthetic harmony. His idea of circular openings over the principal arches 'to improve the appearance of the heavy mass of masonry' was not taken up.[44]

On the north side of the ante-chapel, he partly filled in Carter's arch, remodelling the area beyond in conjunction with his other changes to make another vestibule and a tiny vestry under the stairs going up to the north aisle gallery (the old vestry, shifted since Carter's day, being lost to the enlargement of the adjoining Brooke Hall). In the Chapel itself, his chief difficulty was to accommodate a new organ, which was too big for the existing gallery. This instrument, purchase of which had been delegated to the Bishop of London, was by one of the leading makers, Joseph Walker.[45] Blore's response was to remove the gallery altogether and adapt the north aisle gallery, where governors and senior officers then sat, for the new organ. He transferred the carved woodwork from the old organ gallery front to the new, incorporating the uprights as part of the cladding to what are presumably iron supports. Two tiers of new collegiate-style pews were set against the south wall of the chapel for the Master and Preacher and those displaced from their perch over the north aisle (though Herkomer's painting shows pensioners here). The Master's and Preacher's seats were distinguished by canopies with the 'Jacobethan' ornament favoured by Blore at the Charterhouse and elsewhere. Similar canopies were provided for the seats used by the Schoolmaster and his assistant on either side of the sanctuary.

These alterations allowed Blore to call time on the pretence that the base of the tower could be part of the chapel proper. Taking out the seats from the vaulted area on the south side, he made it into a screened-off ante-chapel or vestibule. The nave itself he realigned to the newly revealed archway from the ante-chapel, instead of to the entrance from Chapel Cloister and the east window. In a further refinement, he removed a porch which had been put up at the entrance (Chapel Cloister then still being open to the air), and created the present porch or lobby, originally with inner and outer doors. This involved moving Kinsman's doorway (see Ill. 82). It is assumed that it was Blore who replaced the broad, asymmetrical south window with the present three-light one. He also installed the font (dated 1843).[46]

In the north part of the building, the boys' seats in front of the scholars' bay were turned to face the Master's pew, and family pews for staff were fixed in the gallery there, which was given a new Jacobean-style front with an arcaded screen beneath. A new approach to the gallery, from the organ loft, was provided through an exterior turret, built into the corner where the 1825 extension met the Chapel wall, cutting across the windows there.

This left one problem spot, the corner presided over by Sutton's monument, complained of on account of its gloom and the monument's inaccessibility, hemmed in as it was by the scholars' benches. Blore left the monument in place and the seating too, but put a window in the east wall, taking advantage of the extra light available since the demolition of the adjoining house and its replacement by the low-level Day Boys' Lodge (page 76), separated from the chapel by a 6ft gap.[47] This and the main east window were soon fitted with stained glass (see below).

It was found that the tower was in a poor state, owing to decay in the principal timbers. The upper rooms there were in any case no longer in use, and accordingly Blore cut back the upper part on the north side, building a new north wall only a little way in front of the medieval original to take the weight of the cupola. He remodelled the parapet all round, with bartizan-like features at the corners and other fussy detailing, largely destroyed when the parapet was rebuilt in its present plain manner, in the late nineteenth or early twentieth century. A similarly ornamental parapet survives on the remnant of the cut-down part of the tower (Ill. 81). The north aisle was re-roofed, and the wall separating the tower from Brooke Hall and the Reader's apartment above was rebuilt, slightly to the east.[48]

With the departure of the school to Godalming in 1872, the schoolmasters' seats on either side of the sanctuary were removed, and the boys' benches in front of Sutton's tomb were replaced by more substantial pews with decorated ends, since removed.[49] (Although the sale of the old school site to the Merchant Taylors included 'free daily use' of the chapel, in practice it was attended by Merchant Taylors' School only once a year.)[50] The present altar rails date from the 1872 remodelling.[51]

In 1875, the back of the sanctuary was altered and embellished, and a watercolour copy of Francesco Francia's *Pietà* in the National Gallery was installed as an altarpiece (painted by the daughter of the Registrar, Archibald Keightley). The alterations, including an ornamental frieze and pilasters, were designed by Phillips & Son of Baker Street, in conjunction with Blore.[52] The *Pietà* was much later replaced by the present painting, Giordano's *Visitation of the Blessed Virgin to St Elizabeth*. This came to the Charterhouse from the collection of one of the governors, O. T. Norris, after whose death in 1973 it was accepted by the government in lieu of tax. Having been acquired by the Guildhall Art Gallery it was returned to the Charterhouse in 1982, and hung above the altar.[53] The more embarrassingly Victorian elements of Blore's decoration were expunged as part of Seely and Paget's work on the Chapel in the 1950s; some of his ornamentation over the south wall seats was probably removed at the same time.

59. The Chapel, looking south, *c.*1840. View by John Wykeham Archer

The 1950s restoration was the first significant work to the Chapel for many years. Nearly a century earlier, in 1863, its setting had been much improved by the removal of the privies and other outbuildings of houses in Charterhouse Square, which had been allowed to encroach right up to the south wall. The cleared passage thus formed was paved, and the buttresses and the boundary wall in Chapel Court were repaired. 1898 had seen the removal, many to Brookwood Cemetery, of the sixteen bodies which had accumulated in the vault under Pilkington's extension before further interments were banned in 1854. The same year, Dove Brothers restored the perished exterior stonework, following a survey by the firm of Aston Webb & E. Ingress Bell, and in 1920 a small brick mortuary was built at the north-east corner.[54]

Post-war refurbishment

The Chapel escaped serious damage in the fire that gutted much of the Charterhouse in 1941, thanks in part to the timely closing of the door from Chapel Cloister. A fire on the organ staircase was quickly put out.[55] Nevertheless, the effects of smoke, damp due to lack of heating, and dust from building elsewhere on site made refurbishment necessary, though almost all the work done was ineligible for War Damage Commission funding. More urgently, structural repair was needed to the tower, which had lost some support with the destruction of the Reader's apartment to the west and was now badly cracked. Consolidation was carried out by Richard Costain Ltd in 1946–7. Stone for the purpose was obtained from the demolition of the Victorian scullery in the north-east corner of Wash-house Court and the removal of the battlements from the north front to Entrance Court, while bricks were salvaged from the clearance of the remains of the Master's Lodge on the south side of Chapel Court. Demolition of what was left of the Reader's apartment exposed the monastic sacristy turret and window in the west wall of the Treasury; the lower part had always been visible in Chapel Cloister. The turret was largely rebuilt in brick, with a pointed red-tiled roof, and steel ladders instead of stairs going to the third stage. There is some reconstructed rubble-stone externally towards the top, and inside is an area of very old, narrow red brick.[56]

In the Treasury, the vaulting was at risk of collapse, and had to be taken down and reset. The squint in the south wall was uncovered during restoration work, and the medieval windows were reopened in the west and north walls.[57] The Chapel windows were restored with artificial stone. Inside the Chapel, work continued in the mid-1950s with a new heating system and some de-Victorianization, including the stripping of varnish from the woodwork and alterations to the sanctuary and seating.

Fittings and Furnishings

The Chapel retains some of its original furniture, notably the communion table and pulpit. Both are of oak. The structure of the pulpit, which together with the Reader's pew cost £10, was made by Thomas Herring and Edward Mayes. Various decorative additions cost extra. These were the carvings, done by Francis Blunt, and 'pendalls' made by Jeremy Wincle: perhaps the twisted 'spindles' or balusters for the handrail of the steps. A needlework cloth for the pulpit was made by Anthony Weekes, one of the pensioners; considered to be worth £15 9*s*, this was the most valuable of the Chapel furnishings. The pulpit, originally free-standing, has been much altered and diminished, having lost its sounding-board, steps and supporting post. While the main panels are original, some of the mouldings are not and the whole has been adapted to stand against the south wall (where it is awkwardly entered from the pews), and opened up to allow a seat for the preacher to be fitted. This arrangement, together with the replacement of the support and removal of the stairs, dates from 1872.[58]

60. Communion table of *c*.1613

The communion table, probably by other craftsmen than the pulpit, appears to have survived intact, though there is a reference to 'cuttinge the communion table' when the sanctuary was altered in 1635.[59] It has thirteen legs, in the form of Corinthian columns, and is ornamented with carving including Sutton's arms. More artistically sophisticated are the carvings of a decade later on the front of the organ gallery and the additional carvings supplied by Tobias Priest in 1726 (described above).

The seating has been variously altered and renewed, but some of the pew-ends are the originals, made and carved in oak by James Ryder. Others are nineteenth century or later replicas in pine. More of the old seating, with turned legs, survives in part in the ante-chapel. At the west end of the north aisle, separating the Chapel from the vestry lobby, is a screen and doors with pierced carved panels of foliage, thought to be of the late seventeenth century. In the scholars' bay, the plain seating of 1825 remains. The panelling is of various periods, much renewed in part. Most is mid- or late nineteenth century, some being installed in 1872 when the school left. Its present height seems to have been set by Blore; it was formerly much lower, leaving space for wall monuments above.[60]

The Moses and Aaron reredos

Of the ornate reredos or commandment table erected in 1636, only the figures of Moses and Aaron and fragments of the architectural backing survive. But the various components listed in the accounts, and the design of other examples, allow a general impression of the ensemble's appearance to be formed.[61] Marble, alabaster and ashlar work are mentioned; the surviving pieces are alabaster. Essentially, it comprised two white marble tablets carved with the Commandments, flanked by Moses and Aaron, an exceptionally early instance of this subsequently conventional tableau. The plinth was ornamented with a cherub's head in the centre, and the figures were raised on what were described as 'lamps otherwise called quartwooses', that is, cartouches—probably meaning here some sort of brackets or corbels rather than panels. The Commandments tablets were probably round-headed, with the head of a cherub in the clouds described as 'over' them perhaps in the spandrels between. The whole was surmounted by a cornice with 'the half round and Jehova in the clouds'. This cornice was topped by an urn and a pair of incense bowls.

The figures, with the remains of the piers behind them and a length of bead-and-reel moulding, show how well executed the design was, though there is some awkwardness in the raised arms of the two patriarchs, used as a framing device. This seems to place the sculptor in the Elizabethan tradition of figure work, whose stylized stiffness was then giving way to a more naturalistic approach. Aaron, who carries a censer, has a mitre and belted tabard, both elaborately worked; Moses, a toga-like robe and sandals.

The sculptor was John Colt. The elder John Colt, a Huguenot from Arras, died at an advanced age in 1637 and it is therefore probable that it was his son who made the reredos. The son was at the Charterhouse in 1660, repairing monuments in the Chapel. His uncle Maximilian Colt also had some connection with the Charterhouse, signing for the organist Cosyn's stipend in 1636.[62]

In 1637, Colt was paid for a second assemblage for the Chapel, now entirely lost. This is harder to envisage from the pieces specified, and the material is not stated, but it may have been an addition to the earlier reredos. It incorporated figures of the twelve Apostles and six cherubim heads (with six cartouches). Reference is made to four spandrels, four 'swelling' friezes, seven panels 'on each side of the case' and cherubims' heads 'on the outside of the case'. It was also decorated with further ornamental panels or 'tapherels', two of them 'of each side the wainscott'. Probably in connection with the installation of this piece, a joiner was paid the substantial sum of £35 for unspecified work around the altar.[63]

It is probable that these Laudian pieces were taken down during the Civil War or Interregnum; somehow, the two figures escaped destruction and were lost sight of until discovered in a basement at Sutton's Hospital in 1977.[64]

Stained glass

As originally fitted up, the five principal windows of the Chapel had panels of painted glass: the king's arms in the east window, and smaller panes for the side windows, two with the king's arms and two with Sutton's. The supplier was named Richard Butler. There was no religious stained or painted glass until 1844, when the two east windows were filled with glass by the painter Charles Clutterbuck, who the year before had been engaged to restore and paint the chimneypiece in the Master's drawing room. It was intended to have stained glass throughout, but the only other window to receive it was that in the ante-chapel. This glass, with a conventional figure of Christ, was designed by William Wailes of Newcastle-upon-Tyne, and carries the date 11 June 1853.[65]

Clutterbuck's windows may have been his earliest painted glass commissions.[66] The smaller window by Sutton's tomb, showing Christ bearing the Cross, was paid

61. Moses and Aaron from the lost reredos of 1636, by John Colt

62. North aisle and organ gallery, looking towards the vestry; 63, 64. Carving on organ gallery supports by John James, 1626

65. The Chapel in 2003, looking east

66. East window by Charles Clutterbuck

for by the new Master, Archdeacon Hale; it was removed in 1871, not long after his death. The surviving window, given by the schoolmasters and scholars, shows the Crucifixion. The glass is mounted on hinged wooden panels some way from the external tracery and glazing of the window; this was done in 1855, when the glass had to be removed for repair.[67] In this fine piece, Christ occupies the middle light, with Mary Magdalene at his feet and a centurion to one side. In the two left-hand lights are onlookers and behind them one of the two crucified thieves, the other being shown in side-view in one of the right-hand lights. Also on the right are the soldiers dicing for Christ's garments. The severe cropping may be the result of Clutterbuck's having adapted an originally rectangular design to the pointed lights.

Clutterbuck's glass was unpalatable to the taste-formers of *The Ecclesiologist*, which denounced the use of a landscape format as debased, and found the 'cinque-cento looking figure in thick hose … in such a scene … in very bad taste'. It was also critical of the colour, particularly the 'large mass of blue, in the Bearing of the Cross [presumably referring to the other window], which quite puts the remainder of the window out of tone'.[68] Deterioration and extensive areas of restoration make it difficult now to imagine the original effect, but a more appreciative contemporary found that 'the twilight gloom occasioned by the brilliancy of the dark blue, contrasts with the small patches of white here and there, and awakens feelings of reverence'.[69]

Made at Clutterbuck's workshop in Stratford, east London, the glass seems to have been poorly fired, and only a few years on the paint was lifting. Deterioration may have been the reason why the companion window was removed. Further damage was caused by wartime bombing. The window's restoration in 1955, by James Powell & Sons, involved the replacement of many missing or damaged pieces, and other parts had to be repainted, including the head and shoulders of Christ.[70] Further restoration was carried out in 2001.

Monuments and Memorials

The Chapel has one spectacular monument and several others of more than passing interest. Most are modest in scale, which reflects the fact that most of the august figures associated with the administration of the Charterhouse have been governors rather than resident

67. Sutton's monument seen through the Chapel arcade. Undated photograph

officers, and naturally have their monuments elsewhere. Lord Ellenborough is the exception. A number of officers are commemorated, but Francis Beaumont's small monument of *c.*1630 did not start a tradition. John King (d. 1737), Master from 1715, who was interred in the Founder's vault, left £500 for a marble memorial to be set up, but his wishes were never carried out.[71] His successor, Nicholas Mann (d. 1753), took care to have a memorial put up to himself (over the door to the ante-chapel from Chapel Cloister) in his lifetime. The next Master to have a monument in the chapel was Philip Fisher (d. 1842): a Gothic tablet, probably made on the death of Mrs Fisher, who predeceased him. The Brothers, of course, have usually lacked the resources to afford elaborate memorials, and it would not have been thought appropriate for them to be commemorated in the Chapel in any case. Only one has a memorial there: William Cusens Neats, who died in 1927, leaving £5,000 to the Hospital.[72] Besides, the governors, particularly in the seventeenth and early eighteenth centuries, were not necessarily keen to permit additional monuments. Henry Levett, Physician from 1713 until 1725, was allowed a large memorial, and a slab over his grave in the nave, next to that of Preacher John Patrick (d. 1695). Thomas Walker (d. 1728) and Andrew Tooke (d. 1731), successive Schoolmasters, were commemorated by large memorials, and Walker also had a slab marking his grave in the north aisle.

In 1628, it was ordered that burials in the Chapel or graveyard should only be for those who were governors, officers, staff or pensioners at the time of their death, and that 'no woman or woman kinde' should be interred in either place.[73] The rule was not strictly adhered to, and at least three women were interred beneath the Chapel: Thomas Walker's wife and daughter, who both died in 1736, and the Reader's wife, Sarah Dicken, who died in 1852 and has a small memorial in the north extension. Other women are commemorated, including Fisher's wife and former Matrons—one, Elizabeth Jeffkins (d. 1856), with a particularly fulsome epitaph. Similarly, the Chapel has several memorials to other relations of officers of Sutton's Charity, such as Edmund Fisher (Philip Fisher's grandson), who died aged nineteen in 1842, and seven-year-old Archibald Keightley, presumably the son of the Registrar of the same name. His small memorial is by John Mallcott.

68. (*top*) Captain
69. (*bottom*) Congregation in chapel
70. (*right*) Vanitas group with Time and *Homo Bulla*

Sutton's Monument details

Edward Blore found it desirable to rearrange many of the monuments and memorials 'in a manner less calculated to disfigure the chapel'.[74] The result is that a number are displayed, loosely 'themed' to no particular effect in the north extension or in the obscurity of the organ gallery staircase. The old positions of some are shown in J.W. Archer's view of the chapel (Ill. 59).

Burials beneath the Chapel are marked by several large black slabs; Matthew Raine's is marked by a small stone with his initials. Besides those to Patrick, Levett and Walker is one (in the tower extension) to the Manciple James Sidgrave (d. 1707), who has no mural memorial.

Sutton's monument

Thomas Sutton's body, removed from Christ Church, Newgate Street, was reinterred on 12 December 1614 in a vault at the north-east corner of the Chapel.[75] The great monument which stands above the vault was completed by November the following year. Costs of making and erecting it, as set out in an indenture of 1613,[76] amounted to £366 15*s*, but the Charterhouse accounts and their final receipt show £400 paid to the makers, Nicholas Johnson (or Jansen), Edmund Kinsman and Nicholas Stone. Stone was responsible for the carving, and the extra seems to be accounted for by his small monument to John Law being added to the contract. While the principal pieces are certainly by his hand, others may have been involved, as for instance in the less assured figures of the cherubs at the top. Johnson is thought to have been responsible for the overall design.[77]

Executed chiefly in alabaster with limestone and black marble, picked out with paint and gilding, it is a monument of exceptional richness, the carved decoration replete with symbolism and heraldry. Sutton's effigy on the altar-tomb, clad in a fur-lined robe, with a ruff, is flanked by captains in armour, referring to his military appointment, who act as supporters of the inscription. Above are reminders of transience: a Vanitas group with skull and hour-glass, Time and his scythe, and the image of man as bubble (the 'Homo Bulla' of Erasmus). The piers supporting the canopy are decorated with trophies of war, and above the canopy is a bas-relief panel showing Sutton's pensioners and the officers of the charity gathered for a sermon in the Chapel. At the sides are female figures of Faith and Hope and two boys, one with a spade, the other with a mop over a skull. These last represent Labour and, less obviously, Rest. Their places were swapped for those of Faith and Hope during the restoration of the monument in the 1950s. The stage above contains Sutton's arms and crest, with figures of Peace and Plenty. The ensemble is crowned by Charity and children, with cherubs on skulls to either side.

71. John Law

72. Oliver Walford

73. Francis Beaumont

74. Lord Ellenborough

75. Andrew Tooke

76. Matthew Raine

Other Monuments

Around the monument is the wrought-iron railing made by William Shawe in 1615–16.[78] The front section was originally close up to the base of the monument, with a rebate in the stonework for the centre post. It was almost certainly moved to its present position as part of the Laudian changes to the Chapel in the mid-1630s. A new length of railing (at some point made into a gate) was inserted at the side to make up the gap, and the floor within the railings was paved in black and white.

The monument was repaired, painted and gilded in 1715–16, and was in need of a major overhaul in 1807, when it was recommended that 'all the mutilated parts of the carved Figures, Mouldings and other carved work' be reinstated, the inscriptions recut and the gilding and colouring renewed. The ironwork was painted blue in 1811.[79] A drawing of the early 1840s shows the tomb brightly coloured and gilt, no doubt accurately, for a contemporary noted that it 'strikes attention by the colour and the gilded spikes of the railings'.[80] The colours are now much more muted, and the captains' armour has been changed from the original white to black; the railing too, is black. The tomb was restored again in 1951, by Cecil Thomas. Some of the missing or broken pieces were left unrestored, and the arrangement of the figures on the main cornice was misguidedly altered.[81]

Other monuments

John Law (d. 1614). Law was one of Sutton's executors. The monument is by Nicholas Stone, and was included in the contract for Sutton's monument undertaken by him with Nicholas Johnson and Edmund Kinsman (Ill. 71).[82] It was mounted at the east end of the south wall, but is now over the archway to the ante-chapel. The angels are characteristically Stone's: long-necked, with diminutive wings and no arms.

Francis Beaumont (d. 1624). Beaumont was Master of Charterhouse and, like his predecessor, Peter Hooker, was buried in Sutton's vault.[83] His monument (Ill. 73) was commissioned by his niece, Lady Cramond, and installed sometime after February 1629. Beaumont is depicted at his prayer desk, between bookcases serving as pilasters. The monument was originally fixed on the east wall of the north aisle but moved in 1842 to make way for the new window there and remounted directly opposite Sutton's tomb on the stub of the old chapterhouse north wall.[84]

Henry Levett (d. 1725). A large and conventional marble memorial, topped by a painted coat of arms. It was originally set between and below the windows on the south wall of the Chapel, but is now on the east wall of the north extension.

Andrew Tooke (d. 1731). Tooke's monument, an unsigned baroque cartouche framed by drapes, is now obscurely placed in a corner of the north extension, but was made for greater prominence (Ill. 75). The two children's heads, one asleep, one awake, are naturalistically carved.

John Christopher Pepusch (d. 1752). The composer was organist at the Charterhouse, where he died, from 1737. In 1765, his pupil Benjamin Cooke, organist at Westminster Abbey, obtained permission for a memorial to be erected by the Academy of Ancient Music, of which Pepusch had been a founder member.[85] It was put up in 1767, on the north wall, and consists of a marble tablet and a decorative pendant carved in high relief with a lyre, laurels and music manuscript. Edward Blore was probably responsible for relegating it to the organ gallery stairs, together with a small tablet to a later organist, the composer **William Horsley** (d. 1858), remembered for his setting of *There is a Green Hill Far Away*.

Matthew Raine (d. 1811). By John Flaxman. Raine was Schoolmaster from 1791 until his death, and his monument, on the south wall, celebrates his Christianity and Classical learning (Ill. 76). It was paid for by the schoolboys, and the inscription was devised by his friend Samuel Parr, who composed the epitaph for Dr Johnson's monument in St Paul's.

Thomas Ramsden (d. 1813). Ramsden was the son of the former Master, William Ramsden, and though not an officer of the Charterhouse was 'a Carthusian by birth, education and attachment'. A surgeon at Christ's Hospital, the Foundling Hospital and Barts, he died at 45, only a few years after his father, which may explain why he was allowed a burial place near the Chapel entrance and a large memorial—a Classical composition with a draped urn in the pediment—on a prominent place on the south wall, next to that of John Law. The memorial is now on the east wall of the north extension, with those of former physicians to the Charterhouse.

Edward Law, Baron Ellenborough (d. 1818). An old Carthusian and governor of the Charterhouse, Ellenborough served as Lord Chief Justice of England. He was interred in the Founder's vault. His monument (Ill. 74), executed by Sir Francis Chantrey in 1818, is now mounted on the south wall, where the monuments of John Law and Thomas Ramsden originally were.

Oliver Walford (d. 1855). In the north aisle, under the organ gallery, with an extravagant architectural surround of coloured marble (Ill. 72). The portrait of Walford, who was Usher for many years, was sculpted by William Behnes.

Chapter Cloister and adjoining rooms

The short range connecting Master's Court with the Chapel and tower was largely destroyed in the 1941 fire, though Chapel Cloister on its south side escaped with reparable damage. Before the fire, the rooms here consisted of Brooke Hall, and the Reader's apartment on two floors above. Brooke Hall was named after Robert Brooke, a royalist who was sacked as Schoolmaster in 1644 but returned to the Charterhouse at the Restoration and was allowed to live here gratis. The room was enlarged and refitted for the use of the Master and other officers in 1718. A decorative overmantel with Sutton's arms, carved by James Dryhurst, was installed in 1726 (Ill. 77).[86]

After the war, it was suggested that the Brooke Hall site should not be used for Brothers' accommodation, as Sir Charles Peers had recommended, but left as open space, leaving just the cloister standing. In the event it was rebuilt as a muniment room, becoming a billiard room after the transfer of most of the archives to the Greater London Record Office in 1983. It has since been fitted up for meetings as the Wesley Room, named after the Old Carthusian John Wesley. One floor only of the Reader's apartment was rebuilt, as Brothers' accommodation, its exterior design being inspired by Kip's view of the long-demolished original by Francis Carter.

77. Chimneypiece in Brooke Hall. Overmantel by James Dryhurst, wood-carver, 1726. *Destroyed 1941*

Lord North's bowling alley and the 'gallery next the garden'

The post-war investigations demonstrated that the south cloister walk ran some distance south of where it was thought to have run, and that the nave or south aisle of the Chapel was the priory chapterhouse. The north aisle, being built over the cloister walk, was therefore shown to be post-monastic. Since the north aisle is clearly the 'enlargement of the Chappell' on Carter's plan, it has subsequently been assumed that its structure is Carter's.[87] What, however, of the walling immediately east of Sutton's Hospital, identified in 1915 by the Royal Commission as the remains of the outer or cell-side cloister wall? These consisted of three pieces. First was a length of ragstone rubble wall forming part of the north wall of the porter's lodge at Merchant Taylors' School. Second was a length forming the retaining wall of the north basement area of the headmaster's house there, and third was a shorter length, further east still at the corner of the school site.[88] It was the fact that these lengths of wall were on the same line as the north wall of the north aisle, and evidently part of the same original structure, that had allowed them to be misidentified as part of the outer cloister wall. But even if Carter had built the north aisle he could not have been responsible for them.

In fact, the identification of this long stone wall as the outer cloister wall had been made well before 1915. George Wardle recognized it as such in 1886 (at least as regards the part within Sutton's Hospital), and R. H. Carpenter's plan for Lawrence Hendriks shows it as such too.[89] But there can now be little doubt that the entire length of wall from the Great Staircase compartment to the south-east corner of the Merchant Taylors' School site was originally built by North. Much of it has been demolished or rebuilt, but pre-war photographs and the Royal Commission investigators' description confirm that it was of stone rubble-work, although latterly much reconstructed or refaced in brick, or, in the case of the easternmost portion, cement-rendered. Preacher's Stairs, a spiral staircase in a polygonal turret (rebuilt after the Second World War), was presumably part of the same building phase, and must in any case pre-date Carter's work: it is not mentioned in the accounts of the building works in 1613–14 and, besides, would then have been old-fashioned.

Corroboration of North's activity here is supplied by Maurice Chauncy. This range was the only part of the house to impinge on the cloister garth, where the monks' own cemetery was, and it can therefore only have been here that, as Chauncy recorded, North's workmen turned up the body of Prior John Batmanson as they dug foundations. This must have been in 1547 (sixteen years after Batmanson's burial, Chauncy states).[90] The exact spot was

78. Chapel Yard before the Second World War, showing the north side of Brooke Hall and the Reader's apartment above. At the end, at ground-floor level, are the Library window and the doorway to the Norfolk Cloister. The wall on the extreme right, separating Chapel Yard from first Merchant Taylors' School and then the Medical College of St Bartholomew's Hospital, was demolished in the 1950s

probably at the site of Preacher's Stairs, or to the west, where the structure reached furthest into the garth. Prior Luscote and others are known to have been buried in this corner too, and some of their graves were discovered during the post-war excavations.[91] A skeleton found lying east–west under the floor of the Great Staircase compartment in the nineteenth century was no doubt that of a monk.[92] North's south-walk range included the bowling alley and gallery complained of by the Bassano brothers (page 39), and Chauncy's date fits with their claim that North built his gallery within two years of Henry VIII's death (January 1547).

79. View by Rudolph Ackermann across Upper Green in 1816, showing the Chapel (before the addition of the north or scholars' bay), Brooke Hall range and the turret of Preacher's Stairs. To the left of the Chapel is the house in Rutland Court bought by the hospital in 1794 and later replaced by Day Boys' Lodge; the porch-like structure gave access to a passage through the house into the court itself

The north aisle of the Chapel was evidently adapted by Carter from part of North's building, and the fact that the range continued east of the Chapel, crossing the Howard House boundary on to the site of what was to become Rutland House, explains why there was originally no window in the east end of the north aisle. The stone-built east wall of the aisle (thought by the Royal Commission investigators to be fourteenth-century work belonging to the priory church) may have been the east wall of the bowling alley, although originally the alley may have gone further east, immediately in front of the Bassanos' cells. A brick-arched doorway in this wall, assumed by the investigators to be of seventeenth-century date, is therefore presumably part of North's work too, and must have been blocked up when he hived off the south-eastern part of the Charterhouse, sometime before the sale to the Duke of Norfolk was agreed in 1564.

North's gallery over the bowling alley can be identified as the 'gallery next the garden' mentioned by Norfolk in 1572 (page 156), and the 'long gallery to the garden' named in the December 1612 repairs list (pages 62–3).[93] Repairs were then needed to the gutters and tiling on its north and south sides, confirming that the structure was aligned east–west. Norfolk gives no details of it, but as he was recalling an incident there in 1569 he was clearly not referring to his own gallery, the Terrace or Norfolk Cloister, then unbuilt. Some confirmation is given in the building accounts of the Howard House conversion in 1613–14, where one of the carpenters' jobs was to take down the wainscot in the 'gallery next the chapel'.[94] Another job was the blocking up of an old doorway in the 'passage' between the Great Hall and the Chapel, which can only be explained by the existence of a building on the site of Chapel Cloister or Brooke Hall (and now of the Wesley Room). The 'passage' may have been the old bowling alley itself, which had presumably been rendered redundant by the Earl of Suffolk's new bowling alley north of Wash-house Court (page 58), or more probably it was the narrow prototype of Chapel Cloister shown on Carter's plan, an arcade or colonnade with a vestibule at its east end opening on to the present ante-chapel at the base of Chapel Tower. The footings of this structure may have been the 'Foundations of an aisled nave of uncertain date', found west of Chapel Tower (presumably under the

80. The Chapel and Brooke Hall range from the north, showing Redmond Pilkington's scholars' bay and Edward Blore's remodelling of Chapel Tower. The stone wall east of the Chapel, part of Lord North's south cloister walk range and subsequently part of Rutland House, served as the north wall of Day Boys' Lodge. At the left are houses on the east side of Charterhouse Square. From Radclyffe's *Memorials of Charterhouse* (1844)

floor of Chapel Cloister) and noted by Alfred Clapham. The vestibule and line of piers are shown on the plan of the priory in Hope's *History of the London Charterhouse*, not quite as Carter's plan shows them; the text does not mention them.[q] Carpenter's plan, an adaptation of Carter's, shows them as features now removed, with no suggestion as to their date.[96]

Little of the original stonework of North's long range is now left on the Sutton's Hospital side. As noted above, most has been rebuilt in brick. The north-aisle wall was largely demolished for the building of the scholars' bay in the 1820s, but a small portion remains on view above the 1920s mortuary, patched with later brickwork. The wall east of the Chapel is plainly seen in C. W. Radclyffe's early 1840s view of the Charterhouse from Upper Green (Ill. 80). The taller part of it was by then the north wall of Day Boys' Lodge, a ground-floor building, later adapted by the architect Edward I'Anson as the Merchant Taylors' School lodge, and from the 1930s the lodge house of the Medical College of St Bartholomew's Hospital (page 76); a portion of the stonework is still there, much restored. The lower part of the wall shown by Radclyffe, with a doorway, belonged to an adjoining room which closed off Rutland Place from Sutton's Hospital. Ackermann's earlier view shows the wall incorporated into what had been part of Rutland House (Ill. 79). As for the basement-area retaining wall at the headmaster's house, this may point to a change in level in North's range at this end, reflecting the lower level of the monastic east cloister, relative to the west (page 24).

The 1941 damage revealed the south wall of Brooke Hall to be, like the north wall, built of stone. As it lay on the outer (south) edge of the cloister walk it may incorporate some monastic work from the sacrist's cell and St Agnes's chapel on the north side of the priory church.[97]

Carter's plan (Ill. 30), it may be concluded, shows that his original idea was for the adaptation of Lord North's bowling alley and the 'gallery next the garden' for living rooms and the north aisle of the Chapel. This was altered in the execution, by the creation of Chapel Cloister and

[q] The plan was prepared from Hope's notes and drawings, after his death, with the help of W. H. Knowles.[95]

by the enlargement of Chapel Tower, obviating the north entrance Carter shows. For the rest, he seems to have retained the existing work; significantly, although the building accounts mention the demolition of the north wall of the (unenlarged) Chapel they do not specify the building of a new one, and, while they refer to brickwork in 'new' buildings between the Chapel and Great Hall, most of this brick was evidently for hearths and chimneys.

North's bowling alley and gallery are both mentioned in the 1565 inventory, where the gallery is described as hung with red and green cloth and containing only a table, form and court cupboard. The room sequence is corroborative here, part of it comprising the Hall, the half-pace or landing at the stairhead, the Great Chamber, an entry, and then the long gallery over the bowling alley. This is consistent with the gallery having been approached at the west end via a lobby or passageway close to the precursor of the early Jacobean Great Staircase. A later section of the inventory goes from 'Lady Worcester's chamber' and her maid's chamber to the chapel, then immediately to an entry going 'towards' the bowling alley, followed by 'my Lord's closet' and other chambers. This short sequence (listed between the main rooms in the house – including the Hall and Great Chamber – and the kitchen area away in Wash-house Court) is consistent with the bowling alley having been on the south cloister walk, and seems to offer confirmation that the chapterhouse had become Lord North's chapel, as has long been thought probable.

In 1588, no bowling alley is mentioned, perhaps because it contained nothing to list (as was the case in 1565, when it was only referred to incidentally) or had been put to other use. Nor is the chapel mentioned in 1588, possibly because it had been turned over to another use or because there was some reason to exclude it from the inventory. The gallery next the garden is not listed as such. It may have been omitted because it, too, was empty. But more probably it was the 'highe gallerie used for the wardrope'. As the wardrobe lists begin the 1588 inventory, nothing can be deduced regarding the high gallery's location from the sequence of rooms listed. The high gallery, as it

81. View towards the south-east in 2009, showing the north side of the chapel, rebuilt Brooke Hall range and Preacher's Stairs turret

happens, is followed by the 'bedchamber at the end of the hall', identifiable as the later Withdrawing Room shown on Carter's plan. That adjoined the music gallery overlooking the Great Hall. But the music gallery would have been a strange place to store bedding, and too small anyway. The contents listed include ten featherbeds and pallet beds, each with a bolster, five mattresses, six livery beds, seven mats, and two complete bedsteads with their canopies, besides other items of furniture and equipment, including a cord running along the gallery, presumably for hanging items of bedding and reached by means of the eleven-rung ladder also listed. On the other hand, the gallery over the bowling alley would have been eminently suitable for storing, airing and repairing such material. As a place of recreation, or as a reception room, the gallery had probably been superseded by the Norfolk Cloister; there was, in any case, another long gallery on the first floor of what is now Master's Court. Use of the high gallery as a wardrobe may be related to the insertion of a double-width doorway or archway in the upper wall of the Great Staircase compartment, which may once have been a way in to the gallery from the Great Staircase or its precursor.[r]

Chapel Cloister

Chapel Cloister itself was one of Carter's most stylistically interesting additions to the Charterhouse, with its Italianate open stonework arcade recalling the monastic cloister of old. Such an open arcade or cloister was a fashionable idea of the time, appearing at various great houses including Hatfield House and Audley End, and Carter himself had recently worked at Trinity College, Cambridge, where the new, cloistered Nevile's Court was completed in 1614. There, as at the Charterhouse, the top storey over the cloisters was originally gabled. Carter's plan shows a different arrangement to that actually adopted, with a narrow covered way with what appear to be glazed windows to Chapel Court, leading to a porch or vestibule before the ante-chapel at the base of the tower. As suggested above, this was probably an existing feature of Howard House. The main building abutting is shown divided into small rooms on the ground floor, evidently for pensioners, and larger rooms above, presumably for a member of staff. Instead of the narrow passageway, and perhaps inspired by it, Carter built a broad cloister walk

82. Doorway to the Chapel from Chapel Cloister. Edmund Kinsman, mason, 1613. Above is the monument to Master Nicholas Mann (d. 1753). On the right inside the doorway is the remnant of the door burned in 1941

with an open arcade, extending the first floor of the residential building over it, with three gabled dormers, finished in plaster, to face Chapel Court. This upper floor was destroyed in the mid-1770s, when a second floor was added to what was then the Receiver's apartment (Ill. 42).[99] Later this apartment became the Reader's house, with boarding accommodation for a few boys (known as Dickenites after the Rev. Charles Dicken, Reader from 1838 to 1861).[100]

Inside, the chief feature of Chapel Cloister is the carved stone doorway leading to the ante-chapel, the work of Edmund Kinsman. The door itself, perhaps pre-dating Kinsman's surround,[101] was partly burned in 1941 and is now mounted in the small lobby between Chapel Cloister

[r] This opening is shown in an undated eighteenth- or nineteenth-century sketch of the wall when it was stripped of plaster, showing traces of several partly overlapping openings in the east stair compartment wall. The opening must have predated the building of the east–west wall at the north end of the old Entrance Hall between the Great Staircase and Chapel, which has been external since the restoration by Seely and Paget and clearly was designed to be external, with windows on two levels. This wall butts across the filled-in arch. The exact configuration of this area is therefore unclear. The ground-floor window, which could be sixteenth or seventeenth century, was reopened in the late 1830s to give borrowed light to the Entrance Hall. This and the similar first-floor window are seen in the view of the burned-out building in Ill. 3.[98]

W
E

and the ante-chapel. Inset into the top of the door surround is a plain white marble tablet to Nicholas Mann, Master from 1737 to 1753, framed by consoles and a cherub, these florid decorative pieces being separately made in limestone; the panel with the cherub is a post-war replacement.

The cloister remained open until the arches were glazed in 1847, and in 1867 the Surveyor, George Perry, oversaw the addition of matching blind arcading on the wall opposite, where the doorway to the Wesley Room has a Carter-period door surround.[102] The nineteenth century saw the cloister fill up with mural monuments, and there are several earlier memorial slabs in the floor. Monuments to Thackeray and his friend John Leech, installed in 1866, were destroyed in 1941.[103] Most of the surviving works are very minor, the chief exception being that commemorating Major-General Sir Henry Havelock and other Old Carthusians who died in the Crimean War and Indian Mutiny, erected in 1864 by the Charterhouse Military Memorial Fund. Made using a variety of coloured marbles, it resembles a Classical columbarium for cinerary urns, its grid of individual compartments enclosed in an architectural frame (see Ill. 84).[104] A large tablet on the north wall, of white marble with a variegated marble surround, commemorates Dr Augustus Page Saunders, Schoolmaster in 1832–53, after whom Saunderites house was named.

84. Detail of the Military Memorial, Chapel Cloister

83. Chapel Court from the south, 2010

85. (*top*) Wash-house Court in 2000, looking south
86. (*bottom*) Wash-house Court in 2003, looking north-west

CHAPTER V

Wash-house Court

Though it has been variously altered and much patched, the west front of Wash-house Court is strongly evocative of the priory on the eve of its suppression, enough of the original decoration being left intact to suggest the piety, pride and prosperity which then characterized the house. The bold diapering, picked out in black headers, is fashionable enough for a secular magnate's house and, while the symbols of the cross emphasize the building's religious purpose, the initials IH are those of the recently appointed prior, John Houghton. Built in the early 1530s, it would not yet have lost its newness when the priory closed.

The brick-built west range and its continuation along the north side of the courtyard comprised the last phase of building in Wash-house Court before the priory came to an end. Dendrochronology gives the felling date 1530 for timbers in the roof and upper part of the structure of the west range; this and Houghton's initials are convincing evidence for the building date.[1] There is similar diapering on the courtyard elevation of this range, too, and some survives on the outer elevation of the north range, though this wall was much restored and reconstructed in the nineteenth century. The boundary wall opposite the west front is built in the same diapered brickwork, suggesting that it, too, belongs to this early sixteenth-century phase. Similar work survives further north along the boundary wall and on the west side of Charterhouse Mews.

As regards the early building history of the other Wash-house Court ranges, evidence is slight, and the present elevations are the product of numerous phases of alteration, repair and restoration. The evolution of the buildings before Sutton's Hospital cannot be established in any detail; nor can much be said about their internal layout and functions. It is possible that the east range, entirely rebuilt a few years after the priory's closure, was the earliest. A substantial part of it is thought to have been taken up by the guest-house, or part of the guest-house (see page 29), which seems to have pre-dated the building of the Little Cloister in 1406. The stone-built eastern portion of the north range may have been part of the monks' kitchen, communicating with the back of the frater on the west side of the Great Cloister.[2]

Before the Second World War, Wash-house Court had several original fireplaces, chamfered ceiling beams and other old features. Very little historic fabric now survives inside other than at the north-west corner, where it includes a small wooden staircase on the north side of the slype (page 47 and Ill. 51) and a fireplace on the first floor. Both seem to be post-monastic additions. In the south range, a section of rubble-stone in the east face of the slype made after the Second World War may be the remnant of the west end of a building tentatively identified by archaeologists as the guests' kitchen.[3]

Room use, alterations and the 'dole-hatch'

The priory water-supply plan shows nothing of the structure of Wash-house Court, much of which would not have existed when it was drawn, but its presence is implied in annotations and what may be additions to the drawing. Three features in particular refer to Wash-house Court or buildings on its site. As this part of the plan is right at the edge of the roll, these features may have been fitted in with little attempt at topographical accuracy. But the position of the main gate, also at the edge, suggests that they are more or less in the right place. First is the buttery tap, shown at the south end of the Little Cloister's west side. The buttery, managed by two lay brothers,[4] probably stood south of the guest-house. North and west of the buttery supply pipe the plan shows another pipe going to a tank or vat probably representing the brew-house.[5] Finally, some way south of the brew-house, is a cistern 'by the kychen doore'. This may have been the door to the guest-house kitchen referred to above.

What state Wash-house Court was in when Sir Edward North acquired the Charterhouse can only be guessed. But it had probably suffered some damage. In the first place, all the contents, including such fittings as wainscot and glass, would probably have been stripped out by the king's agents, which may be the explanation for the absence of various rooms (including the kitchen, and the hall and chambers of the guest-house) from the king's commissioners' inventory of 1539 (see page 33). This was probably followed by a period of neglect before the site was taken over by the Tents officers. Their occupation is likely to have been as casually destructive as any short-term occupation (pages 36–8) of requisitioned premises by industry or the military. Even so, it is fair to assume that the kitchens, bakehouses, stores and laundry shown in Wash-house Court on Francis Carter's 1613 plan (he labels it the Kitchen Court) show some continuity of use from the priory. The 1539 inventory names a sequence of places, some if not all of which must have been in Wash-house Court: laundry, brew-house, malt house, new brew-house, bakehouse, store house, boulting house, fish kitchen, larder and buttery. When the laundry was established in the south range (on the site of the supposed guests' kitchen) cannot be determined. The only definite evidence of the whereabouts of a laundry at the priory is on the water-supply plan, where one is shown off the south walk of the Great Cloister, some way east of the chapterhouse. This was probably replaced by one or more monk's cells late in the priory's history (pages 35–6). It is likely that North's laundry, whether of monastic origin or not, was in Wash-house Court. Some of the places in the 1565 inventory, notably a hen-house and a fish-house 'in' the laundry and a chamber 'over' the laundry, suggest that the whole court may have been referred to as the laundry, while the actual wash-house was only part of the ground floor. A reference to Lavendry Court in the Ridolfi plot evidence extracted from the Duke of Norfolk's man Barker (see page 47) must refer to Wash-house Court, and the room sequence of the 1588 inventory is compatible with the Howard House laundry (listed both in its own right and indirectly through a chamber 'over the landrie') having been the wash-house labelled on Carter's plan.

While the basic layout of service rooms shown by Carter may have been of long standing, the sequence of individual pensioners' rooms on the ground and first floors of the west range was part of his conversion. Twelve chimneys built in the 'kitchen court' in 1613–14 may have corresponded with the twelve chambers fitted up where 'cole-houses' were said to have been—going by Carter's plan, these were in the west and south-west of the court, where three large stacks served six corner fireplaces on the ground and first floors.[6] Apart from that, the works in Wash-house Court recorded at the time of the conversion are minor—repaving and new windows. A prominent mullioned window on the north side of the Great Kitchen recorded in old views may have been the remnant of the twelve-light 'great window' made for the kitchen at that time (Ill. 90). It looked out on to a small paved yard, probably screened by a wall from the privy garden.

Beyond the wash-house, kitchen and related rooms it is impossible to do more than speculate about the monastic layout of Wash-house Court. But there is no reason to discredit the long-held assumption that the lay brothers' living quarters were here. If so, they would have occupied the west range—which must therefore have been purpose built—opposite the guest-house and service rooms. That does not explain the broad bricked-up arch on the west front. An early, romantic suggestion was that it led to the burial chamber of John Houghton.[7] It was thought by Gerald Davies (on, he said, the suggestion of the Preacher, H. V. Le Bas), that it might have been a hatch for doling out provisions to the poor, and this possibility was noted by the Royal Commission on Historical Monuments.[8] In fact, this idea had been proposed by George Wardle in 1886, and is suggested on R. H. Carpenter's plan of 1888.[9] It was stated in the 1530s that 'plentye of brede, and ale, & fyshe' was given to strangers in the buttery and 'at the buttery dore' (as well as bread and ale to vagabonds at the gate).[10] But the buttery was probably not on this side of Wash-house Court, besides which neither the size, nor the level nor the construction of the opening particularly supports the dole-hatch theory. In their original record, the Royal Commission investigators noted that the arch 'apparently never continued down to the ground', but it is not clear why they thought that.[11] The plinth which runs all along the west range shows a change in coursing at the blocked opening, indicating that it was formerly interrupted by the archway and that the opening did extend to the ground. Even allowing for the change in ground level (possibly 2ft 6ins lower in the early sixteenth century than in the early twentieth),[12] it is difficult to see how the 'window' would have been suitable for serving from. The archway may, of course, have replaced a smaller opening in the same position.

It is likely that the opening was used in connection with the coal-stores mentioned in 1614 and perhaps there during the latter years of Howard House.[13] The 1590 survey describes a large (40ft by 17ft) burned-out building in the stable yard, formerly used as a coal-store, a replacement for which would have been needed when the house was fully occupied again a few years later.[14] Whatever its original purpose, the archway is a post-monastic insertion. The plain, unmoulded bricks of the arch itself, the abrupt, squared edges of the sides and absence of a rebate for a frame suggest as much.

Above the coal-stores may have been 'the chamber called knaves hall' in 1588, where low-ranking male servants presumably lodged, and where the Carthusian lay brethren may formerly have slept. This perhaps extended along most of the west range, with Lord Thomas

87. Wash-house Court. Pre-1941 view looking north-east, showing scullery addition of 1864. The first-floor windows blocked with stone belong to what was once the Duke of Norfolk's bedchamber

Howard's (the future Earl of Suffolk's) wardrobe in the roof space above. That there was no chimney in Knaves' Hall is suggested by the presence of a charcoal brazier, as well as the need to build so many chimneys in 1613–14 for the new pensioners' rooms in that area. There is a brick fireplace of sixteenth-century or seventeenth-century date in the west wall of what would have been this large room. Its exact date is uncertain, however, though it seems to be post-monastic because the stack serving it interrupts the decorations in the brickwork.

In the course of the history of Sutton's Hospital, the pensioners were gradually moved out of Wash-house Court and much of it was taken over for staff accommodation and offices. In particular, in 1768 the Registrar's apartment or house in the south-west corner of Master's Court was extended into the south range of Wash-house Court. Two cellars were dug to provide storage for the Registrar, and pensioners' rooms on the ground floor of the west range were made into offices for him and his clerk. Further alterations were made to the house in 1789, and it may have been then that a second floor was added.[15] (Later enlargement of the house is described below in connection with the conduit house.) It was probably from about this time that Wash-house Court took on the name Poplar Court, from a poplar or poplars planted in the courtyard. This had gone out of use by the mid-nineteenth century. The name Abbot's Court also enjoyed some currency in the early to middle nineteenth century when Wash-house Court became firmly established as the proper name.[16]

John Houghton's initials

The question of the letters IH on the west side of Wash-house Court has been much commented on since the nineteenth century.[17] Do they stand for John Houghton, or for the name Jesus in Greek (commonly abbreviated as IHS or IHC after capital iota, eta, sigma)? The issue only arises because of reluctance to accept that Houghton could have

88. Wash-house Court, west side, in 1996. In the background, flats on the Barbican Estate

been party to a piece of apparent self-advertisement. This reluctance may stem from a misunderstanding of the thinking behind such an inscription, in which questions of record, responsibility and prioral authority may have outweighed any suggestion of personal aggrandizement. The debate was reignited by Gerald Davies and E. Margaret Thompson, who were strongly opposed to the idea that they were Houghton's initials, and their view has been more than once uncritically repeated.[18] Previous scholarly writers, notably Lawrence Hendriks and Basil Champneys, did take them as such and this became the accepted view.[19] Much earlier, in the 1830s, William Hale referred to the letters as IHS. But he was guessing the sometime existence of the S (as William Roper confirms), and had no inkling that the building dated from Houghton's time.[20] He merely saw IH(S) as pointing to its monastic origin. Nearly thirty years later, however, he 'would willingly assume' the letters to be Houghton's initials.[21] Among later writers, David Knowles was inclined to accept the letters at face value given the widespread practice of signing such buildings at that time; the archaeologists Bruno Barber and Christopher Thomas also assume that they stand for Houghton. Recently, the present Master of Sutton's Hospital has argued against this view.[22] It is difficult to reach a final conclusion because the brickwork to the right of the H may have been replaced: it carries no trace of any initial or of the diapering which otherwise runs along the wall (see Ill. 89). A century ago, the Royal Commission investigators thought that the H had been reset, and the whole wall has been subject to much repair and restoration. Any thought that I and H alone were meant to stand for Jesus suggests unlikely false naivety on Houghton's part. As noted above, the pattern of the surviving decoration implies an originally symmetrical design, with the initials balanced by something to the right where the later chimney stack was built, perhaps the date of building. A further clue may be the cross below the initials, the head now missing. Its position in the ensemble seems to fit better with IH than IHS.

89. Wash-house Court, west front. Drawing by John Wykeham Archer, *c.*1840

Some distance from these decorations is a V-shaped pattern which has been identified as the image of the Sacred Heart.[23] This is not certain. Although there is evidence of medieval Carthusian devotion to the Sacred Heart, there is no record of an altar or chapel dedicated to it at the London Charterhouse. Unlike the initials and crosses, which interrupt the bonding with specially cut bricks and incorporate curves, the shape is wholly angular and has more in common with the abstract diaper patterning.

The north elevation

Stylistically similar to the west front, the north front is a less authentic survival. Some patching up was necessary when the disused structure built on to the north wall was pulled down in the late 1830s (Ill. 90). Part was then said to have been used as a larder, and a note on an earlier plan shows it as the 'old Bakery'. Carter's plan shows a group of rooms here, and the bakehouse ovens; the long, ground-floor space he shows on the north side of the ovens was originally an open yard, and was again by 1820, north of which was the Manciple's house, replaced by a new apartment in the east range of Preacher's Court.[24]

In 1872, the east end of the north range of Wash-house Court was demolished for the rebuilding of the Great Kitchen. The new kitchen was situated immediately west of the screens passage at the end of the Great Hall (its present position), with a new scullery, larder and cook's apartment beyond, behind the gabled front in 'Tudor' style shown in Ill. 136—the work of the Charterhouse Surveyor, George Perry.[25]

By the 1890s there was perhaps a feeling that the venerable buildings of the Charterhouse deserved better than this utilitarian sort of replacement. In March 1893 it was agreed that R. H. Carpenter, an Old Carthusian who

90. Preacher's Court from the west in the early 1840s, showing the unrestored north range of Wash-house Court, with the Great Kitchen window at the junction of the new and old buildings

had acted as an honorary architect to the hospital for some years, would produce a joint report with Perry on the exterior condition of both Wash-house and Master's Courts. Carpenter died suddenly a few weeks later and the report considered in May was probably more the work of his friend and partner Benjamin Ingelow, who went on to restore the entrance front to Master's Court. Trial work on Wash-house Court, carried out by Dove Brothers, met with the governors' approval in November 1893 and the north front was then tackled. Further repairs to Wash-house Court were made by Doves before the First World War, including work on the south and east ranges in 1911.[26]

The post-war works

Reinstatement of Wash-house Court was the first major phase of the post-war work at the Charterhouse, the main contractor, Richard Costain Ltd, starting work there in April 1949. Use was made of timber, doors and mantelpieces salvaged from the demolished buildings in Preacher's Court (Ill. 51). The whole of this phase of work, including the new porch at the Brothers' entrance adjoining the north range, was completed in March 1951.[27]

The 1941 fire had swept through the east and south ranges, and, although much of the north and west escaped relatively lightly, the roof over the middle of the west range was destroyed. Wooden floors in the north and west, and the wall timbers in the west slype and the adjoining staircase were retained; and at the north-west corner (in Room 11) enough of the seventeenth-century cornice survived for a facsimile to be made. Perry's 1872 building on the site of the Great Kitchen was demolished and rebuilt to match the rest of the north range.

More reconstruction was carried out in the south range, where the south front and canted corner had to be rebuilt. The large chimney stack on the south wall was demolished and the fenestration altered. Utilizing an old blocked doorway in the inner wall, a slype was made to link Wash-house Court with the little triangular courtyard on the site of the Registrar's house. The walls of the slype into Master's Court, which had contained timber framing, were rebuilt in brick. Among other changes, the ground-floor addition filling the north-east corner of the courtyard (built in 1864 as a 'vegetable room' or scullery: Ills 40, 87) had been removed in 1946. The doorway to it from the east range was replaced by a window.[28] As part of a general tidying up of the north courtyard elevation, matching windows were put in at either end, that at the west taking the place of a doorway. The stone plinth was extended, too. Two first-floor windows were reopened on the east side, and the stone window openings around the courtyard were restored, mostly with artificial stone.

On the west front, the southern of the two large chimneys was rebuilt (the other has since been rebuilt too) and the smaller stack between them was demolished above eaves level; the other chimney, towards the south end, also appears to have been rebuilt at this time. Additions to the fenestration at first-floor level further eroded the old character of the exterior. Two new ground-floor windows were inserted on the north front.

Inside, the restored ranges were divided on new lines between staff quarters and service rooms on the ground floor and pensioners' rooms above. A seventeenth-century-style oak staircase, copied from one in the architects' own offices at 41 Cloth Fair, was made for the rebuilt north-east corner (Ill. 49). One of two wooden chimneypieces brought from the Old Hall at Cley in Norfolk (where Seely and Paget had been working) was also installed here. In contrast, for the new stone service stairs in the south range they provided metal balusters in the Contemporary style, with a simple design that they also used at Lambeth Palace. Adding to the variety of approach, in the top floor of the taller east range, the lower parts of the new roof trusses were left exposed (as was also done in Master's Court), the timber being finished with an adze to suggest antiquity.[29]

Perhaps the least praiseworthy part of the work was the utilization of so much of the west range ground floor for services. A large room behind the putative dole-hatch was made into a boiler-house for heating and hot water, and between this and the new slype in the south range were placed a transformer room and switch room. The originally coke-fired heating system was converted to oil in 1952, when storage tanks were installed in the cellars of the recently demolished buildings on the west side of Preacher's Court.[30]

91. The conduit house in 2010, looking south

The conduit house

Near the south end of Wash-house Court, adjoining the inner gateway in Entrance Court, is the conduit house built to Francis Carter's design in 1614, possibly on the site of the 'cistern by the kitchen door' shown on the water-supply plan (see Ill. 13). Brick-built with stone dressings, it consists of a cross-vaulted chamber with an upper floor served by external steps; the original roof was topped by a weather-vane. The conduit house remained in use after 1767, when Sutton's Hospital reluctantly abandoned its failed private water supply in favour of New River Company water, the cost and difficulty of reinstating the old system leaving little choice.[31] But by the late nineteenth century the building was disused, and in 1887–8 was absorbed into an extension to the Registrar's house at the south-east corner of Master's Court, losing both its distinctive roof and its separate identity. The new building (Ill. 41), nominally Tudor in style and faced in red brick, was designed by George Perry. After the Second World War the conduit house re-emerged when the burned-out Registrar's house was demolished, to be restored about 1950 by Seely and Paget as a strong-room with a store-room above. On grounds of cost, the roof, its design based on the old one as depicted by Kip, was clad in copper rather than lead.[32]

92. Master's Court and the Great Hall in 1996

CHAPTER VI

Master's Court

Master's Court was largely built by Sir Edward North in the mid to late 1540s to contain the principal private and state apartments of his house. Shown as the Middle Court on Francis Carter's plan of 1613, Master's Court was so named because until the Second World War the Master of Sutton's Hospital had his residence here. The Master's Lodge occupied much of the east range and, later, half the south range, together with a wing to the east, formerly 15 Charterhouse Square.

Most of the pensioners' accommodation and the school being adapted from outbuildings, these rooms were little affected by the conversion of Howard House in 1613–14. Subdivision and alteration took place over the following three centuries, but the north range, with the Great Hall and Great Chamber, survived relatively unchanged between then and 1941. More or less the entire interior of the south, west and east ranges was destroyed in 1941, and if any historic elements survived they were not considered worth restoring after the war. The one exception is an early seventeenth-century plaster relief of Faith, Hope and Charity from an overmantel in the Master's Lodge. These three ranges today, but for their much-restored outer walls, are in effect new buildings. This is not the case with the north range, but even there the fire did severe damage and the surviving fabric was altered pragmatically in the course of post-war restoration. Various further interior alterations were made in 1989–91, including the conversion of offices, staff accommodation and infirmary rooms into flats and bed-sitting rooms for the Brothers.

North's quadrangle was an enlarged rebuilding of the monastic Little Cloister of 1406, extending about 30ft further east and south (Ill. 15). The north range was built using a significant part of the earlier foundations; the west range to a lesser extent, probably because of the slighter nature of the monastic buildings on that side, thought from archaeological evidence to have been timber-framed.[1] The shallower south range was probably raised on new foundations, though there were previous buildings there too, traces of which were excavated after the Second World War. On the east side, use was again made of the monastic work, the front of this range following the line of the original east wall of the priory church, and the side of the chapel of SS Michael and John the Baptist to the south. A portion of the chapel wall itself remains, a patch of neat ashlar amid the rubble-work with which most of Master's Court is faced.

The courtyard elevations

Restoring the courtyard elevations of Master's Court was one of the most important elements in Seely and Paget's restoration of the Charterhouse. Not that their carefully scraped and pointed surfaces necessarily replicated their Tudor appearance, for they were probably limewashed or plastered from the start, remaining covered until 1755, when they were stripped as the preliminary to refacing in grey brick. At the same time, the roofs were relaid with slate.[2] Perhaps because of particular respect for the antiquity of the building, or the awkwardness cladding would have entailed with regard to the windows, the front of the Great Hall was merely re-rendered. But the other sides, and the staircase tower in the north-west corner, were covered in brick, tied in place by iron hooks fixed to horizontal wooden battens nailed to the old masonry. Segmental and elliptical gauged arches were provided for the windows, nearly all of which, on the east range at least, were replaced with wooden sashes. The work was done by William Conduit, a bricklayer regularly employed at the Charterhouse.[3]

This refronting was carried out while the Master's Lodge was being enlarged and remodelled internally, and was perhaps done as much to achieve a stylistically 'polite' look, commensurate with the Master's status, as to avoid periodic repairs to the render. As pre-war photographs show (see Ill. 39), the Georgian treatment was dignified and not unsuccessful visually. It is not certain from the records whether its design was by Benjamin Timbrell, the Surveyor to the Hospital, who died in 1754, or his son-in-law and successor, Charles Evans, who had been his assistant for some years. Evans is more likely to have been responsible, as he had taken over much of Timbrell's workload and made drawings for new works at this period, but there is no clue as to whose idea the refronting was. In a report on Master's Court in 1749, Timbrell had merely recommended repairs to the roofs and render.[4]

93. Old entrance hall, Master's Court. Early twentieth-century view looking east into Chapel Cloister. The wooden column was fitted in 1869.[16] *Burned out 1941*

Entrance Court front

If the inner Master's Court elevations were intended by Seely and Paget as a genuinely historical recreation, the same cannot have been true of the south front facing Entrance Court. This had been altered in the nineteenth century, by Edward Blore and others, and had already acquired an inauthentic, Tudoresque appearance with mechanical detailing. The post-war alterations were appreciable: removal of the battlemented parapet and addition of a dormer-windowed attic storey tiled in the vernacular manner; recasting of the central gabled bay over the entrance to provide a window at the new attic level, insertion of a first-floor window through the eastern main chimney stack; reconstruction of the octagonal chimneys as square; demolition of a chimney towards the east end of the range; and the introduction of statuettes and a cross to decorate the gables. Against these can be set only the reinstatement of the long-lost gables at either end of the range as an attempt at historical restoration.

In making these changes, the architects were motivated chiefly by the wish to add another floor, but their readiness to alter the building contrasts with the deference generally shown by them towards the monastic relics uncovered at the Charterhouse. Not surprisingly, they were keen to get rid of the nineteenth-century additions, such as the crenellation added by Blore in 1842. It is not certain quite how extensive was Blore's work on the front at this time, but it probably included replacement of the windows and entrance arch, and perhaps the reconstruction of the brick chimneys on the two main stacks. However, he did nothing to alter the west end of the front, which had been rebuilt in brick in the later eighteenth century, probably in 1789, for the new Registrar's house (Ill. 22).[5] This was finally refronted in 1894 by Benjamin Ingelow, to blend in with Blore's work.[6]

The finials on the gables were carved in 1953 by Michael Groser.[7] They are: on the western gable, a greyhound (Sutton's crest), flanked by a gownboy and a pensioner; on the centre gable, representing the Salutation, a cross, St Elizabeth and the Virgin Mary; on the east gable, a lion, James I, with an orb and sceptre, and his consort, Anne of Denmark, holding a dove.

94. Reception room in south range of Master's Lodge, 1816.
This room was partitioned out of the eastern half of the Tudor long gallery

Rooms in Master's Court

Successive inventories of Howard House give indications of the interiors which once existed in the south, east and west ranges. But few of these can be confidently matched with the rooms shown on Carter's plan, and there is scope for conjecture, made the more unresolvable by the partial nature of the inventories, the varying sequences in which rooms were listed, and changing room names and uses. Illustration 25 sets out the more secure identifications. For part of the building at least, the post-Sutton room uses can be matched fairly convincingly with an inventory of the Hospital made in 1617. The first floor of the Master's Court east range was then occupied as the Master's lodgings, the rooms comprising 'first chamber', 'great chamber', bedchamber (presumably the southernmost room), man's room and study. These last would have been the tiny rooms shown by Carter between the bedroom and great chamber. In the study were a table and chair, in the man's room little more than a chair, stool and round table—he slept in a truckle bed in the Master's bedroom.[8] The 'first chamber' was panelled up to the ceiling, with an architrave, and had a wooden fire-surround with a decorative plaster panel in the overmantel, depicting the figures of Faith, Hope and Charity (see below). Accounts for 1615 mention 60 yards of wainscot for the Master's chamber, which may refer to the panelling of this room.[9]

The 'great chamber' seems to be synonymous with the later 'large drawing-room', remodelled in 1754 by the Surveyor, Charles Evans, as part of a general improvement and enlargement of the Master's Lodge.[10] Illustrations 95 and 96 show the fireplaces in the drawing rooms, destroyed in 1941. The two chimneypieces may have been swapped round at some point, as were the portraits (of Thomas Sutton and the antiquary Daniel Wray) in the overmantels.[11] In 1754, the carver James Dryhurst was paid £24 for carving 'to the chimneypiece' in the Master's great room, work which actually seems to relate to the small drawing room piece, with Sutton's greyhound crest at the top and (then) his portrait beneath. This chimneypiece was that

95. Chimneypiece in small drawing room, Master's Lodge. *Destroyed 1941*

96. Chimneypiece in large drawing room, Master's Lodge. *Destroyed 1941*

said in 1829 to have been in the 'New Governors' Room' (the large drawing room).[12] The elaborate gilded picture frame in the overmantel of this chimneypiece was commissioned from the carver Sefferin Alken in 1748 for the Sutton portrait later reinstalled in the chimneypiece of the large drawing room, and it is likely that the overmantel was designed in 1754 by Evans purposely to accommodate this frame and picture.[13] The lower part of this chimneypiece was thought by the Royal Commission on Historical Monuments to have been late seventeenth-century work, the columns of the overmantel perhaps reused from an earlier piece.[14] The other chimneypiece, which had some generic resemblance to that in the Great Chamber (Ill. 112), had been covered over in white paint before the mid-nineteenth century, when the Master, Archdeacon Hale, had it stripped and the arabesque work regilded.[15]

After the Second World War, it was decided to rehouse the Master in the Physician's house at the gate, instead of reinstating him in Master's Court. The governors' room was placed in the south range, east of the archway, and fitted with panelling salvaged from two seventeenth-century houses, 62 and 63 Bartholomew Close. West of the arch, the ground-floor rooms were let as offices. The rest of the south range and the whole of the east were used as accommodation for the Brothers. A new brick stair turret was built at the east end of the south range, projecting into Chapel Court, and a lift was installed at the north end of the east range. Fittings salvaged from the Thackeray Room in Preacher's Court (page 172) were reused on the first floor of the bay overlooking Charterhouse Square.

East of the main stairs, a new ante-room was created at the end of Chapel Cloister, replacing the former entrance hall at the north end of the east range of Master's Court (Ill. 93). The fireplace here, with the Faith, Hope and Charity overmantel, was salvaged from the first floor of the Master's Lodge.

15 Charterhouse Square

East of Master's Court, Chapel Court was formerly closed on the south side by a wing later known as 15 Charterhouse Square. Carter's plan shows it following the irregular frontage to the square, and closed off from what was to become Rutland House by a party wall with a chimney. This building, probably part of North's work, occupied the ground south of the priory church, including the site of the 'pulpit house' used by Alvise Bassano in the 1540s (page 35). It was distinguished by a double-height oriel at one end, looking into what was then Charterhouse churchyard, and it is possible, therefore that

97. Faith, Hope and Charity overmantel from Master's Lodge, now in entrance hall between Great Staircase and Chapel Cloister

the upper room here was the 'gazing chamber' listed in the 1565 inventory. Carter shows it communicating with the long gallery.

The building was treated as a separate house early on in the history of Sutton's Hospital, and at one time was on lease to the Receiver, John Clarke, who absconded with a substantial amount of the Hospital's money during the Civil War. In the 1650s it was taken by the new Registrar, Edward Cressett, who as a married man was barred from living within the Hospital proper. When he later became Master, however, the house was allowed to become an extension of the Master's Lodge. This arrangement ended in 1660 when Cressett resigned and his son took the old house on lease.[17] It was later occupied by various officers of the hospital, undergoing enlargement and partial rebuilding in the eighteenth century.[18] In 1838, the house was again united with the Master's Lodge, and, after Master Philip Fisher's death in 1842, was rebuilt to Edward Blore's designs as part of his remodelling of the Master's Lodge for Fisher's successor, Archdeacon Hale. It was burned in 1941 and subsequently demolished.

The Faith, Hope and Charity overmantel

After the 1941 fire, the plaster overmantel in the Master's old 'first chamber' on the first floor, latterly used as a museum, remained clinging to the wall (under wraps) until 1953. Taken down for restoration, it was reinstalled in its present position in the ante-room or entrance hall on the floor below.

Nothing is known for certain of the work's provenance, but it was probably commissioned for the room in the early years of Sutton's Hospital, either as part of the original fitting-up of the Master's lodgings in 1613–15 or some years later. No identifiable reference to it is made in the surviving records of building works, possibly because it was privately commissioned. Stylistically, it is thought most likely to date from the 1620s or 1630s, perhaps therefore from the Mastership of Sir Robert Dallington in 1624–38.

The composition is closely based on a drawing by Maarten de Vos of the three Theological Virtues, engraved by Hieronymus Wierix in 1572, following a design by G. de Iode, and depicts Charity in a pose derived from the traditional religious image of the *Virgo Lactans*, flanked by Faith (with plumed helmet and chalice) and Hope (with anchor). A small boy offers up a bowl of fruit, representative of earthly charity. The scene has been modified so that Faith, in the engraving with her back to the viewer and head in profile, has been brought round a quarter-turn. Hope too has been altered, from her original mannish pose (right leg bent sharply at the knee across the left, right foot on the anchor shaft).[19] Before the war, the figure of Faith held a staff or a cross (as in the engraving), but this was not replaced during restoration. Hope is shown with a crow, associated with her in the Roman era because of its call resembling the Latin 'cras' ('tomorrow').

The snail and scallop shell in the foreground may be the signature motif of the sculptor. Who he was is a matter of conjecture. Two possible candidates are Kelham Roades and James Leigh, who did much plasterwork at Sutton's Hospital in its early years. Roades was paid almost £40 for unspecified tasks in 1628, and smaller sums in 1630 and 1631, but there is nothing else to indicate that it might be his work.[20] A third possibility is George Ubanke or Huebanke, a master plasterer who also figures in the accounts in the late 1620s and early 1630s for unspecified work.[21]

The north range

Most of the interior layout of Howard House has been destroyed, but in the double-pile north range of Master's Court the essential arrangement of rooms survives. This was the nucleus of the house from Lord North's day, with the double-height Great Hall in front and the Great Chamber behind on the first floor, beneath which was a low-ceilinged room, not, as might be thought, the Parlour but probably Lord North's private room or closet, now the Library. To the east, the Great Staircase only replaced the original stairs there in the early seventeenth century. To the west, extending into the west range of Master's Court and the north end of Wash-house Court, were the kitchens and related service rooms, now much reduced in extent, as well as almost entirely rebuilt.

The north range is readily recognizable on the anonymous late sixteenth-century panorama entitled 'The View of the Cittye of London from the North towards the Sowth'. This shows the windows along the north wall of the Great Chamber, a dormer above and the short gabled wing at the west end containing the Great Chamber alcove; the gable at the east end of the Great Chamber is also shown. There is no indication of the Norfolk Cloister, though this existed by the time the drawing for the engraving was made, apparently between the late 1570s and the late 1590s.[22]

It is clear from the medieval water-supply plan and the post-war excavations by W. F. Grimes that the north range derives its layout from that of the priory and is raised in large part on the old foundations. Roughly speaking, the Library corresponds to the site of the frater, and the Great Hall to Cell A, the original prior's cell. In both cases, the rooms cover a larger area than these precursors. Their east walls either follow the line of the inner wall of the Great Cloister walk or go beyond it, while the hall extends further west than the small structure of Cell A itself. Its front wall is on the line of the outer north wall of the Little Cloister walk, the cloister being the basis for the larger courtyard of today. The cellars, entered from the hallway just beyond the west end of the Library, derive from an undercroft to the frater, though the medieval structure itself has been almost entirely replaced or obscured.

North's reason for building his hall, closet and great chamber in this place was probably that it was next to existing kitchens and bakehouses (with the exception of the 'flesh kitchen', which, for reasons of propriety in a house where the professed brethren were not to eat meat, was situated outside the gate). But there may already have been a hall here, which North largely or completely rebuilt, extending it and raising it in height.

The Great Hall

At 49ft long and nearly 28ft wide, the Great Hall is a fair-sized example of the private or institutional hall of late medieval to early modern date. Inventories show it to have been sparsely furnished during the North and Howard House period, containing little more than the tables and forms appropriate to a servants' dining room. But it would have been fitted up with hangings and other furnishings when the owner or tenant was in residence and it was wanted for banquets, masques or other entertainments.

The Hall has the conventional plan, with an oriel at the high end and a screens passage, screen and gallery at the other. It has windows only in the front wall, explained by its backing on to the Library and Great Chamber, but its chief peculiarities are an irregular façade and a false-ceilinged hammerbeam roof. In its early days it may have gained some additional light from a window in the east end, uncovered after the Second World War (Ill. 105), and from oculi high in the gable ends. It is not certain, however, that the east window was ever external. If it was, it may mean that the building was detached from the east range of Master's Court, and that the precursor of the Great Staircase was in an external turret. In the medieval hall tradition, there was originally no chimney, and smoke from a central hearth or brazier would have escaped through a louvre on the roof. The louvre turret is shown on the 'Agas' map, and survived, albeit largely reconstructed, until burned in 1941.

The façade's appearance has never been satisfactorily explained. Two phases of building must have brought about the disunity of the upper and lower windows, a disunity compounded by the slightly unequal heights of the left-hand and middle windows, a curious error in such prominent and close-set features. The prevailing interpretation, based on the windows, has long been that the building was raised in height by North or Norfolk, the upper windows being added at this time.[23] However, it is unlikely that the back of the double-pile range would originally have been higher than the front, and therefore the Hall was probably its present height from the time that North was first building. Tree-ring dating of the timbers carrying the floor of the Great Chamber, and of what remains of the old roof timbers there, confirms that the wood was felled in the early to middle 1540s, and that the structure is therefore part of North's work. The date of the remaining original pieces of the Hall roof could not be established.[24] One possibility is that the upper windows are later insertions, in which case they were bound to be offset from the main windows because of the positions of the roof trusses. Another is that the two large arched windows are insertions, replacing the lower portions of an original series of rectangular windows in order to aggrandize the building or improve the natural light. Either way, if these large windows were reused from the priory church (which Seely and Paget conjectured might be the case), that might account for the discrepancy in height and for their being so close-set.[25] Windows of this width could have existed on the south side of the church, or in the south and west sides of the chapel of SS Michael and John the Baptist. Not being so tightly juxtaposed, a difference in height there would not have been noticeable.

The main structure, as revealed after the fire, was built using 'a mass of heterogeneous material, mostly robbed from the monastery'. Though, unfortunately, no investigation was made of the foundations, this seemed to dispose both of Gerald Davies's theory that it originated as the sixteenth-century refectory, built under William Tynbygh (prior, 1500–29), and R. H. Carpenter's theory that it was the prior's 'guesten hall'.[26] It also seemed to explain Maurice Chauncy's remark that North had made a banqueting hall out of the church. Chauncy's actual words were 'de ecclesia triclinium suum fecit', and it was Paul Paget who suggested that this might mean that North built his hall out of the stones of the demolished church. David Knowles did not entirely endorse this suggestion, questioning 'whether *ecclesia* could be used in a purely material sense' to mean the stones of the church.[27] Chauncy might actually have been referring to temporary use of the old church as a dining room, and it may be significant that he used the word *triclinium* rather than *aula*, which might be the more obvious word for a hall. Or Chauncy's remark may have been prompted by the location of the dining chamber listed in 1565, which may have been in the east range of Master's Court; this occupied part of the church site and incorporated some of the old fabric left standing.

The front is largely rubble-stone, with tile for filling in and levelling courses, and brick-arched heads to the large windows, all of which, no doubt, is post-suppression. Rubble from the church must have been used, for one stone, found behind the buttress when that was worked on in 1950, was carved with the Popham family arms.[28] It would have come from one of the two chapels on the south side of the church paid for by Sir John Popham in the mid-fifteenth century (see page 26).

The band of stone quatrefoil panels below the windows, running the full extent of the face, including the porch and oriel, is unlikely to have been purpose-carved for North, as the rest of his exterior walls are simply done using the demolished materials to hand, with no comparable ornament. If it was reused, it may have been from the inner wall of the Little Cloister, the lower part of which was partly exposed in 1929, when it was described as being built of flint and tile.[29] But it might derive (reused or partly *in situ*) from an earlier guest hall in the same place, the building of which would account for the prior's move from Cell A to the former Bishop of Lincoln's house on the south side of the Great Cloister (page 29). This was an obvious site for a hall, being adjacent to the kitchens and the guest chambers elsewhere in the Little Cloister. The east end of the present hall at least, including the oriel, must be North's or Norfolk's work, for it is built over the south-west corner of the Great Cloister and therefore cannot be of monastic origin. The west side of the oriel coincides with the line of the outer edge of the Little Cloister walk, including the east wall of Cell A, and the west wall of St Anne's chapel. Grimes's plan of the historic core buildings shows an unexplained thickening of this wall at the corner of Cell A, and a return wall running off to the east, also unexplained but pointing to alterations here which could relate to the supposed guest hall.[30] Early on, Archdeacon Hale was of opinion that the Hall must have been built during the reigns of Edward VI and Mary I, on account of the scraps of stained glass remaining in the oriel, but later decided it was monastic. The glass includes the arms of the Lord Protector, the Duke of Somerset, and 'some fragments of a regal coat of arms containing the arms of Castile and Arragon'.[31]

Whatever the building's origins, it is impossible to say who was responsible for the second post-suppression phase of building. North had ample opportunity to improve upon his initial work. He not only owned the Charterhouse

Great Hall

98. (*right*) Looking east from music gallery in 1996
99. (*above, right*) Screen and screens passage in 1996
100. (*bottom, left*) Screens passage doorways in 1996
101. (*above, left*) Access gallery in 1996
102. (*bottom, right*) Fireplace in 1940

for many years but over two periods (separated by the Duke of Northumberland's brief ownership), with visits from Elizabeth I during the later period. On the other hand, the Duke of Norfolk installed the present screen, and spent heavily on other improvements to the house. In favour of Norfolk's having installed or embellished the oriel is the possible punning intention behind the motto 'Thynke and Thanke' carved on the window-side of the oriel arch, 'Thomas Norfolk' being the form of the duke's name which appears (as the monogram TN) on the Great Hall screen. It has also been thought, in view of the high quality and late Gothic character of the oriel arch, that it was reused from the priory.[32] Davies was certain that the oriel had been cut back, since the angle of view of anyone standing in it made it impossible for them to read the motto. He may have been correct, but had no evidence, claiming first that this was done in the eighteenth century and then in the nineteenth.[33] Any such change must have been much earlier, for Francis Carter's plan shows the oriel as it is today.

The porch was part of the building in North's day, as the stonework of the sides shows, but it was later remodelled with a Classical arch and quoins. This was probably done in the early years of Sutton's Hospital. Carter may have designed it: his plan shows attached columns on either side of the porch entrance, whether existing or proposed. Another possibility is that the front was designed and executed by Richard Maude, who succeeded Edmund Kinsman as mason to the Hospital in the mid-1620s. In 1628, Maude, who had carried out various unspecified works the previous year, contracted for, among other things, the outer door of the porch and the stonework of the sundial at the top of the buttress.[34] A master mason and surveyor of Oxford, he was responsible there for part of Canterbury Quadrangle at St John's College in 1631–2, and later worked at other colleges.[35] Again in 1628, John James was paid for carving the king's arms, possibly those mounted over the porch.[36]

Standing in the Great Hall today, the impression is of an Elizabethan or Jacobean room with an altered roof, and only closer inspection, particularly of the doorways, might suggest an earlier date. This is because of the visual dominance of the carved wood on the screen and side gallery, and of the chimneypiece. Of these three items, the screen, which carries the date 1571 as well as Norfolk's monogram, is by some way the oldest. The date has been confirmed by tree-ring analysis, making clear that Norfolk was not merely embellishing an existing feature of North's.[37] The architectural design and figurative carving are characteristic of the period, though the work as a whole is plainer and coarser in workmanship than the nearly contemporary screen in Middle Temple Hall (1574). The upper level has demountable panels which allow the gallery behind[s] to be open to the Hall or shut. Various alterations have been made, the most obvious being the makeshift adaptation of the north end to take the later access or communication gallery. The doorways have probably been altered on several occasions, while the cornice over the figures on the gallery level was added in the mid-nineteenth century by Edward Blore.

The access gallery runs along the north wall, at a slightly higher level than the music gallery at the end. It was obviously built to give a direct thoroughfare between the Great Staircase and the first floor east of the Hall, avoiding the need to pass through the Great Chamber. Until the Second World War, it continued beyond the Norfolk screen, cutting off a portion of the music gallery, and Carter's plan confirms that this was the original arrangement.[39] Dendrochronology has shown that it cannot be earlier than 1607, while the absence of Sutton's insignia in the decoration suggests that it was among the last alterations to Howard House as a private residence.[40] It was probably made about the same time as the Great Staircase, for the Earl of Suffolk. The carved decoration is in a similar style to that of the now-destroyed balusters of the Great Staircase, though not an exact match.

The third dominating feature of the Hall, the chimneypiece, is well documented. Made of Caen stone, it is the work of the mason Edmund Kinsman, and was installed in 1614 as part of the Howard House conversion, when two large openings to the Upper Hall, later fitted with removable panels, were also made on either side. The centrepiece has Sutton's arms and crest, below which is a cartouche with a salamander in flames, symbolizing enduring faith. Sutton's post as Master of the Ordnance in the North Parts is commemorated by two wheeled cannon, with powder barrels and cannonballs, at the sides. The carriages and powder barrels are stone, while the cannon and balls are wood. Jeremy Wincle, who undertook wood-carving elsewhere in the buildings, was responsible for these features, familiarity with both wood and stone being usual in skilled carvers of the period.[41] The iron grate, an early example for burning coal, is decorated with Sutton's crest. It was formerly in the Great Chamber, changing places with the Hall grate after the Second World War.[42]

The roof is a curiosity. Of the five trusses, only the hammerbeam brackets are original, the upper parts, in so far as they still existed, having been destroyed in the fire. These brackets incorporate traceried spandrels and pendants carved with cherub heads and foliage. The roof's

[s] The gallery was for many years used as a study by the hospital organist, being restored to its original state in the early nineteenth century.[38]

present form is largely due to Seely and Paget, and loosely based on what existed before the fire: the original open roof having long been ceiled in flat along the sides with a central barrel-vault. This seems to have been one of the alterations overseen by Carter in 1613–14. Possibly the original plasterwork was decorated, but if so it did not survive long enough to appear in any illustrations of the room. James Leigh, who produced ornamental plasterwork for the schoolhouse, was paid for the 'ceilings in the hall' in 1614, but the records give no more detail than that.[43] No record of the concealed timbers seems to have been preserved, beyond Gerald Davies's impression of 'a great jumble of beams and rafters which resulted from the heightening of the roof' and which 'would have been unsightly and unpresentable'. This supposed 'heightening' was part of Davies's theory that the Hall had originated as Prior Tynbygh's refectory. In fact, what he must have seen was a mixture of the old beams and the 'new roof' to the Hall, for which the builders Locke & Nesham of Theobalds Road were paid £355 in 1842.[44] This was part of the extensive work done by them at the Charterhouse under Blore. Clearly, it did not involve complete replacement of the old structure. Davies's account in any case seems to confuse the raising of the roof itself (presumably, through increasing the pitch) and the raising of the walls carrying it. His observation that the lower part of the lantern had 'mouldings and arched openings which were never meant to be hidden, and which were once external' suggests that Blore did raise the pitch of the roof, concealing the base of the old lantern, replacing or remodelling the upper part to give the simple, glazed structure that survived until 1941.[45]

Blore made internal alterations to the Hall in the early 1840s. To the 'disjointed' ceiling he added ribs and panels to give visual unity, work which, after the war, Seely and Paget dismissed as a 'most unsatisfactory' solution.[46] He put similar ribs under the side gallery too, and may also have been responsible for its curved soffit, which appears to have replaced a flat, sloped ceiling. He also opened up the archways in the screen, taking out the fanlights, doors and central serving-hatch. At the opposite end of the Hall, he put Sutton's portrait into a new frame with Jacobean gingerbread trimmings. These changes were the last significant alterations to the Hall's appearance before the devastation of 1941.

Restoration by Seely and Paget

Secure under a temporary roof, the burned-out hall stood empty for some years after 1941, the remains of the panelling, screen and side gallery having been taken to Godalming for safe keeping. The only work done for some time was the laying of a concrete floor in 1946, following an attack of dry rot. But the all-important reconstruction of the roof had to wait, delayed by the post-war steel shortage. Meanwhile, work on the exterior carried on in the late 1940s, with the render stripped off—revealing the long-lost quatrefoil band—and the stonework restored, using masonry salvaged from the demolished battlements over the old long gallery fronting Entrance Court.[47] Repairs to the windows were made in 1952. The oriel was in particularly bad condition, and required much restoration with plastic stone, as well as a new concrete roof. Opportunity was taken to make changes of detail, including replacement of the curved cornice with a conventional Classical one.[48]

Replacement of the roof took place in 1955–6 and there, again, aesthetic considerations took precedence over literal restoration. A new open hammerbeam structure had been considered (disregarding the hall's appearance since 1614), but was unaffordable. Instead, it was decided to have plaster ceilings on the old lines—but decorated. The model which Seely and Paget had broadly in mind was the ceiling in the Great Chamber of Herringston House at Winterborne Herringston in Dorset, exactly contemporary with Carter's work at Charterhouse (though far more ornate than could seriously have been envisaged).[49] This, also, was to prove too expensive. Faced with the prospect of replicating the bleak pre-Blore look, Seely and Paget eventually, with the help of the architect Albert Richardson (involved as a member of the Royal Fine Art Commission), reached an ingenious and fairly successful compromise. The long beams linking the hammerbeam ends, which had carried the plaster vault, would be set back, to leave a narrow strip of flat ceiling along the sides, freeing the hammerbeam ends and pendants as they would have been in the original roof. The new plaster vault, as well as thus having a wider span than the old, would have a shallower, elliptical profile. And it would be carried on arched timber ribs to give the visual unity which Blore had sought.[50] The existing pendants were retained, with new turned drops at the ends of the hammerbeams.[51]

Externally, the roof was covered in the red tiles used elsewhere in the restoration, instead of the pre-war slates, but to save money the lantern was not replaced, while the chimneys between the Great Hall and Great Chamber were rebuilt to a much reduced height.[52] This placed the burden of relieving the bareness of the roof on the sundial, rising from a rebuilt parapet of plain brickwork. It was accordingly embellished with a pediment and pilasters, on the authority of Kip's view.

The salvaged panelling had been 'split and broken in every direction and resembled nothing more than a heap of firewood'.[53] To keep the cost down, new panelling in pine was matched to what could be used of the old oak.

103. Gownboy dining-hall (now Library), before the departure of Charterhouse School to Godalming in 1872. A former pupil recalled that 'it always reminded me of the lower deck of a man-of-war'[61]

The screen and the side-gallery front were similarly addressed.[54] Cork tiles on the floor and recessed lights in the flat ceilings were concessions to modernity, though the lights proved inadequate and were replaced in the early 1990s by brass chandeliers along the middle of the room. The new panelling and the need to use oak rather than the intended steel for the roof trusses helped push up the final cost of restoring the Great Hall to £19,018, almost 50 per cent more than the estimate.[55]

The Library

The room known since the late nineteenth century as the Library, or more recently the Old Library, is described in the 1588 inventory as 'the lowe rome called the auditors hall', suggesting that it was then used in connection with accounting, presumably by the senior servants, including Lawrence Bannister, William Dix and William Cantrell. The room is slightly less low-ceilinged today, owing to the insertion of concrete beams above the old timber beams as part of the restoration of the Library and Great Chamber in the 1950s. In 1588 it would have been much more private than today, when it has several entrances and exits and serves as a thoroughfare between different parts of the buildings. Auditors Hall was not its original designation: it was probably Lord North's closet, and had then an inner room. It may have subsequently been used as the Parlour, which is listed in close proximity to the hall in the 1573 and 1583 inventories. But this is not certain, as the Parlour then may have been North's 'Parlour Chamber', which was also listed close to the Great Hall in 1565 but must have been on the first floor, as it had a garret over. No parlour (other than the 'summer parlour' in the garden) is mentioned in 1588.

Exactly how the room related to the Great Hall and other parts of Howard House before the creation of Sutton's Hospital is not known, nor can it be said for certain how far west it extended. Carter's plan shows it closed off at that end by a wall aligned roughly on the long

104. Library in 1996, looking east towards monastic doorway uncovered after Second World War (page 140)

axis of the screens passage of the Hall, beyond which wall was a pantry, and this complete separation of the room from the service quarters may always have existed. The pantry may have been Carter's creation or proposal, and the 1583 inventory shows the parlour possibly adjoining the buttery. Whatever the case, the main entrance to the room would have been from one end of the Hall (and therefore destroyed when the two large openings in the north wall of the Hall were made in 1613–14) or through the doorway in the east wall rediscovered after the Second World War (see below). The scholars' or gownboys' dining hall, as the room became, was not only low-ceilinged but at a higher level than the Hall, up steps, and therefore known as the Upper Hall. There is no obvious reason for this change in level, which did not reflect the floor levels of the monastic structures.

Carter's plan shows the present-day space between the Library and the Norfolk Cloister, which was then used as a staircase compartment serving the upper-level walk, opened up as an alcove (the presumed original purpose of the space above, see page 144). At the front he shows what may be an archway, and at the back a solid wall blocking the way to the Cloister. As he shows a window at the side which seems never to have existed, his drawing must show a proposed arrangement only. In the event, a doorway was made in the north wall of the room and the would-be alcove became, in effect, an extension of the Cloister, allowing direct access for the scholars between the school and their dining hall.

Illustration 103 shows the room in its last days as a dining hall, its appearance then little changed since the early seventeenth century. While the shell and proportions of the room belong to Howard House, little else in the picture does. Possible clues to its original appearance are, however, given by the inventories. Those of 1573 and 1583 suggest a single window, each mentioning two curtains and a single rod. This might account for the need to put in the present four stone windows in 1613–14, while the listing of fire-irons in 1565 and later shows that there was always a fireplace.[56] The panelling and bench-seating along the wall, and some of the furniture shown, probably dated from the establishment of the hospital. The chimneypiece and the doorway to the Norfolk Cloister, carved by Edmund Kinsman in 1613–14, each take up the full height of the room, while the exposed ceiling beams add to the ship-like impression of low headroom. These last date from Lord North's day. The oak columns were installed in 1750, by Michael Babb, carpenter. They may have been like-for-like replacements, though Carter's plan shows a single pillar, beneath the partition between the Great Chamber and the ante-room. Whether or not this ever existed, it is clear that the floor structure above was considerably altered during the 1613–14 conversion. The accounts mention partial new joisting and new 'summers' overhead too. This may have been done in part because of structural decay, but the unequal spacing of the beams is obviously determined by the need to avoid Carter's new chimney and fireplace in the south wall. As the 1941 fire revealed, at this end of the room the joists rested directly on top of the cross-beam, instead of being morticed into it as with the closer-set beams west of the fireplace.[57] This suggests a different phase of work, though tree-ring analysis indicates that the beams, including the unmorticed one at the east end, are all likely to have been felled in the early to mid 1540s.[58]

The room remained a dining hall until the departure of the school in 1872, when it was fitted up as the Library. It was damaged by the 1941 fire, but the principal roof beams and the columns survived with a scorching, and the room was not entirely gutted (Ill. 5). Its restoration in the 1950s went further than the level of damage alone justified. In the first place, the room was enlarged by rebuilding the west wall further west, so that it could be entered from the screens passage in the Great Hall (there having long been a doorway in the north end of the passage, probably since the reconstruction of the Great Kitchen and associated changes in 1872). The surviving panelling and the bench seats, integral to the room's historic character, had been put by for reinstatement but this was not done. Changes were made to the floor and ceiling levels which have significantly altered the room and its relation to the spaces adjoining, particularly the Hall and Norfolk Cloister. The ceiling beams were dropped to accommodate new reinforced-concrete beams above (so as not to affect the floor level in the Great Chamber), and the floor was lowered by nearly 18ins, bringing it level with the hallway to the west and the Great Hall, the chimneypiece being reset lower down to match. To compensate for the overall dropping of the room, the window recesses (though not the windows themselves), were extended to allow the cills to be lowered. At the east end, a partition to create an ante-room like that upstairs was proposed but finally abandoned. Instead, the floor at that end was further lowered so that monastic tiles and stonework that had been found there could remain on view. The Jacobean doorway leading to the Cloister (where the floor level was also dropped, irrelevantly, to the monastic cloister level) was therefore lowered drastically. A balustrade and steps between the two floor levels in the Library had to be provided, which prevented full use of the room and led to falls by the elderly residents. Eventually, in 1962, the sunken area was floored over to provide a level surface throughout, but the north door remains too low down.[59]

A further change resulted from the discovery of a blocked-up doorway of medieval date in the east wall. Seely and Paget were seized with the idea that this was a monastic doorway which had led from the cloister walk into the cloister garth.[60] In fact it is at too high a level, and it is not certain that the wall is even on the exact line of the inner wall of the west cloister walk (page 156). Probably the doorway was moved there by Lord North from elsewhere in the priory, and it became redundant with later changes. Reinstatement of this doorway, leading into the Great Staircase area, was the only change to the room by Seely and Paget to offset an overall loss of character and historic integrity. But it also made it a thoroughfare rather than the backwater it had once been, giving the room at times the restless air of a foyer.

Rooms West of the Library

The exact organization of the area immediately west of the Library is impossible to trace with certainty, though the buttery, pantry, larder and kitchens were clearly here from the time of Lord North, and the cellars remain a constant. The original purpose of the broad brick arch separating the kitchen from the entrance hall is not ascertainable. Somewhat over-restored, it may be late monastic work or later.[62] Carter shows in its place only a small doorway apparently connecting the pantry with a lobby giving on to the cellar stairs and the pantry door of the screens passage.

This area of the Great Hall range has been extensively altered structurally since Howard House days. The Great Kitchen and other rooms were more or less completely rebuilt following the departure of the school, less catering being required. It was then that the open fire for roasting, which probably dated back to Lord North and possibly to the priory, gave way to gas.[63] Apart from the kitchen archway, the only historical features of interest are in the present Manciple's office, designed by Seely and Paget as a tea-room, where two niches or aumbries were revealed by the post-war restoration. They may be of monastic origin, but if so were reused, as the wall is part of the north addition to the range (incorporating the alcove in the Great Chamber), attributable to the Duke of Norfolk. What exactly the rooms here were in the sixteenth century is not known, but it was very probably here in 1588 that the ewery, buttery and outer chamber to Auditors Hall were situated. As part of the fitting up of the tea-room, Seely and Paget installed one of two fireplaces removed by them to the Charterhouse from Cley Old Hall in Norfolk, which they restored in the late 1940s.[64]

Blore's entrance to the Great Chamber range from Preacher's Court was replaced by a glazed outer porch executed in Clipsham stone. Its design, with three round-arched openings, was based on Carter's Chapel Cloister. Behind the porch, the west wall of the range was rebuilt in 1951, with a new buttress at the corner of the projecting north bay.[65] A recent addition, on the west side of the Great Chamber, is the Millennium Clock, made by Gillett and Johnston to a design by a former Surveyor to Westminster Abbey, Peter Foster, himself a governor.

On the first floor, the present Common Room is the descendant of the Withdrawing Room to the Great Chamber listed in 1565. It appears as a withdrawing room in the 1583 inventory too, and is so labelled on Carter's plan. However, it was a bedchamber in 1588. From its position and size, as well as the tapestry hangings kept for it in the Wardrobe, and the elaborate folding table and large cupboard there, it was an important room. Davies called it the Duchess's Withdrawing Room, though he doubted this name's accuracy, suggesting rather implausibly that it was really for the use of musicians playing on the Great Hall gallery. He mentioned that it had always been the organist's private room since the seventeenth century.[66] After the Second World War the room was fitted up by Seely and Paget as the Brothers' lounge.[67] As part of the work, a passageway and stairs to the attic at the west end were removed, and the doorway to the side gallery of the Hall was blocked. Another doorway, from the stair turret in the corner of Master's Court, was also filled in, and a new one made in the west wall. In the south wall, the remains of a stone-shafted window which had been uncovered were made an internal feature, and a single shaft was also exposed on the outside wall. This window must date from Lord North's initial building work in the 1540s, and was presumably blocked when the stair turret was built, probably by the Duke of Norfolk. The doorway in the north wall is one constant in the history of the room. Made of Reigate stone, it may be of monastic origin but is unlikely to have been the doorway to a cell, being higher and wider than the surviving doorways in the Great Cloister. The fireplace in this room, with painted tile-work showing horses and foliage, was designed by Seely and Paget.

The corner stair turret was probably added by Norfolk to give direct access from the courtyard to his bedchamber on the west range of the quadrangle. It is brick-built, like the Norfolk Cloister. Before the Second World War it was faced in the same eighteenth-century brick as the east, west and south sides of the courtyard, with a plain parapet, and the tall, nine-light window in its south side had been partly blocked and given an arched head. The window was uncovered and restored as part of the post-war work, when it was found that one of the lights retained its original glass.[68] An extra storey was added to the turret, under a hipped roof, and a new oak staircase was fitted.

The Great Staircase

Though it was reported in 1947 that the Great Staircase had only been 'damaged', it seems in fact to have been entirely destroyed. Early on it was decided that its replacement would be plain, though built 'to the same form'. In the event, the new stairs were differently aligned and appreciably smaller.[69]

105. Landing of main staircase in 2003, showing doors to access gallery and Great Chamber ante-room, and remains of window uncovered after Second World War

106. Upper landing from east
107. Upper landing from west

Great Staircase in 1940

As explained above (pages 56–7), the Great Staircase was almost certainly made for the Earl of Suffolk in the last years of Howard House, and not, as long thought, for the Duke of Norfolk. Mention was made, too, of the billiard room, which appears to have existed here at first-floor level in 1588, with the implication that the original staircase to the Great Chamber must have been comparatively small.

Structurally and stylistically, the Great Staircase showed a strong affinity with other early seventeenth-century great stairs, in the pattern introduced in the very early seventeenth century, as at Knole (*c.*1605), a new reliance on cantilevering allowing the newels to be cut short, to great spatial effect.[70] The design was slightly more advanced than the great staircase at Knole, with its plainish turned balusters, but very close to that of John Bucke's much grander stairs at Hatfield House (*c.*1610). It was of two flights, the newel posts being carved in a similar manner to the Hatfield stairs, with trophies of war, musical instruments, foliage and ribands, and the balusters with grotesque heads in the form of terms. Various alterations were made to the staircase and its compartment over the years, beginning with the probable replacement of the Earl of Suffolk's arms by Sutton's greyhound crest in 1628 (page 57); Rowland Buckett was paid for colouring the stairs the following year.[71] The spiteful-seeming alteration would have been in response to Suffolk's behaviour over the manors of Littlebury and Hadstock. Sutton had granted them to him conditionally on his paying £10,000 to the executors within a year of Sutton's death, but he had neither paid up nor relinquished them before he died in 1626, and the matter was not resolved until 1633.[72] The matching greyhound finials on the newels may have been part of the 1628 alterations, for there is no record of their being added as part of the conversion work of 1613–14; the originals could have been lions like those at Hatfield, holding heraldic cartouches, which are strikingly similar to the lions over the gate at Howard House (Ill. 131). In all probability, at least part of the motive for building these grand stairs at Howard House was the same as at Hatfield: their intended use by the sovereign.

Kip's view shows that, by 1720, the staircase was lit by a window facing Master's Court at first-floor level (Ill. 34). A small, offset window lit the ground floor. In the later eighteenth century, a doorway and new window above was inserted, with steps up from Master's Court, opening onto the lower landing. This arrangement gave access to the Great Chamber and the Receiver's apartment, as it then was, over Chapel Cloister, without the need to pass through either the Great Hall or the Master's Lodge.[73] In 1841, as part of his makeover of the buildings, Blore undid this alteration, removing the door into Master's Court and

108. Great Chamber, view from east in 1996

replacing the window. Inside, he continued the balustrading of the stairs across the landing under the new window, replicating the old carved work. He also substituted 'a neat and appropriate' Jacobean-style ceiling for the existing plain one.[74]

The stairs and stair-hall were essentially as Blore left them when they were wrecked in 1941. In the 1950s, Seely and Paget provided a light-oak staircase which is a smaller, stripped-down version of the old, in a different position, set against the east and north walls of the new entrance hall (Ill. 48). This allowed the whole of the space to be rearranged. A new doorway was opened into Master's Court, taking the place of the door from the hall porch as the principal entrance to the 'house'. It has windows each side and a new stone panel, continuing the quatrefoil band on the hall. Inside, the ground floor was opened up and the north door replaced by a window. The newly discovered blocked-up doorway opening on to the Library (see above) was reinstated, while the doorways on the east wall were reset slightly to the south, opening into new anterooms on the ground and first floors.

On the first floor, the window in the north wall was reduced in size. Adjoining the door to the side gallery of the Hall, another discovery—the remains of a window probably dating from the time of Lord North—was left exposed (Ill. 105). At the head of the stairs was hung the present lantern, incorporating a panel with the Duke of Norfolk's arms salvaged or copied from the ruined Great Chamber ceiling.

The Great Chamber

In size, shape and position, the Great Chamber is characteristic of such rooms in the late medieval and early modern large house. Long but broader in proportion than a long gallery, it occupies the north side of the Great Hall on the first floor, approached via an ante-room from the principal staircase of the house off the dais end of the Hall. There are therefore no windows on the south wall, where there is a single large fireplace towards the far ('high') end. At that end is a deep recess or alcove on the north side, opposite which a doorway leads to a former withdrawing room, a standard arrangement of rooms. The chief features are the ornate heraldic ceiling and the chimneypiece, a ceiling-high architectural construction, richly painted.

This present-day appearance is deceptive, for the room has changed in several important respects since the sixteenth century, and it was restored after the Second World War from little more than a gutted shell. Here as elsewhere in the Charterhouse, the combination of successive alterations with practical and financial constraints ruled out a recreation of the room at any one stage of its development, even if that had been the aim. Though it must date from the 1540s, the first known documentary reference to it is as the 'Throne Room', where Elizabeth I held court when she came to the Charterhouse in November 1558, soon after her accession, and where the Privy Council probably convened during her five-day stay.[75] The inventory made at Lord North's death gives some clues to its then appearance. In the first place, from the sequence of entries it appears to have taken up the whole length of the space now occupied by the present room and the ante-room. That is, it was entered directly from the landing at the top of the stairs where the Great Staircase was later built. From the north wall of the ante-room a doorway gives on to a small lobby leading outside to the upper terrace walk of the Norfolk Cloister. This, of course, postdates Lord North's occupation, but the lobby itself was probably built by him as a recess to the Great Chamber (see page 157). At the west end, again as now, was the door to the Withdrawing Chamber (much later occupied by the organist of Sutton's Hospital and now the Brothers' common room or lounge). Despite its size (over 70ft long by 23ft wide), the Great Chamber contained just one set of fire-irons and a single pair of curtains. Two fire-backs are listed, however, confirming that the two fireplaces shown on Carter's plan existed then. In 1588, the room, listed as the Great Dining Chamber, was apparently still its original length, but entered now from a room described as the 'room over the screen at the east end of the hall', where there was a billiard table (see page 53). At the west end of the room, North's Withdrawing Chamber had become a bedchamber. The 1588 inventory also gives details of the wall hangings here, a set of seven 9ft-deep tapestries called the 'Wilderness' suite, making a run of 72ft. At the time these were in the Wardrobe, and the room itself was empty apart from one long table, so the inventory gives no further evidence about windows or fireplaces; but, allowing for at least two doorways and two fireplaces, the hangings would have needed all the available wall space. The recess at the east end may have been completely walled up at this time, or may have had a doorway into the stair compartment there, giving on to the upper walk of the Terrace or Norfolk Cloister.

Like Elizabeth, James I held court in the Great Chamber on his accession in 1603 (see page 55). It is possible that the room had by then been reduced in size to create the 'outward chamber' shown on Carter's plan of 1613, or was soon to be so reduced. The partition shown by Carter, apparently involving the loss of one of the twin columns on one side of the eastern chimneypiece, recalls the equally ham-fisted adaptation of the Great Hall screen to make way for Lord Suffolk's access gallery (see Ill. 46). This was essentially the arrangement up to the Second World War. Only the western fireplace and chimneypiece exist today, the eastern chimneypiece having long been destroyed, perhaps when the ante-room was partly rebuilt in the eighteenth century.

The Great Chamber after 1613

The Great Chamber was in a dilapidated state when it came into the hands of the governors of Sutton's Hospital. One gable end, brought down by the wind, had recently been rebuilt, but there was probably weather damage to the room, and the ceiling had to be reinforced with ironwork. (Later 'an unseemly post' was put in to support the outward chamber or ante-room ceiling, removed when the ceiling was repaired in 1668.)[76] In 1808, Smythe also described two pillars, 'half Gothic half Grecian', apparently put in since 1611 to support the ceiling at the west end of the room, near the alcove.[77] Today, the upper part of the north wall at the east end of the building is appreciably thinner than lower down, with an external offset, which may be due to rebuilding at the same time as the gable, or when the buttresses against the wall were built.[78] It is not known when this was, but they appear to postdate Carter's plan and were old enough to be badly decayed by 1734.[79]

From the start, the Great Chamber was used for the governors' assemblies, and became known as the Governors' Room. The existing decorative treatment seems to have been retained, but painted glass with Sutton's arms was put in the windows. As in Tudor times, the walls were lined with tapestries. An eight-piece set of 'fine hangings' was acquired from Edmund Traves in 1615 at a cost of £148 8*s*, for the '2 great chambers'—presumably meaning the Great Chamber and ante-room, which at this time would have had the same ceiling treatment at least as the Great Chamber itself. These were each six Flemish ells deep, the Flemish ell (three-quarters of a yard) being the usual measure for such hangings. This works out at 13ft 6ins, much deeper than Philip Howard's

109. Tapestry in Great Chamber, depicting the Queen of Sheba's visit to King Solomon. Part of the set purchased for this room in 1615

Wilderness hangings, and would have taken up almost all the available height, the room being 17ft high (the deep cornice, restored after the war, dating from *c.*1840).[80] The hangings gave the Great Chamber the alternative name Tapestry Room, often used before the Second World War; their faded and shrunken remnants hang in the room today. They are believed to be of Flemish make. Two have been identified as showing the Queen of Sheba's visit to Solomon, and the arming of David by Saul.[81]

Improvements made in 1626 included the setting up of some sort of carved decoration incorporating cherubs' heads, and in 1657 a new portrait of Sutton was ordered to be hung in the room; this is thought to be the one now in the Great Hall. (There were two portraits of him at the Charterhouse by 1685, the other being that now at Charterhouse School).[82] In 1750, the ante-room and attic above were partly rebuilt and another floor added to the lobby leading to the upper Terrace walk (Ill. 43). This was demolished after the Second World War, and the present roof constructed.[83]

Despite being architecturally the finest and historically the most evocative room in the Charterhouse, the Great Chamber proved something of a white elephant. It was too big for the governors' meetings, and by 1639 it seems to have been superseded, for some meetings at least, by a room in the Master's lodgings.[84] For a few years from 1734 the scholars appear to have put on a play there each year. Although it was still called the Governors' Room it had ceased to be used for their meetings by 1754 or 1755, when it was adapted for the scholars' use, perhaps as a temporary measure while the schoolhouse was being renovated.[85] Meetings were in any case frequently held at Whitehall, and had been intermittently since the early days of the foundation. In 1767, there was talk of making the Great Chamber into an infirmary, and by the early nineteenth century it was effectively redundant, used only for the Founder's Day dinner. Such was the indifference with which it was regarded that the ceiling was subjected to a 'lamentable and ever-to-be-regretted white-washing'.[86] Half of the cornice had disappeared and the chimneypiece was 'clouded by the murky filth of centuries'. In the late 1830s, demolition was considered, but eventually more than £350 was spent on renovation. This included £37 for the restoration of the ceiling by John Jay of London Wall.

The design was modified to include panels noting its restoration in the year 1838.[87]

Only a couple of years later, the Great Chamber was further restored and altered by Edward Blore, whose new building in Preacher's Court abutted the room, blocking the window in the alcove. To compensate, Blore put a new window in the west wall, which he rebuilt, over the pensioners' entrance to the Great Hall range from Preacher's Court. For this he copied the style of the existing lights, and reused the old glass, some panes of which have pre-1840s graffiti. Fortunately for the post-war restorers, the old masonry was left in place and merely covered up. The windows in the rest of the north wall seem to have been replaced at this time, and other structural work included the rebuilding of the chimney and the alteration of the roof at the west end from gabled to hipped. As with Blore's work elsewhere at the Charterhouse, the contractors were Locke & Nesham.[88]

In Blore's view, the recent work in the Great Chamber had left it 'incomplete in its decorations', and he proposed further restoration of the ceiling and cornice to their original appearance, and other improvements. The surviving tapestries were mounted in frames, Jacobethan-style overdoors were fitted, and the room repainted and papered, with coloured emblazoning to the ceiling, the work being done by Crace & Son.[89] With little alteration, so the room remained until 1941.

Post-war restoration

Reinstatement of the Great Chamber was one of the original aims of the post-war rebuilding scheme, as approved by the Estates Committee following the initial report by Sir Charles Peers. Like the Great Hall, it was soon covered by a temporary roof, and in 1949 the west wall and bay on the north side were rebuilt. Full restoration took place over several years from 1951. It was decided not to restore the wall between the Great Chamber and the former ante-room, the latter having been a library (with a small vestibule) since the late eighteenth century, housing the collection of an antiquarian Old Carthusian, Daniel Wray, who died in 1783.[90] Instead, the Great Chamber was to be extended to 60ft long, leaving enough space for a new ante-room to buffer it from the Great Staircase and way through to the Terrace walk. It was also decided not to reinstate the storey over the former Wray Library.

Much of the structure had been destroyed, including the floor and most of the roof. A reinforced-concrete floor was laid, with some consequence for the restoration of the Library beneath (see above), and a new hipped roof constructed. Part of the north wall had to be rebuilt, with a long concrete lintel inserted. The old parapet was taken down and not replaced. As on the front of the Hall, the restored wall was left stripped of render, removal of which also exposed the poor state of the buttresses. The north windows were restored with artificial stone and reglazed, two of them using the old glass. Demolition of the Manciple's house in Preacher's Court had uncovered the alcove window, which was duly restored. Blore's west window was repaired, but the decorative stepped gable-head above was destroyed. In the ante-room, a new east window was put in, matching the Library window below.[91]

In the former Wray Library, the damaged fireplace and overmantel were not replaced, leaving the decorative restorations in the enlarged Great Chamber to focus on the ceiling and the painted chimneypiece. While the alcove ceiling was intact enough to be restored, the rest had to be replicated in fibrous plaster, incorporating fragments salvaged by the contractor, G. Jackson & Sons, in 1952.[92] It is hung with chandeliers of Seely and Paget's own design, decorated with a star motif picked up from the chimneypiece. The cornice, which had been made of oak, was also copied in fibrous plaster, from a surviving piece. The same pattern of cornice was fitted in the ante-room, with a plain ceiling. Both floors were laid in Yugoslav oak, so that the Great Chamber could be used for dancing.[93]

The ceiling

The design of the Great Chamber ceiling is based on a large repeat pattern of squares and circles connected by straight lines, enlivened by a wave pattern intersecting the circles but leaving the squares clear. Leaves decorate the points of intersection of the curved ribs, while the decoration of the squares is heraldic: arms and crests in the centre of the panels and rampant lions at the outer corners. The ceiling of the alcove is similar in pattern, but more conventional in having foliage at the corners of the squares, the lions being set in half-square panels at the front and back. Perhaps to avoid a too-rich effect, it was decided when the ceiling was restored in the 1950s to gild the curved ribs but not the straight, emphasizing the curvilinear forms (deriving from Gothic tracery) but obscuring the full geometry of the design and diluting what might have been a dazzling richness of ornament. A profusion of gold was probably the original (or at least the pre-Sutton's Hospital) effect, for the room was referred to in 1612 as the 'gilded chamber'.[94]

110. Ceiling in recess at west end, with fourth Duke of Norfolk's arms, thistles, and (top) Tudor rose

GREAT CHAMBER CEILING IN 2009

QVI

111. Heraldic panels on main ceiling relating to Duke of Norfolk. Left to right: lion rampant of the Mowbrays, Dukes of Norfolk to 1476; Norfolk's quartered arms; the Howard winged crest

From the Howard motifs decorating the square panels, it has naturally always been assumed that the ceiling was the creation of the Duke of Norfolk and more or less contemporary with the 1571 screen in the Great Hall. That is probably so, and a possible candidate for the work is the London plasterer Henry Watson (*c.*1518–75), to whom payment of £3 for work probably at Howard House is recorded in the 1572–3 accounts of the receiver-general of Norfolk's estates.[95] This may have been an instalment for a substantial contract or payment for another job.

Differences between the (remade) main ceiling and the (original) alcove ceiling suggest that the two are of slightly different date, and raise the possibility that the original decoration may have been altered during the duke's ownership. In particular, one half-square panel at the side of the alcove (the matching one on the other side is now obscured by a pelmet) contains half of a Tudor rose. There are no roses elsewhere in the ceiling. It is debatable whether the rose, naturally a common motif in sixteenth-century ornament, was always confined to this panel or pair of panels, or whether it is a survival from an earlier scheme of decoration, perhaps over the main ceiling too, otherwise replaced by Norfolk's heraldic devices. If the latter, the ceiling might conceivably date from Lord North's period of ownership. However, the additional foliage of the alcove ceiling consists of thistles, suggesting a connection with Norfolk's intended marriage to Mary, Queen of Scots, may put the rose in a different light. If Norfolk was really alluding to the possible future union of England and Scotland, they were dangerous ornaments indeed, recalling the misuse of the royal arms in interior decoration by his father, Surrey, for which he was executed. In that case, they could only date from after the death of the duke's third wife in 1569. This would accord with the supposition that the alcove itself was built by him to replace an earlier alcove at the other end of the room, taken to provide access to the new Norfolk Cloister at the top of stairs from the formal garden (page 157).

Support for the possibility that the thistles refer to Mary Stuart comes from the fact that, sometime after Norfolk's return from the Tower in August 1570 Robert Cooke, Clarenceux King of Arms, set out for him a pedigree on vellum, with Norfolk's arms on one side and Mary's on the other, 'largelye painted'. Cooke also set out the duke's pedigree 'in glasse in the Wyndowe of the Great Chamber at the Charterhowse', with his arms quartered with those of his attainted great-grandfather Edward, Duke of Buckingham, a descendant of Edward III.[1]

The three devices which fill the square panels are Norfolk's quartered arms, the Howard winged crest, and the lion rampant of the Mowbray Dukes of Norfolk, each enclosed by the garter and the first two surmounted by a ducal coronet (Ill. 111). The coronet over the lion badge is either of unorthodox type or was replicated from a mutilated original. Before the fire, the decoration also included the Howard arms (as in the first quarter of the duke's arms) in a roundel, again enclosed by the garter; these were presumably omitted from the restoration by Jacksons because the originals were destroyed or too damaged to reproduce. The half-square panels along the sides of the main ceiling carry the duke's motto, *Sola Virtus Invicta* ('Virtue alone is invincible'). Before 1941, two panels corresponding to these contained references to the restoration of the ceiling in 1838.

[1] The story is told by Strype in his edition of Stow's *Survey of London*, but wrongly, attributing Cooke's role to William Dethick, then York Herald. This incorrect version was repeated by Mark Noble in his *History of the College of Arms* (1805) but corrected by Sir Anthony Wagner in *Heralds of England* (1967).[96]

The chimneypiece

Artistically, the Great Chamber chimneypiece is one of the most important features of the Charterhouse, even in its present heavily restored state. Before the war it was obscured with generations of dirt, and probably layers of varnish and local restoration. The 1941 fire left it scorched and water-damaged, some of the panels split, the joints opened and the paintwork badly blistered. Cleaning and restoration, a lengthy and expensive task undertaken by A. Robin Ashton, was begun in 1955 and hastily completed in readiness for the royal opening of the restored buildings in 1958, which led to some cracking. The work included the reinstatement of missing sections, including two entire panels on the right side, based on those on the left.[97] Much of the original colour has been lost, and subsequent experimental restoration has not significantly improved upon Ashton's work.

The chimneypiece, together with a similar one at the other end of the room, is shown on Carter's plan of 1613. It is first referred to in late 1626, more than a decade after the conversion of Howard House, when the painter Rowland Buckett was paid £50 for various works: gilding the organs in the chapel; mending, painting and gilding the wainscot in the Great Chamber; and 'Guildinge and payntinge the Chymney peece' there.[98] Unquestionably, the chimneypiece itself predates Sutton's Hospital, and there is great uncertainty over how much of the painting is by Buckett. As W. Haig Brown remarked in the 1870s, the 'most cursory view would suggest the strange disparity of the different portions of this work', and his description confirms that their mixed artistic qualities are not the result of the post-war restoration. Parts, in his opinion, were 'gross and clumsy', while the scenes of the Annunciation and Last Supper were 'not without merit'. These last were described by the critical Robert Smythe in 1808 as 'extremely well performed'.[99]

The overmantel has long been thought earlier than the lower portion, on stylistic grounds, and may date back to the Duke of Norfolk's alterations, though an earlier or later date cannot be ruled out. Its architectural design recalls that of a chimneypiece in the large drawing room of the Master's Lodge, decorated with arabesque work, which was destroyed in the fire (Ill. 96). The geometrical pattern employed in the centre of the overmantel was much used in Elizabethan design, and versions of it decorate the panels on the upper stage of the Great Hall screen, as well as the Great Chamber ceiling. The stone fire surround, which has a shallow, angular arched top, also recalls the lost fireplace in the Master's Lodge.

The oval centre panel contains the Stuart royal arms and the cipher CR for Carolus Rex, and the four panels framing the oval contain representations of the Evangelists. At the sides are tall, round-headed panels containing allegorical figures identifiable as Plenty (with a cornucopia) and Peace or Victory (with a palm frond), both of them of Moorish appearance, together with fanciful arabesques and Italianate grotesquerie. The columns are painted with head-and-shoulder depictions of the Apostles or other saints, in roundels. Beneath, Sutton's monogram and arms, supported by putti, are painted over a background of similar fanciful ornament to that of the side panels. On either side are scenes of the Annunciation and Last Supper. In the entablature at the top are four boys' faces, so animated and individual that they would seem to have been done from life. Four more images on the curved cornice supporting the overmantel are of the Elements. Below, the chimneypiece incorporates images of Faith, Hope and Charity and, in the arched panels between the columns on either side, figures traditionally identified before the fire as a soldier and an Amazon, or Mars and Minerva, and now difficult to make much of. Faith, Hope and Charity, which appear fuzzily restored, were probably poor images to begin with, or had been poorly restored, Haig Brown describing them as 'rather rude'.[100]

How many phases of work are represented, and how much is attributable to Ashton's restoration, is impossible to say without scientific analysis. It was apparent to Alfred Clapham and his colleagues at the Royal Commission on Historical Monuments (as it had been to Smythe) that the Stuart and Sutton arms were not part of the original decoration, though Clapham's brief account is evasive and unresolved.[101] The oval panel with the Stuart arms and CR is said to be inscribed on the back 'Painted by Rowland Buckett in 1626', and is similar in treatment to Sutton's arms and monogram below. But it is not now clear whether the endorsement is Buckett's own or, as the phrasing suggests, a later annotation; and there is reason to doubt that the painting itself can be of 1626. Even allowing for extensive restoration, the oval panel appears poorly integrated with the decorative scheme as a whole, and less well executed than other portions of the overmantel, notably the Apostle roundels and the round-headed panels, which are reminiscent of Buckett's work elsewhere, such as his earlier painting of the chapel gallery and Dutch organcase at Hatfield House. Just as at Hatfield, there is a marked contrast between the technically accomplished, or at least facile, Italianate grotesquerie and the stodgier handling of the realistic subjects in the roundels, which supports the view that these are all Buckett's work.[102]

The oval is usually described as bearing the arms of Charles I, but this is based on its supposed date. It is hard to believe that the republican governors, meeting in this

GREAT CHAMBER CHIMNEYPIECE DETAILS:

113–8. Clockwise from top: portrait heads on cornice; Stuart royal arms with CR cipher, and four Evangelists; Thomas Sutton's arms and monogram; Last Supper; Annunciation; panel on right-hand side with figure of Victory or Peace

112. The chimneypiece in 2009

room during the later years of the Civil War and the Interregnum, would have tolerated the royal arms so prominently displayed on the chimneypiece. The charity was brought under close scrutiny by the republican government, with a view to purging it of its perceived Catholic and Royalist taint, and the board of governors was packed with prominent Parliamentarians, including Cromwell himself. In the same period, the royal arms were taken down elsewhere on the site and those of the Commonwealth put up. For these reasons alone, it is almost certain that this panel is not by Buckett but was done at the Restoration, the CR standing for Charles II. Haig Brown stated that it was placed there 'about 1660', but probably had no more than this rationale to support his claim.[103] Very probably, as he surmised, the centrepiece was originally an emblazonment of the Duke of Norfolk's arms.

Unlike the rest of the panels, the Last Supper (deriving from Da Vinci's painting), is painted on canvas stuck on to the wood, and is in very good condition. This may have been completely redone in the 1950s, either by Ashton himself or another painter employed by him, but it repeats the original treatment of figures drawn in gold on a black background. (In contrast, the figures of Faith, Hope and Charity were black on a gold background.) It is strikingly different in artistic technique and style to the restored lower panels.

There seems no reason to connect the Christian iconography of the overmantel with Philip Howard's intermittent occupation of Howard House between 1578 and 1585, or his reception into the Roman Catholic faith. There is nothing specifically Catholic in the scenes of the Annunciation and Last Supper, such subjects being common enough in work commissioned by unwaveringly Protestant householders. Their style, in any case, points to a later date. As for the boys' faces, however, these seem not to fit with the overall decorative scheme and its religious, allegorical and heraldic elements. Though perhaps much restored by Ashton, they have a freshness and vivacity lacking from the other figurative paintings, pointing to their being a distinct phase of work. From their dress, the boys do not appear to be scholars of Sutton's foundation, and, given their individuality, they may possibly depict the fourth Duke of Norfolk's sons—Philip (born 1557), Thomas (1561) and William (1563)—and his stepson George Dacre (1562). If so, they must date from before George's death in May 1569 (page 43). Under the duke's plans for his family, George's three sisters were to marry the Howard boys, while George was to have married their sister Margaret.

CHAPTER VII

The Norfolk Cloister and Old Schoolhouse

The Norfolk Cloister is the remnant of the Duke of Norfolk's chief work at Howard House, a great 'gallery' which extended all along the west side of the Carthusian cloister, with a high-level walk, real-tennis court, bathing-house and banqueting room. What survives is about half the original 263ft-long brick-vaulted passage which was the structural and functional core of the complex, thought to have been built in 1571. The other half was pulled down in 1873 for the building of Merchant Taylors' School, together with the old Charterhouse schoolhouse alongside, built in 1613–14 from the shell of the tennis court.

In its original form, the cloister probably gave access to the tennis court, but its essential function (beyond that of status symbol) was as a promenade: for exercise, contemplation and conversation. It was a garden building, albeit a sophisticated one, with windows on the east side looking onto the old cloister garth, by then converted into the formal garden which was one of the glories of Howard House. On this side, the elevation was a symmetrical, Classical composition with decorations in raised brick-work. Unlike today, the principal access was not from what is now the Library at the rear of the Great Hall but from

119. Norfolk Cloister, east side, before demolition of northern half. Note third canted bay and gateway at north end, added about 1859

the garden itself. Inside, the building would have been plastered throughout and finished with ornamental painting and gilding, or decorated with hangings. Alcoves on the blind west side provided secluded places to sit, and the doorway there gave access to the smaller privy garden, with its more intimate summer parlour. The architectural treatment on this side was less formal too, and apparently less advanced. On the upper level was a 50ft covered gallery, entered from the main house or by way of stairs from the garden, beyond which was an expanse of open terrace, a fair-weather counterpart to the vaulted passage. Flanked by battlemented parapets and more ornate features with sculptural decorations, this terrace broadened out alongside the tennis court, no doubt affording a view of the play below. Beyond, steps gave on to the garden later known as the Wilderness. It was, in short, a building designed for pleasure; and for weightier matters too, whether affairs of state or business talk. A glimpse is given in a letter of 1603 from one George Bowes to the last Howard owner of the house, the Earl of Suffolk: 'At my last attendance on you in your terrace walk at Charterhouse I did impart my opinion of gold in Scotland, and that by his Majesty's motion to my uncle then ambassador there, I had bestowed two journeys to view the aptness in those mountains for gold and other minerals'.[1]

Long before its partial demolition in 1873 the cloister had lost much of its original character through decay and rebuilding, inside and out. The surviving portion is today a melancholy place, redolent more of monkish austerity than worldly extravagance, power politics and pleasure. Even so, as a rare survival it is of considerable interest.

The building's original name was 'the Terras', a word used to describe a raised walk, or a gallery or colonnade open on one or both sides. It became known as 'the Cloister' or just 'Cloisters' after the creation of Sutton's Hospital. The name Norfolk Cloister may have been coined by R. H. Carpenter, who uses it on his 1888 plan drawn for Hendriks's *The London Charterhouse*. Gerald Davies referred to it as Norfolk's Arcade; earlier, Augustus Hare, in *Walks in London* (1878), called it the Brick Cloister. At some point in the nineteenth or twentieth century the name Queen's Walk was coined for the upper terrace: Elizabeth I may have set foot on it during her final visit to the Charterhouse, in 1603.

Although garden galleries were common in Tudor England, they were often built of timber and so have not survived.[2] Few were of a scale comparable with the Norfolk Cloister. One was the Water Gallery of 1536 at Hampton Court: over 170ft long, this combined the functions of jetty, boathouse and 'recreational riverside grandstand'.[3] Something similar to the Water Gallery existed at Arundel House in the Strand: a two-storey building with semi-octagonal bays at the sides, and a watergate. Here is a possible link with the Norfolk Cloister, for the Arundel House gallery may have been built or completed (after 1604) by the Earl of Suffolk.[4] Another comparable structure was the terrace at Lambeth Palace, probably built in the 1540s for Archbishop Cranmer. About 190ft long, this led from the palace alongside the privy garden to a small banqueting house, and had a central semicircular bay on each side. It was covered on top with lead, providing a high-level walk. Inside, the passage was open to the garden only, through an arcade.[5] Outside London, a broadly similar, though L-shaped, gallery was at Sir Nicholas Bacon's house at Gorhambury, Hertfordshire, built about 1577. A cloister with a timber-built gallery above, extending from the house, it was 160ft long in all.[6] The Norfolk Cloister was longer and perhaps more ambitious than any of these. A later building in some respects comparable is the stone cloister at Aberglasney House, Carmarthenshire, built for the Bishop of St David's in the early 1600s.

A gallery for recreational use was more or less de rigueur in a great Tudor house, and by Norfolk's time the 'long gallery' (as it was retrospectively to become known), often hung with portrait paintings, was well established as one of the principal rooms. At Howard House, there was already such a gallery in the south range of what is now Master's Court. The garden gallery was in some ways similar, though likely to retain the historic function of the gallery, originating in the medieval alley or pentice, as a corridor for access rather than a room in its own right. In the case of Norfolk's Terrace, access to the tennis court and other rooms at the far end was presumably one, but not the main, function.

Garden galleries often had the character of a cloister, long before the Dissolution and the conversion of many monasteries into great houses. At Howard House, the Terrace's position was determined by the largely demolished Carthusian cloister, and in building it Norfolk made use of some of the remaining monastic fabric.

The monastic structure

Although the Norfolk Cloister is essentially an Elizabethan brick building, the west side of the vault is carried on the stone wall which was the front of the monks' cells north of the frater. The extant portion comprised the fronts of Cells B, C and D, while the demolished part included the fronts to E, F and G. The wall still incorporates the complete entrance doorway and serving-hatch of B, and the serving-hatches to C and D.

Next to B doorway is the front of another hatch, at the level of the Elizabethan floor, which was lowered about

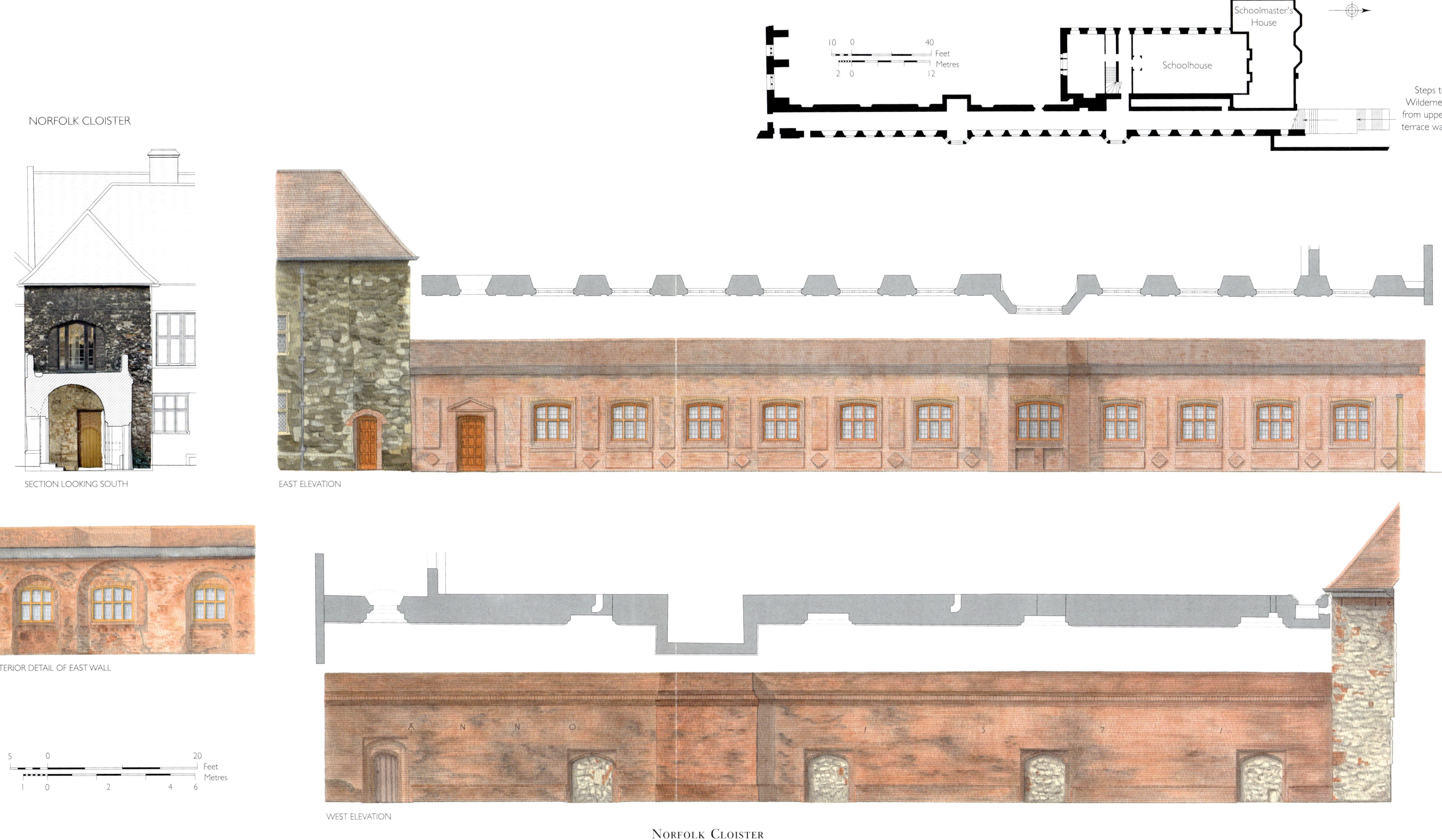

120. The surviving portion in 2009, with (*top*) plan of complete cloister and school buildings in 1825

121. (*right*) Interior elevation in 2009. Composite photograph, showing remaining fabric of the monastic Great Cloister, areas of post-Dissolution robbery of masonry, infill, and reconstruction for the fourth Duke of Norfolk

nine inches to the monastic pavement level during restoration of the building in the 1950s. It has been suggested that this was a refuse hatch, but it is more likely that it was taken from another cell after the suppression and reset here for another purpose.[7] It gives on to a straight, brick-lined shaft, now blocked, which emerged through a small arched opening on the west side of the wall, probably of late eighteenth- or early nineteenth-century date. This may have had something to do with the old drainage system replaced in the 1820s.[8]

What is striking about the face of the wall today is the almost complete obliteration of the doorways to C and D cells and, going by the priory water-supply plan, additional doorways opening on to the gardens of B and C. These features were presumably taken for reuse elsewhere, and this appears to have been done carelessly, without regard for the wall itself, which may have been left ruinous and only patched up with stone later. Cell B entrance may have provided a useful short cut between the east and west sides of the grounds, and so was spared. Destruction was more sparing towards the north. The entrances to Cells E and G remained intact (see below), while G itself, the north-west corner cell, was seemingly adapted as a termination to the Terrace and tennis court. From its dimensions, it is probable that the tennis court utilized some of the monastic walls or their foundations.

The cell-front wall itself had probably been built in stages, as the actual cells were built. At least three years separated the building of B and C, for instance. This could explain some of the variation in the masonry seen today. In its original state the wall may have been rather higher, but there is no archaeological evidence to show how high the cells were, or whether the presumed upper floors were in the roof-space or were of full height. All that is recorded of the building of the cloister walk is that its pavement and ceiling (*pavimentum cum celatura claustri*) were not installed until after the death of Prior Luscote in 1397, at which time many cells on the east and south sides of the cloister had yet to be built.[9] The only clue to its form is a series of what seem to be large filled-in holes at the top of the surviving stone wall, possibly the sites of sockets for beams or stone corbels. One such site, at Cell B, is filled by a single stone which might be a cut-back corbel. The level does not suggest a very lofty structure.

122. (*top*) Norfolk Cloister, looking south, *c.*1840. Remains of Cell E entrance to right
123. (*bottom*) Norfolk Cloister, looking north, before demolition of northern half in 1873

W. F. Grimes took the east wall of the Norfolk Cloister and that of the Library to be on the line of the monastic inner cloister wall, and even hinted vaguely that the masonry of the inner wall might be hidden behind Norfolk's brickwork. It is not clear if his location of the inner wall was anything more than an assumption, and he did not comment on the fact that it would have made the west cloister walk significantly wider than the other three, whose width was proved by the discovery of traces of the inner-wall footings.[10] He may have based his conclusion chiefly on the discovery of a doorway of late fourteenth-century appearance in the Library wall. In fact, this was almost certainly not left *in situ* from monastic days but moved there by North (page 140), and the wall itself may therefore be entirely of North's day. Whether it is or not, there is no reason to think that the Norfolk Cloister incorporates any *in situ* monastic masonry other than that clearly visible on the west side, and it is probable that the inner cloister wall had been demolished many years before construction of the brick cloister began, as Maurice Chauncy's testimony implies (page 34).

Inside and out, the wall is patched with stones salvaged from elsewhere in the priory. At least three of these have deeply incised X marks, of unknown purpose, one in the blind arch at the south of the building, and two inside. From their positions, they appear to have been cut before the stones were moved.

The Duke of Norfolk's Terrace

In one of his last confessions, Norfolk described how, in September 1569, he was at Howard House when a Dr Francis and a Master Caldewell paid an afternoon call, 'as though they had come to see how I did after my physic' (real or feigned illness having kept him from court). Walking with Norfolk 'in the gallery next the garden', Francis warned him that he was likely to be taken to the Tower: 'this sudden news did mercilessly appal me, and indeed I was so amazed, as I knew not what to do'. With none of his advisors in the house, he eventually decided to leave for Kenninghall, relying on friends and his own 'humble letters' to mollify the queen, an act of folly that did nothing to avert his eventual downfall.[11]

If Norfolk's 'Terrace' was built, like the screen in the Great Hall, in 1571—in the last days of his residence at Howard House, where he had returned from the Tower to house arrest—it cannot have been the 'gallery next the garden'. This was almost certainly the gallery on the site of the monastic south cloister walk, built by Lord North in the 1540s, the evidence for which is discussed elsewhere (see pages 110–5). Evidently the Norfolk Cloister replaced it, and it may not be too fanciful to speculate that the trauma Norfolk experienced in the earlier gallery was one reason for superseding it with one of the grandest garden galleries of the Elizabethan period.

The earliest definite reference to the new edifice is in the accounts of the receiver-general of the late duke's estates for 1575–6, in which the last £80 of their £560 bill for building 'lez Tarres apud Howard house' is recorded as having been paid to 'Hugoni Drewe et Arden Bricklaiers'.[12] As suggested above (page 46), the full cost of the building must have been far higher than £560, making it a very expensive undertaking. It next appears in the 1588 inventory, together with a chamber at the end of the 'tarris' and a 'bathinge house' beneath that. No contents of the cloister itself are listed.

Two years later, the Crown survey of Howard House calls the cloister a 'long gallery', and describes it as being paved with Newcastle stone on the floor and upper terrace. Rainwater was soaking through the paving 'to the great decay of the vault', which might explain why the cloister had apparently been empty in 1588. This was to be a recurrent problem, never fully solved.[13] Also in 1590, the 'vamors' or vauntmures (parapets) of the terrace were in bad condition, 'for that yt overhanges to the daunger of the overthrow of the same'. The cost of remedying this was put at the substantial sum of £80, though the surveyors added that they thought the structure could only be kept dry by covering it with lead or a 'close roof', which would have cost £300. The parapets were described as 'battlements' nearly 30 years later, when they were raised in height to 4ft, having perhaps been cut down after the 1590 survey.[14]

Four structures connected with Norfolk's Terrace are mentioned in the survey, only one of which survives. First is the tennis court built on to the west side towards the north end (discussed separately below). Secondly, there was a two-storey 'square house' (a building with a flat roof or parapet), measuring 26ft by 21ft, at the north end of the terrace, comprising the 'bathing house' and chamber above, apparently adapted from Cell G. While it cannot be identified in the 1565 inventory, it may have been any of several outbuildings listed, or disused. Neither chamber nor bathing house contained much in 1588: a cupboard and window-boards, and a tin cistern or bath probably for use after tennis. But the hangings stored in the Wardrobe for use in the upper room suggest that it was used for entertaining, as a banqueting room, a term with less grand and formal connotations than today. The walls were high, the hangings being mostly over 11ft deep. That would be far too deep for the upper floor of a typical Carthusian cell, usually only a loft inside a pitched roof, so the upper floor had presumably been rebuilt by Norfolk in conjunction with the Terrace. In 1590, the lead of the roof was sagging and the parapets were decayed. The building was evidently later incorporated into the house occupied by the Preacher and Schoolmaster of Sutton's Hospital, for two decayed old windows there had to be replaced (in brick) in 1613–14, and the shape of the cell is clear in the footprint of the house, shown on Francis Carter's plan (Ill. 30). In 1839, Archdeacon Hale recorded that a cell doorway here had been discovered some years earlier when the Schoolmaster's house was rebuilt.[15]

The third structure was another 'square house': the short extension to the Great Chamber range at the south end of the cloister. This contained the 'pair of stairs going up to the terrace' taken out in 1613–14 when the way through from what is now the Library was made.[16] These terrace stairs were approached from the surviving door on the east side. There would not have been a way through from there to the cloister itself, hence the need for the second door on the east side, opposite the site of Cell B. The ground floor of this wing has now been vaulted over as an extension of the cloister, while the first floor consists of a lobby giving on to the terrace, and a cupboard to one side. As straight jointing between it and the main house shows, this shallow 'wing' was an addition, probably built to make an alcove in the Great Chamber, which would have been superseded by the existing alcove at the west end of the room when the Norfolk Cloister was built. Constructed, like the house itself, with reclaimed monastic stone, it could date from any time between North's building of the Great Chamber range in the mid-1540s and his death twenty years later. In 1590, the roof was so decayed as to need replacement.

On the ground floor on the west side of this staircase 'wing', beneath the cupboard, is a sealed void. Walled off from the passageway with undisturbed monastic masonry, it can never have been open as Carter shows it on his plan. Conceivably it contained a chute serving a garderobe in the cupboard area above, but it is more likely that it was simply left as a void because it was not needed, the purpose of the new wing being the recess on the first floor.

The broad archway leading to the terrace, roughly built with reused stone, was presumably formed about 1571 to give access to the upper walk of the duke's new Terrace. It would have opened onto the fourth adjunct mentioned in 1590, a 'little gallery', 12ft wide and extending 50ft along the terrace.[17] In 1590, this too needed re-roofing, and it was probably pulled down not very long after the survey, as there is no subsequent record of its existence. Faint marks on the north wall of the staircase wing may be the trace of its pitched roof. The little gallery was probably intended to run all the way to the chamber at the end of the terrace, and if so must have been cut short at Norfolk's attainder (as with the tower of Kenninghall church, which he is said to have then been rebuilding).[18] Like the 1590 surveyors, the builders would have known that there was no sure way of waterproofing the vault other than with a roof such as that provided by an upper gallery, or sheet lead, expensive as either would have been.

Everything else about the building points to a no-expense-spared project, including a feature which some trouble was taken to remove in the 1950s: a series of iron bars crossing the passage just above the springing of the vault (Ills 122, 123).[19] A couple of remaining stumps show that they were of square section, set diamond-wise and fixed in place as the brickwork was laid; structurally superfluous, their intended purpose is unclear. *Chronicles of Charter-house* (1847) notes 'traces' of a flat ceiling immediately above the windows, which might have been carried on these bars.[20] However, the 1590 survey makes no mention of any such ceiling, and it must have gone by 1751, when the cloister was replastered and the cross-bars, along with cornices, lamp-irons and other features, were painted.[21] J. W. Archer's (Ill. 122) view shows a small boss in the centre of each bar, perhaps relics of a decorative treatment, and a few of these are just discernible in enlargements of later photographs. None were left on the bars remaining in the 1950s.

The two elevations

Although the west face of the Norfolk Cloister has 'ANNO 1571' fixed on it in iron characters, there is room for doubt about the last figure, described in 1839 as a replacement put up on the assumption that the cloister was built in the same year as the similarly dated screen in the Great Hall. It has been argued that it can only have been nought or one;[22] but Norfolk was not executed until 1572 and the work may have carried on into that year. Though the bricklayers' contract was not fully paid off for several more years this may reflect nothing more than late payment. In any case, the iron date is only evidence for the west front; this seems to have been built subsequent to the main structure and therefore might date from the late 1570s, when Philip Howard was in possession of the house and carrying out his own improvements. This side, facing the former privy garden, is plain apart from the date, a doorway and a roughly spaced series of shallow, arched recesses with plain-chamfered sides. Purely ornamental, these recesses may have been sites for seats, cisterns, or plants, and were probably finished with plaster, perhaps with painted designs.

The east elevation, which looked on to the much larger formal garden, is decorated with raised pilasters and oblong and diamond panels, and has hollow-chamfered brickwork to the sides of the windows. This essentially Classical treatment is unusual for its apparent date, and contrasts with the more old-fashioned west side. A symmetrical composition, it was divided into thirds by two canted projecting bays (these being matched by projecting rectangular bays on the west side of the building). The canted bays were mirrored, each having an extra-broad pier on its outer side and a standard narrow pier on the other (see plan in Ill. 120).[23] The surviving (south) bay has been partly rebuilt, but has traces internally of windows on the angled faces. A drawing of 1750 by Benjamin Timbrell confirms that there were windows on the sides of the north bay too. It also shows a pedimented doorway instead of a window immediately north of the north bay, similar to the doorway surviving at the south end of the building.[24]

Owing to the disappearance of the upper parts and other changes, the fronts cannot be compared fully. On the east side, the window heads have been rebuilt, together with everything above. Timbrell's drawing shows conventional six-light mullion-and-transom windows and a string course at the base of the parapet. These windows were still in place in the early nineteenth century, when they were described as 'projecting'; their glass had gone by then. A Victorian photograph shows that one of them survived until the north half of the cloister was demolished.[25] On the west side, the parapet is recent and the plinth appears to be an addition. Kip's view (Ill. 34) shows what may be a tall shaped pediment rising from the projecting bay—presumably a relic of the original superstructure. Gainsborough shows the same feature, with a stone urn or other feature on top (see frontispiece).

Style apart, there is evidence that the two fronts are of different date, including a slight difference in size and colour between the bricks; the fact that the west parapet is set back from the outer wall; and the absence of bonding between the two concentric brick surrounds at the doorway on the west side. All point to the west front being a later cladding. This seems to be confirmed by the construction of the inner face of the projecting west bay, which is in stretcher bond, suggesting that it was built as a temporary, half-brick-thick closure, pending construction of a permanent façade: a hiatus which may have had something to do with the duke's attainder and execution.

The east elevation raises questions too, chiefly because its style is more suggestive of the seventeenth century than the sixteenth. But there is no compelling physical or documentary evidence for later reconstruction or remodelling of this front. Straight joints between the piers and the walls beneath the windows, and the clumsy intersection of the splayed sides of the piers with the springing of the vaulting over the windows, are better explained by the builders' method of working rather than as later alterations. Probably, the piers were left toothed on their outside faces and upper sides until the vault was laid and the centering struck, the low walls under the windows, the splays and the façade itself being built as a separate stage of the work. The straight joints and irregularities left inside the cloister would have been completely concealed by plaster. As for the east front's comparatively advanced design, its symmetry at least reflects the structure of the vaults and piers and cannot have been altered later.

The cloister since 1611

Little was done to the building during the conversion of Howard House in 1613–14, but in 1618 there was concern about its condition and repairs were put in hand. As in 1590, the problem was rainwater. Accordingly, the terrace was relaid with stone (lead and 'plaster' having also been considered) and new parapets were built, with lead-lined gullies; the steps to the Wilderness were also relaid. At £376 12*s* 3*d* this was a big outlay for a non-essential structure.[26] Repairs made in 1641 included repaving and renewal of lead pipes and cisterns on the terrace. James Selby, bricklayer, was paid £47 10*s* 5*d* for 'work done about the cloister', described as amounting to 950½ yards at a shilling a yard. The relatively low cost and casual description seem to rule out any possibility that this was much more than repairs and repointing.[27]

In 1618, the governors had justified the expensive repairs on the grounds that the building was 'not only a great ornament to the hospital but very commodious for the Master, officers, poor men and children'. All these may have been entitled to use it then, but a few years later keys for the upper terrace and Wilderness garden were issued to the senior staff—Preacher, Surveyor, Schoolmaster, Physician, Receiver, Steward, Auditor and Usher. Gainsborough shows boys playing on the terrace, on to which a door opened from the schoolhouse. The cloister below was the way to the scholars' dining hall from the schoolhouse, and cannot have been much used by the pensioners, if at all. From Victorian times, and probably much earlier, it was also used as a covered playground, where a sort of cricket and a violent kind of football were played, and for watching sports matches on the school green. The southern square embayment, called Middle Briers (perhaps by corruption of 'bower'), was used until 1836 as a tuck-shop, which moved in that year to a basement room in the new schoolhouse.[28] By the early nineteenth century, attempts to keep the glazing in repair had been abandoned and, with the removal of the frames, the windows remained gaping holes until the 1950s. The interior was replastered in 1751 and 1779, but maintaining the plasterwork proved as futile as mending the windows.[29]

The lost northern part was adapted as lavatories and washrooms, known as 'Cocks', the windows being partly bricked up. It is not clear quite what form the north end of the cloister originally took. Carter's plan is sketchy and uninformative about the entire building, omitting the windows and showing the main passage broadening out alongside the old tennis court, which it can never have done. As later drawings show, the vault actually continued at the same width all the way along, and there was a void or passageway between the two structures. The length of 263ft stated in 1590[30] shows that the vault went no further than the north end of the tennis court, where there were steps down to the Wilderness from the terrace. Some changes were no doubt made when the former Schoolmaster's and Preacher's lodgings were rebuilt on a larger scale as the Schoolmaster's house, in 1829. A third canted bay (see Ill. 119) was a Victorian addition, built about 1859; the previous arrangement was quite different (see plan in Ill. 120).[31] North of the new bay, the terrace was extended some way beyond the north end of the Schoolmaster's house. At the corner, an angled gateway linked the end of the building with a straight wall running north to the property boundary alongside Wilderness Row. This wall was built in 1821, when part of the Wilderness was incorporated into the school playground.[32]

The stretch of cloister alongside the schoolhouse appears on a plan of 1825 by Redmond Pilkington.[33] He shows a narrow passage north of the entrance to the schoolhouse from the cloister—perhaps the old tennis court entrance—and a door at the top end (Ill. 134). In 1847, the Surveyor, Ebenezer Perry, proposed to turn this unused space into a store for shoes and cricket bats.[34] It may originally have had no function other than its structural one of carrying the terrace alongside the tennis court. Drawings made by Timbrell a century earlier suggest that the shoe-room passage may then have been sealed off from the schoolhouse entrance.[35] Gerald Davies recalled that there was 'a considerable portion of one of the cottage cells here', used by the school groom for keeping 'his utensils, and wares which he had for sale'. As with much else, he was vague about it, identifying it in one place as Cell E, in another as either F or G.[36] This store-cupboard may in fact have been Perry's passage; the cell entrance, which belonged to Cell E, is shown on both Pilkington's plan and J. W. Archer's later sketch (Ill. 122). It was similar to that of Cell B, going by a description of 1847 (an 'equilateral arch within a square head, the spandrils being filled by quatrefoils'), but much mutilated.[37] Perry recommended rebuilding the west face of the Norfolk Cloister, but merely the repair and repointing of the east. With his shoe-room idea, this was part of a schedule of proposed repairs and improvements, turned down in favour of cheaper 'temporary' repairs, thus saving the 1570s wall.[38]

The northern half of the cloister was sold along with the rest of the school site to the Merchant Taylors' Company, who took possession in 1872. George Currey, Master of Sutton's Hospital, made some attempt to prevent its demolition, prompted less by antiquarian concern than loss of access to his garden from the terrace, which he had hoped he might continue to use. Edward I'Anson, as the Merchant Taylors' architect, replied that his plans were too far advanced to alter, and that he considered the cloister to be 'of no great age' and not part of the medieval buildings. In fact, he must have been aware of the west wall's age. In 1870, the antiquary and ecclesiologist Mackenzie Walcott noted that the cloister retained three cell doorways, one of them with a 'turn' or serving-hatch (i.e., Cells B, E and G), and this must still have been apparent when I'Anson began work a couple of years later.[39] It is, however, difficult to see how the cloister could have been incorporated into the new school without great inconvenience, because of its blocking the light between the school green and the schoolhouse site (although this fact had not deterred E. W. Trendall years before in his scheme for enlarging the old schoolhouse, as described below). The partial demolition attracted little public attention, though an Old Carthusian and former assistant master, H. W. Phillott, denounced it in a letter to *The Builder* as a needless 'act of barbarity'.[40]

Leading nowhere, the remaining portion now had no use for the Hospital, and it was let to the Merchant Taylors' School at a nominal rent in return for their undertaking to keep it in repair.[41] At the north end, a store-room was created by walling off the last bay and a half (also cutting off access to the old privy garden door), sometime before 1910. The rest provided a sort of pavilion for watching sports on the green. In 1907, a proposal to adapt it as a rifle range was rejected.[42] During the Second World War, the cloister was used for storing corned beef from Smithfield Market, and after the war by students at the Medical College of St Bartholomew's Hospital for parking bicycles, and for storage during restoration of the Great Hall. An early scheme by the architects Seely and Paget to build living accommodation over the terrace was soon abandoned. In the late 1950s, a restoration grant was obtained from the Ministry of Works, on condition of limited public access.[43]

As part of the restoration by Seely and Paget, the doorway and hatch to Cell B were fully revealed, and the floor was lowered to the monastic level, although no trace of the ancient surface remained; the existing intact flagstones were relaid. The iron bars across the vault were hacked out. The chief improvement was the installation of timber-framed windows, designed by Seely after a failed attempt to find an illustration of the originals.[44]

The tennis court

No trace remains today of the Duke of Norfolk's tennis court, which was converted into the original Charterhouse school in 1613–14. It was probably an open walled enclosure, perhaps with a viewing gallery from the terrace over the cloister, an arrangement which would have provided sufficient light. The internal dimensions were 93ft 6ins by 30ft. There was no standard size for tennis courts, but that would have been large enough for 'major' tennis, being comparable in size and proportion to the Tudor courts at Hampton Court and Whitehall Palace. At Howard House there may have been some utilization of existing monastic walls or footings, partly dictating the size of the court, which must have corresponded closely in length to the combined plots of Cells E and F. The rooms shown on Carter's plan at the south end must relate to the school as then proposed, though they may possibly have been existing ancillary rooms.

Tennis was of great importance as a royal and aristocratic game, and features in two of the most famous anecdotes about the duke. One describes a scene in 1565 when he and the Earl of Leicester (despised by Norfolk as a parvenu) were playing before Elizabeth I, probably at Hampton Court. Leicester took a napkin from the queen's hand to mop his face. Outraged at this overfamiliarity, Norfolk threatened to hit him with his racket. In the other, related by William Camden, Norfolk is said to have let the queen know, in a stormy interview in 1569, that when in his tennis court at Norwich 'he thought himself in a manner equal with some kings'.[45]

Norfolk granted a life-hold lease of the Howard House court to Anthony Norton at the nominal rent of 2*s* 6*d* a year, with all 'benefites comodities profits allowances and advantages'—presumably fees or tips from players or payments for services relating to the game. The date of the grant seems to be unrecorded. In July 1578, Philip Howard made out a new grant by way of reward to his groom of the chamber Luke Bateman, to run for Bateman's lifetime after Norton's death. Norton was still alive but had assigned his interest to Humfrey Ward, and Bateman's grant obliged him to allow Ward to keep the court on for 'a reasonable rent' after Norton's death. Accordingly, in 1584 Ward took an assignment of it from Bateman at £6 13*s* 4*d* a year, with a covenant to keep it in repair and let Bateman inspect it with workmen once a year. Bateman also had a 'little tenement' between the back yard and the privy garden, perhaps a house or a store used in connection with the court.[46]

The schoolhouse

Conversion of the tennis court into the schoolhouse in 1613–14 was not carried out as on Carter's plan, which shows a single-storey building, subdivided into a large schoolroom and four smaller rooms, dormitories perhaps, the latter grouped at one end round a central chimneystack. Instead, the walls of the court were raised in height and the whole was roofed over, with a gable at the south end: at the other end, the building abutted a house for the Preacher and Schoolmaster, enlarged from the bathing and banqueting house described in the 1588 inventory and 1590 survey. A first floor was put in, and this and the attic were fitted up as dormitories, the attic

124. Undated scheme, probably 1830s, for enlargement of old schoolhouse and Norfolk Cloister. E. W. Trendall, architect

125. Old schoolhouse, and Schoolmaster's house. From Radclyffe's *Memorials of Charterhouse* (1844)

being lit by gabled dormers along each side. Two stone doorways and 22 stone windows were inserted, this work being carried out by Edmund Kinsman.[47]

On the ground floor were a schoolroom and a smaller hall, 60ft by 30ft and 20ft by 30ft respectively. They were separated by a lobby with a 'fine oak staircase'. Gerald Davies described the schoolroom as 'a really noble room … whose richly decorated ceiling was supported by eight lofty oak columns, square in section. This ceiling divided into panels was decorated with the arms of the first Governors of Charterhouse … It was, of its kind and date, amongst the finest ceilings in England'.[48] The 'upper end' was ornamented with the royal arms. Most of the plasterwork was by Kelham Roades, the coats of arms being supplied by James and Abraham Leigh.[49] Davies, however, would not have known the room at first hand, as he did not start school here until 1856, after it had been subdivided.

Upstairs, the first floor and attic were described in 1750 as 'two long low pitched Rooms one over the other, which are lined with rows of Cabins on both sides with walls made of lath & plaster', and this was probably the original arrangement. Each cabin was occupied by two boys, apparently sharing a bed.[50] These dormitories, where the boys were locked in at night, despite the risk of fire, were in a bad state, the partitions and windows broken and the doors removed: a scene of 'horror and wretchedness'.[51] Benjamin Timbrell recommended demolition, drawing up plans for a new building, as well as for improving the existing one. Repairs were ordered, but only in 1803–5, with the erection of a new schoolhouse (page 70), was the old building substantially improved, with new 'airy' dormitories allowing a bed for each boy.[52] Illustration 119 shows it essentially as altered at that time, the east wall alongside the terrace rebuilt and the attic made into a full second floor. On the ground floor, the large schoolroom was divided into a writing school and a dormitory for senior boys.[53] A picture of the writing school in 1862 shows the room dominated by four massive tapering columns of square section, with Classical capitals.[54]

The Schoolmaster's house was rebuilt in 1829 as part of the improvements to the Hospital designed by Redmond Pilkington (see Chapter IX). This was during the reign of Dr Russell, when the school roll was greatly increased. It was no doubt in response to this increase that the architect E. W. Trendall produced an unlikely scheme for hugely enlarging the schoolhouse with extra

126. Scholars' hall in old schoolhouse, looking north-east, not long before demolition in 1873

floors, and creating a matching block at the north end of the Schoolmaster's house: his plan also suggests wings extending towards Pensioners' Court. The ensemble—institutional-looking in a perfunctorily Tudor style—included an enormous extension of the Norfolk Cloister alongside the proposed new block, sacrificing the possibility of ground-floor windows on that side of the building (Ill. 124). The ground floors of the school blocks were to comprise dining halls, perhaps doubling as classrooms, and the upper floors dormitories for a total of about 150 boys.[55]

With the collapse of Russell's expansionist policy, there was no need for so many beds. But by 1860 improved finances allowed a modest increase in the number of boarders, and in 1862–3 more accommodation, including a buttery and dormitories, was provided in a large extension to the schoolhouse, designed by P. C. Hardwick, on the south side of Scholars' Court, as the area between the schoolhouse and Pensioners' Court was known.[56] Meanwhile, the scholars' hall at the south end of the schoolhouse had been remodelled in the mid-1840s by Edward Blore, the alterations including a new chimney-piece bearing Sutton's motto *Deo Dante Dedi* ('God giving, I gave'), a ceiling, 'adorned with arabesque shields and scrolls', and new supporting pillars.[57] These last were probably removed by Hardwick in his later work on the schoolhouse. The ruthlessly Victorianized hall is shown in Ill. 126.

The schoolhouse (or 'Gownboys') was demolished along with the northern part of the cloister in 1873. Kinsman's west entrance doorway, carved with the names of pupils leaving in the late eighteenth and early nineteenth centuries, was re-erected in the new Charterhouse School at Godalming. A fireplace also found its way to Godalming, where it was installed in the house called Hodgsonites.[58] The Schoolmaster's house and Hardwick's buttery block survived, adapted into the new Merchant Taylors' School described in Chapter XI.

CHAPTER VIII

The Gatehouse and 17 Charterhouse Square

It was at the gate of the Charterhouse that one of Prior Houghton's arms is usually said to have been fixed after his dismemberment at Tyburn in 1535.[u] After two days, the monk Maurice Chauncy relates, the arm fell, was retrieved by two lay brothers and buried, together with Houghton's bloodstained shift, in a chest 'in a secret subterranean place'.[1]

The gateway, with the precinct wall adjoining, was by then well over a century old, having been built on the instruction of two Continental priors sent in 1405 by the general chapter of the order to visit its English province. This physical separation of the priory from the churchyard was particularly intended to keep out women, something which the monks had supposedly hoped to achieve in stages, initially by confining female worshippers at the church to the new chapel of St Anne and Holy Cross at the west end. Public attendance at the church, male and female, was the legacy of its origin as a cemetery chapel, and something which the monks were wary of challenging in case it provoked violent protest (or loss of monetary support) from the townspeople.[2] It had received a fillip from Pope Boniface IX, who in 1399 granted a seven-year indulgence to penitents visiting the priory on the feasts of the Assumption and Annunciation and giving alms for the upkeep of the church. This ordinance specifically allowed women to enter both church and cloister.[3] The wall was also meant to keep the monks in, only the prior and proctor having legitimate occasion to go into the world beyond, after the London monks were denied the *spatiamentum*, or weekly walk outside, by the provincial visitors.[4] Before the gate and wall were built, the priory register records, monks had gone as far as the outer gate of the cemetery in order to meet funerals.[5]

Women may officially have been banned, but laymen continued to attend the church. From the gate they would have crossed the courtyard to a door on the south side of the chapel of St Anne and Holy Cross.[6] But the gate was doubtless situated here less for their convenience than because there was already a footpath or cartway here, going towards the gardens, outbuildings and lay brothers' quarters, partially developed as these must then have been.

Only with the removal of render in the late 1950s did it become certain that the gatehouse is the original, its front continuous with the precinct wall adjoining and faced with the same chequerwork of Reigate stone and knapped flint.[7] It is shown on the fifteenth-century water-supply plan as a building no wider than the gateway itself (lacking the porter's lodge at the side), with a timber-framed upper storey and oriel (Ills. 12, 13). The stonework has been much renewed; an elevation drawn in 1697 (Ill. 127) shows slender shafts below the stops to the arch moulding: the stops have long since been replaced. The oak doors, with pointed panels still retaining some tracery, are probably also original: somewhat shortened because the surrounding ground level has risen. One contains a wicket, with a speaking-grill and an iron lion's-head knocker probably of eighteenth-century date. Gerald Davies, who assumed that the archway itself was a sixteenth-century rebuilding, recorded a Charterhouse tradition that the doors were removed to the main gate from the inner gateway at the west corner of Entrance Court

127. Gatehouse and Physician's house, drawn in 1697

[u] The *Chronicle of Grey Friars*, however, states that it was at the gate into Aldersgate Street, and the inner gateway in Entrance Court is also sometimes assumed to be the place.

128. Gatehouse. Late nineteenth- or early twentieth-century view

(which retains the iron pintles on which they would have hung).[8] This inner gate was probably built in the early sixteenth century to close off the lay portion of the priory, and would have become redundant once the Charterhouse was in secular hands.

The gatehouse is referred to in the monastic accounts of the 1490s as the 'porter's lodge and chambers over', and additional security was evidently provided by dogs, for the accounts also mention kennels in the courtyard for two mastiffs.[9] The Tents Office accounts in the 1540s record the employment of John Ellis as porter at the 'great gate', and a 'note of things at the Charterhouse' in 1580 mentions bedding left at the 'porter's lodge'. However, there is no clue to the building's size and shape after the water-supply drawing until the Crown survey of Howard House in 1590.[10] This gives the dimensions of the 'gatehouse' as 20ft broad (the depth of the gateway) by 75ft long. This would have been essentially the house shown on Kip's view (Ill. 34), although by that time various alterations had taken place (and the building shown appears to be under 75ft wide). The gatehouse, which had been shored up as 'like to fall' in 1614, was allocated as lodgings to Thomas Barker, first Physician to Sutton's Hospital, and then to Barker's son William, who succeeded him in his post. The house was entered by a doorway in the south side of the archway, the porter's lodge being entered by another on the north side (roughly in the place of the present door there), where a room with a large fireplace occupied what is now the pedestrian entrance to Sutton's Hospital. In order for Barker junior to have his wife and family live there with him, the house had to be physically separated from the rest of the Hospital site by blocking up the entrance and making a new one at the front, opening on to Charterhouse Square.[11]

In the 1620s, Barker's successor, Lawrence Wright, was recompensed for repairs or improvements he had carried out to the house, which in 1631 he complained was 'much decayed in the Tymber and other mayne parts'. In 1633, he took on the lease of the house next door, which had been occupied by Sir William Monson (page 55) and then by Thomas Heyward, the first Registrar of Sutton's Hospital. Heyward was allowed to sublet the 'gatehouse'

129. (*right*) Gatehouse and 17 Charterhouse Square in 1997

130. Bracket beneath canopy over gateway

itself to Sir John North, but it remained the official Physician's house, and was rebuilt as such in 1716.[12]

The porter's lodge owes much of its present arrangement to the Surveyor, Ebenezer Perry, who oversaw a major remodelling and partial reconstruction of the building in 1848. Until that time, it comprised two low floors and contained several small rooms. Perry opened up the main room next to the archway, and the space above, to make the present pedestrian entrance from the square.[13] To the rear, a clock was mounted over the doorway, where one of the little upper windows had been. A number of large, peg-like brackets high on the south wall of the pedestrian entrance probably date from this period and are thought to have been for fire-buckets.

Although the front to Charterhouse Square was stripped back to stone and brick as part of the restoration of Sutton's Hospital by the architects Seely and Paget (with a new plain brick surround to the entrance on Charterhouse Square), the back and side of the porter's lodge retain their old stuccoed decorative treatment, with battlements and mechanical details in the 'Tudor' style. This actually predates Perry's work, and was probably introduced by Redmond Pilkington in the 1820s or early 1830s, when the lodge was extended. Outside the carriage entrance, the iron lamp standards, with cannon bases, were bought in 1817, following the installation of gas in Charterhouse Square.[14] The lanterns, though still for gaslight, are not the originals. Inside the arch itself, the protective bollards, labelled 'St James Clerkenwell', have been set in place since the Second World War.'

17 Charterhouse Square

Charles Goodall, who became Physician in 1691, found his new home 'unfitt & inconvenient' and by 1694 had spent £200 on repairs and improvements. After his death in 1713 it was decided that it would be cheaper in the long run to rebuild than to make further repairs. The cost of a new house, together with refurbishment of the porter's lodge, was estimated at about £800. The new Physician, Henry Levett, was willing to put up some of the money, and it was finally agreed in 1716 that he would stand half the cost.[15] The house was built that year, the date being recorded on the rainwater heads.[16]

Levett supplied the plans for the governors' approval, and these may have been drawn up by the hospital's current Surveyor, if there then was one. Westby Gill acted in this capacity in the 1720s and 1730s, but whether his involvement went back to 1716—he was then in his mid-30s—is not known. Whoever designed it, the result was a building perfectly judged to express its dual identity as a part of Sutton's Hospital and a private residence in a well-to-do London square. Unlike the various (now destroyed) eighteenth-century extensions and alterations to the buildings within the gates, including the Master's Court fronts, Levett's house is free from any suggestion of institutional stricture. The façade is executed in mellow, plum-coloured brick, with quoins, gauged window-heads and plain string courses in orange-red. The six bays read as two houses, the three adjoining the gate being slightly set back to allow for a basement area and having slightly taller windows on the first floor than those over the gate. Set close up to the gate, the doorway is in the same position as that of the previous house.

The wooden lion brackets carrying the flat hood over the main gate predate the house and have been attributed to the time of either Lord North or the fourth Duke of Norfolk.[17] The stylized lions, holding cartouches, are similar in execution to the lion finials on the staircase at Hatfield House (*c.*1610), and may be part of the embellishments to Howard House carried out for the Earl of Suffolk about this time or a few years earlier. The hood itself, which may have been reconstructed, is integral with the wooden cornice running across the north half of the

131. (*top*) 17 Charterhouse Square, first-floor landing in 1996
132. (*bottom*) 17 Charterhouse Square, rooms on first floor in 1996

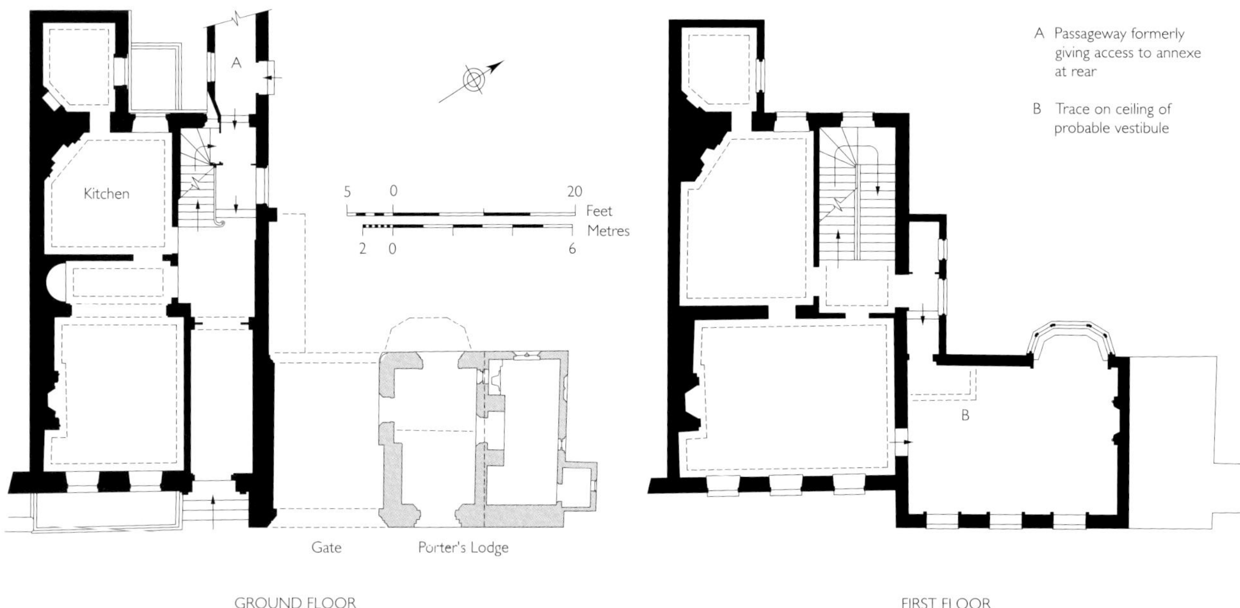

133. 17 Charterhouse Square, ground and first-floor plans in 2009

building. A similar cornice, with the hood and brackets, are shown on the 1697 sketch, and presumably survived because of the demarcation between the house itself, on which Levett was spending his own money, and the gate and lodge, for which he had no responsibility and with which he had no right to interfere.

The house continued to be occupied by successive Physicians to Sutton's Hospital (latterly styled Medical Officers) until the Second World War, though not in unbroken sequence. Matthew Raine, Schoolmaster from 1791, was living there for some years in the early nineteenth century.[18] After the war, it was decided to make it the Master's residence, instead of reinstating him in Master's Court. This break with tradition was made in a convenient interregnum between the death of the old Master, the Rev. Dr Edward Schomberg, in 1952, and the appointment of Canon John Macleod Campbell in 1954. It was in part due to the new Registrar, Norman Long-Brown, who was closely involved in the re-planning of the hospital. A flat for the Medical Officer and his family was provided in what remained of Preacher's Court.[19]

In general, the house has been little altered, the only significant exterior change being the addition in 1907 of the oriel window at the back of the first-floor room over the gate, looking on to Entrance Court. This was designed by the Hospital's surveyor, Herbert Steward.[20] Inside, the open-string staircase, the panelling and probably the plaster cornices in the principal rooms are original. In the ground-floor dining room the marble chimneypiece is probably that installed by George Burnill in 1753.[21] On the first floor, the chimneypiece in the west room was probably reinstalled here from elsewhere, as it carries a monogram not relating to any of the Physicians or other senior officers. The entrance passage was fitted with a screen at the far end in 1831; the doors to this have since been removed, but the fanlight remains.[22]

At the rear of the house is a two-storey building which must be the 'back office' insured for £40 in 1716. It was originally detached from the house but connected to it in the middle of the nineteenth century by a corridor. The building's exact purpose is uncertain. It appears to have had a great deal of natural light. Four large window openings occupying most of the side elevation to Entrance Court have long been blocked, as has the middle one of the first-floor windows on the front. Since the war the building has been walled off from the house and corridor. It has recently been leased to the Paviors' Company and refurbished as its administrative headquarters.[23]

CHAPTER IX

Pensioners' Court and Preacher's Court

Between 1825 and the early 1840s, the area north-west of Wash-house Court underwent complete transformation. The accretions of buildings around the privy garden and Great Court made way for new accommodation for pensioners and staff around two large courtyards. At the west corner, the stables and other ancillary buildings were also rebuilt. The original schoolhouse survived, but the enlarged and adapted Schoolmaster's house at its north end was pulled down and rebuilt. Other staff houses were also replaced. Much of this rebuilding survives today, but much else has been altered or demolished, through the redevelopment of the school site for Merchant Taylors' School in the 1870s, and more extensively through the restoration of Sutton's Hospital in the 1950s.

Reconstruction on this scale became necessary on account of the character and dilapidation of the existing buildings. In any case, they held none of the historical associations which have served to preserve the main ranges of Howard House from demolition, even after severe damage. However, the work would have been impossible without the great increase in revenue enjoyed by the charity at this time, and the efforts of one man: Archdeacon William Hale Hale (1795–1870). Hale became Master in 1842 and retained the post until his death. His practical influence at the Charterhouse went back to 1823, when he was appointed Preacher during the Mastership of Philip Fisher, a scholar who left much of the administrative burden of the post to his deputies, latterly to Hale.[1] It was Hale who both brought the establishment more or less up to date and subsequently defended it against well-meant but, to some extent, misinformed criticism.

Architecturally, the work was first in the hands of Redmond William Pilkington, who succeeded his father William as Surveyor in 1824, and later those of Edward Blore. Ebenezer Perry, brought in to install new drains in 1832, had a humbler role in overseeing lesser works during much of this period of change, and remained Surveyor until his death in 1850, when he was succeeded by his son George.[2] Of the two main architects, neither Pilkington nor Blore displayed great flair or originality, but Pilkington's overall conception was sound, and his forced resignation was not due to any serious failure of his scheme. Blore was brought in to complete the redevelopment, and in style and planning he had little to add, though his work here, including his quite interesting treatment of the junction between the new and ancient buildings, has been unnecessarily destroyed. So too has much of the extensive, mostly cosmetic work of embellishing and restyling which he carried out elsewhere in the buildings.

In Hale's words, the pensioners' quarters by the early 1820s were no better than 'an undisciplined workhouse', and the redevelopment was accompanied by a transformation in the institutional regime.[3] Rebuilding had been under discussion as early as 1813, and in 1820 plans were drawn up by William Pilkington for new buildings immediately north of Wash-house Court, on the site of the privy garden and the west part of the Great Court. Three detached blocks of pensioners' rooms (80 in all, accounting for all pensioners) were to make up three sides of a quadrangle, the fourth being provided by servants' or other staff houses built against the Norfolk Cloister.[4]

New plans by Redmond Pilkington (Ill. 134), deriving from this scheme but on a grander scale, were carried out in stages from the summer of 1825, and in the following year a large quantity of salvage from the old buildings, including bricks, roof tiles, panelling, chimneypieces and paving, was disposed of at auction.[5] The new plans called for the obliteration of the three main ranges of pensioners' rooms (the Howard House stables, the Wren–Woodroffe building and the old bowling alley), the stables and several houses built for members of staff. The layout also involved closure of the original burial ground and its extension of 1817 immediately to the north, the space being incorporated into the northern of two new quadrangles. A replacement burial ground was provided north of the new buildings.[6] The quadrangles came to be known as Pensioners' Court and Preacher's Court, but were originally referred to simply as the north and south quadrangles and are shown as such on a plan as late as 1863.[7] A subsidiary court, later called Scholars' Court, was formed between the east range of the north quadrangle and the old schoolhouse. Preacher's Court, to the south, was not completed as originally intended, and never acquired a south range.

The main structural work was carried out by William Webb (bricklayer), John Barton (mason) and David Freeman (carpenter).[8] First to be built were stables, coach-

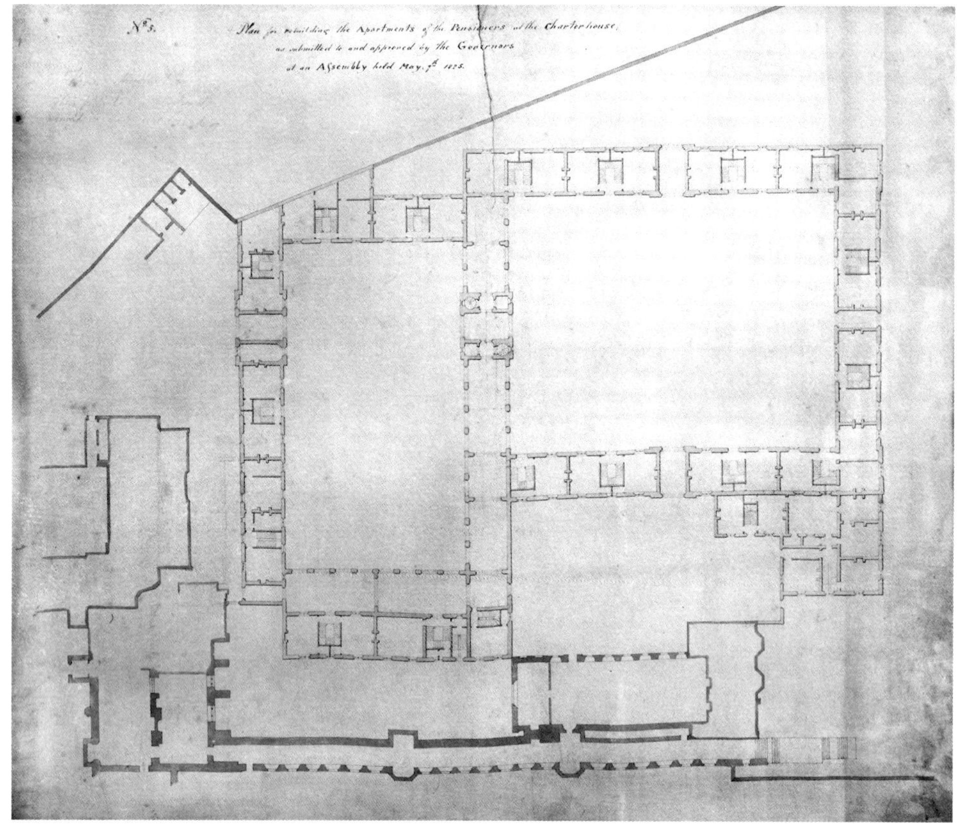

134. Plan by Redmond Pilkington for Pensioners' and Preacher's Courts, *c.*1824 (North is to the right)

houses, workshops, stores and houses for the cook, butler and laundress. These occupied a long triangular plot at the edge of the site, west of the north quadrangle.[9] Later, in 1839, one of the houses was converted into an infirmary for boys with infectious disease.[10] It was demolished with other parts of this group when the northernmost strip of the ground (including part of the burial ground and Master's Garden) was taken for the construction of Clerkenwell Road in the late 1860s; the remainder survives as Stable Court, the coach-houses and stables having since been converted into garages and staff accommodation.

Pensioners' Court was begun shortly after the stabling, and a view of it was exhibited by Pilkington at the Royal Academy in 1827.[11] It comprises one-room-deep, two-storey ranges in the Tudor style then thought particularly appropriate for such institutional buildings, regardless of their historical antecedents. The strictly orthogonal planning, simplified, repetitive detail and pale-yellow brick convey the sense of efficiency within a tight budget; the loss of the original battlemented parapets in the 1950s, however, in favour of low eaves under slate, spoils the formality of the style, making the paraphernalia of hoodmoulds seem superfluous. The most interesting part of the ensemble was the cross-range dividing the two quadrangles, where the ground floor was given over to a fine arcade (now glazed in and subdivided), with a central gatehouse to admit carriages, rarely as this can have been needed. Two winding staircases, placed diagonally at front and rear corners of the gatehouse, were crowned by turrets, one with a bell rung before meal-times.[12] The effect was possibly a little odd, and as early as 1857 the Surveyor, George Perry, was looking for a reason to remove the 'two unsightly Turret erections', on the grounds that they caused the fireplaces in the rooms below to smoke. The north turret was subsequently demolished; the other survived and was rebuilt in 1985.[13]

Little in the way of ornamentation was called for to relieve the façades: simply carvings in the arch spandrels of the entrances to Preacher's Court, Scholars' Court and Stable Yard (the Sutton arms) and to the new burial ground (slightly naive skulls and crossbones). The courtyard was laid out with gravel walks and grass, with a large lamp standard in the centre.[14]

Most of the pensioners' rooms were arranged in groups of four around a common staircase. Each had a fireplace and a closet or recess. Originally, the entrances to the staircases from the courtyard were open, but doors were fitted in the mid-1840s to make the stairs less cold and draughty.[15]

Work on Preacher's Court to the south began in 1828, in the same Tudor style, beginning with the east range, of which about two-thirds was completed to Pilkington's design. This block, only the north half of which survives, is three storeys high and two rooms deep, with a ground-floor arcade in continuation of the cross-range. It contained the Preacher's residence, and rooms for sick or infirm pensioners and the woman who attended them.[16] The northern part of the west range, which also survives, was begun in 1829. It is of three storeys, but only one room deep and has no arcade. The new houses for the Scholars' Matron and Schoolmaster were built in the same year, the latter a late addition to the scheme.[17]

The exact circumstances in which the programme came to a halt in 1830 are unclear, but they obviously had something to do with the personalities of the architect and his effective patron, the Preacher, William Hale. The governors' decision against more building for the time being was ostensibly on grounds of cost, but it was really the consequence of Hale's criticism of the work so far. According to Pilkington, no complaints had been voiced about the buildings until, in May that year, Hale (acting out of a self-declared 'sense of public duty alone') suddenly 'opened a full and general denunciation of the whole work that had been done under my direction, bad alike as to character, workmanship, and material'. The architect Joseph Kay, surveyor to the Foundling Hospital and clerk of works to Greenwich Hospital, was asked to make a survey of the Preacher's house, and then of all the new buildings.[18] Kay did find some evidence of poor workmanship and materials, including defective party walls and flues in the Schoolmaster's house, and was mildly critical of the interior joinery. Perhaps the most serious faults were in the Matron's house, where the cellar was waterlogged and there were problems with the sanitation.[19] (This was apparently to do with a parallel programme to replace the old drainage system, which Pilkington was never able to carry out. Instead, Ebenezer Perry was brought in, designing a more sophisticated and expensive system than Pilkington had planned.) But Pilkington was able to mount a thorough and essentially convincing defence of his work, with testimonies from expert witnesses in support of both design and workmanship, and he exposed Hale's ignorance of building matters with relish. Part of the trouble seems to have stemmed from his refusal to allow certain changes to the work without express approval from the governors. There was, too, a sub-plot of disgruntlement on the part of the hospital's own bricklayers, Henry Munn and William Elston, who had not been allowed to tender for all stages of the work; and Pilkington may have been correct in asserting that the petition they got up (asking that they be allowed to tender for future works and that a clerk of works be appointed to

135. Preacher's Court, looking north-east, late nineteenth or early twentieth century

136. Preacher's Court, undated view looking south-east, before 1941 fire. Left to right: Manciple's house range, pensioners' entrance and west window of Great Chamber (Edward Blore, architect, 1840–1); gabled front of scullery and cook's apartment (George Perry, surveyor, 1872); north range of Wash-house Court

prevent disputes) bore the marks of a put-up job.[20] The upshot was that Pilkington resigned and payment of certain bills was delayed while defects were put right, the dispute dragging on for some while. The final cost of Pilkington's new buildings came to £46,319 5*s* 1*d*, including his own fees.[21]

In July 1834, the rebuilding project resumed, with Edward Blore appointed to draw up plans for its completion.[22] Blore came up with designs for a three-storey south range to Preacher's Court, two rooms deep, enclosing a shallower courtyard than that planned by Pilkington. It was set aside. In 1838, Ebenezer Perry was asked to prepare plans for completing Preacher's Court. Work was deferred, chiefly because of expenditure on the Great Chamber that year. Perry's scheme also was set aside, and in 1839 Blore was asked for fresh designs for the west side of the court, which were duly executed.[23]

What Blore came up with was a slightly more decorative version of Pilkington's existing block, stepped forward in response to the kink in the site boundary at this point (Ill. 137). The Master's (Philip Fisher's) initials and the date 1840 were carved over the door.[24] The building (demolished after the Second World War) was contracted for by the firm of Locke & Nesham, who went on to execute Blore's subsequent work in Preacher's Court and elsewhere at Sutton's Hospital. It provided two-roomed apartments for three pensioners on each floor. One (on the ground floor, left of the entrance) was the model for Colonel Newcome's room in *The Newcomes*. It was then occupied by Captain Thomas Light, whom Thackeray visited when writing the final chapters. When the building was demolished after the Second World War, the fireplace and other fittings from the room were installed at the south end of Master's Court, in the first-floor room in the bay looking out onto Charterhouse Square. A commemorative tablet mounted under the window of Light's room has been reset in the Admiral Ashmore Building, which occupies the site of Blore's range, close to its old position.

Plans by Blore for completing the east side of Preacher's Court were approved in 1840 and the work was finished the following year, entirely closing off the former privy garden.[25] The new extension, which had been intended for a dispensary, linen room and under-housekeeper's apartment, was in the end fitted up for the Manciple. As he was a single man, the second floor was left incomplete, remaining so until the appointment of a married successor in 1854.[26]

On the face of it, the decision—whether on aesthetic or cost grounds—not to have a south cross-range to close Preacher's Court, as Pilkington had originally proposed, seems a bad one. Pilkington's plan had at least been devised to avoid too detrimental an effect on the historic buildings to the south, but now Blore's extension butted right up against the Great Chamber, entirely blocking the window in the north alcove there. As this was not a well-lit room, a replacement was essential, and the west wall offered the only possible place for it. Blore's new window was large but heavily mullioned and transomed, in keeping with the old windows in the Great Chamber. Externally, it was crowned by Gothic ornamentation and a rather feeble pediment with the inevitable Sutton arms, the best that he could do to express the importance of the room behind. For the rest, Blore continued Pilkington's arcade, breaking forward slightly to suggest a gate tower, with an oriel window. Under the Great Chamber window, however, he had to reduce the arcade to little more than a shallow porch so as not to block the window to the ancient Great Kitchen, one identifiable feature among a jumble of openings and accretions along the north side of Washhouse Court (Ill. 90). This corner was not fully sorted out until the rebuilding of the kitchen by George Perry in 1872. It was not an easy problem to resolve (Ill. 136). The work of both Blore and Perry was ruthlessly excised by Seely and Paget.

Pensioners' Court and Preacher's Court survived essentially unaltered until Seely and Paget's restoration. But there was some modification and modernization. An early change, to the east range, concerned the extra ventilation needed with the introduction of gas. Modifications to the basement of the Preacher's house, as it then was, were made following his complaint in 1861 that, because of the lowish ceilings and low setting of the casements in the (iron-framed) windows, a servant in the kitchen was obliged to work with her head in hot, fume-laden air. The floor was lowered, conventional sash-windows fitted, and a full basement area opened up. Other basements were

137. Preacher's Court, late nineteenth or early twentieth century, looking north-west. On the left is Edward Blore's addition to Redmond Pilkington's buildings, demolished after the Second World War. The plaque commemorating Thackeray's visits to Captain Light was put up under the window left of the doorway

138. Pensioners' Court, looking north-west, late nineteenth or early twentieth century. Entrance to burial ground on right, beneath creeper

subsequently modified in the same way.[27] New baths were installed in 1915, and electric lighting was adopted in the 1920s, many years after it had first been contemplated on safety grounds: though there was some gas lighting, many pensioners were still using candles or oil lamps.[28]

The buildings survived the Second World War largely undamaged, and this was no cause for celebration on the part of those responsible for the post-war reinstatement of Sutton's Hospital. On the contrary, there was from the start a strong animus against these relics of what had long been seen as a particularly barren period of architecture. (The writer Augustus Hare, in his *Walks in London*, first published in 1878, dismissed Preacher's Court and Pensioners' Court as 'miserable works of *Blore*'—Pilkington had already been forgotten.) Sir Charles Peers, whose 1943 report on the Charterhouse buildings was the starting point for the eventual restoration under Seely and Paget, had no good word to say for the buildings. He declared that they should be demolished, regardless of the fact that their replacement would not attract a farthing from the War Damage Commission. The Master of the day was in agreement. Even the sentimental associations with Colonel Newcome could not overcome his antipathy to Blore's west range, 'by far the most inconvenient and also the ugliest' of the pensioners' quarters.[29] The architects, too, were determined to destroy the nineteenth-century ranges, justifying the demolition of Blore's on the grounds that they were of no merit and more use as a source of timber and fittings than as standing structures.

This may have been nonsense, but the prevailing contempt for nineteenth-century architecture was such that it carried the day, despite second thoughts on the part of the Hospital. The Blore ranges were pulled down in 1949 and 1951. Once it became apparent that the adjoining Pilkington ranges of Preacher's Court must be retained on cost grounds, Seely and Paget at first wanted to remove the top floors, reducing the buildings to the height of the cross-range. Instead, the buildings were simply repaired, and at Paget's insistence windows were made in the

139. Pensioners' Court in 2000, looking north-west, showing post-war alterations by Seely and Paget

exposed south ends to improve their appearance.[30] A flat for the Physician was provided in the east range, so that the Physician's house at 17 Charterhouse Square could become the new Master's Lodge.

With improvements to the garden in Preacher's Court, including rock gardens to disguise the entrances to air-raid shelters, new beds, a dwarf wall and a pergola, the space took on a much more informal appearance than hitherto. In the 1970s, under the direction of the Master, Oliver Van Oss, the appearance of Preacher's Court, Pensioners' Court and the old burial ground (by then the Master's Garden), were further transformed by an ambitious scheme of ornamental planting, some of which remains.[31]

The more extensive Pensioners' Court, which had been used in part for storing the contents of the war-damaged buildings,[32] had to be dealt with after Preacher's Court. Statutory power was obtained to allow the restored buildings to be let commercially,[33] and in 1956 the buildings were converted into flats, maisonettes and offices, with garages in the cloister arcade.[34] Roofs, parapets and chimneys had survived the war in poor condition, and for reasons of cost or taste the buildings were re-roofed with eaves instead of parapets, but the London County Council insisted that elevations should be otherwise unaltered, with no external plumbing added.[35] Careful tenant selection, property management and restrictive clauses in leases (no mats to be shaken after 9 a.m., and never out of windows) were intended to produce an Albany-like atmosphere.[36]

Admiral Ashmore Building

The Admiral Ashmore Building actually consists of two separate buildings, large and small, on the west and south sides of Preacher's Court. They were built in 1999–2000, providing flats for additional Brothers and freeing the entrance range to Pensioners' Court for conversion into an infirmary. The name commemorates the Admiral of the Fleet Sir Edward Ashmore, chairman of the governors of Sutton's Hospital from 1981 to 1996.

140. Preacher's Court in 2001, looking north-west: the Admiral Ashmore Building

New building on this scale was made possible by the rise in the Hospital's income in the late twentieth century. After the war, it had been assumed that 45 pensioners at most could be maintained, and by the late 1970s the number fell below 30. But by 1990 revenues had risen 40-fold since 1960 and expansion was possible. The west side of Preacher's Court, where successive generations of buildings had stood since the fourteenth century, offered the only obvious site for new accommodation. Only the cellars under Blore's building survived here, utilized in the early 1950s for storing heating oil but redundant since the adoption of gas-fired boilers.

What might have been a simple commission to earlier generations proved a difficult problem at the turn of the twenty-first century. How to reconcile the style of a new building so close to the dissimilar styles of the sixteenth-century Wash-house Court and the early nineteenth-century Preacher's Court? Initial designs were intended to harmonize with Preacher's Court and another was prepared subsequently in a cottage-like style intended not to detract from Wash-house Court.

None of the early designs having proved acceptable, Michael Hopkins & Partners were commissioned. Their solution was a four-storey building on the west side and a smaller, three-storey block on the south side, where the drive widened to enter the court. Both eventually had to be reduced by one storey, to lessen their impact on neighbouring buildings outside the Charterhouse.

While the arrangement of the blocks seems ideal, the external appearance is severely plain, perhaps to avoid competing with the neighbouring buildings. They are of red brick, in deference to Wash-house Court, with colonnaded walkways on the ground floors facing the court, perpetuating the tradition of the cloister at the Charterhouse. Beyond that, they have no particular affinity with the earlier buildings, being essentially minimal neo-Georgian, with bare parapets and without modelling and recession in the façades. Internally, the arrangement bears some similarity to the collegiate layout of Pensioners' Court, with pairs of apartments on either side of a central stairway; the south block includes a common room on the ground floor.

CHAPTER X

Rutland House

When Lord North wrote of his 'house in Charterhouse Yarde', he was probably referring not to the future Howard House but to another house fronting the north side of Charterhouse churchyard.[1] This second house was retained by the North family when the great mansion itself was sold to the Duke of Norfolk in 1565. It had a history of being divided and reunited, but was permanently made into one in 1631, under the name Rutland House. By that time it comprised a collection of buildings and outbuildings extending from Howard House to Aldersgate Street, though the core of the house remained along the north side of Charterhouse Yard, or Square. Rutland House has one particular claim to fame. Sir William Davenant's *The Siege of Rhodes*, long regarded as the first English opera, was staged there in 1656.[2] It was no grand venue: the room where the performance took place, somewhere at the Aldersgate Street end, was awkward and cramped.

The precise origins of Rutland House are obscured by the difficulty of identifying houses in which North had an interest, variously described in the sixteenth century as being within the priory or the priory precinct; or in the churchyard, which was outside the priory itself but could be considered as inside the (outer) precinct. The site of Rutland House was entirely within the inner precinct. One of the two component houses must have originated as the former Prior's House, built in the early 1490s, for the Bishop of Lincoln and occupied after the suppression of the priory by Alvise Bassano (pages 28, 35). The other was no doubt built by North, and may be identified as the house at the east end of the Charterhouse described as newly built in a deed of 1563. It was, according to one account, 'prepared' for the use of his second wife should he have predeceased her (they married about 1561, not long after the first Lady North died in 1560).[3] The 1563 deed also refers to another house, then or lately occupied by Nicholas Heath, Professor of Divinity (presumably the deprived Archbishop of York). By this time, North had long since gained vacant possession of the Bassanos' cells and other buildings at the south-east corner of the priory, and it is possible therefore that Heath's house was the former Prior's House.[4]

North's son Roger, the second Lord North, added to or partly rebuilt the buildings on the Rutland House site in 1576, the bills for brickwork, masonry, roof-tiling, glazing, plastering and paving coming to £213 7*s* 6*d*. If he had done any previous building there, it is unrecorded: his pre-1575 accounts do not survive.[5] Roger North died in December 1600 'at his house called the Charterhouse', and the property passed to his grandson Dudley North, then still a minor. Dudley, who was married that year, took up residence, but spent much of the next couple of years with the English forces in the Netherlands.[6] He was plagued by depression, and one activity that he took up between then and about 1607 (when he was 25) in an attempt to shake it off, was building: 'I chose to entertaine my mind to build in dividing my *London* house where (in al events) there would be least losse, and then I lived many years in the lesser part'.[7] The greater part he let to Roger Manners, fifth Earl of Rutland. In his personal reflections, North also recorded 'an unhappy accident of the greater house at [Charterhouse] turned into my hands, at such time when I was thoroughly resolved for thrift'.[8]

The Earl of Rutland had been released from the Tower in August 1601, having been imprisoned for involvement in the Earl of Essex's rebellion. A Catholic, he was one of a number of Essex's supporters to receive help from the uncle of Thomas Howard (the future Earl of Suffolk), Henry, Earl of Northampton. Thomas obtained his grant of Howard House that year, and it may have been through Northampton that Rutland's tenancy of the neighbouring house was arranged. Rutland's estates had been confiscated and he had been heavily fined, so rented accommodation was a necessity. The family accounts contain entries for cleaning the place and transporting his things there from the Tower. He could not have taken up residence at once, for until January 1602 he was effectively under house arrest at his uncle Roger Manners' residence at Uffington, Lincolnshire. But he was living there in November, paying a yearly rent of £100. After his death in 1612, his brother Francis, the sixth earl, gave up the tenancy, which may have been the 'unhappy accident' to which Dudley North referred, although the family were apparently still in residence the following summer.[9]

Dudley's son, also Dudley, the politician and writer who became the fourth Baron North, was born at the Charterhouse in late 1602, and the inventory of the (lesser) house made in 1608 includes a nursery with a red-upholstered high chair which must have been his or a sibling's.[10]

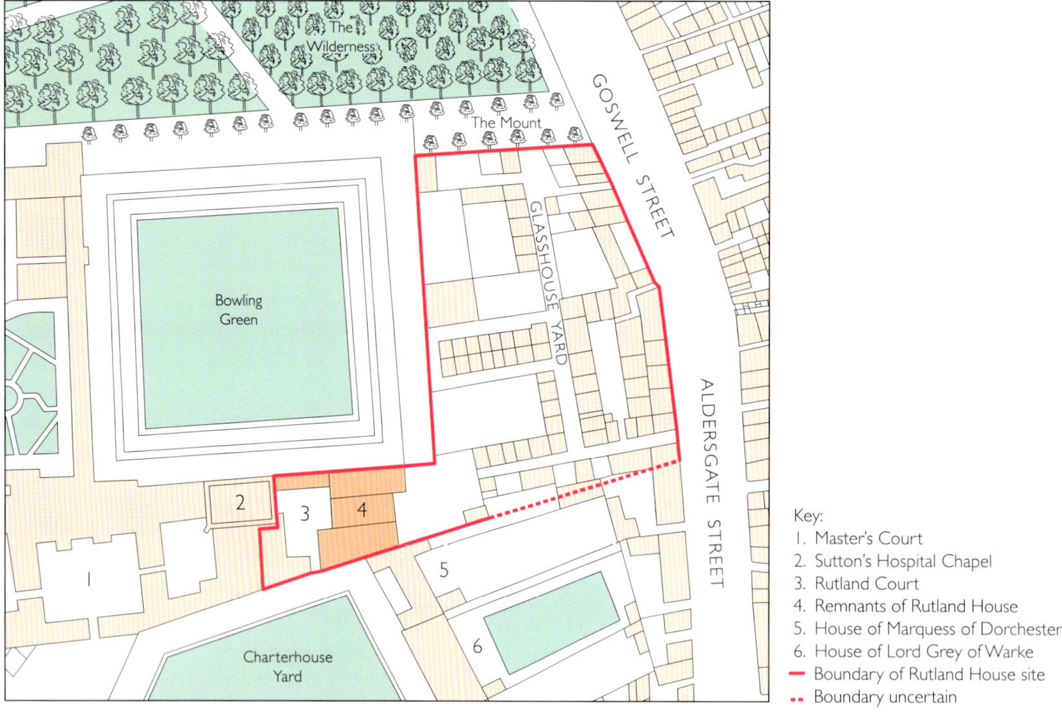

141. Rutland House site after the Restoration, showing small houses etc in and around Glasshouse Yard. Redrawn from Ogilby and Morgan's map of 1676

The property remained two distinct houses, both substantial enough to be described as 'capital messuages or mansion houses' when, in January 1631, they were bought for £4,500 by the sixth Earl of Rutland, from the third Lord North and his son. North was still living in the smaller house himself, and the other was in the occupation of Sir Christopher Nevill.[11] Thereafter, the houses were brought together as Rutland House. On the sixth earl's death in 1632 Rutland House passed on a life interest to his widow, Cicely, who occupied it until she died in 1654, the freehold passing in due course to the earl's grandson, George Villiers, second Duke of Buckingham, a royalist whose estate was sequestrated. In 1650, the Committee for Compounding ordered the seizure of the countess's plate and household goods there, and in the following year sold the reversion to George Thorn and John Hopkins, who took possession on her death. At this point Sutton's Hospital briefly considered buying the property, which would have reunited the old priory precinct.[12]

It is difficult to obtain much of an impression of Rutland House other than that it was a sprawling agglomeration of buildings, less coherent than Howard House. Like Howard House it seems to have had little architectural and stylistic formality, perhaps reflecting the third Lord North's attitude to building:

> I hold the same opinion of Verses as of Ayres in Musick, or Houses, that let them bee delightfull and pleasant to the first appearance with conveniency to the designe, and for the fantasticated rules of Art, Architecture, and proportion, let them observe that list: and commonly who most affects them, most faile in the generall delightfulnesse and use.[13]

Besides the 1608 inventory, there is one made of the late sixth Earl of Rutland's goods there in 1634. More than 40 rooms are listed, including a hall, great chamber (served by 'great stairs') and gallery, mostly furnished well but not extravagantly. The hall itself contained little more than three old forms; more forms, a court cupboard and a couple of tables were contained in a parlour within the hall. There was a dining room on the first floor, on the other side of the stairhead from the great chamber. The gallery contained only a few pictures, which included a descent from the cross and one of Mary Magdalene washing the Saviour's feet, both large paintings, and portraits of 'Mr Tresham' and Jocelyn Percy.[14]

Little of this can be tied to the depictions of the buildings on maps and in views of the Charterhouse generally.

Deeds show that the gallery ran along the south front of the house, over the gateway on Charterhouse Square, just to the west of where the entrance to Rutland Place now is.[15] On the west side of the gate, partly under the gallery, was a vaulted structure described as a 'cloister' or cellars, possibly the 'cellar' described in the inventory as next to the laundry. This may have been of monastic origin, for Robert Smythe in the early nineteenth century writes of there being remnants of the priory in Rutland Court.[16] (Rutland Court was the predecessor of Rutland Place, in a slightly different position.) It is not clear whether it can have been the 'Cloyster goeing to the garden' listed in the 1608 inventory, when it contained a settle at either end and unspecified maps and pictures. It is more likely that the 1608 cloister was a garden gallery somewhere further east, where it would have been nearer the open ground along Aldersgate Street.

The Siege of Rhodes, relating the defeat and expulsion from Rhodes of the Knights Hospitallers by the Ottoman Turks under Suleiman the Magnificent in 1522, was the most ambitious of a series of theatrical and musical entertainments held at Rutland House from May 1656. Its originator and promoter, Sir William Davenant, described it as 'a representation by the Art of perspective in Scenes', with a narrative sung as recitative to musical accompaniment; as with the other 'representations', its form was contrived so as to evade the Puritan ban on overtly dramatic performances. The backdrops were the work of Inigo Jones's former assistant, the architect John Webb. The room where it was staged, described in the title to the first printed edition (1656) as being in 'the back part of Rutland House in the upper end of Aldersgate Street', was a far cry from the purpose-built theatre near the Charterhouse which Davenant and his partner William Cutler had planned to build. They had promoted this on a joint-stock basis that February, trying to raise £4,400 in sixteen shares of £275, but failed to get enough investors to complete the work. Instead, a room at Rutland House had to serve. Descriptions and Webb's own drawings fail to give a clear picture, but the stage was at the end of a relatively long and narrow room, with the musicians concealed by drapes in some kind of high-level gallery, described as a 'louver hole'. The stage itself, raised three feet, was 11ft high, 22ft 4in wide and 15ft deep. It was, going by Webb's drawings for the rather deeper stage at the Cockpit theatre in Drury Lane, to which the *Siege of Rhodes* transferred, simply provided with a mixture of fixed and movable scenery. At the Cockpit, where the Rutland House scenery would have been reused, there were three pairs of fixed wings and a series of removable back shutters. Webb's Rutland House frontispiece, of which an elevation by Webb survives, would also have been adapted for reuse at the Cockpit.[17] The seating, said to be for as many as 400, was cramped and arranged along the sides, facing across the room or at an angle.[18]

With the Restoration, the second Duke of Buckingham regained possession of Rutland House, using the garden as the site of an unsuccessful manufactory of rock-crystal glassware in association with the French glassmaker John de la Cam.[19] Having failed to sell the property, he relinquished it to his creditor John Eaton, a mercer. Eaton sold a half share, for £900, to a resident of Charterhouse Square, James Nelthorpe. As the price suggests, the time for private mansions in this area was well past, and Rutland House itself was soon broken up among various tradesmen owners, and the gardens were built over with little houses. The Presbyterian minister Matthew Sylvester lived in part of Rutland House in the 1680s, holding religious meetings there with the assistance of the elderly Richard Baxter. But the congregation declined after Baxter's death in 1691 and Sylvester left Rutland House the following year.[20]

Rutland House disappeared by stages. Most of the eastern part of the site had been redeveloped by the time of Ogilby and Morgan's map of 1676. The old (Prior's House) part west of the entrance from the square, which had been acquired by James Nelthorpe's brother, Sir Goddard, was replaced by two completely new houses (13 and 14 Charterhouse Square) in 1688.[21] The range on the other side of the gateway, left by James to his son John in 1696, was probably rebuilt or remodelled in the eighteenth century. The building here was finally demolished in 1825 for the creation of Rutland Place and Day Boys' Lodge (see page 76). This building, the work of the headmaster of Charterhouse School, John Russell, survives at least vestigially, having been remodelled by Edward I'Anson in the 1870s as the porter's lodge of Merchant Taylors' School (see page 181). For the rest, Rutland House has left no trace, and its site no longer makes any claim to be considered part of the Charterhouse.

142. Former Merchant Taylor's School Headmaster's house (now Dean Rees House), Rutland Place entrance and porter's lodge. View from the north, 2009

143. Detail of frieze on front of former Headmaster's house

CHAPTER XI

Merchant Taylors' School

In May 1866, the decision was finally taken to move Charterhouse School out to the country (see page 75). Arrangements for the disposal of the 5½-acre school site followed swiftly. Offer of first refusal having in effect been given to the Merchant Taylors' Company, which wanted the site for its own school, negotiations over price were soon concluded. The company's offer fell far below the hoped-for £120,000, and in July the figure of £90,000 was agreed, without restrictions as to future development. But it was six years before the Company could take possession of most of the ground, because Charterhouse School had to find itself a new site and erect the necessary buildings.

Like Charterhouse, Merchant Taylors' School had come under the scrutiny of the Clarendon Commission on public schools, which recognized the importance of keeping such day schools in the metropolis.[1] It too found itself having to choose between finding a new home and improving its existing accommodation, built on a cramped site in Suffolk Lane in the City, blighted by industrial pollution. It was a difficult decision, and the offer of the much larger Charterhouse site, with its spacious playground, tipped the balance in favour of moving.[2] So extensive was the site that it was possible for a large portion (two acres) to be given over to commercial development, raising funds for new school buildings. Accordingly, in 1868, the Merchant Taylors' Company took a first tranche of ground, alongside Wilderness Row, which they let on building leases, mostly for warehousing, and eventually sold.[3] The development coincided with the widening of Wilderness Row as the eastern end of the new Clerkenwell Road.[4] The company acquired the remainder of the site in June 1872, by which time their surveyor, Edward I'Anson junior, an old boy, had drawn up preliminary plans for the school.[5]

At first it was intended only to adapt the existing buildings, but the plans were later revised on much more ambitious lines. Most of the existing buildings were then demolished and replaced by a large range on the west side of the green, on the site of the Writing School and the northern half of the Norfolk Cloister. The Schoolmaster's House, refaced and re-fenestrated, and the recent buttery building were absorbed into this range, adapted as classrooms and a library. Two gate lodges were also provided: one on the north side of the green at the bottom of Foresters' Hall Place, linked to the new building by a cloister, and one on the south at the top of Rutland Place, a major remodelling of Day Boys' Lodge (page 76). In Rutland Place, the former Usher's house of Charterhouse School was allocated to the headmaster, and the smaller house next door adapted as bachelor accommodation for under-masters.[6] The Duke of Edinburgh laid the foundation stone of the new school in June 1873, and it was formally opened by the Prince of Wales on 6 April 1875. Browne & Robinson of Worship Street were the builders.[7]

Assembly hall building

Although best known for his pioneering office buildings in the City, I'Anson had a large practice and worked in a variety of styles. The idiom he used here was a Franco-Flemish Gothic, in other words the Gothic normally employed for public schools at the time, with an added mercantile tinge. The high point of his design was the main building largely comprising the assembly hall. Built of red Suffolk bricks, copiously dressed with Portland stone relieved by some touches of terracotta, it dominated the playground and towered above the rest of the Charterhouse behind. The row of nine plate-traceried windows lighting the first-floor hall, the dormers in the steeply pitched roof, the Ypres-style tourelles at the corners and the exaggerated height of the flèche on the roof all added to the tone of a Flemish guildhall. This building was among the grandest school and college halls of its period. Yet it also contrived to look isolated and lifeless, perhaps because of rigid symmetry and lack of relief along the front, apart from a first-floor balcony on brackets over the Aberdeen granite columns of the triple entrance. Only the gabled classroom block set back to its north helped give the context it needed.

The ground floor of the hall block was taken up by a spacious entrance hall communicating left and right with large classrooms (the Mathematical School and Writing Room), and at the back by a corridor leading to classrooms in the wings. All the upper portion was taken up by the hall itself, imposing in its dimensions (93ft by 50ft) and endowed with an open timber roof and a vast traceried window filling the south end. It was the roof which

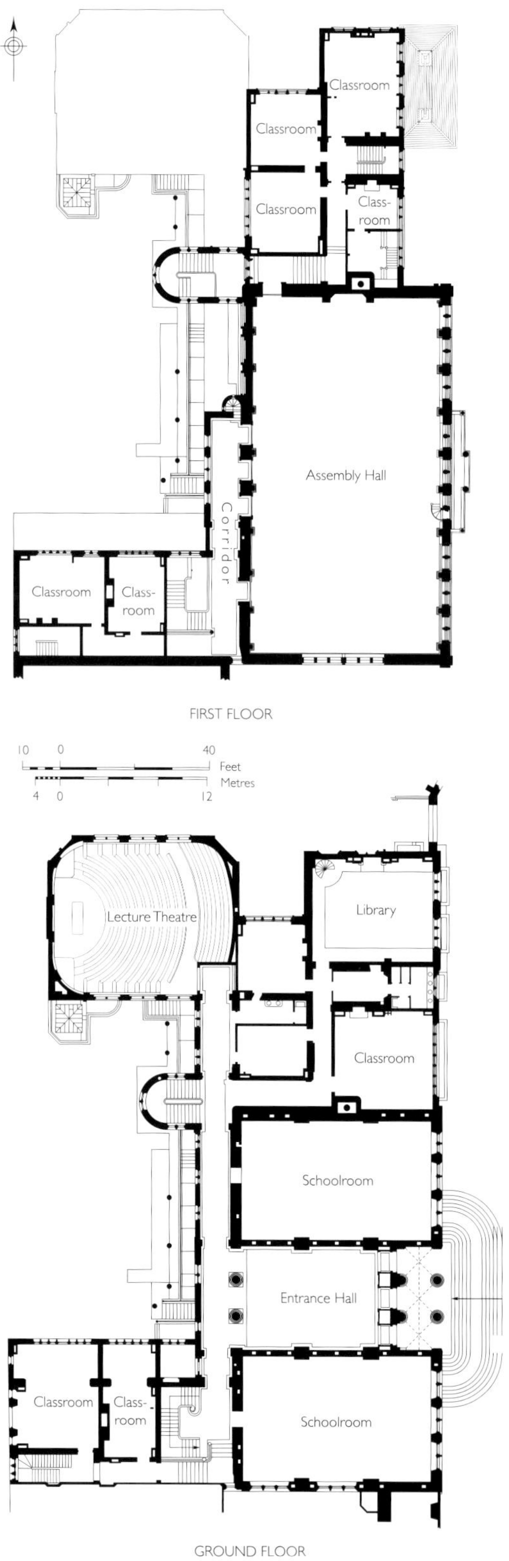

144. Main school building, ground and first-floor plans

145. Main school building in the late nineteenth century, seen across school green. Left: Norfolk Cloister and Preacher's Court east range. Right: classroom block adapted from the Schoolmaster's house of Charterhouse School, and new cloister giving covered access to Foresters' Hall Place entrance. *All demolished except Norfolk Cloister and part of Preacher's Court range*

particularly impressed the *Building News*: 'We have not again the everlasting open hammer-beam principals of Westminster Hall transposed, but the roof has a freshness about its design; the principals show below the boarded ceiling as open-work ribs of light and elegant form, while the visible portion of roof is closely boarded with stained and varnished deal'. It also admired the 'rich panelled oak dado … a credit to the joiners'.[8] At the north end stood a massive stone fireplace, carved by Thomas Earp, and there was a sturdy organ gallery midway along the west wall.[9] The window glass was mostly plain; only the great south window originally had stained glass, in the form of a roundel depicting St John the Baptist (artist unknown). One window in the east wall was filled with stained glass in 1899 to designs by Heaton, Butler & Bayne depicting Edmund Spenser and Bishop Lancelot Andrewes, two of the school's most famous alumni.[10] The company also commissioned for the hall, from Thomas Woolner, an 'heroic sized' marble statue of Sir Thomas White, one of the school's founders, exhibited at the Royal Academy in 1878.[11] This was taken by the school to Northwood in 1933.

Internally, the construction of I'Anson's buildings involved a good deal of ironwork, seemingly used in the candid manner adopted by Sir Gilbert Scott in the main staircase of the recently built Midland Grand Hotel at St Pancras. Several of the staircases were carried by iron girders 'of a dark chocolate colour, contrasting forcibly with the stone steps', while in the Mathematical School and Writing Room the ceiling joists sat on doubled plate girders, 'between each pair being the warm-air chamber, with perforated metal casings forming the soffits'.[12] But the iron ties proposed by I'Anson for the assembly hall roof were objected to and omitted, with the result that the piers on the front of the building moved slightly out of plumb. A gale in October 1877 caused further movement, and though a full set of tie-rods through the trusses was avoided a couple had to be inserted.[13]

The heating and ventilation system proved the least satisfactory aspect of the buildings. It was installed by Wilson W. Phipson, who had also provided the apparatus for the Albert Hall. Air was warmed by hot-water pipes and distributed around the building through brick air-passages, while foul air was extracted through shafts. Hot-water

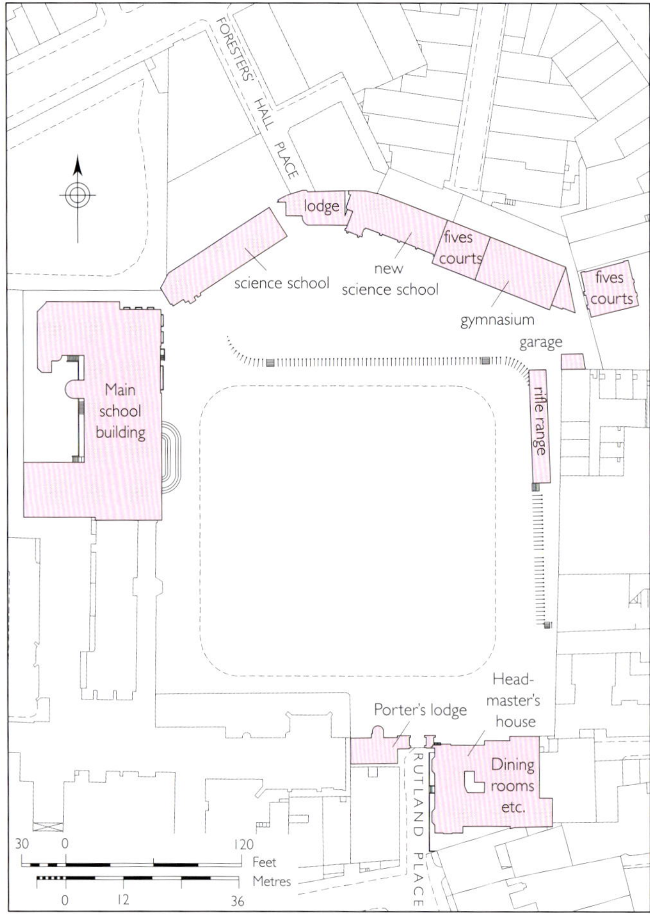

146. Plan of Merchant Taylors' School in 1927

pipes beneath the assembly hall warped the wooden flooring, and the system left some rooms hot and stuffy, others cold and draughty. Phipson made successive modifications, and a consulting engineer was called in, whose proposed remedies in 1877 seem to have had little effect. Gradually the hot-air system was replaced by steam pipes, but the whole was still unsatisfactory ten years later.[14]

I'Anson's buildings seem to have commanded no great affection. The future architect Charles Reilly, a pupil in the 1880s, preferred the great blank wall of the warehouses in Goswell Road backing on to the site, 'the most impressive piece of building the school possessed'. 'For the rest', he remembered, 'the school buildings, though expensive and well built as I see now, with their great polished red granite columns to the entrance block and the lofty windows and high pitched roof of the great hall over them, were hard and unfeeling and without any compensating efficiency in the way of sun and air'.[15]

In its new premises, Merchant Taylors' School quickly proved a success, and with success came expansion. The increased numbers of staff and pupils required more room than had been anticipated, and the headmaster was soon urging a reluctant Company to sanction enlargements to the classrooms.[16] The first substantial addition, built in 1884, was a gymnasium on the north-east side of the site, for which I'Anson produced plans based on that recently erected at the City of London School.[17] Of yellow stock bricks and red-brick dressings, with Gothic-arched windows, it had a high, hipped roof with a lantern on the ridge (Ill. 152).

This was I'Anson's last work for the school. He had resigned in 1883, to be succeeded by Walter Hilton Nash, who had spent some time in I'Anson's office during the 1870s, when the original school designs were being prepared. Nash's first major task was a new science school to contain a physics laboratory and natural history museum.

147. View alongside main school building towards Sutton's Hospital. Undated, probably early 1920s

148. Assembly hall, looking north *c*.1875, the organ not yet installed on the gallery. Tie-rods were later fitted through the two trusses from which the gasoliers hang

149. Assembly hall, looking north, after installation of tie-rods in late 1870s, showing Thomas Woolner's statue of Sir Thomas White

150. Assembly hall, looking south. Undated view

151. Merchant Taylors' School before building of new science block in 1926–7, showing old science building, entrance from Foresters' Hall Place, and blank wall admired by C. H. Reilly

After long delays, the first section of this was put up in 1891. The building stood on the north side of the green, partly on the site of I'Anson's cloister, in a harmonizing Tudor style of red brick with stone dressings. The second phase was not built until 1906–7, when one bay was added to the west and four to the east.[18]

Headmaster's house

Although the Company had often been slow to release funds for additional buildings, and had quibbled over costs, it was unusually prompt and generous in providing a decidedly large new three-storey house for the headmaster (Ills 142, 143). Designed by Nash, it was built in 1894 by Dove Brothers at a cost of more than £9000. The house occupies the site of the old headmaster's house and under-masters' residence at 1 and 2 Rutland Place.[19] In a rather more English style than the earlier buildings, and faced in brighter red brick than the lodge opposite, it has shaped gables, two sets of bay windows and a corner turret with copious detail. Two lively stone frieze-bands run along the Rutland Place front, the upper one enriched with a continuous wave of acanthus leaves, the lower with tailor's scissors, Tudor roses and the lamb emblem of St John the Baptist, patron saint of the Merchant Taylors.

The house included a dining room, morning room, study and first-floor drawing room, plus ten bedrooms and a generous number of bathrooms, dressing-rooms and water closets. But it was not well liked by the headmasters who lived there, despite, or perhaps because of, its size. Dr Baker, its first occupant, complained that the rooms were too dark, and iron casements were substituted for the original timber ones to let in more light. His successor, John Arbuthnot Nairn, found the house so inconvenient, and the heating, lighting and cleaning bills so high, that he moved his family out in 1914, staying there by himself during the week in term time.[20] The building survives

152. Merchant Taylor's School. View taken immediately after Ill. 151, showing gymnasium of 1884

as part of the Charterhouse Square campus of Barts and The London School of Medicine and Dentistry (the former Medical College of St Bartholomew's Hospital).

By the early decades of the twentieth century, sport had become an indispensable element of a public-school education, and in that respect Merchant Taylors lagged behind its peers. Additional playing fields were acquired at Bellingham in South London, but there was no space to expand at Charterhouse, and the area had become even more industrial since the 1870s. Such concerns prompted Nairn to suggest in 1910 that the school should be moved out of central London.[21] In the hopes of increasing the value of the site by improving access, in 1924 the Company bought the plot on Goswell Road occupied until 1909 by the church of St Thomas, Charterhouse.[22]

In 1925, the Company decided against moving. The church site was utilized for fives courts, and it was agreed that another science block should be built next to the gymnasium.[23] Designed by R. H. Mew, surveyor to the Company since 1905, it was built in 1926–7. Large windows produced well-lit classrooms and laboratories, while the red brick and stone dressings, timber mullions and transoms matched the existing buildings on the site. Two years later there was another change of mind, and a new site for the school was acquired at Sandy Lodge, in Northwood, Middlesex. Proposals in 1929 for the purchase of part of the site for the City of London School for Girls, then in Carmelite Street, came to nothing. In June 1933, the recently vacated school was taken over by the Medical College of St Bartholomew's Hospital.[24]

Of the old school buildings, only the Rutland Place lodge and the headmaster's house survive. Much of the rest was bombed in the Second World War and subsequently replaced by the medical college, though the gymnasium survived until recently, when it was demolished for the redevelopment described in the following chapter.

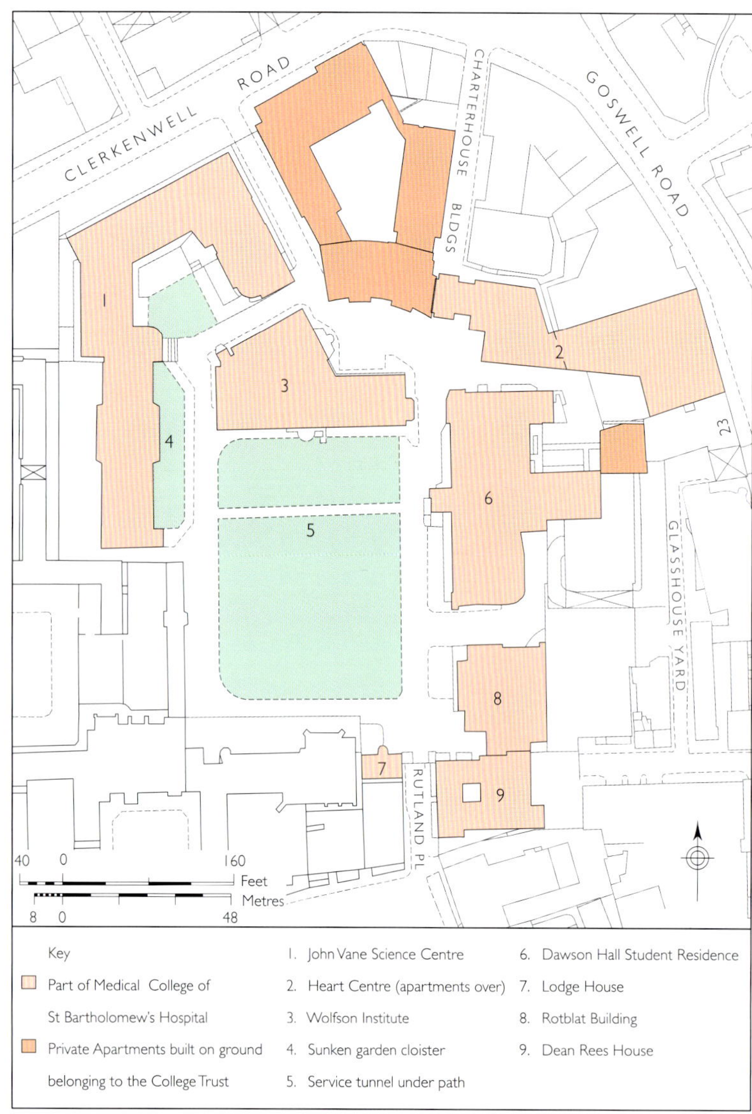

153. Barts and The London School of Medicine and Dentistry, Charterhouse Square campus (former Medical College of St Bartholomew's Hospital). The medical school and associated buildings in 2009

CHAPTER XII

Medical College of St Bartholomew's Hospital

The site of Merchant Taylors' School has been occupied since the mid-1930s as a medical college, which for most of this time was known as the Medical College of St Bartholomew's Hospital. Following reorganization of medical education in London, the site is now correctly the Charterhouse Square campus of Barts and The London School of Medicine and Dentistry. For convenience, it is here referred to by the former college name.

By the time of its move to the Charterhouse, the medical college was the largest in the country, with some 600 full-time students and over 80 teachers. Part of the University of London's Faculty of Medicine since 1900, it had obtained its own charter of incorporation in 1921. Physically, however, it was spread around the various departments at Barts itself. The new site at the Charterhouse enabled the pre-clinical school to be brought together, just a short walk from the hospital. The adaptation was put in the hands of the architect Henry Vaughan Lanchester and his young partner Thomas Arthur Lodge, highly regarded specialists in the design of hospitals and other large public buildings. Lodge in particular won the admiration of the college dean, (Sir) William Girling Ball, as 'a brilliant man of ideas' and master of detail. The necessary alterations and new building were estimated to cost £75,000, on top of the £130,000 for the site. As the university was unable to contribute financially, an appeal for funds was launched, and the Merchant Taylors' Company agreed to grant the college a mortgage for part of the purchase price, recouping most of the remainder from the appeal fund.[1]

Plans were drawn up in 1933–4, and the building contract was awarded to Wilson, Lovatt & Sons Ltd in January 1935. Work was completed the following year. The main school building was adapted for the physiology and pharmacology departments, with a large experimental laboratory built on at the rear. The assembly hall itself became the students' dining room, known as College Hall. Its High Victorian architecture was by then utterly out of fashion, and Ball, annoyed at soot and dirt falling from the lantern, urged Lodge to 'knock the damned thing off'. The architects' own style was expressed in the plans they drew up in 1937 for a students' residence on the east side of the old school green, a severe stone-faced block in the current stripped-classical manner. It was never built, thanks to the outbreak of war as much as to lack of funds.[2]

The anatomy school and biology department were adapted from the former headmaster's house and dining rooms at the rear, where laboratories, a museum and X-ray and photographic rooms were provided, and an extension was built containing a dissecting room and lecture theatre. The old and new buildings are now known respectively as Dean Rees House and the Rotblat Building, after Dame Lesley Rees, warden of the college before the merger of 1995 (see below), and Joseph Rotblat, Professor of Physics at Barts.[3] The theatre was partly built on the site of the east cloister walk of the priory, and the rediscovered doorway to Cell T was preserved *in situ* inside a cupboard there. On the north side of the green, a new flat-roofed, single-storey brick building provided laboratories for physiological and organic chemistry. To the rear, the chemistry and physics departments took over the former Merchant Taylors' science schools. Additional laboratory space was provided in a plain, neo-Georgian 'tower' built as an extension to the physics block east of the Clerkenwell Road entrance.[4]

During the war, the college was evacuated to Queens' College, Cambridge. Bombing raids in October and December 1940 destroyed the roof of College Hall, the chemistry department and half the physics department. More extensive damage was done in January 1941, when the physics department took a direct hit. In May, College Hall was hit again and the physiology department burnt out, leaving the college in a precarious state. Not only did it need substantial funds to put right the damage, but it still owed the Merchant Taylors £50,000.[5]

At least twice this sum was needed for repairs, but Ball saw the opportunity to replace the old buildings completely. Lodge drew up a layout providing for phased construction to be undertaken as funds permitted, and Ball sought permission from the University to pull down the damaged blocks and begin the foundations of the future buildings. Given the wartime situation, there were bureaucratic hurdles to overcome before work could begin (supposing that any builder could be found to undertake it). But in February 1942 Ball commissioned sketch plans for the new buildings from Lodge. Two ranges were proposed: a students' hostel with a swimming pool, on the site of College Hall, and an L-shaped block for the departments of physics, physiology and chemistry, adjoining the biochemistry laboratories, part of which was to stretch across the middle of the green. This scheme would have worked out cheaper than reinstating the original buildings, but Sir Walter Moberly, chairman of the University Grants Committee, was concerned that Finsbury Borough Council might object to building on the green. Nevertheless, Lodge pressed on with detailed plans.[6]

Further bomb damage occurred in July 1944. Difficulty was found in getting contractors to make repairs, and Lodge himself had become demoralized, showing little interest in the damaged buildings and arranging only the most cursory protective measures with tarpaulins. Informed in November that building licences would not be granted owing to scarcity of materials and labour, Ball began to lose heart himself. He died in July 1945 and it was left to his successor, Dr (later Sir) Charles Harris, to oversee the rebuilding.[7]

For the students who returned in May 1946, temporary accommodation was provided in some of the partially restored buildings. College Hall, effectively a roofless ruin, was patched up sufficiently for the basement to be used. The green was cleared of an air-raid shelter, concrete barrage-balloon anchors and a base for winding-gear. But relations with Lodge had so deteriorated that at the end of 1946 he was replaced by Easton & Robertson, a well-known practice with considerable experience in institutional buildings. The firm, later Easton & Robertson, Cusdin, Preston & Smith, was to oversee almost complete redevelopment between then and the mid-1960s.[8]

Preliminary plans for rebuilding were ready in 1947. Student accommodation was the most urgent requirement and the part of the scheme most likely to receive an early licence. For this reason, the hostel was built on the already vacant east side of the green. The University had set aside £100,000 for building, to which was added war-damage compensation of nearly £190,000. These preliminary figures were already outweighed by the estimated costs of £204,500 for the hostel and £487,000 for the science blocks.[9]

Dawson Hall Student Residence

Exigencies of licensing and supply led to the hostel design changing from a steel frame to reinforced concrete and back to steel before the go-ahead was given in June 1948. Work did not begin until the new year, with Humphreys Ltd as contractors on a tender of £192,997, and dragged on long after the intended completion date. The new building, known by the same name as the pre-war dining hall, College Hall, was finally opened in April 1952. It was designed for 100 students, but with dining and recreation rooms for the whole college. Early plans for a glass curtain-wall (thought appropriate to the 'forward-looking spirit' of the occupants) were abandoned on cost grounds, and instead the seven-storey building is faced in buff (or 'grey-brown') Buckinghamshire bricks with minimal Portland-stone dressings. The principal elevation is classically composed, its overall formality offset chiefly by the handling of the top floor, intended for female students. This has French windows opening on to a wavy balcony under a canopy on struts with a forward rake.[10]

As completed, the residential part of the building comprised six floors of bed-sitting rooms on either side of spinal corridors, the much wider ground floor containing the communal and ancillary rooms: kitchens and dining rooms to the north, social rooms to the south, divided by a spacious foyer and the main staircase and lifts. An extension was built on to the north side in 1954–5, and in 1963–4 a new boiler-house was added at the rear, serving the whole site. Work then began on the east wing, completed in 1966, which provided 102 more student rooms.[11] A service tunnel constructed in 1949 under the green connects the building with those on the west side of the site.[12]

College Hall has since been renamed after Sir Anthony Dawson, first chairman of the Medical College of St Bartholomew's Hospital Trust.

John Vane Science Centre

Because of objections from Sutton's Hospital, supported by the Royal Fine Art Commission and the London County Council, one of the main components of the post-war redevelopment, a seven-storey science building crossing the green, had to be rethought.[13] The problem was resolved when Sutton's Hospital offered to sell part of the Master's Garden alongside Clerkenwell Road, with a proviso that the green must remain open space. The deal was concluded in 1952. In addition, the college acquired the adjacent sites of Foresters' Hall and Foresters' Hall Place off Clerkenwell Road, and the sites of bombed warehouses and tenements in Clerkenwell Road, Goswell Road and Union Place. Fresh plans were prepared, and the newly acquired sites, cleared in 1953, were made into a car park, off Clerkenwell Road, and two hard tennis courts fronting Goswell Road.[14]

The new science block, partly built on the Foresters' Hall and Master's Garden sites, took many years to complete. It consists of a range fronting Clerkenwell Road of four storeys over a raised basement, two shorter splayed wings at the rear creating a small open 'quadrangle', and a long west extension on the old College Hall site (Ill. 156). Trollope & Colls' tender of £58,698 for the north range, containing physiology laboratories, was accepted in 1951, building being completed in 1954. This was followed by the pharmacology department, part of the histology

154. Dawson Hall in 1995, view from south-west

156. John Vane Science Centre in 2009, view from north

laboratories and an animal house, completed in 1955.[15] The first two phases of the west extension were built in 1961–3, containing the departments of radiology, physics and zoology, the library, and a linear accelerator in the basement, the reinforced-concrete housing and armoured doors for which remain. The south end was closed by a temporary wall and staircase, pending future extension. Formal opening took place in May 1964.[16]

Externally, the building is in the same style as the hostel, faced in the same buff brick, the two main ranges comprising the west wing each with a penthouse floor under a cambered, copper-covered roof. On the east side of the building the area is laid out as a garden, with an open-sided cloister, off which runs the service tunnel to Dawson Hall (Ill. 11). The outstanding architectural feature of the building is the staircase at the junction of the northern block with the long west range, built around a harp-shaped well. A further addition at the south end of the west range was eventually built *c.*1996. Harmonizing well with the earlier work, it was designed by Michael Squire & Partners.[17]

The Science Building, as it was for long known, is now named after the pharmacologist Sir John Vane (d. 2004), whose discovery of how aspirin works paved the way for the development of new anti-inflammatory drugs.

155. John Vane Science Centre in 2009. Staircase

Wolfson Institute of Preventive Medicine

The Wolfson Institute was built in 1990–2, on the site of the pre-war biochemistry laboratories on the north side of the green. Almost entirely funded by external donations, including £1m from the Wolfson Foundation, it operates as a centre of excellence in the study of epidemiology and preventive medicine. Designed by Carl Fisher & Partners, the two-storey building has a facing of dark brick with orange-brick bands, and metal porticoes in the postmodern manner typical of the period (Ill. 157). The ground floor is occupied by laboratories, a freezer-store and offices. On the first floor are a common room, library, seminar room and more offices.[18]

Recent development

Following the changes to medical education recommended in the Todd Report (1968), preparations were made for the amalgamation of the college with The London Hospital Medical School as the Medical Faculty of Queen Mary College, University of London. This was to involve transfer of the pre-clinical school from the Charterhouse to a new site at Queen Mary College in Mile End. Plans were

157. Wolfson Institute and apartments in 2009, view from east

well advanced by 1973, but due to the financial stringencies of the period it was not until 1985 that full funding became available. However, St Bartholomew's was determined to resist the sale of the pre-clinical school premises at the Charterhouse, on which the grant depended, and in 1988 a new scheme was agreed by which the three colleges—Queen Mary, Bart's and The London—formed a confederation while retaining separate identity and funding. The pre-clinical students of Bart's and The London duly moved to Mile End, leaving the way clear for the whole of the Charterhouse site to be used for medical education and research.[19]

Plans for building on the bomb-site car park by Clerkenwell Road were drawn up in the late 1980s, initially for a science park with some student and staff accommodation. Funding was to have come from the sale of the Goswell Road tennis courts. The scheme was deferred when the property market slumped in the early 1990s and it was decided to proceed with a students' hall of residence and recreational facilities instead.[20] This scheme, too, was subsequently shelved.

Meanwhile, the college was affected by the reorganization of London health services and medical education set out in the Tomlinson Report of 1992, which proposed the closure of St Bartholomew's and the merger of its medical college and that of The London with Queen Mary and Westfield College. Although Barts was eventually saved following a public campaign, the merger took place in 1995 and the freehold of the college site was transferred to the Medical College of St Bartholomew's Hospital Trust, which let the land and buildings to the merged colleges at a peppercorn rent. In 2004, the trust obtained planning consent for redevelopment of the car park and tennis court sites, together with the pre-war science 'tower' and the late-Victorian gymnasium of Merchant Taylors' School (page 184), as a cardiac research centre and private and social housing. Thornsett plc was chosen as developer, and the new flats (marketed as 'Charterhouse the Square') and research centre were built in 2006–8 by Ardmore, to designs by Capital Architecture. The Heart Centre occupies the ground and basement levels of two adjoining blocks north of Dawson Hall and 23 Goswell Road.

A small housing block at the back of 23 Goswell Road remains to be built at the time of writing (2009).[21]

In 2005, an inscribed stone was set up by the trust at the south-west corner of the medical college green, on the site of the monks' burial ground. This commemorates the Carthusian monks and lay brothers, the London Charterhouse and the much later occupation of the site successively by Charterhouse School, Merchant Taylors' School and the medical college.

'The Panther Hunter'

On the lawn near the main entrance to the John Vane Science Centre is a marble version of a celebrated work of 1845–6 by the Danish sculptor Jens Adolf Jerichau (Ill. 1207). Usually known as 'The Panther Hunter', it exists in several versions, though the original no longer survives, and a small-scale edition in terracotta was also produced. Of four marble copies made, two were acquired by English collectors, and the medical college marble is presumably one of these. One was shown at the Great Exhibition in 1851 (where it was 'one of the most noted works', winning a gold medal) and subsequently acquired by Baron Carl Hambro, the Danish-Jewish merchant banker. The other was commissioned by Sir Francis Henry Goldsmid, a prominent Anglo-Jewish barrister and MP, who commissioned other work from Jerichau.[22]

On the evidence of a photograph taken in the late 1940s or 1950s, the group was formerly mounted on a decorative pedestal just inside the porch of the College Hall building, having presumably been left there or elsewhere on the site when Merchant Taylors' School moved away in 1933, as Victoriana of little merit.[23] It has stood on the lawn for many years, though apparently not until some time after the opening of the Science Building.

Jerichau, a favourite pupil of Thorvaldsen, moved away from the master's static neo-Classicism towards greater naturalism and dynamism, and the Panther Hunter, which made his international reputation, vividly marks this development.[24] The hunter has a new-born cub under his arm and is on the point of killing or being killed by the attacking mother. (His spear is now missing.) The statue, which has also been described as representing a hunter and lioness, may have been inspired by the legend of Phalaicos, tyrant of Ambracia, killed by a lioness after the goddess Artemis contrived that he should find her cub while out hunting.[25]

158. 'The Panther Hunter', by Jens Adolf Jerichau, in 2009

APPENDICES

Note on transcripts

A very few clearly unintended repetitions or similar minor errors have been silently corrected. Manuscript corrections and insertions are indicated as such (^ ^). Original spelling has been preserved exactly, but for clarity i, u and v have where necessary been amended to j, v and u in accordance with present-day usage. The letter y used for thorn has been left as in the originals. Initial double-f is given as capital f, but otherwise capitalization has not been modernized; it is, however, open to interpetation in very many instances, particularly in Appendix III, where the distinction between upper and lower case is particularly vague. Words contracted or abbreviated with conventional symbols for particular letter combinations have been silently expanded, as have some other contractions or abbreviations where the spelling is more or less certain or apparent from other entries in the document. Where there is uncertainty, missing letters are supplied inside square brackets, using the most likely or modern spelling. Frequently used contractions and abbreviations with easily understood meanings, however, have mostly been left as they are, but without any of the original marks of abbreviation other than full-stops or colons. They include 'cont' for containing; 'dd' for delivered; 'de' and 'di' for demy/demi or dimidium; 'dos', 'doss', etc for dozen; 'It', 'Itm' and (Appendix I) 'Itme' for Item(e); 'ob' for obolus (halfpenny); 'Lo': and 'La': for Lord and Lady; 'Md' for Memorandum; 'M^{r}' and 'M^{ris}' or 'M^{res}' for Master and Mistress; 'n^{l}' for nihil or nil; 'w^{ch}' for which; 'w^{t}', 'wth' or 'wth' for with. Punctuation marks elsewhere, being used inconsistently and often unnecessarily, have generally been omitted except where they are helpful to the sense of entries.The layout is essentially as in the originals, though gaps have been closed or regularized. Main and marginal headings have been emboldened for emphasis.

Footnotes are supplied to explain obsolete or unusual words or usages (only the first instance being annotated in each transcript), where the spelling may mislead, and where the reading of a word is uncertain; some biographical and other historical notes are also given. Definitions are mostly taken from the *Oxford English Dictionary*, but use has been made of other sources, including Rosemary Milward, *A Glossary of Household, Farming and Trade Terms from Probate Inventories*, 1986.

APPENDIX I

North House Inventory, 1565

Transcript from Bodleian Library, North MS b.12, ff.15–47, 97–101r. By permission of the Bodleian Library

This is much the fullest inventory to have survived of the contents of the mansion called North House and subsequently Howard House. It was made, for probate purposes, on the death there of Edward, first Baron North on 31 December 1564. It is possible that it includes the contents of some rooms in the part of the Charterhouse excluded from the forthcoming sale to the Duke of Norfolk. Although the document as a whole is not dated, North's plate is described as having been weighed and valued on 4 January 1564/5. Marginal notes show the distribution of many items to individuals, in some cases specifying that these were legacies, which implies that others may not have been. Those concerned are nearly all identifiable as North's immediate family, servants or executors. In a few instances, the marginal notes and striking through show that items already belonging to these individuals had been included in the inventory by mistake.

Comparison with the inventory of things remaining at Howard House in 1588 (Appendix IV) suggests that Lord North's establishment had been a somewhat simpler and less pretentious one than that of the Earl of Arundel (Philip Howard), whose own household even so was probably reduced from that of his father, the Duke of Norfolk in the late 1560s. There are, for instance, very few paintings listed in 1565 (though North did have several framed maps and poems). Hardly any of his wall hangings were thought to merit much description, and the bedding was apparently plainer than the finest of that listed in 1588.

The document is in two parts, bound into a volume of North family manuscripts at different points, hence the large gap in the folio numbers. The second part is damaged in part by damp and staining, but very little has been lost altogether; missing text is indicated by dots. In making the fair copy, folios 34 and 35, as originally numbered, were accidently transposed; this has been corrected in the transcript. The record of things 'Att the Charterhowse' ends with oddments of jewellery and a stock of servants' badges found in Lord North's closet or private room, and the remainder of the document, not given here, lists the contents of a farm belonging to North at Hoxton. At least two writers compiled the document, accounting for some of the variation in abbreviations, spelling, etc.

A very few uninformative right-hand-side marginal jottings in minute handwriting, comprising sub-totals and totals repeated in arabic numerals (presumably for aid in totting up), have been omitted, together with the check marks ('ex' for *examinatur*) written against both the sub-heading totals and some individual valuations. Similar small omissions have been made to the notes in the left-hand margins in the interest of clarity. For the same reason, a few word-endings and abbreviations using ambiguous signs and symbols have been rationalized, rather than expanded: e.g. abbreviations for 'weighing' (given in the transcript as w^{g}), pounds weight (^{lli}), *quarterius* or *quarterium* (qt^{r} and variants). Crosses marking certain items in the armoury, of unknown significance, have been left in place.

[f.15r]

Att the Charterhowse/

In the hall there

Inprimis a longe table of fyrre wth ij trestles wth a forme of the same being olde	vj^{s} viij^{d}
Item twoo tables of waynescotte wth v trestles	xij^{s}
It one longe Forme of fyrre	vj^{s}
It thre longe Formes of oke	x^{s}
It thre shorter Formes	v^{s}
It a paire of great Andyrons[1] of yron	xvj^{s}

1 Andirons: decorative stands for supporting burning logs in a fireplace (fire-dogs)

	It a payre of Creepers[2]	vj^{s}
	It a Fire Fork	xij^{d}
To my la: North[3]	It a Cradle of yron for sea coale[4]	xxvj^{s} viij^{d}

1

[f.15v]

	It twoo candle plates	ij^{s}	To my la: North j
	It a Frame wth the Kinges armes	ij^{s}	
	It a Mappe in a frame of wainescott	xij^{d}	
	Summa iiij^{li} xiij^{s} iiij^{d}		

In the half pace at the stayer heade

	It a courte cupborde[5] of wallnutte tree	vj^{s}
To my la: North	It a latten[6] plate to sett candles in	xij^{d}
	Summa vj^{s}	

In the great chamber

dd to my L: Dyer[9]	It twoo peces of hanginges of the storie of Kinge David & Gol[iat]h[7] cont. lxxx elles fleemyshe[8] at iiij^{s} v^{d} the elle	xiiij^{li}
	It one pece more of the same storye cont xxx^{ta} elles at iij^{s} vj^{d} the elle Fle[mish]	v^{li} v^{s}
	It v peces of hanginges of the storie of Tobie[10] cont Cxl elles Flemishe at iij^{s} vj^{d} the elle	xxiiij^{li} x^{s}
	It three olde wyndowe carpettes of parke worke[11]	xxvj^{s} viij^{d}
To my La: North	It a table of fyrre with iij trestles	xiij^{s} iiij^{d}
To my L: Dyer	It a faire turkye Carpett cont vj yeardes longe & iij yeardes brode	x^{li}
To Mr Applegarthe	It a drawing table of wainescott wth a frame cont v yeardes longe	xxiij^{s} iiij^{d}

2 Small fire-dogs

3 North's widow, his second wife, Margaret

4 Fire-basket for coal

5 Shelved cupboard or dresser, originally without doors, for displaying plate or earthenware, etc

6 Latten: brass or similar alloy

7 Partly obliterated by water damage

8 Flemish ell (standard measure for wall tapestries) = 27ins; English ell = 45ins

9 Sir James Dyer, Lord Chief Justice of the Common Pleas, Lord North's co-executor with Sir William Cordell. He lived near the Charterhouse, and for some years had a house at Carlton in Cambridgeshire, near North's seat at Kirtling

10 Tobias, son of Tobit, whose encounter with an angel is a popular subject in Christian art

11 Decorated with park-like scenes or subjects

[f.16r]

Recipient	Item	Value
To my L: Dyer	It a Turkye carpett cont iiij yeardes qt^{r} longe & ij yeardes qt^{r} brode	v^{li}
To my La: North	It a longe Forme of Fyrre	vj^{s}
To my Lo: Dyer	It a courte Cupborde of wainescott It a Turkye Carpett upon the same table cont iij yeardes longe & a yeard iij qt^{r} brode	vj^{s} lx^{s}
	It a shorte table of wainescott wth a chest valued at	iij^{s} iiij^{d}
To Mr Kydd	It an old Turkye carpett cont in lengthe iij yeardes and in breadthe a yeard iij qt^{r}	xx^{s}
To the M^{r} of ye Rolles[12]	It a faire chaire of clothe of gold frynged about with venyce gold[13] & silke	xxx^{s}
To my la: Northe	It a chaire of wallnutt tree the seat & backe of yellowe satten of bruges & ymbrodered wth blacke velvett	xx^{s}
	It a chaire wth a grene frame the seate & backe of purple sarcenett[14] quylted	xxiij^{s} iiij^{d}
To my La: North	It twoo spanishe Chayres the seate and backe of clothe of gold & damaske	xl^{s}
To my L: Dyer	It a picture of Kinge Henrye the viijth wth a curten of sarcenett It a paire of Flaunders Andyrons of ~~yron~~ Latten It a paire of yron Tonges & a forke	xx^{s} l^{s} ij^{s}
To Mr Applegarthe	It ij^{o} backes of cast yron	x
	It a steele glasse[15] covered wth crymsen satten	xv^{s}

2

[f.16v]

Recipient	Item	Value
	It twoo old windowe Curteynes of saye[16] & a curteyne rodd	v^{s}
	Summa lxxvij^{li} ix^{s}	

In the entrie

Recipient	Item	Value
To my La: North	It an oyster boorde[17] of waynescott wth a frame	ij^{s} vj^{d}
To Mr Tho: Northe[18]	It a skrene of wyckers	xx^{d}
	Summa iiij^{s} ij^{d}	

12 Sir William Cordell, co-executor of Lord North's will and Master of the Rolls 1557–81

13 Venice gold: gold thread

14 Very fine, soft silk material

15 Mirror of polished steel

16 Say: a fine, serge-like woollen cloth, sometimes part silk

17 Osyter-board: a narrow board or table for preparing oysters

18 North's second son, the translator Sir Thomas North

In the longe gallarie over the bowling alleye

	It hanginges of redd and grene	xj^{li}
	saye cont CCCxxxvj yeardes	
To my La: North	It a Courte Cupbord	iiij^{s}
	It a longe table of deale boorde	vj^{s} viij^{d}
To my La: North	It a shorte Forme	xvj^{d}
	Summa xj^{li} xij^{s}	

In the wthdrawing chamber to the great Chamber

	It vj peces of hanginges wth	
To my L: Dyer	brode Flowres cont C^{xx}iiij v ell	xxx^{li} xvj^{s} viij^{d}
	Flemishe at iij^{s} iiij^{d} the ell	
	It a Chaire of purple velvett richlye	
	ymbrodered wth goold wth my L: armes	x^{li}
	& a longe quyshen of purple velvett	
	& ymbrodered wth gold wth my L. armes	

[f.17r]

	It a Turkye Carpett cont iij	
To my La: North	yeardes iij qt^{r} de longe & a yearde	xl^{s}
	& a half brode	
	It an other Carpett of turkye worke	
To my La: of Worc[19]	cont ij^{o} yeardes iij qt^{r} longe & a yeard	xl^{s}
	& a half brode	
	It a windowe Carpett of parke	
	worke cont ij yeardes longe & a yearde	xij^{s}
	de brode	
	It a close chaire[20] of black velvett	xx^{s}
To my L: Dyer	It twoo lowe stooles covered wth crymzin	
	velvett fryndged about wth sylke	xvj^{s}
	and ymbrodered	
	It a lyvery Cupborde[21]	vj^{s} viij^{d}
	It a litle table upon a frame	v^{s}
	wth turned pyllers	
	It a longe windowe Curteyne	
	of blewe buckeram[22] wth a	v^{s}
	Curteyne rodd of yron	
To the M^{r} of	It a paire of Andyrons of yron	
the Roolles	bossed wth latten wth a paire	xij^{s}
	of Creepers & a paire of tonges	
	Summa lj^{li} xiij^{s} iiij^{d}	

In the ynner rowme called a privie rowme

Item a lyttle Cupborde and ij	
Curteyn roddes of yron	iiij^{s}
Summa patet	

3

19 Christian, Lady Worcester, daughter of Lord North and his first wife Alice; married William Somerset, third Earl of Worcester

20 Commode

21 Livery cupboard: cupboard for storing provisions, especially those for allocation to servants

22 Buckram: a fine linen or cotton fabric; also a coarse linen or cotton fabric stiffened with size or gum

[f.17v]

In the dyning chamber

Recipient	Item	Value
To Mr Atturney	It v peces of parke worke & one of ymagerie cont $\overset{xx}{\text{vj}}$ v elles at xiij^{d} ob le ell	vij^{li} vij^{d} ob
	It a longe Carpett of thr[o]wne[23] englyshe making cont v yeardes de longe & a yearde iij qt^{r} brode	vj^{li} x^{s}
	It an other thr[o]wne englyshe carpett old cont iiij yeardes longe & one yearde de brode	xiij^{s} iiij^{d}
	It ij half shorte turkye carpettes for wyndowes	viij^{s}
	It ij ^old^ broken turkye carpettes	xx^{d}
	It a faire table of wallnutt tree standing upon a frame turned wth vices[24]	iiij^{li}
	It an old table painted sett upon a frame	v^{s}
	It ij^{o} longe formes & ij shorte formes	viij^{s}
	It a lyverey Cupbord	v^{s}
	It a lytle table wth a cupbord wth Locke and Keye	iiij^{s}
	It x wallnutt tree stooles at xiiij^{d} the pece	xj^{s} viij^{d}
	It one longe quyshene of clothe of baudkyne[25] lyned wth old velvett	xiij^{s} iiij^{d}
	It an other old quyshyne of counterfecte[26] clothe of gold lyned wth buckeram	viij^{s}
	It a faire large Chayre covered wth redd clothe enbrodered wth blacke velvett	xv^{s}

[f.18r]

Recipient	Item	Value
To Mr Millysent	It an other old Chaire of redd clothe wth E & A[27] fryndged	vj^{s}
To Mr Tho: North	It a grene Chaire seat & backe of grene cloth ymbrodered wth blacke velvet fryndged wth grene sylke	iiij^{s}
	It an other lowe chaire of redd clothe ymbrodered upon wth blacke velvett	iiij^{s}
To Mr Atturney	It a lytle lowe stoole of blacke velvett ymbrodered wth redd velvett	ij^{s}]
To Mr Tho: North	It a Chaire of wallnutt tree broken	ij^{s} vj^{d}
	It ij waynescott stooles	ij^{s}
	It a paire of playing tables[28] of wallnuttree	v^{s}
	It a paire of virginalles lyned wth grene satten of bruges	xxx^{s}

23 Made with thrown (twisted) threads, perhaps thrown silk
24 Spirals
25 Baudekin: a rich silk material
26 Counterfeit
27 For Edward North and his first wife, Alice
28 Tables with integral boards for games such as draughts; backgammon had probably not yet been introduced to England

To Mr Atturney	It a table of the picture of Lucrecia[29]	viij^{d}
	It ij^{o} wyndow curteyns of buckeram	vj^{s}
	& an other of saye wth ij^{o} roddes	
	It a Chesse bord wth the men of bone	iij^{s} iiij^{d}
	It ij yron backes in the chymneyes	x^{s}
	It a paire of yron Andyrons a paire of creepers & a paire of tonges	ix^{s}
	Summa xxvj^{li} viij^{s} j^{d} ob	

In the chamber next the dyning chamber

To my La: North	It v peces of hanginges of the passion, whereof fower lyned wth Canves & one unlyned cont vj^{xx} elles at ij^{s} the ell	xij^{li}

4

[f.18v]

To Peter Rosewell	It an old pece of a windowe carpett	xvj^{d}
	It a Courte Cupborde	iij^{s} iiij^{d}
	It a table wth a frame	viij^{s}
	It a paire of old yron Andyrons and a paire of crepers	v^{s}
	Summa xij^{li} xvij^{s} viij^{d}	

In the ynner chamber next the gasing chamber

It vj peces of hanginges of sundry sortes old and muche worne wth twoo old wyndowe Carpettes cont lxxxxiiij elles	C^{s}
It an old lyverey Cupborde	ij^{s}
It a Curteyn of grene saye and redd wth an yron rodd	ij^{s}
Summa Ciiij^{s}	

In the chamber commonlye called the gasing chamber

To my la: Northe	It viij peces of hanginges of brode leaves whereof vij lyned & one unlyned cont Clxvij elles at xx^{d} the ell	xiij^{li} xvij^{s} ij^{d}
	It a Courte Cupborde	viij^{s}
	It ij^{o} windowe Curteyns of redd & grene saye wth a curteyn rodd large & bygge	xiij^{s} iiij^{d}
	It an old broken silke curteyne wth a Curteyne rodd	ij^{s}

29 Lucretia, whose rape by the king's son led to the founding of the Roman Republic

[f.19r]

Recipient	Item	Value
To the M^{r} of the Roolles	It a paire of Andyrons of yron bossed wth latten & a paire of creepers	xij^{s}
	It a faire large bedsteade paynted redd & yellowe gold wth bases of Damaske	vj^{li}
To the M^{r} of the Roolles	It a bedd of downe wth a fustian tyke wthout a boulster	iiij^{li}
	It a feetherbedd wth a stryped tyke[30] wth a brysell[31] bolster	lx^{s}
	Summa xxviij^{li} xij^{s} vj^{d}	

In the gallary next the gate

Recipient	Item	Value
	It a Courte Cupborde	v^{s}
To the M^{r} of the Roolles	It ix wallnutt tree stooles at xv^{d} the pece	xj^{s} iij^{d}
	It a waynescott chayre	ij^{s}
	It a longe table peced[32]	v^{s}
To M^{r} Wm Gerrard[33]	It a Commpter table wth vj Aumbris[34]	xxvj^{s} viij^{d}
To the M^{r} of the Roolles	It a Clocke wth all appendmentes	xl^{s}
	It a table wth my Lordes armes & myne old Ladies armes	xx^{s}
	It the hanginges aboute the gallary of redd & grene saye cont CCCiiij yeardes	vij^{li} x^{s}
To Mr Sootherton	It a mappe sett in waynescott of England Scotland & Ireland	iij^{s} iiij^{d}
To Hunter my L: Dyers servant	It an other mappe sett in waynescott verye small of London	viij^{d}

5

[f.19v]

Recipient	Item	Value
To Mr Necton[35]	It vij tables wth poesies sett in frames of waynescott	iiij^{s} iiij^{d}
	It a mappe of thysle of wighte	v^{s}
	It a printed paper of geneologie	ij^{s} vij^{d}
	It a geneologie in frenche sett in a Case of waynescott	iij^{s} iiij^{d}
	It iiij hatchementes for a Tente	xxvj^{s} viij^{d}
	It certen bookes vizt Sir Thomas ~~E~~[?] Mores workes betwyxt hym &	

30 Tick: cover or case

31 Presumably, stuffed with hogshair (bristle)

32 Repaired with new material, or made up from more than one original

33 Servant of Lord North

34 Ambries (cupboards or lockers): perhaps here referring to drawers or other compartments

35 William Necton was one of Lord North's servants named in his will, and was later employed by the Howards. In the 1580s he was receiver-general of the late Duke of Norfolk's estates and is referred to in a dispute between the keeper of Howard House and Robert Sackville over tenancy of a dwelling there (see page 52)

	Frythe & Tyndall[36]/ A booke of Statutes of Kinge Henry theighte bechas Cronycle[37]/ an old cronycle/ A great booke of statutes from the begyning of King Edvard the iij^{d} to the xxvth of Kinge Henry the viijth/ viij bookes of statutes of Kinge Henry the viijth/ A Testament in englyshe of Erasmus translac[i]on	xxiij^{s} iiij^{d}
	Summa xvj^{li} ^ ix^{s} j^{d} ^	

In the parlo[u]r chamber

	It one pece of hanginges of Imagerye of the xij signes[38] cont xxxvj elles	lxvj^{s} viij^{d}
	It v peces of hanginges of the ix worthies[39] cont Cxxv elles at xviij^{d} thell	ix^{li} vij^{s} vj^{d}
[f.20r]		
	It iij other peces old of Imagerye cont lxv elles at [—]	lxxv^{s}
	It an old windowe carpet of yrishe worke	iiij^{s}
	It iiij Curteynes of redd & grene saye for windowes wth ij ^yron^ roddes	xij^{s}
	It a lytle pece of tapstrye wth floweres	iij^{s}
	It a Courte Cupborde	v^{s}
	It a table with vices of yron	xx^{s}
To M^{r} Wm Gerrard	It a grene table clothe upon the same table	x^{s}
To the M^{r} of the Roolles	It a turkye Carpett cont ij yeardes de qt^{r} longe cutt & worne	vj^{s} viij^{d}
	It a folding table wth a frame & an old Carpett wth old Flowers	viij^{s}
To M^{ris} Gerrard	It a chaire of grene clothe frindged wth grene sylke	vj^{s} viij^{d}
	It a lytle wainescott chaire old	ij^{s}
ij^{o} formes to M^{ris} Gerrard	It ij joyned Formes of wainescott and one stoole	v^{s}
To my La: of Worc	It a wycker skrene	xij^{d}
	It iij quyshins one of tapstrie and thother of old velvet	ij^{s}
	It a bedsteade painted redd & yellowe	xxx^{s}
To the M^{r} of the Rolles	It the testor & seelor[40] wth paynes of redd velvet & clothe of tyshewe & the vallaunce of crymsen velvet and bawdkyne frynged wth yellowe & redd	x^{li}

36 Referring to the controversy in the late 1520s and early 1530s between More and the Protestant reformers John Frith (burned at Smithfield in 1533, following prosecution by More) and William Tyndale

37 Perhaps Lydgate's *The Fall of Princes*, based on the original work by Giovanni Boccaccio (John Bochas)

38 The signs of the Zodiac

39 Great figures from pagan, Jewish and Christian history, held to typify the ideals of chivalry

40 Celure, or canopy, of a bed

	sylke wth v curteyns of yellowe and redd damaske	
To the M^{r} of the Roolles	It a Featherbedd wth a brasell[41] tyke cont ix qt^{r} nume[ro] 2 wth his boulster	~~lx^{s}~~ iiij^{li}

6

[f.20v]

To the M^{r} of the Roolles	It an other Featherbedd cont x qt^{r} num[er]o 3 wth his bolster	liij^{s} iiij^{d}
	It a pallett of canves	ij^{s}
To Mr Waters	It a Coverlett of old bawdkyne lyned wth buckeram broken	iij^{s} iiij^{d}
To the M^{r} of the roolles	It a faire large quylte of crymzine turkye silke lyned wth buckeram	iiij^{li} x^{s}
	It a Cipres[42] Chest	xxvj^{s} viij^{d}
	It a paire of yron Andyrons a paire of creepers & a fyer shovell	viij^{s} vj^{d}
To my La: of worc	It a standyshe[43] covered wth leather wth Counters	ij^{s} vj^{d}
	Summa xlv^{li} x^{s} x^{d}	

In an ynner chamber to the parlo[u]r chamber

	It old hanginges of buckeram torne	xij^{s}
	It an old bedsteade of oke wth selor & testor of old bruges satten paned wth grene & whyte & fringed aboute wth whyte & grene sylke	xiij^{s} iiij^{d}
	It an old featherbedd mothe eaten & broken wth ij boulsteres one of flockes & thother of featheres	xvj^{s}
	It a redd & whyte blankett	iiij^{s}
	It a table & two trestles	ij^{s}
	It a presse of waynescott wth iiij Awmbries	xv^{s}
	It a blacke byll[44]	viij^{d}
To Mr Tho: North	It a walking spade[45]	viij^{d}
	Summa lxiij^{s} viij^{d}	

41 Bristle

42 Cypress-wood

43 Standish: inkstand or stand for writing materials generally

44 As a spade is listed next, this might seem to have been a billhook for garden or farm use. However, no other such tools are listed in the inventory. The black bill was a standard military weapon, a polearm with a hooked blade, often with spikes or barbs too, used by foot soldiers for dragging men in armour off their horses. A number are listed among the contents of the armoury, below

45 This term is obscure

[f.21r]

In my Lordes beddchamber over the pastrie

To M^{ris} Mary Scrope[46] as parte of her legacye dd to Sir G bowes	It iiij peces of hanginges of flowres cont $\overset{xx}{\text{vij}}$ elles Flemyshe at [—]	x^{li} x^{s}
	It iij other small peces of tapstrie	xiij^{s} iiij^{d}
	It iij peces of buckeram under the windowes	ij^{s}
	It iij old Curteynes of saye redd & grene wth iij yron roddes	vj^{s} viij^{d}
To Mr Percyvall Bowes	It a picture of our Ladye	v^{j}
	It a lytle close Cupborde wth an Awmbry	iiij^{s}
To my Lord Noarth	It a lytle lowe table	xvj^{d}
To the M^{r} of the Roolles	It an old great damaske cheste	xx^{s}
To my Lord North	It a large Cipres Cheste	xl^{s}
To the M^{r} of the Roolles	It a faire large quylt of crymzine Satten	xij^{li}
	It a bedsteade of wallnutt tree wth a base of yellowe & blewe saye frindged wth blewe & yellowe Crule[47]	xxxiij^{s} iiij^{d}
To M^{ris} Ma: Scrope dd to Sir G Bowes being parte of ~~a~~ [~~illeg~~] her legacye	It the selor & testor of blewe satten & yellowe & dooble vallaunce fringed wth blewe & yellowe silke wth v curteynes of blewe & yellowe sarcenett	ix^{li}
	It a quylte of blewe & yellowe satten	x^{li}
To my Lord North	It an old Coverlett wth flowres	xxvj^{s} viij^{d}
	It an old pallett of strawe	ij^{s}
To M^{ris} Ma: Scrope as parte of her legacye dd to Sir G: bowes	It a featherbedd cont x q^{r}teres nume[ro] 4 wth a boolster	iiij^{li}
	It an other Featherbedd wth a bolster cont ix qt^{r} nume[ro] 5	iij^{li} x^{s}
To my Lord North	It a woolle matteres	viij^{s}

Summa lvj^{li} xvij^{s} x^{d}

7

[f.21v]

In the garrett over the parlo[u]r chamber

It a great Lanterne of glasse	v^{s}
It a Fishe nett	xij^{d}
It a bell wth a frame & a Clapper	xx^{s}
It an old Clocke wth plumettes of lead & a dyall belonging to the same	viij^{s}
It a great table for a gynne[48] & the pulles[49] belonging thereunto	xx^{s}
It Cages hampers wth other old Lumber wth a tent frame	x^{s}
It ij^{o} Trunckes	vj^{s} viij^{d}

46 Lord North's granddaughter, daughter of Henry, Lord Scrope and North's daughter Mary. Scrope's second wife was Margaret Howard, sister of the fourth Duke of Norfolk, the purchaser of North House

47 Crewel: a thin worsted yarn

48 An engine or mechanical device, possibly connected with the bell or clock listed above

49 Pulls or handles (not pulleys)

	It ij old chestes one shippe[50] & an other square	x^{s}
	It a bare hyde[51]	xxv^{s}
	It twoo clothes sackes[52] one xx^{s} & thother xiij^{s} iiij^{d}	xxxiij^{s} iiij^{d}
To Mr Necton——	It an old feld table for the tent	x^{s}
	It an old bare hyde	v^{s}
	It an old boorde	vj^{d}
	It iij Casementes of yron for windowes wth a clapper of a bell	iij^{s} iiij^{d}
	Summa vij^{li} xvij^{s} x^{d}	

In the woodhowse in the backe yearde

	It Clvij deale boordes at iij^{s} iiij^{d} the pece	xxvj^{li} iij^{s} iiij^{d}
	It iij plankes wth other old timber wth a roller & a longe ladder wth xxxij steppes	x^{s}
To Mr Thrower——	It a waggen wth iiij^{or} wheeles	xl^{s}
	Summa xxviij^{li} xiij^{s} iiij^{d}	

[f.22r]

In the Laundrie

To Wm Salmon——	It a longe table wth iij trestles & ij Formes	iij^{s} iiij^{d}
	It ij Leaden Cesternes one greater & thother smaller	iiij^{li}
	It an old Aumbrye	ij^{s}
To my La: North——	It one old hoggeshead & iiij tubbes & a washing stoole	vj^{s}
To the M^{r} of the Roolles ij qt ^ viij^{s} 4^{d}^ & To my La North ij qt viij^{s} iiij^{d}	It baye salte[53] by estimac[i]on ij qt^{r}/viij^{s} iiij^{d}	xvj^{s} viij^{d}
	Summa v^{li} vj^{s}	

In the henne howse within the Laundrye

	It ij^{o} old Cowpes	iij^{s}
	It v troughes wth small leade	v^{s}
	Summa viij^{s}	

In Moother Jones chamber

To my La: North——	It a lyttle bagge of feathers	viij^{d}
	Summa patet	

50 With a convex top?

51 Bare hide: hide either undressed or stripped of hair, used as protective covers or tilts

52 Clothesacks: bags for clothes

53 Sea salt

In the chamber at the stayre heade over the Laundrye

	It a great frame for turkeye Carpettes	v^{s}	
my Lady Noorthes————	~~It a byrde cage~~	~~viij^{d}~~	vac
	Summa patet		

8

[f.22v]

In the chamber over the Laundrie

To Wm Salmon————	It a cheste bounde wth yron olde	iij^{s} iiij^{d}
	It a bedstead of boordes	xij^{d}
	It a paynted seelor & testor of canves	xx^{d}
	It an old coverlet & a paire of blankettes	iiij^{s}
	It an old Featherbedd a matteres & ij boolsteres & a flocke boolster	xij^{s}
	It twoo old doores & ij trestles	ij^{s}
	Summa xxiiij^{s}	

In the Fyshe howse in the Laundrie

It a stockfyshe[54] Andvell & a hammer	ij^{s}
It a Cherne a lanterne of horne a wyndowe wth yron hyndges wth other Lumber	iij^{s} iiij^{d}
Summa v^{s} iiij^{d}	

In the backhowse

It an old moulding boorde[55] a forme iij trestles wth a lyttle trowghe	xx^{d}
It an old oven lydde of yron	ij^{s} vj^{d}
It a Trivett wth iij feete	xvj^{d}
Summa v^{s} vj^{d}	

In the moulding howse

It ij trowghes a moulding borde wth theire covers a brake[56] ij^{o} tubbes	xxvj^{s} viij^{d}
Summa patet	

In the bulting[57] howse

It a bulting bynge[58] wth an old hutche[59]	iiij^{s}
Summa patet	

54 Fish dried unsalted in the open air, which had to be softened by beating, typically with wooden bars (stocks)

55 For kneading dough or preparing pastry; the trough listed with it was presumably also for kitchen use

56 A wooden tool for kneading dough

57 Boulting: sifting flour to remove the bran

58 Bin

59 Box

[f.23r]

In the brewehowse

It ij stellings[60]	v^{s}
It xiij yeast Tubbes	iiij^{s} vj^{d}
It whereof some wth a tonell[61]	
It iiij half pypes	iiij^{s}
It iij gutters & a paire of slinges	v^{s}
It a great Keele Tunne[62]	lx^{s}
It ij Coole backes[63]	xxxiij^{s} iiij^{d}
It a worte Tonne & a mashe Tonne with ij peces of leade loose	lxvj^{s} viij^{d}
It a brewing panne of copper wth leade aboute yt	xij^{li}
It a boyling Furnes to seethe brawne[64] in sett in Lead	liij^{s} iiij^{d}
It ij brewing Kettles[65] one of latten & an other of copper	v^{s}
It iij stycke forkes ij Rudderes[66] wth other necessaries	xx^{d}
It a fyer forke & cole rake	xij^{d}
It a lytle forme	vj^{d}
It a borde bedstead & an other forme	ij^{s}
It an old Featherbedd a mattres a Coverlett & a boulster	xij^{s}
It a q^{r}tr of hopps	v^{s}
It iij brewing baskettes & a stocke[67]	viij^{d}

Summa xxiiij^{li} xix^{s} viij^{d}

In the Tayleres workehowse

It an old cutting borde standing wth iiij trestles ij stooles & an old case[68] chest & an old cast yron windowe	iij^{s}

Summa patet

9

[f.23v]

In Hughe wooddes[69] chamber

It an old carpenteres bedstead wth a Testor of buckeram	iij^{s} iiij^{d}

60 Probably stells (stands) for barrels

61 Tonel: a kind of cask or barrel

62 Shallow, wide tub to cool liquids

63 Shallow vats for cooling the wort in brewing

64 Bran

65 Brew kettles: large side-handled pans for boiling wort and hops

66 Paddles for stirring mash

67 Reading uncertain. Stock: trough or similar container

68 Uncertain. Perhaps cash (casse)

69 Servant of Lord North

It a matteres a featherbedd & ij bowlsteres & a pillowe	xx^{s}
It a Coverlett of dornix[70] & a whyte Rugge	v^{s}

Summa xxviij^{s} iiij^{d}

In John Fearnes chamber

It a bedstead wth a painted celer	ij^{s} vj^{d}
It a Featherbedd ij boulsters one of feathers & thother of flockes & a redd coverlet	xj^{s}
It a lytle borde wth ij trestles & other Lumber	xij^{d}
It a great Sawe	v^{s}

Summa xx^{s} vj^{d}

In Mr Jones[71] chamber

To Mr Rosewell my L: Dyers servant

It certen paynted clothes cont xl yeardes	x^{s}
It ij boordes wth iiij trestles	ij^{s} vj^{d}
It a wainescott stoole	vj^{d}
It a bedstead wth pillers wth selor of waynescott	v^{s}
It a Featherbedd a boulster & a pillowe of downe	xxvj^{s} viij^{d}
It ij Coverlettes one of redd & thother old of Imagerie	vj^{s}

Summa ~~xlix^{s} viij^{d}~~ l^{s} viij^{d}

[f.24r]

In the bakers chamber

It a bedstead of boordes very olde	viij^{d}
It an old Matteres ij bolsters of feathers & ij blanckettes	ix^{s}

Summa ix^{s} viij^{d}

In Ralphe Walkers chamber

It a featherbedd a boulster of flockes a blanckett & a Coverlett	vj^{s} viij^{d}

Summa patet

In Gabriell Emersons chamber

It a bedstead wth pilleres wth the selor of mockado[72]	iij^{s}
It a featherbedd of ymagery old & a Rugge	xij^{s}
It an old settle & a joyned stoole	iij^{s}
It ij old boordes wth iiij trestles	xx^{d}

Summa xxix^{s} viij^{d}

70 Dornick: a kind of figured linen originally made at Doornik (Tournai)

71 Thomas Jones, servant of Lord North

72 Mockado: a woollen imitation velvet

In the Smythes Forge

It a great Andvyll of yron	x^{s}
It a byckhorne[73] a slegge[74]	ij^{s}
It iiij paire of tonges wth vj puntches & [—]	iij^{s}
It a vice	iiij^{s}

[f.24v]

It a paire of bellowes for a smythe	x^{s}
It a trusse[75] to shoe a horse	ij^{s} vj^{d}
Summa xxxj^{s} vj^{d}	

~~Item~~	
Item certen seacoles by estimac[i]on	lxvj^{s} viij^{d}
It certen old yron	nll
Summa patet	

In the storehowse for tymber worke

It xxxviij bundelles of lathe	xxv^{s} iiij^{d}
It xxxv Fatholtes[76] at iij^{d} le pece	viij^{s} ix^{d}
It iiij dooz single Clapborde[77]	vj^{s}
It certen tymber wth other old Lumber	lx^{s}
Summa C^{s} j^{d}	

Note that parte of this Lumber is my Lady Northes

It an old haye for conyes[78]	ij^{s}
Summa patet	

In the gardiners chamber

It an old bedstead broken	xij^{d}
It an old broken featherbedd wth a pillo	v^{s}
Summa vj^{s}	

In the Myllhowse

It the frame of the ij mylles wth 4 stones & other furniture to the same	xij^{li}
Summa patet	

73 Bycorne or bickhorn: a type of anvil with tapered projections at each end

74 Sledge-hammer

75 Uncertain. Perhaps a version of the close-fitting pair of breeches known as a trowse, worn to protect the legs when shoeing

76 *OED* suggests that fatholts were staves for casks, which seems to be confirmed by the following entry here

77 Pieces of split oak, imported from north Germany, used for making barrel-staves

78 A net for rabbit-catching

[f.25r]

In the sommer parlo[u]r wthin the garden

It a large plancke boorde x^{s}
It xxvij deale bordes at iij^{s} iiij^{d} a pece iiij^{li} x^{s}
It a Carpenters gynne xx^{s}
It a horslytter[79] wth the shaftes iiij^{li}
wth all his apparell
Summa xxiij^{li} vj^{s} viij^{d}

In the stylling howse

It vj Stylles lx^{s}
Summa patet

In the hen howse

To the M^{r} of the Roolles — It a horslytter wth his furniture vj^{li}
lyned wthin wth grene clothe
Summa patet

In Robert Tompsons chamber

It a bedstead of boordes old xij^{d}
It an old featherbedd a bolster x^{s}
& ij blanckettes
Summa xj^{s}

In Thomas Wilkyns chamber

It an old bedsteade xij^{d}
It an old broken mattres a bolster vj^{s}
& an old whyte Coverlett
Summa vij^{s}

11

[f.25v]

In John Morryce chamber

Item an old broken bedstead xij^{d}
It an old featherbed a bowlster a x^{s}
blankett a flocke bolster & a Coverlett
Summa xj^{s}

In the Stable

It v C boordes of oke at iiij^{s} v^{d} le C xxij^{s} vj^{d}
It sixe sadles bridles wth thappurt[enances] xxx^{s}
at v^{s} the pece
Summa liij^{s} vj^{d}

79 A litter slung on poles, carried between a leading and a following horse

In the lofte over the stable

	It a saddle of blacke velvet wth the bridle & the harnes belonging thereto	xl^{s}
To the M^{r} of the Roolles	It old harnes of velvet for the moyle[80] very bare[81] wth gilt bosses	v^{s}
	It a chest of wainescott old iij bordes wth iiij trestles & other Lomber	xij^{s}
	Summa lvij^{s}	

In the plomerie

My la. North hath one bell besydes thes ij^{o} wch rem[ain] her[e]	It ij belles wth Clappers weying lvl^{lli} at iij^{d} ob the lli	xiiij^{s} vij^{d} ob
	It certen broken pypes of Leade weyeing ix^{lli} q^{r}t^{r} wth a pece of a gutter at ix^{s} le lli	iiij^{li} iij^{s} iiij^{d}
	It x gunnes great & small wth chambers	liij^{s} iiij^{d}

[f.26r]

	It a mowlde to flote lead in	xx^{s}
	It ij plankes	iiij^{s}
	It a cradle frame & a candle mold wth broken tubbes & other old Lumber	x^{s}
To my La: North	It a doore of wainescott wth hindges and hookes	iiij^{s}
	It certen tallow by estimac[i]on	xij^{s}
	Summa x^{li} xv^{d}	

In the entrie by Mr Pigottes[82] chamber

To Mr Sootherton	It a bedstead wth pillers carved wth a testor of waynescott	xv^{s}
	Summa patet	

In the woodhowse

	It ij^{o} yron slynges[83] upon stockes wth theire chamberes & wheeles	v^{li} v^{s} viij^{d}
	Summa patet	

In the Armoreres working howse

	It v drie Fattes[84] one broken, an old forme & an old doore	iiij^{s}
	Summa patet	

In the garner

To Mr Waters	It iiij q^{r}teres of otes	xj^{s}
	It viij b[ushels] of maulte	x^{s}

80 Mule

81 Threadbare

82 Edward Pigott, servant of Lord North

83 Sling: a type of cannon

84 Dry-fats: barrels or casks for dry goods

It ij skryves[85] one for wheat & thother for maulte	x^{s}
It ix sackes	xx^{d}
Summa xxxvij^{s} viij^{d}	

12

[f.26v]

In the chamber next the garner

It a bedsteade wth pillers wth a Testor of bawdkyn	viij^{s}
Summa patet	
It a glasse lanterne at the gate broken	iij^{s} iiij^{d}
Summa patet	

In Mr Cosyns chamber

It a boorde bedsteade	xvj^{d}
It a featherbedd two bolsters & a pillowe	xxiij^{s} iiij^{d}
It ij^{o} Coverlettes one redd & an other of Carpett worke	ix^{s}
It a selor of buckeram	xvj^{d}
It twoo stooles one wallnutt tree & an other waynescott	xx^{d}
It a presse of bordes wth a plancke afore the windowe	xx^{d}
Summa xxxviij^{s} iiij^{d}	

In the next Lodging

^Thes^ ij^{o} forme is my Lord Northes/ideo canc[ellatur]	~~It ij Formes~~	~~xx^{d}~~
	Summa patet	nll

In the porteres Lodge

It a square table wth the frame	ij^{s}
It a featherbedd ij bolsters & a mattres	xv^{s}
It an old Coverlet & a blancket	v^{s}
It a paire of old playing tables wth men	xx^{d}
It an old broken stoole	ij^{d}
Summa xxiij^{s} x^{d}	

[f.27r]

In Mr Pigottes chamber

It a bedstead of wainescott wth pilleres wth the vallance of old buckeram	viij^{s}

85 Scry: a sieve

To Webster my L: Dyers servaunt	It a featherbedd & a boulster	xviij^s
	It ij^o pallettes of strawe	iij^s
	It a redd woollen Coverlett & a whyte blankett	x^s
	It a wainescott chaire broken	xij^d
	It a litle boorde wth ij^o trestles	vj^d
	Summa xl^s vj^d	

In Mr Brigantynes chamber

It a bedstead wth pilleres	x^s
It a joyned Chayre	iij^s iiij^d
It a little table wth folding feete	iij^s iiij^d
It a Courte Cupborde	iij^s
It old hanginges of redd & grene buckeram	x^s
It a blue & redd Curteyne of buckeram wth a curteyne rodd	ij^s
It a paire of Crepers	xij^d
It a bedsteade of boordes	xvj^d
It a presse of wainescott broken	viij^s
It a pece of old hanginges of red saye	ij^s
It ij old joyned stooles	xij^d
Summa xlv^s	
It a Lanterne of glasse hanging in the ynner yearde	v^s
Summa patet	

13

[f.27v]

In Applegarthes chamber

	It an old bedstead wth pillers	v^s viij^d
	It a featherbedd & ij boolsters	xxv^s
To Mr Wateres[86]	It a broken woollen mattres	ij^s vj^d
	It a Coverlett a rugge & a blanckett	vj^s viij^d
	It an old lyvery Cupborde	viij^d
	It a wainescott table wth ij^o trestles	ij^s
	It an old Curteyne of saye	xij^d
	It a remnaunt of blue buckeram & an old forme	viij^d
	Summa xlv^s ij^d	

In Mr Thomas Northes chamber

It a wainescott bedsteade wth pilleres carved	xv^s
It the testor selor & vallaunce of redd saye wth v curteynes of the same	x^s

86 Servant of Lord North

	It a featherbedd & bolster wth a brysell tyke cont 7 qt^{r}	liij^{s} iiij^{d}
	It an other lesser featherbedd wth his bolster sore worne 7 qt^{r}	xvj^{s}
To Mr Necton	It ij pillowes of downe	iiij^{s}
	It ij woollen blankettes	iiij^{s}
	It a strawe bedd	xvj^{d}
To the M^{r} of the Roolles	It a Coverlett of flowers	xx^{s}
	It certen old hanginges	vj^{s} viij^{d}
	It ij^{o} stooles	xvj^{d}
To Mr Tho: North	It a broken chaire of wallnutt tree	ij^{s}
	Summa vj^{li} xiij^{s} viij^{d}	

[f.28r]

In the Rose[87] chamber

It hanginges of redd & grene saye	xxvj^{s} viij^{d}
It a windowe curteyne of old buckeram wth an yron rodd	xx^{d}
Summa xxviij^{s} iiij^{d}	

Brass remayning in the garrett

It v brasse pannes great & small weyeing lxxviij^{lli} at vij^{d} le lli	xlv^{s} vj^{d}
It iij Kettelles great & small wth yron bandes w^{g} lxxiiij^{lli} at vj^{d} le lli	xxxvij^{s}
It a great brasse pott wth a chafer[88] wth a bale[89] w^{g} lxvj^{lli} at iiij^{d} le lli	xxij^{s}
It ij broken brasse pottes wth other broken mettle w^{g} xxviij^{lli} at ij^{d} ob the lli	v^{s} ij^{d}
It ij^{o} yron Trivettes w^{g} xv^{lli} at j^{d} ob le lli	xxij^{d} ob
Summa v^{li} xij^{s} vj^{d} ob	

brasse owt of the Laundrie

It twoo great brasse pottes w^{g} v^{XX} vj^{lli} at iiij^{d} the lli	xxxv^{s} iiij^{d}
It a great panne w^{g} xxvj^{lli} at vij^{d} le lli	xv^{s} ij^{d}
It a kettle wth an yron bale wey[ing]^{e} xij^{lli} at iiij^{d} the lli	iiij^{s}
It an other old kettle w^{g} xvij^{lli} at iiij^{d} le lli	vj^{s} iiij^{d}
Summa ~~lx~~ lx^{s} ij^{d}	

14

87 Or Rofe (roof)

88 Container for burning charcoal or other fuel beneath the pot

89 Hooped handle

[f.28v]

Brasse in the Kychen

	It a great Caudron of brasse wth	xxij^{s} viij^{d}
	ij ringes w^{g} lxviij^{lli} at iiij^{d} le lli	
	It iij old kettles w^{g} xliiij^{lli} at iiij^{d}	xiiij^{s} viij^{d}
	It iij pannes ij great an other	xix^{s} x^{d}
	smaller w^{g} xxxiiij^{lli} at vij^{d} le lli	
	It a kettle wth a handle & a	iij^{s} viij^{d}
	panne in the plomerie xj^{lli} at [—]	
	It iij brasse pottes w^{g} iiij^{xx} xij^{lli}	xxx^{s} viij^{d}
	wth a chafer wthall at iiij^{d}	
	It a broken chafer & a broken pott	iij^{s} xj^{d} ob
	w^{g} xix^{lli} at ij^{d} ob	
	It an old kettle remayning in the	iij^{s} iiij^{d}
	backhowse w^{g} x^{lli} at iiij^{d}	
	It iij shreading knyves, a Clever	xvj^{d}
	& a bread grate	
	It a butchers Axe	vj^{d}
	It a latten candlesticke hanging	vj^{d}
	Summa Cj^{s} j^{d} ob	

Pewter going abrode[90] aboute the howse

	It pewter vessell going aboute the	
	howse w^{g} xj^{xx} x^{lli} at v^{d} ob	v^{li} v^{s} v^{d}
	le lli	
	It ij^{o} old pottes & a Cullender	ij^{s} viij^{d}
	w^{g} viij^{lli} at iiij^{d} the lli	
	Summa Cviij^{s} j^{d}	

[f.29r]

In the pastrie

	Item an oven lydde of yron	iij^{s} iiij^{d}
To my La: North——	It a fylling Ladle of brasse	xij^{d}
	It a hand peele[91]	iij^{d}
	Summa iiij^{s} vij^{d}	

In the Spicerie

To my La: North——	It a spice morter standing in	x^{s}
	a blocke wth a pestle of yron	
	It a presse wth leaves lockes and	x^{s}
	hynges	
	It a chest of wainescott old & broken	ij^{s}
	It a pyle of weightes wth theire	xiij^{s} iiij^{d}
	ballance w^{g} xx^{lli} [—]	
	It certen boordes & shelffes aboute	iiij^{s}
	the spicerie wth a forme	
	It a wafer panne of yron	iiij^{s}

90 Dispersed

91 A small fire-shovel, or a wooden shovel or slice for use in baking

To Mr Necton	It a perfume panne	viij^{d}
	It an yron to roste apples	xij^{d}
	Summa xlv^{s}	

In the drie Larder

It ij planckes & ij pa[i]rre of trestles	xij^{s}
It a bynne for otemeale	xx^{d}
It a Cupbord called a meat Awmbrye	v^{s}
It an old Cheste	iij^{s} iiij^{d}
It ij^{o} newe Flaskettes[92]	xviij^{d}

15

[f.29v]

given to Mr Tho: North ij^{o} firkins j spent in the howse j to John Waters & j other sold to my la: North	It v firkins of butter hole at xij^{s} the firkyn	lx^{s}
	It a hoggeshead of vergiewse[93]	v^{s}
	It ij emptie hoggesheads & iij Rundelettes[94]	iij^{s}
	It Rackes for cheses	ij^{s}
	It a brasse Chafer	iij^{s} iiij^{d}
To my Lord North	It a morter of Alabaster wth a woodden pestle	ij^{s} vj^{d}
	Summa iiij^{li} xix^{s} iiij^{d}	

In the wette Larder

It iij old planckes & ij bordes	ij^{s} vj^{d}
It a hoggeshead a powdring tubbe[95]	xx^{d}
Summa iiij^{s} ij^{d}	

In the wette Larder yearde

It a Cesterne of Leade wth a partyc[i]on	xxxiij^{s} iij^{d}
It a Musterd querne	xij^{d}
Summa xxxiiij^{s} iiij^{d}	

In the Kychen

It a chopping bord, & a longe dressing bord/an other shorter borde & an old boorde standing upon feete	xv^{s}

92 Probably here (and in the pantry, below) referring to long, shallow baskets or similar containers, not to little flasks

93 Verjuice: the juice of unripe fruit, used in cooking and medicine

94 Runlets: small casks

95 For salting meat

[f.30r]

To my La: North———	It a stone morter & a pestle	ij^{s} viij^{d}
	It ij old boordes in the skulley yeard	viij^{d}
	It ij^{o} old frying pannes	xvj^{d}
	Summa xix^{s} viij^{d}	

Iron worke in the Kychin

	It x spyttes weyeing vj^{xx} xiiij^{lli} at j^{d} ob le lli	xvj^{s} ix^{d}
To my L: Dyer———	It a great grydyron w^{g} xxxvj^{lli} at j^{d} ob le lli	iiij^{s} vj^{d}
	It a longe Trivett weyeing vj^{xx} viij^{lli} at j^{d} the lli	x^{s} viij^{d}
	It ij^{o} yron rackes wth [—] weyeing v^{xx} xij^{lli} at j^{d} ob le lli	xiiij^{s}
	It an other paire of rackes greater weyeing ix^{xx} lli at j^{d} ob le lli	xxij^{s} vj^{d}
	It old Trevettes & old grydyrons w^{g} all iiij^{xx} at j^{d} le lli	vj^{s} viij^{d}
To my La: North———	It iij drypping pannes wth ij^{o} yron handles a pece	iiij^{s}
	It an old latten basen w^{g} vij^{lli}	ij^{s} iiij^{d}
	It a lytle square trivet w^{g} xiiij^{lli}	xiiij^{d}
	Summa iiij^{li} ij^{s} vij^{d}	

In the buttrie viz in the first Rowme

It a Table wth a frame	iiij^{s}
It a Cupbord wth Awmbries & lockes	vj^{s}
It a bynge for breade & a chipping knyfe	v^{s}

16

[f.30v]

Itm ij^{o} shelves and a Chippinge borde	ij^{s}
Itm A pottell[96] wyne pott	ij^{s} vj^{d}
Itm A pottell Ale pott	xx^{d}
Itm A pynte wyne pott	x^{d}
Itm ij^{o} pewter cruses[97] wth eares	xij^{d}
Itm iiij^{or} pewter saltes[98]	xij^{d}
Itm ij^{o} blacke Jackes[99] of pottelles	ij^{s}
~~Summa~~	

96 Of the capacity of a pottle, i.e. 4 pints (approx. 2.3 litres)

97 Term applied to various sorts of jar or pot, including drinking vessels

98 Salt cellar

99 Black jack: large tarred leather jug or tankard for beer, etc

In the plate house w^{t}in the butterey

Margin	Item	Value
	Itm A table wth ij^{o} Tresselles	iiij^{s}
	Itm A Chest for plate	iij^{s} iiij^{d}
	Itm A lyttell shorte chest bound w^{t} Iron	iiij^{s}
To my La: North	Itm A bread Bynne wth A partic[i]on in ye myddes	iij^{s} iiij^{d}
	Itm A plate Baskett	xx^{d}
	Summa xlij^{s} iiij^{d}	

In the Buttrye viz in the second rowme

Item iij^{re} longe beare stales[100] & a pulley	x^{s}
Item A stoole Joyned and a broken chayre	xvj^{d}
Itm one Iron harthe	xiij^{s} iiij^{d}
Summa xxiiij^{s} viij^{d}	

In the wyne seller

Itm ij^{o} Joyces[101]	iiij^{s}
Summa patet	

In an other wyne seller

Itm iij^{re} wyne stalles	x^{s}
Itm A Racke for cheses	ij^{s}
Itm an olde Aumbry & an olde borde	xij^{d}
Itm ij^{o} treyes	viij^{d}
Summa xiij^{s} viij^{d}	

[f.31r]

In the pantry

Margin	Item	Value
	Itm A Breade Bynne wth iij roumes	vj^{s} viij^{d}
	Itm an Aumbrye	xij^{d}
	Itm A Table of bordes wth ij^{o} Tresselles	xij^{d}
	Itm a longe settle of waynescott	vj^{s} viij^{d}
	Itm ij^{o} olde Chestes	xx^{d}
	Itm shelves aboute the pantrye	xx^{d}
To my L: dyer	Itm a latten panne to put broken dryncke in wth ij^{o} handelles	xij^{s}
	Itm a payre of flaggon budgettes[102]	xij^{d}
	Itm latten Candellsticks there viz of A large sorte iiij^{or} payre at ij^{s} iiij^{d}	ix^{s} iiij^{d}
	Itm vj payre of a lesser sorte at ij^{s} payre	xij^{s}
	Itm vj odd olde Candelsticks verye smale	ij^{s}
	Itm A payre of large pewter Candelstickes	iij^{s}
	Itm ij^{o} payre of a lesser sorte	iiij^{s}
	Itm A newe flaskett	vj^{d}
	Itm A Case w^{t} broken knyves	xx^{d}
	Itm viij Chargers whereof one square weyeinge xxxvij^{lli} at vj^{d} the pound	xviij^{s} vj^{d}
	Summa iiii^{li} ij^{s} viij^{d}	

100 Beer stalls (stands for casks)

101 Joists or similar lengths of timber

102 Leather flagons

In my Ladye worce[s]tors Chamber

Itm a beddstead of waynescott w^{t} pyllors w^{t} the bases of grene Saye	xiij^{s} iiij^{d}
Itm A Testor and Selor of Taffata sarcenett withe doble vallaunce wth my Lordes Armes ymbrodered at the heade wth v curteynes of redd sarcenett	iij^{li}

17

[f.31v]

	Itm A bedd of fustyane stuffed w^{t} downe and a boulster	iiij^{li}
	Itm ij^{o} pyllowes of downe	v^{s}
	Itm A fetherbedd w^{t}out A bolster	xij^{s}
	Itm A matteres	iij^{s}
	Itm A white Iryshe Rugge	iij^{s}
	Itm A redd coveringe	vj^{s}
	Itm A coveringe of sylke Imagerye	xxxiij^{s} iiij^{d}
	Itm A payre of fustyane blanckettes	xiij^{s} iiij^{d}
	Itm A iiij^{or} square table wth a frame	v^{s}
	Itm A Courte cupborde	iij^{s}
my Lord Northes	~~A Chayre of waynescott covered wth clothe and ymbrodered~~	~~xx^{d}~~
	Itm olde velvett quyshions one of roses & the other w^{t} flowers	ij^{s} viij^{d}
	Itm ij^{o} wyndowe Curteynes of grene and redd saye wth ij^{o} Iron roddes	vj^{s}
	Itm A basone and Ewer of pewter old	iij^{s} iiij^{d}
	Summa xij^{li} x^{s} iiij^{d}	

In the Inner Chamber called the maydes chamber

Itm A beddstead olde wth pyllors	iiij^{s}
Itm A Selor and Testor of clothe of bawdkyn	x^{s}
Itm a fetherbedd a boulster and A pyllowe	xxvj^{s} viij^{d}
Itm A woollen blanckett	xx^{d}
Itm A coverlett of Tapestrie lyned	iiij^{s}
Itm A presse of waynescott	xij^{s}
Itm an old chayre w^{t} A backe	xvj^{d}
Itm A longe newe borde	viij^{d}
Summa l^{s} iiij^{d}	

[f.32r]

In the Chapple

It a great standert[103] bound wth yron redd	xxvj^{s} viij^{d}
It a vestment of grene velvet wth awbes & the furnyture thereof	xiij^{s} iiij^{d}

103 Standard: large chest or packing-case

To Mr Heathe	It a paire of Regalles[104] wth the table & frame	lx^{s}
	It a vestment of redd & grene fustian of Napes[105] wth the furnyture	vj^{s} viij^{d}
	It an Aulter clothe of hayre	xij^{d}
	It a Corporas Case[106]	viij^{d}
	It ij Curteynes of redd & grene saye	xij^{d}
	It ij curteyns roddes of redd & grene sarcenet wth ij^{o} curteynes roddes	vj^{s} viij^{d}
	It a paire of latten Candlestickes for the Chapple	iij^{s}
	It ij Crewettes of pewter & a paxe of pewter	vj^{d}
	It a Corporas clothe of Calowcoret[107] clothe & ij tape girdles	viij^{d}
	It ij^{o} Aulter clothes of grene & redd fustian of Apes[108]	xvj^{s}
	It an Alter clothe of hayre	xij^{d}
	It ij^{o} Aulter clothes of dyaper[109]	iiij^{s} vj^{d}
To Mr Sootherton	It ij^{o} longe quyshens of downe covered wth velvet	iiij^{s}
	It ij^{o} quyshe[n]s wth roses & one wth Flowers	v^{s}

18

[f.32v]

It a Table of waineocott wth a cupborde standing Aulterwyse	v^{s}
It a bible in lattyne & a boke of St Jheromes epistles in parchement	xxvj^{s} viij^{d}
It an englyshe bible and twoo communion bookes	xvj^{s}
It x formes after deske fashion long & shorte	xx^{s}
It iiij^{or} foolding boordes wth yron henges	x^{s}
It a lecterne & a deske	xij^{d}
It a carved creast wth boordes & turned pilleres & ij seare clothes[110] & other Lumber	iij^{s} iiij^{d}
It ij trestles	viij^{d}
Summa xl^{li} xvij^{s} iiij^{d}	

104 Pair of regals: a small organ with a keyboard for one hand and bellows worked by the other

105 Fustian of Naples: a kind of cotton velvet

106 Case for a corporal-cloth (on which the consecrated elements for the Eucharist are laid out, and with which their remnants are covered)

107 Calicut (calico)

108 Variant of fustian of Naples

109 Diaper: linen cloth textured with a self-coloured ornamental weave in diamond or other pattern

110 Cerecloths: waxed cloths used as winding-sheets for burials, but perhaps here referring to protective covers for furnishings or other items

In the entrie going towarde the bowling alleye

	It a great chest bounde wth yron	x^{s}
	Summa patet	

In my Lordes Closett

To Mr Necton	It the hanginges of redd & grene saye wth a boorder old	xv^{s}
	It a presse wth viij leaves full of writing boxes	lxvj^{s} viij^{d}

[f.33r]

	It a great yron Chest	x^{li}
	It a small yron Chest	iiij^{s} x^{s}
To my Lady of Worc	It a fyne Compter[111] wth boxes	iiij^{li} x^{s}
	It a shorte Venyce Chest	x^{s}
	It a gardyvian[112] chest bounde wth yron	xx^{s}
	It a lytle chest plated wth yron	v^{s}
	It a chest of wainescott wth ij^{o} boxes belowe at the ende	vj^{s} viij^{d}
To my La: of worc	It a Trunke wth locke & keye plated wth yron	v^{s}
	It ij^{o} olde gardyviances	viij^{s}
To my La: of worc	It a Flaunders Caskett[113]	x^{s}
	It a lytle steele Cofer	x^{s}
To Mr Johnes	It a lytle old Cassocke[114] plated wth yron wth diverse boxes	iij^{s} iiij^{d}
	It a boxe ~~of~~ for billymentes[115]	xx^{d}
To Mr Johnes Wateres Necton Thornton & Cosen[116]	It iij paire of weomens gloves perfumed one wth pearle & gold at v^{s} and thother ij^{o} at ij^{s}	vij^{s}
	It iij paire of new gloves of the wch ij paire of oxfordes making	ij^{s}
To Mr Johnes & Waters	It ij paire of knyves one of Scottishe making at xij^{d} a paire	ij^{s}
	It a pyn pillowe of crimsen satten ymbrodered wth golde & an other of tawney velvet imbrodered wth gold	iiij^{s}
	It ij Cogniz[a]unces for a foteman & ij^{o} lesser scuchyons	iiij^{s}

19

111 Counter: a table or desk for counting money and keeping accounts; also applied to a side table or dresser

112 Gardeviance: portable safe or chest for meat or valuables

113 Flanders was a centre for the manufacture of high quality chests and caskets, often elaborately worked with carved ornament

114 Presumably an error for a word such as casket or casson

115 Biliments: ornamental items of women's headgear or neckwear

116 Servants of Lord North

[f.33v]

	It Muffleres boundgraces[117] & a partelett[118]	ij^{s} vj^{d}
	It a Case for a nest of goblettes	xvj^{d}
	It a case of knyves of Allyphantes tothe[119] typte wth sylver	xx^{s}
To my La: of Worc	It an other case of knyves of Dancaster[120] making	iij^{s} iiij^{d}
	It an olde stoole of wainescott	viij^{d}
	It ij Crosbowes wth cases of leather one bigger an other lesser wth theire quyveres & rackes the best xxx^{s} & thother xiij^{s} iiij^{d}	xliij^{s} iiij^{d}
To my La: of Worc	It ij^{o} old Lutes	x^{s}
	It a pyle of weightes wth a paire of ballances	xx^{s}
To my La: of Worc	It certen psalter bookes & prayer bookes ij covered wth velvet & clasped wth sylver & one covered wth redd tynsell[121] & a claspe of silver	xxvj^{s} viij^{d}
	It ij^{o} other psalter bookes covered wth velvet being wrytten in parchement	viij^{s}
	It iij englyshe bookes of partes of the bible	ij^{s} vj^{d}
	It iiij^{or} old bookes in latten	vj^{d}
To my La: of Worc ij Necton iij & Thornton j	It vj doos of fyne case trenchers whereof 3 dos square & 3 dos round	viij^{s}
	It a grene Clothe	iiij^{s}
To Alex Roswell & Gysse	It a yearde of white carsey[122]	ij^{s}
	It one pece of fyne canves ell brode cont xxxvj elles at xvj^{d} thell	xlviij^{s}
	It an other pece of canves fyner of ij elles brode cont 4 elles de at iij^{s} the ell	xviij^{s}

[f.34r]

To Alex Roswell & Gysse	It xj elles of courser canves of an ell q^{r}t^{r} brode at ij^{s} vj^{d} the ell	xxvij^{s} vj^{d}
	It a pece of holland of xv elles & a half at xvj^{d} le ell	xx^{s} viij^{d}
	It an other pece of holland cont xxj elles at ~~xxj^{d}~~ xvj^{d} le ell	xxviij^{s}
	It ij^{o} bowes	iij^{s} iiij^{d}
	It an old chaire of needle worke	x^{s}
	Summa xliij^{li} viij^{s} viij^{d}	

117 Bongrace: a curtain-like veil or other shade, worn against the sun as part of a woman's headgear

118 Partlet: item of clothing for the neck and upper chest, especially covering a woman's low décolletage

119 Ivory

120 Doncaster

121 Tinsel: cloth such as satin or silk interwoven or brocaded with gold or silver thread, or thinly coated with gold or silver

122 Kersey: coarse woollen narrow cloth, usually ribbed

In the ynner rowme in my Lordes Closett

	It a presse full of boxes	xxvj^{s} viij^{d}
To my L: Dyer	It a reading glasse	iij^{s} iiij^{d}
	Summa xxx^{s}	

My Lordes Apparell

Gyven by wyll to my Lord North	It a parliament Robes furred wth mynivere wth all his apparell	x^{li}
	It a faire velvet gowne wth a garde ymbrodered faced wth sables & furred wth squyrelles	xij^{li}
	It an other gowne of velvet faced wth unshoorne velvet wth x payre of Aglettes[123]	x^{li}
To Sir G Alington	It an other velvet gowne wth a garde ymbrodered faced wth marternes[124] & lyned throughe wth squyrelles worne	viij^{li}

20

[f.34v]

	It a damaske gowne wth ij^{o} burgoni[an][125] yardes of velvet faced wth velvett	vj^{li} viij^{s} iiij^{d}
	It a gowne of taffata & faced wth taffata wth a small welte of velvet & lyned wth cotton	xl^{s}
To M^{r} brigantyne	It a gowne of grograyne[126] sore worne furred wth old squyrelles	xx^{s}
To Mr Holmes	It a Jacket of velvet wth a garde ymbrodered	xxxiij^{s} iiij^{d}
To M^{r} brigantyne	It an other old velvet Jackett layed on wth iij parchement lases	xiij^{s} iiij^{d}
To Sir G: Alington	It a ryding Cloke of velvet garded wth iij burgonyon yardes	iiij^{li} iiij^{li}
	It a Cassocke of blacke damaske garded wth velvett	xv^{s}
	It a Jerkyn of russet satten furred wth Lambe & edged wth luzernes[127]	x^{s}
	It a Jerkyn of blacke satten wth sleves	xv^{s}
To Mr Thornton	It a Jerkyn of blacke satten wth sleves edged wth Martyrnes & furred wth lambe	x^{s}
To Mr Waters	It an other of blacke satten edged wth conye	viij^{s}

123 Aglets: ornamental tags or pendants; otherwise metal points at the ends of laces

124 Martens

125 Burgundian

126 Grogram: a coarse fabric of silk or part silk, often stiffened with gum

127 Lucerns, i.e. lynx-skins

To Mr Waters	It an old peced Dooblet of blacke satten	iiij^s
	It an other old satten Dooblett lyned wth whyte cotton	ij^s
To Mr Millysent	It a Cloke of pinke wth sleves wth a garde of velvet	xxvj^s iiij^d
Given to Wm Johnson by my L: Dyer	It an old Cloke of clothe for the rayne	xiij^s iiij^d
	It a newe coote of clothe	xij^s
To Wm Johnson	It iij redd petyecootes of clothe	vj^s viij^d
To Mr Tho: North	It an night gowne of clothe faced wth foynes[128] & furred wth whyte Lambe	viij^d

[f.35r]

	It ij paire of hoose the best ij^s And thother xx^d	iij^s viij^d
To Sir G Alington	It a skeyne[129] wth gylte hyltes & locks & chape[130] gilte wth a shethe of velvet	xiij^s iiij^d
	It an armyng sworde wth a gilte pommell	x^s
	It an other armyng sworde wth a pommell of yron vernyshe	iij^s iiij^d
To Mr Thornton	It a woodknyfe[131] wth a horneheaste[132] russett vernyshed	vj^s viij^d
To Mr Millisent	It a skeyne wth a skaberde of velvet	v^s
To Sir G: Alington	It a woodknyfe wth hiltes & pommell of yron wth a skaberd of velvett	v^s
	It an other woodknyfe wth a broken pomell covered wth velvett wth a paire of compasses	iiij^s
	It a halmeste[133] banded aboute ~~wth~~ the hilt	v^s
	It a short slavye[134] blade wth the hyltes of Latten	iiij^s
To Mr Waters	It a hatt of blacke velvet wth a bande of goold	v^s
To Mr Millisent	It a velvet Cappe	iiij^s
To Mr Johnson	It a velvet night cappe	xij^d
	It a satten night cap^p lyned wth velvet	xvj^d
	It an other velvet night cappe	ij^s
	It iiij paire of old shoes of velvet & a paire of velvet slyppers iiij paire of leather shoes & v paire of old buskyns	[—]
	It a lytle bell	xij^d
	Summa lxvij^li iij^s viij^d	

21

128 Foin: fur of the weasel or similar animal

129 Skene: a dagger or short sword

130 Chape: metal mounting of sheath or scabbard

131 Wood-knife: a short sword or dagger, used originally when hunting, for cutting up carcases, but also as a weapon

132 Horn haft

133 Unidentified word; reading uncertain

134 Unidentified word, reading uncertain. Perhaps connected with slave, meaning to tear away or split, and slive, to cut off, slice or split

[f.35v]

In the pantrie chamber

Recipient	Item	Value
	It a bedstead of wainescott wth pillers	lx^{s}
To the M^{r} of the Roolles	It a featherbedd wthoute bolster cont 8 qt^{r}	xl^{s}
	It a faire large Covering paned wth grene velvet & redd damaske wth roses of venys goold	xij^{li}
To my La: North	It an other course Coverlett of grene Flowers	xxiij^{s} iiij^{d}
	It a redd Rugge	xviij^{s}
To the M^{r} of the roolles	It an other featherbedd wth a course boolster cont [—] qteres	xlvj^{s} viij^{d}
	It one whyte blanckett	iij^{s} iiij^{d}
	It a selor & testor of grene velvet & redd damaske wth roses of venys gold wth v curteyns of redd & grene sarcenet & dooble vallaunce wth the fryndge of grene & redd silke	x^{li}
To the M^{r} of the Roolles	It a large redd Rugge	xv^{s}
To my La: North	It a table wth ij^{o} leaves upon a frame wth an Awmbry in yt	xij^{s}
	It a turky carpet ij yerdes longe & an ell brode	xij^{s}
	It a courte Cupborde	vj^{s}
To my La: North	It a turky carpet upon the same Cupborde	xij^{s}
	It a spanyshe chaire ~~sell~~ seat & backe of clothe of gold & damaske	xx^{s}
	It a Jewell chest covered wth blacke velvett & barred wth steele & iij Lockes	v^{li}

[f.36r]

Recipient	Item	Value
To M^{ris} Alington	It a chest covered wth blue velvet ymbrodered wth silver lace	xl^{s}
To the M^{r} of the Roolles	It a quyshine of crymsen satten ymbrodered wth venys goold	xxvj^{s} viij^{d}
	It a cristall glasse covered wth crimzin satten ymbrodered wth gold	xv^{s}
	It an other looking glasse covered wth grene velvet ymbrodered wth silver	xiij^{s} iiij^{d}
	It an other looking glasse gilded standing in a case of woodd	xv^{s}
	It a combe case of whyte & blewe bubell[135] wth the combes & other the appurtenaunces	iiij^{s}
	It ij^{o} Canapye clothes one whyte & thother wth blue taphata wth parchement Lace of gold the whyte xx^{s} & thother v^{s}	xxv^{s}
	It half a yeard of clothe of gold	x^{s}
To Mr Foster	It a great chest of wainescott wth handles of yron	x^{s}

135 Presumably bubble or bauble; precise meaning uncertain but perhaps referring to a type of glass

To my La: North	It a close chaire covered wth grene clothe	xx^{d}
To my La: of worc	It a womans chaire seat & backe of tawnye velvet wth E & A	xv^{s}
To Mr Millisent & Mr Necton	It iij lowe stooles covered wth tawnye velvet ymbrodered wth silke	vij^{s} vj^{d}
	It a windowe carpet wth Flowers	x^{s}
	It ij^{o} old quyshens one of roses the other of flowers	ij^{s} viij^{d}
	It ij^{o} wyndowe curteynes of redd & grene saye wth a curteyn rodd	vj^{s}
To the M^{r} of the Roolles	It one chest bounde wth flat yron bandes	xx^{s}

22

[f.36v]

To Mr Necton	It a flaunders chest wth yron bandes	xiij^{s} iiij^{d}
To the M^{r} of the Roolles	It vij peces of hanginges of brode leaves & one of parke worke cont $\overset{xx}{\text{viij}}$ xv elles at ij^{s} iiij^{d} thell	xx^{li} xiij^{s} iiij^{d}
	Summa lxiij^{li} v^{s} ij^{d}	

In an Inner Chamber next to the pryvie beinge the maydes Chamber

Itm A beddstead of waynescott wth pyllers and bordes	v^{s} viij^{d}
Itm A lyttell Jacke[136] of wood for a bason	xij^{d}
Itm an olde Skryne	xij^{d}
Summa viij^{s} viij^{d}	

In an other maydes Chamber

Itm A beddstead of waynescott w^{t} pyllors	iiij^{s}
Itm A footepace[137] w^{t} ij^{o} leaves	vj^{d}
Itm A lyttel Courte Cupborde	ij^{s}
Itm an olde presse of waynescott	x^{s}
Itm olde paynted clothes	iij^{s} iiij^{d}
Summa xix^{s} x^{d}	

[f.37r]

In the brushing chamber

	It a table of deale wth ij^{o} trestles	iij^{s} iiij^{d}
To Mr Gysse	It an old chest broken	xij^{d}
	It old paynted clothes	xij^{s}
	Summa xvj^{s} iiij^{d}	

136 Stand

137 Probably meaning a small platform or step of two levels on which to set the feet

In an ynner rowme

To my La: North	It ij^{o} powdring tubbes wth covers	xx^{d}
	It vj casementes of yron wth other old yron	v^{s}
	It a litle hand baskett	iiij^{d}
	Summa vij^{s}	

In the gentleweomens chamber

It a bedstead of wainescot w^{t} pillers	x^{s}
It the selor & testor of blacke velvet & damaske old & worne frindged wth silke	viij^{s}
It old hanginges of buckeram liiij yerdes	xiij^{s}
It a pallett of strawe	xij^{d}
It a featherbedd wth a broken bolster & a pillowe	xviij^{s}
It a white woollen Coverlett	iiij^{s}
It a blacke yrishe mantle	ij^{s} vj^{d}
It a longe settle of wainescott	iiij^{s}
It a litle turned chayre for a Chylde	iiij^{d}
Summa l^{s} x^{d}	

23

[f.37v]

In the entrye goeinge downe the kytchen

Itm a pece of Bockerame	xij^{d}
Summa patet	

In the entrye by the wardroppe

Itm vj waynescott bordes for wyndowes	vj^{s}
Itm A trussing frame[138] for a chayer	v^{s}
Itm A Chamber stoole w^{t} a panne	iiij^{s}
Itm A skrene of wycker wth other lomber	ij^{s} vj^{d}
Summa xvij^{s} vj^{d}	

In the wardroppe

To M^{r} Wm Gerrard	Itm an olde fetherbedd w^{t} A bolster peced	xv^{s}
	Itm an other fetherbedd w^{t}out A bolster	x^{s}
To the M^{r} of the roolles	Itm A felde bedd w^{t} pyllors of wallnuttree wth Joyntes	xiij^{s} iiij^{d}
	Itm A Canapie for the same trust bedd of chaungable[139] taphata the toppe of yeallowe satten ymbrodered with blacke vellvett	v^{li}
	Itm A Quylte of chaungable taphata Agreable to the same trust bedd	iiij^{li}

138 Probably referring to a demountable chair

139 Shot: showing different colours according to viewpoint

	Itm A Chest of waynescott cresse[140] pannell	vj^{s}
To El. denham[141]	Itm A longe paynted chest	iij^{s} iiij^{d}
To Agnes Knight	Itm an other playne shorte chest	iiij^{s}

[f.38r]

	It a high wainescott Cheste	vj^{s}
	It an other cheste creaste pannell	v^{s}
	It a great Cheste	vj^{s} viij^{d}
	It a litle lowe settle of wainescott	ij^{s}
To Mr Tho: North	It a spynning wheele	ij^{s}
To the M^{r} of the roolles	It a close stoole wth joyntes lyned wth grene Clothe wth a cover of grene clothe	viij^{s}
	It a lyttle standing deske	iiij^{d}
	It an old Casket bounde wth yron	ij^{s} vj^{d}
To my L: Dyer	It a Capp panne[142]	vj^{s}
To my La: of worc	It a picture of Kinge Edward the vj^{te} the picture of Quene Mary the picture of our Lady a picture of Christe & a picture of Mary Mawdelen	viij^{s}
	It an old gilte target & a Javelyne	iij^{s} iiij^{d}
	It vj Curteyn roddes of yron great & small	ij^{s} vj^{d}
	It an old table wth a paire of trestles & an old joyned stoole	iij^{s}
To my La: North	It ij^{o} whyte yrishe Rugges	viij^{s}
	It an old tawney yrishe Mantle	iij^{s} iiij^{d}
	It a great presse carved wth iij floores	v^{li}
To my La: North	It ij presses plaine pannell	xlvj^{s} viij^{d}
To the M^{r} of the roolles	It iiij pyllowes of downe and one of featheres	xiij^{s} iiij^{d}
	It a sumpter clothe[143] wth my Lordes armes	xiij^{s} iiij^{d}
To Mr Necton	It an old turkye windowe carpet worne cont a yeard iij qt^{r} longe and a yearde brode	vj^{s}

24

[f.38v]

To the M^{r} of the roolles	Itm an other Turkey carpett a yearde and iij^{re} qr^{ters} longe and yearde broad	viij^{s}
	Itm a shorte Turkey carpett ij^{o} yeardes longe redd & yeallowe	x^{s}
To Mr Necton	Itm an other olde Turkey carpett broken ij^{o} yardes long and a yarde q^{ter} broade	vj^{s}
	Itm an other Turkey carpett redd of a yarde longe	v^{s}

140 Crest: referring to raised panelling

141 Servant of Lord North

142 Meaning uncertain; possibly referring to a type of helmet (pan)

143 Covering for a pack- or baggage-horse

	Itm A great coverlett of flowers lyned w^{t} Canves	xxxiij^{s} iiij^{d}
	Itm vij peces of olde blue bockerame	vj^{s} viij^{d}
	Itm a Clocke of Copper gilte wth the plomettes and his appurtenaunces	iij^{li}
To the M^{r} of the Roolles	Itm a faire large quylte of Turkye yeallowe Caffa[144]	ix^{li}
	Itm A quylte of Callowecowe clothe	iij^{li} vj^{s} viij^{d}
To my La: North	Item A harnesse of blacke vellvett for A Ladyes saddell sett w^{t} gylte studdes and fryged w^{t} blacke sylke and goolde and A Reyne suteable to yt	xxvj^{s} viij^{d}
	Itm ij^{o} plate Candellstickes of latten w^{t} iiij^{or} candell noses[145]	viij^{s}
	Itm A hollyewater stocke[146] of pewter	viij^{d}
	Itm A padlocke w^{t} a key	ij^{s} vj^{d}
	Itm A shreddinge knyfe	iiij^{d}
	Itm A pyllor for a stone bowe[147]	xij^{d}
	Itm A Testor and Selor of bridges[148] satten yeallowe white and grene broken	xxvj^{s} viij^{d}
To Mr Millisent	Itm A pycture of the resurrection in glasse	xx^{d}
	Itm ij^{o} crewetes of pewter	vj^{d}
To the M^{r} of the Roolles	Itm ij^{o} coveringes for wyndowe quyshins of purple satten ymbrodered w^{t} clothe of golde and lyned wth blacke damaske	iij^{li} vj^{s} viij^{d}

[f.39r]

It a litle belle of brasse	vj^{d}
It a ryche Aulter clothe of golde Arras for the upper parte of the aulter	xij^{li}
It an other aulter clothe of gold Arras for the neather parte	vj^{li}
It an upper Aulter clothe of grene & redd velvet ymbrodered wth angelles of gold wth my Lordes armes	viij^{li}
It an other of the same sorte for the nether parte of the Aulter	iiij^{li}
It ij^{o} streamers of grene sarcenet of our Ladies assumpc[i]on	viij^{s}
It a litle Aulter clothe of blue velvet & redd damaske wth a Crucifixe ymbrodered	x^{s}
It an aulter clothe of bruges satten one pane whyte & an other grene	vj^{s}
It a vestm^{t} of bruges satten white & a crosse of velvet redd wth the Awbe & the furniture	x^{s}
It an other vestm^{t} of the same sorte wth the furniture	x^{s}

144 A rich silk fabric

145 Sockets for holding candles

146 Stoup or basin

147 Part of a stone-bow: a cross-bow or similar weapon for firing stones

148 Bruges

	It a vestm^{t} of redd turky satten wth a crosse of grene velvet wth an Awbe & his apparell	viij^{s}
	It an other vestm^{t} of white damaske wth his furniture old	vj^{s} viij^{d}
	It an other vestm^{t} of whyte damaske bawdkyn wth a crosse of redd damaske wth all the furniture	viij^{s}
	It a Corporas case of clothe of tissew	iij^{s} iiij^{d}

25

[f.39v]

	Itm A Canapie of clothe of Bawdkyne wth A pickkes[149] of Tynne	xx^{d}
	Itm a Testor Sellor and doble vallaunce of Crynsen satten rychlye ymbrodered all over w^{t} golde w^{t} v Curteynes of Crymsen sarcenett suteable the frynge redd sylke & goolde	l^{li}
	Itm ij^{o} greate quyshions w^{t} roses	viij^{s}
To Mr Hunter	Itm a greate quyshion of T[u?]rinne makinge	iij^{s} iiij^{d}
To Mr Millisent viij & Mr Sotherton iiij	Itm xij quyshions of tawnie vellvett wth E & A and roses of sylke	xxiij^{s}
To the M^{r} of the roolles	Itm iij^{re} longe wyndowe quyshions of blacke vellvett ij ell longe one yerd longe	xl^{s}
	Itm A longe quyshione of tyssewe and thother syde blewe satten	xx^{s}
	Itm an other quyshion of clothe of golde lyned w^{t} yeallowe brydges satten	vj^{s} viij^{d}
	Itm ij^{o} wyndowe clothes of yellowe and blacke satten of bridges	xiij^{s} iiij^{d}
	Itm iiij^{or} curteynes of sarcenett of dyverse coulores for wyndowes	viij^{s}
	Itm an olde pece of redd saye iiij^{or} yerdes	iij^{s}
	Itm iij^{re} peces of olde carpettes for wyndowes	xx^{d}
	Itm ij^{o} lyttell quyshions thone of nedle worke and thother of E and A	xvj^{d}
To the M^{r} of the roolles	Itm A quyshion of clothe of goolde lyned w^{t} tawnye velvett	xxiij^{s} iiij^{d}
	Itm ij^{o} quyshions of yellowe taphata ymbrodered wth redd velvett thone lyned w^{t} yeallowe bridges satten thother lyned w^{t} redd velvett	xxxiij^{s} iiij^{d}

[f.40r]

To the M^{r} of the roolles	It ij quyshins of clothe of bawdkyne lyned wth yellowe bridges satten	xxvj^{s} viij^{d}
	It iij quyshins of grene damaske ymbro dered wth blacke velvet & lyned wth grene velvet	xl^{s}

149 Pix. The pix-canopy would have gone over an altar

	It one quyshine of gold Arras lyned wth Capha redd	xxvj^{s} viij^{d}
	It a pece of old redd saye hanging over the chymney	ij^{s}
	Summa Cxlix^{li} xviij^{d}	

Naperie in the warderobe

	It a table clothe of damaske wth flower deluces[150] cont xj yeardes longe & iij yeardes brode	liij^{s} iiij^{d}
	It ij towelles wth flower deluces of the same making cont x elles	xiij^{s} iiij^{d}
To the M^{r} of the Roolles	It an other damaske table clothe cont vij yeardes long & iij yeardes brode	xxxviij^{s}
	It a Towelle of damaske worke xiij yeardes longe	xxv^{s}
	It a damaske table clothe of the lyllie pott[151] cont iij yeardes iij qt^{r} long & a yearde iij qt^{r} brode	xij^{s}
	It a towelle to the same vj yeardes longe	viij^{s}
	It a table clothe of the vyne leaves cont v yeardes q^{r}tr longe & ij yeardes q^{r}tr brode	xij^{s}
To the M^{r} of the Roolles	It a towell cont vj yeardes de longe	viij^{s}

26

[f.40v]

To the M^{r} of the Roolles	Itm a table clothe of damaske worke v yerdes longe, and ij^{o} yerdes q^{ter} broade	xx^{s}
	Itm A towell of damaske iij^{re} yerdes longe	iiij^{s}
	Itm A doble cupborde clothe olde of course damaske iij yerdes longe & ij^{o} yerdes broade	vj^{s}
	Itm A fyne damaske clothe of the storye of Jonas[152] vij yerdes di[153] longe ij^{o} yerdes qr^{ter} broade	xlvj^{s} viij^{d}
	Itm A towell of damaske worke of xiij yardes Longe	xxiij^{s} iiij^{d}
To the M^{r} of the Roolles	Itm A Table clothe of damaske worke w^{t} the Kynges Armes of vj yerdes iij^{re} qr^{ters} long and ij^{o} yerdes qr^{ter} broade	xxiij^{s} iiij^{d}
	Itm A Towell suteable to the same cont xv yerdes di long	xx^{s}

150 Fleurs-de-lys

151 Lily-pot: representation of a lily in a pot, a symbol of purity with particular reference to the Virgin Mary

152 Jonah

153 Dimidium or demi, i.e. half, and quarter(ium) are used in combination as follows:

di qr = one-eighth
qr di = three-eighths
di di qr = five-eighths
iij qr di = seven-eighths

	Itm A Banckettinge clothe ymbrodered v yeardes longe di ij^{o} yerdes iij^{re} qr^{ters} broade	xxxvj^{s} viij^{d}
	Itm A dyaper table cloth vij yerdes longe iij^{re} yerdes broade sore worne	xx^{s}
	Itm iij^{re} towelles of Dyaper iiij^{or} yerdes a pece	viij^{s}
	Itm A lyttell towell of Byrdes Ies iij^{re} yardes longe	xx^{d}
	Itm a table clothe of dyaper v yardes longe	v^{s}
To the M^{r} of the Roolles	Itm iij^{re} cupborde clothes of dyaper ij^{o} yerdes longe a pece	vj^{s}
	Itm iiij^{or} coverpanes of damaske worcke of Adame and Eve	xvj^{s}
	Itm one dossen of damaske worcke napkyns of Strawberye blossome	xvj^{s}

[f.41r]

To the M^{r} of the Roolles	It vij napkyns of damaske worke	x^{s}
	It a doss of course napkyns of damaske	xvj^{s}
	It a Cupborde clothe ij^{o} yeardes de longe of course damaske	xx^{d}
	It a dyaper cupborde clothe ij yeardes longe thynne and worne	ij^{s} vj^{d}
To the M^{r} of the roolles	It a Coverpane of stychte clothe	xvj^{d}
To Mr Necton	It one odd napkyn of dyaper	viij^{d}
	It one dooss of diaper broken napkyns	ij^{s}
To the M^{r} of the roolles	It a plaine table cloth iiij^{or} elles longe & ij^{o} yeardes brode	xij^{s}
	It an other plaine table clothe cont iiij^{or} elles long and an elle de brode	vj^{s} viij^{d}
	It an other plaine table clothe cont iiij^{or} elles long and an elle de brode	xij^{s}
	It a thynne plaine towelle iij^{re} elles de longe	ij^{s} vj^{d}
	It a plaine towelle wrought wth silke ij elles	ij^{s}
	It a thynne towelle woorne iij elles longe	xvj^{d}
	It a plaine table clothe iij^{re} elles q^{r}r^{tr} longe	vij^{s} vj^{d}
To the M^{r} of the roolles	It a Cupborde clothe wrought wth blacke silke of fyne holland ij^{o} elles longe	vj^{s}
	It a dooss of plaine napkyns stychte wth blue	viij^{s}
	It an armyng towelle[154] for a butler	xx^{d}
	It a remnaunt of course clothe to putt the dyaper in	xij^{d}
	It one fyne sheete of iij breadthes cont ix elles	xxvj^{s} viij^{d}
	It an other odd sheet of ij breadthes & a half cont vij elles	x^{s}

27

154 A ceremonial towel, worn round the neck or over the shoulder as part of the elaborate ritual of serving the head of a great household at dinner

[f.41v]

	Itm A payre of fyne sheetes of ij^{o} breadthes and a di of xij elles di in the payre	xxx^{s}
	Itm A fyne payre of sheetes of iij^{re} breadthes	iij^{li}
	Itm an other payre of sheetes of iij^{re} breadthes xix elles the payre	xlvj^{s} viij^{d}
	Itm an other payre of ij breadthes cont ix elles di in A payre	xxiij^{s}
	Itm an other payre of sheetes newe of ij^{o} bredthes viij elles in the payre	xvj^{s}
To the M^{r} of the roolles	Itm ij^{o} other payres of sheetes of ij^{o} breades viij elles di in the payre	xxvj^{s} viij^{d}
	Itm an other payre of sheetes of ij^{o} breades di xij elles in the payre	xij^{s}
	Itm one payre of ij^{o} breades & x elles	xv^{s}
	Itm one other of ij^{o} breades ix elles di	xij^{s}
	Itm one other payre of ij^{o} breades ix elles di in the payre	xv^{s}
	Itm one sheete of fyne Callacowe clothe of iiij^{or} breades overthawart[155]	l^{s}
To Mr Necton	Itm a sheete of nettle cloth[156] checkered redd vj elles di	vj^{s} viij^{d}
	Itm ij^{o} playne pillowberes[157]	iiij^{s}
To the M^{r} of the Roolles	Itm ij^{o} fyner pyllowberes	v^{s}
	Itm ij^{o} fyne pyllowberes of the fynest	vj^{s} viij^{d}
	Itm one fyne pyllowbere	iiij^{s}
	Itm one course pyllowbere olde	xvj^{d}
To my La: of Worc	Itm A gowne of Crymsen velvett w^{t}out sleves or lyneinge to yt	iiij^{li}
	Itm A payre of sheetes of hollande ij^{o} breades di and xj elles in the payre	xv^{s}
	Itm A cupborde clothe of nett makeinge	ij^{s} vj^{d}
	Itm iiij^{or} payre of sheetes of white canves of xj elles in the payre	liij^{s} iiij^{d}

[f.42r]

To the M^{r} of the Roolles	It one paire of fustian blankettes of xxiiij yeardes	xvj^{s}
	It an other paire of fustian blankettes of xxiiij yeardes course & worne	xl^{s}
	It a paire of old worne sheetes	ij^{s} viij^{d}
	It ij old sheetes all broken & torne	iij^{s}
	It an old whyte curteyn of lynnene clothe	xvj^{d}

Summa liij^{li} xij^{s} viij^{d}

Pewter remayning in a cheste

To the M^{r} of the roolles ij chargers	It viij great chargers iij dooss of platters a dooss of dyshes ij dooss

155 Overthwart: across

156 Cloth made from nettle fibre

157 Pillowcases

ij gr platt j doss sallet dysh j doss platt j doss sawc & j snowe platter w^{g} iiij^{xx} xij^{lli} at vj^{d} le lli xlvj^{s}	of sallet[158] dyshes twoo dooss sawceres iij snowe platteres[159] & one depe bowlle cont all xj^{xx} iiij^{lli} at vj^{d} le lli	v^{li} xij^{s}
To Mr Goldingham ij chamber pott & to Mr Tyrrell an other	It iiij waterpottes for the chamber a depe bowlle w^{g} xiij^{lli} de at iiij^{d}	iiij^{s} vj^{d}
To the M^{r} of the roolles ij paire ix^{s}	It viij pewter Candelstickes ij paire of ix^{s} & ij paire of vij^{s} ~~the paire~~	xvj^{s}
	It iiij^{or} litle candle plates of latten	ij^{s} viij^{d}
	Summa vj^{li} xv^{s} ij^{d}	

Naperie in the pantrie

	It a table clothe of damaske worke cont vj yeardes de long & ij yeardes q^{r}tr brode	xxx^{s}
To the M^{r} of the roolles	It a Towell of the same making cont vj longe	x^{s}
	It an other table clothe of damaske worke v yeardes qt^{r} longe & a yearde q^{r}tr brode	xxv^{s}

28

[f.42v]

To my L: Dyer	It a damaske worke towell worne iij^{or} yeardes de long	iiij^{s} vj^{d}
To the M^{r} of the roolles	It a table clothe of damaske worke cont vj yeardes longe & ij^{o} yeardes brode	xxiij^{s} iiij^{d}
	It a damaske worke towell iiij^{or} yeardes longe	vj^{s}
	It a damaske worke table clothe sore worne v yeardes longe & ij^{o} yeardes brode	x^{s}
	It a thynne towell of damaske worke iiij^{or} yeardes q^{r}tr long	ij^{s} vj^{d}
To the M^{r} of the roolles	It a damaske worke towell iiij^{or} yeardes de longe	vj^{s} viij^{d}
	It a dyaper table clothe cont iiij yeardes iij qt^{r} longe & a yearde de brode	vj^{s} viij^{d}
	It an other table clothe thynne cont iiij^{or} yeardes iij qt^{r} longe & a yearde de brode	iiij^{s}
	It a table clothe of dyaper broken iiij^{or} yeardes de longe & ij yeardes brode skante	iij^{s} iiij^{d}
	It one dyaper table clothe thynne v yeardes long & a yeard de brode	iij^{s} iiij^{d}
	It a dyaper table clothe of v yeardes longe & worne ij yeardes brode	v^{s}
	It an old diaper table clothe cont v	iiij^{s}

158 Salad

159 Presumably for serving 'snow', a sixteenth-century confection made with cream, egg-whites and sugar

	yeardes longe thynne a yearde de brode	
	It a dyaper table clothe v yeardes longe & ij^{o} yeardes brode	viij^{s} iiij^{d}
	It a dyaper table clothe v yeardes longe & ij^{o} yeardes brode	v^{s}
To the M^{r} of the roolles	It an other dyaper towell of iiij yerdes longe	iij^{s} iiij^{d}
	It an other dyaper towell of 4 yeardes de longe	iiij^{s}
	It an other diaper towell of v yerdes longe	iij^{s} iiij^{d}
	It a damaske worke Towell iiij^{or} yeardes longe broken	ij^{s} vj^{d}

[f.43r]

	It an other diaper towell iij^{re} yerdes long	xx^{d}
	It a Cupborde clothe of diaper cont ij^{o} yeardes q^{r}tr sore worne broken	xij^{d}
	It a cupborde clothe of diaper cont ij yerdes de longe broken & sore worne	xij^{d}
	It an other cupborde clothe of diaper ij^{o} yeardes q^{r}tr longe worne & broken	xij^{d}
	It an other cupborde clothe of diaper a yearde iij qt^{r} long sore worne	xij^{d}
	It iiij^{or} other broken Cupbord clothes of dyaper sore worne	xvj^{d}
	It an other broken cupborde clothe of dyaper	viij^{d}
	It iiij^{or} broken ewery[160] towelles at v^{d} the pece	xx^{d}
	It ij^{o} ewery towelles of dyaper	ij^{s} viij^{d}
To the M^{r} of the roolles	It ij^{o} broken ewery towelles	viij^{d}
	It a dooss of damaske worke napkyns	viij^{s}
To the M^{r} of the roolles	It an other dooss damaske worke napkyns of the lyllye pottes	xij^{s}
	It an other dooss damaske worke napkyns wth flower de luces	viij^{s}
To the M^{r} of the roolles	It an other dooss of diaper napkins	vj^{s} viij^{d}
	It an other dooss of diaper napkyns worne	iiij^{s}
	It a dooss of old diaper napkins broken	xvj^{d}
	It an other doss of old diaper napkins broken	xij^{d}
	It an other doss of the same sorte worne broken	xij^{d}
	It an other doss of the same sorte broken torne	xij^{d}
	It a playne table clothe iiij^{or} elles longe a yeard de brode thyne & broken	iij^{s} iiij^{d}
	It an other plaine table clothe cont iij elles de Longe	iiij^{s}

29

[f.43v]

To the M^{r} of the roolles	Itm an other playne table clothe of iiij^{or} elles longe	v^{s} viij^{d}
	Itm an other playne table clothe of iiij^{or} elles broken	ij^{s}
	Itm an other playne table clothe of the same lengethe	ij^{s}

160 Household department dealing with ewers, table linen, towels, etc

To the M^{r} of the roolles	Itm A playne table clothe of v yerdes ij qrt^{er} longe and ij elles broade	xvj^{s}
	Itm an other table clothe playne of iiij^{or} elles qr^{ter} longe, and an ell & di broade	v^{s} viij^{d}
	Itm a playne towell iiij^{or} elles longe	viij^{s}
	Itm an other playne towell of the same sorte	vj^{s}
	Itm an other playne towell of the same sorte worne of iij^{re} elles	iiij^{s}
	Itm an other towell playne worne, iij^{re} elles longe	ij^{s} vj^{d}
To the M^{r} of the roolles	Itm an other towell playne, iij^{re} elles q^{ter} longe	iij^{s} iiij^{d}
	Itm an other towell playne iiij^{or} elles longe	iij^{s} vj^{d}
	Itm an other towell playne broken iij^{re} elles qr^{ter}	xvj^{d}
	Itm A playne table clothe iiij^{or} elles longe	vj^{s}
	Itm an other table clothe worne and broken iiij^{or} elles	ij^{s}
	Itm ij^{o} Ewrye Towelles thynne	xx^{d}
	Itm x other Ewrye towelles	iij^{s} iiij^{d}
	Itm A playne cupborde clothe ij^{o} elles longe	iij^{s}
	Itm iiij^{or} olde cupborde clothes broken	ij^{s}
To the M^{r} of the roolles	Itm A newe cupborde clothe wroughte w^{t} blue	ij^{s}
	Itm an other cupborde clothe wrought w^{t} a white seame	xx^{d}
	Itm an other cupborde clothe playne	iij^{s} iiij^{d}
	Itm an other cupborde clothe of ell iij^{re} qr^{ters}	xx^{d}
	Itm vij olde and broken cupborde clothes	ij^{s} viij^{d}
	Itm a dossen of playne napkyns thyne	ij^{s} iiij^{d}
	Itm a dossen of napkyns playne much worne	ij^{s}
	Itm iiij^{or} dossen of broken napkyns	n^{l}
	Itm a course playne table clothe of iiij^{or} elles longe	ij^{s}
	Itm an other broken table clothe	vj^{d}
	Itm vj olde broken table clothes	xij^{d}

[f.44r]

	It one plaine table clothe old iiij^{or} elles de longe	iij^{s} viij^{d}
	It iij other broken table clothes old	xviij^{d}
To the M^{r} of the roolles	It ij armyng Towelles wth blacke seasmes	vj^{d}

Summa xvij^{li} xx^{d}

Lynnen going abrode for servauntes

It iiij^{or} paire of course sheetes at iiij^{s} a paire	xvj^{s}
It ij^{o} paire of course sheetes worne & torne	iij^{s} iiij^{d}
It iiij^{or} paire of stronge newe sheetes	xx^{s}
It xvj paire of broken sheetes at ~~xvj^{d}~~ xx^{d} the paire	xxvj^{s} viij^{d}
It one paire of pillowbeares	xij^{d}
It a paire of fyne sheetes broken	ij^{s}

Summa lxix^{s}

In the Armorie

+	It demylaunces[161] viij wth the furnitures at xxvj^{s} viij^{d} the pece	x^{li} xiij^{s} iiij^{d}
+	It an Armor for a man of armes	xl^{s}

161 Short, lightweight lances; the same word (below) describes light horsemen using such lances

+	It v white corslettes[162] at xv^{s} le pece	lxxv^{s}
+	It blacke corslettes ij^{o} at xij^{s} le pece	xxiiij^{s}
+	It a blacke Anamye[163]	xx^{s}
+	It xxvj Almayne Rivettes[164] fullye furnyshed at v^{s} the pece	vj^{li} x^{s}
+	It xliiij almayne rivettes wanting theire gorgettes[165] at iiij^{s} the pece	viij^{li} xvj^{s}

30

[f.44v]

+	Itm ij^{o} Allmayne Ryvettes wantinge hedd peces	v^{s} iiij^{d}
+	Itm xlviij Allmayne Revettes wantinge hedd peces gorgettes and Taces[166] ij^{s} a pece	iiij^{s} xvj^{d}
	Itm x backs w^{t} their brestes for Allmayne Revettes at xvj^{d} the pecc	xiij^{s} iiij^{d}
+	Itm xiij payre of splintes[167] for Allmayne Ryvettes at xij^{d} a payre	xiij^{s}
	Itm x olde backes w^{t} their brestes for demylaunces at xij^{d} a payre	x^{s}
	Itm vj olde heddpeces for demylaunces at viij^{d} the pece	iiij^{s}
	Itm xv payre of old quyshes[168] for demylaunces at viij^{d} the payre	x^{s}
	Itm ix payre of vambraunces[169] for demylaunces at viij^{d} the payre	vj^{s}
	Itm x payre of olde pellraunces[170] for demylaunces at iiij^{d} the pece	iij^{s} iiij^{d}
+	Itm vij coates of plate w^{t} sculles[171] whereof one lyttell worthe at xij^{d} the pece	viij^{s}
+	Itm iiij^{or} newe Jackes or Cootes of plate[172] w^{t} ij^{o} payre of canves sleves bordered w^{t} mayle at v^{s} the pece	xx^{s}
	Itm vj payre of olde broken gauntlettes at vj^{d} the payre	iij^{s}
+	Itm viij plates for iiij^{or} stele saddelles at xij^{d} the pece	viij^{s}

162 Cors(e)let: armour for the upper body

163 Anime: a flexible breastplate or cuirass, made of overlapping plates

164 Almain rivets: German-style light armour, articulated with overlapping plates and sliding rivets

165 Gorget: piece of armour for the throat

166 Tache: buckle or other fastening

167 Pieces of armour for protecting the elbows

168 Cuisses: armour for the front of the thighs

169 Vambrace: protective cover for the forearm

170 Perhaps variant of pouldron, a piece of shoulder-armour

171 Steel skull-caps

172 Jack: a soldier's coat of fence, a sleeveless jacket typically of quilted leather with iron plates

Wepons in the same Armorye

		Itm l pykes whereof ij^{o} onelye lackinge	l^{s}
	+	theire heades at xij^{d} the pece	
Sir Roger Northes———		Itm one Armed pyke	
		Itm blacke bylles w^{t} staves lxxj whereof	xlvij^{s} iiij^{d}
	+	ij^{o} of the holberdes at viij^{d} the pece	

[f.45r]

		It xliiij blacke bylles wthout staves at	xxij^{s}
	+	vj^{d} the pece	
		It xviij light horsmen staves	xxj^{s}
	+	at xv^{d} le pece	
	+	It xxvij Javelyns at xij^{d} le pece	xxviij^{s}
	+	It iiij^{or} heades for bore[173] speares at iiij^{d} le pece	xvj^{d}
	+	It xiij Mases at viij^{d} le pece	viij^{s} viij^{d}
	+	It vij dagges[174] wanting Flaskes and	xxxv^{s}
		charges at v^{s} a pece	
		It v old hornes & one Flaske w^{ch}	x^{d}
		served for hand gonnes at ij^{d} le pece	
		It xxxviij armyng swordes[175] wth sheathes	xxxviij^{s}
	+	at xij^{d} le pece	
	+	It xij daggers wth theire sheathes	iiij^{s}
		It iij paire of sleves of male one	ix^{s}
		paire v^{s} thother ij^{o} ij^{s} a pece	
		It one paire of gloves of flat male	iiij^{d}
		unrevytted	
		It ij^{o} gussettes[176] of male unrevytted	ij^{s}
iij dd to ye keper iij———	+	It [~~illeg~~] vj bowes of yewghe not broken	v^{s}
		It viij broken bowes whereof one shorte	nll
		It one yewghe staffe for a bowe	vj^{d}
		It xxvj sheaves of arrowes wth theire	xxvj^{s}
	+	cases not fully furnyshed	
		It xviij Cases for sheaves of	iij^{s}
		arrowes at ij^{d} le pece	
		It xxvj bowe stringes	nll
		It ij braseres & one shooting glove[177]	iiij^{d}

31

[f.45v]

Item iij qr^{ters} of a fyrkyne full of Serpentyne[178]	ij^{s}
powder	
Itm one olde chest for bowes and an other	iij^{s}
to put in the male	

Summa lix^{li} iiij^{s} viij^{d}

173 Boar

174 Dag: heavy pistol or other hand-gun

175 Arming sword: the medieval cross-shaped sword used by knights, otherwise called broadswords

176 For filling up the gap between two pieces of mail, e.g. at the armpit

177 Bracers: wrist protectors for use in archery; shooting glove also for protection in drawing a bow

178 A kind of cannon

In Mr Nectons Chamber

	Item A Table of waynescott w^{t} A foote	iij^{s} iiij^{d}
	Summa patet	

Cranes[179] in the orcheyearde

To my L. Dyer j To Mr Att[o]rney ij	Itm iij^{re} Cranes at iij^{s} iiij^{d} the pece	x^{s}
To the M^{r} of the roolles	Itm A Signett[180]	ij^{s}
	Summa xij^{s}	

Sugar in the Spicerie

vj loaves dd to my La: North cont xlix^{lli}	Itm xxvij loaves of sugare weyeinge $\overset{xx}{x}$ iiij^{lli} at ix^{d} the pounde	vij^{li} x^{s}
	Itm vj^{lli} of dates	iiij^{s}
	Summa vij^{li} xiiij^{s}	

Lynges and haberdynes[181] in the fyshe chamber

Lynges To Mr Applegarthe & Mr Sotherton xxx^{re} 37^{s} 8^{d} To the M^{r} of the roolles lx 3^{li} 15^{s} my Lady North xl 50^{s}	Itm $\overset{xx}{vij}$ x lynges at vij^{lli} x^{s} the C	viij^{li} ij^{s} vj^{d}
To the M^{r} of the roolles $\overset{xx}{vj}$ 53.4 my L. Dyer lx 25.8 my La: North 40 17^{s}	Itm haberdynes $\overset{xx}{xj}$ at liij^{s} iiij^{d} the C	iiij^{li} xvij^{s} ix^{d}
	Summa xiij^{li} iij^{d}	

Saulte over the ovens

Salte To the M^{r} of y^{e} roolles j q^{r}t^{r} To my La: North j q^{r}t^{r}	Itm ij^{o} qr^{ters} of white saulte	xviij^{s}
	Summa patet	

In the parsone of moltons[182] chamber

given by my L. will to the parson of Mooltone	Itm old paynted clothes	x^{s}
	Itm A beddstede w^{t} coullours w^{t} A selor of waynescott	viij^{s}
	It A fetherbedd w^{t} A bolster a matteres a strawe pallett ij^{o} olde blancquettes and a payre of sheetes	xxxv^{s}
	Itm A lyttell olde table	xx^{d}
	Itm A Joyned stoole	viij^{d}
	Summa lv^{s} iiij^{d}	

179 Kept for food

180 Cygnet: perhaps here referring to a young crane

181 Haberdyne: salt or dried cod

182 Moulton in Suffolk, near the North seat at Kirtling, Cambridgeshire

[f.46r]

In the Tower

To Mr Necton	It a Compter table wth Tylles[183]	xij^{s}
	It a presse of waynescott wth v Flooeres	vj^{s} viij^{d}
	It a settle wth ij^{o} Lockes	iij^{s} iiij^{d}
	It iij great wicker hampers wth boxes	iij^{s}
To Thornton	It a Cheste covered wth blacke leather wth yron bandes	x^{s}
	It an other settle wth ij^{o} lockes	iij^{s} iiij^{d}
To Cosen	It an other cheste of blacke leather wth plate	vj^{s} viij^{d}
To Roswell	It a lyttle bagge of nayles	v^{s}
	It lxxj small barres of yron	viij^{s}
	Summa lviij^{s}	

In a Cipres cheste

To the M^{r} of the roolles	It a saddle clothe of blacke velvet wth the harnes of the same for a moyle frynged wth silke & silver wth all the Apparell	iiij^{li}
	It a Jacke wth plates covered wth velvet	iij^{li}
	It a head pece covered wth blacke velvet wth silver lace	x^{s}
	It a dooblet of crymzin wth sleves of male	xl^{s}
To Mr Gysse	It a face[184] of fyne bridge old	xiij^{s} iiij^{d}

32

[f.46v]

	It a paire of spurres gilte & an other paire of spurres vernyshed partlye gylte	v^{s}
	It one waste girdle wth the hanginges wth gilte bucckles & an other waste girdle of velvet wth the hanginges	iij^{s} iiij^{d}
	It iij turkye bowes[185] ij of steele one of woodd wth a case of arrowes	ij^{s}
To my L. Dyer	It a paire of gloves	viij^{d}
	It a coller & a lyne of blue & white threde for a dogge	vj^{d}
	Summa x^{li} xiiij^{s} x^{d}	

In an Awmbry in the wall in my Lordes bedd chamber

	It ij Flaggons of glasse the one wth a vyce[186]	v^{s}

183 Tills: drawers or other compartments, presumably here for counters

184 Facing for a garment

185 The Turkish bow was a comparatively small, highly efficient bow suitable for use on horseback, recurved (so that the ends curved away from the archer) and of composite construction

186 Vice: a screw-stopper

	It a neast of bowlles of glasse wth a cover gilte	xx^{d}
	It ij bowlles wthout a cover of glas one broken	ij^{d}
	It ij^{o} standing[187] Cupps of glasse wth ij^{o} coveres parcell gilte	ij^{s} viij^{d}
	It certen glasses for waters	vj^{d}
	It a gilte case of redd leather wth a glasse of burroll[188] in the toppe	xij^{d}
	Summa xj^{s}	

[f.47r]

In the Stable

	It one horse called old North	xl^{s}
To M^{r} b [illeg]————	It blacke Dingley	lx^{s}
To Mr Tho North————	It graye Foxe	xxxiij^{s} iiij^{d}
	It baye brewer	xl^{s}
	It sorrell bagnall	xlvj^{s} viij^{d}
To Ric Millisent————	It white Cropley	xxx^{s}
To John Applegarthe————	It white warcoppe[189]	~~iiij^{li}~~ xx^{s}
To Mr Necton————	It graye North	~~xl^{s}~~ iiij^{li}
To Sir G^{o}. Alington————	It blacke Darcye	xl^{s}
	It the Moyle	viij^{li}
To the M^{r} of the roolles————	It the blacke Mylle horse	xv^{s}
	It a white straye from Harrowe[190]	xv^{s}
To Humfrey Applegarthe——	It the gray stoned[191] horse called gaye Elmham[192]	lvj^{s} vlij^{d}
	Summa xxxij^{li} xvj^{s} viij^{d}	

33

[f.98r]

Plate weyed and appreysed the iiijth of Januarie 1564
Gylte plate viz

To my La North as parcell of her/Legacy————	In primis iij bowles wth one Cover weieng Lviij oz at v^{s} vj^{d} le oz	xv^{li} xix^{s}
	Itme iij bowles embossed wth a Cover w^{g} xlviij oz at v^{s} vj^{d} le oz	xviij^{li} xiiij^{s}
To Mr John North as parcell of his legacye————	Itme a standing Cuppe wth a Cover emboste wth iij faces upon the Cover weieng xxxj oz at v^{s} iiij^{d} le oz	viij^{li} v^{s} iiij^{d}
To my L: Dyer————	Itme one other standing Cuppe wth a cover emboste weieng xxx oz iij q^{rters} at v^{s} iiij^{d} le oz	viij^{li} iiij^{s}
	Itme one longe Bowle wth A Cover w^{g} xxxij oz at v^{s} vj^{d} le oz	viij^{li} xviij^{s} ix^{d}

187 Standing on a stem and base
188 Beryl-glass: a mirror
189 Warcop or Warcup was the maiden name of Edward, Lord North's mother
190 Harrow, Middlesex, where North had property
191 Stoned: uncastrated
192 Reading uncertain

To M^{r} Jo: North for parte of his legacy	Itme ij^{o} square saltes wth one cover vj square weieng xxxiiij^{te} oz de de q^{r}ter at v^{s} iiij^{d} le oz	ix^{li} iiij^{s} viij^{d}
To my La North for parte of her Legacye	Itme one dosen of spones wth thappostelles at thendes weieng xxvj oz de q^{r}ter at v^{s} iiij^{d} le oz	vj^{li} xix^{s} iiij^{d}
To the M^{r} of the Rolles	Itme one Spyce boxe wth A Spoone weieng xxj oz de de q^{r}ter at v^{s} ij^{d} le oz	Cxj^{s} viij^{d} ~~ob~~ q^{r}
	Itme ij^{o} quarte pottes wth ij^{o} covers w^{g} lxix oz at v^{s} iiij^{d}	xviij^{li} viij^{s}
	Itme iiij^{re} Ale pottes wth one Cover weieng xlij^{te} oz de de q^{r}ters at v^{s} ij^{d} le oz	xj^{li} ij^{d} ~~ob~~ qr
	Itme one Cuppe of Assaye[193] weieng v oz iij q^{r}ters de at v^{s} iiij^{d} le oz	xxxj^{s} iiij^{d}
	Itme one Casting bottell[194] weieng v oz j q^{r}ter at v^{s} vj^{d} le oz	xxviij^{s} x^{d} ob
	Itme one other Casting bottle weieng vj oz iij q^{r}ters a farthing olde weighte at v^{s} vj^{d} le oz	xxxvij^{s} v^{d} ob de q^{r}
To M^{r} Jo: North as parte of his Legacye	Itme one Bason and one Ewer ^& cover^ wth L Armes weyeng lxxij oz at v^{s} iiij^{d} le oz	xix^{li} iiij^{s}
	Itme one Ale potte wth ij Eares wth A cover weieng xx oz at v^{s} ij^{d} le oz	Ciij^{s} iiij^{d}
	Summa Cxl^{li} ix^{s} xj^{d} ob de q^{r} partis	

34

[f.98v]

As yet the Gylte plate

To M^{ris} Mary Scrope for her legacye and delivered unto Sir George Bowes	Itme ij^{o} Spoones wth Flatt Knoppes wth an E and A at thende weieng iij oz at v^{s} iiij^{d} le oz	xvj^{s}
	Itme one Table for an Alter plated wth Sylver all gilte weieng by estimac[i]on xxvj oz at v^{s} le oz	vj^{li} x^{s}
	Itme ij^{o} Alter candelstyckes weieng xlv oz de q^{r}ter at v^{s} ij^{d} le oz	xj^{li} xiij^{s} j^{d} ~~ob~~ qr
To my Ladye North as parcell of her legacye	Itme one Bason and one Ewer wth an Antyque[195] holding the Spowte weieng iiij (xx) x oz at v^{s} vj^{d} le oz	xxiiij^{li} xv^{s}
	Itme ij^{o} playne pottell pottes wth ij^{o} Covers weieng iiij (xx) oz at v^{s} iiij^{d} le oz	xxj^{li} vj^{s} viij^{d}
ij^{o} saltes wth j cover wei^{g} xli oz to my L Dyer	Itme iij square Saltes wth one Cover weieng lviij oz de at v^{s} vj^{d} le oz	xvj^{li} xxj^{d}

193 Cup of assay: small cup used for a taste (assay) of wine or other liquor

194 Casting-bottle: for sprinkling rose-water, etc

195 Grotesque or impossibly contorted supporting figure

To my La Northe as parcell of her Legacye	Itme one Magdalen Boxe[196] wth wreythed hoopes and A Cover weieng xxvij oz at v^{s} iiij^{d} le oz	vij^{li} iiij^{s}
	Itme one Chalyce wth A patent weieng xxij oz iij q^{r}ters at v^{s} ij^{d} le oz	Cxvij^{s} vj^{d} ob
	Itme one pyxe wth A Cover weyeng ~~xxij oz~~ iiij oz at v^{s} ij^{d} le oz	xx^{s} viij^{d}
	Itme one paxe weieng vj oz de at v^{s} le oz	xxxij^{s} vj^{d}
	Itme one holy water Stocke A sprenckell[197] A Cheyne weieng xviij oz de at v^{s} ij^{d} le oz	iiij^{li} xv^{s} vij^{d}
To M^{ris} Ma: Scroope lxxix^{s}	Itme one powncest cuppe[198] wthoute a cover weyeng xvj oz j q^{r}ter at v^{s} iiij^{d} le oz	iiij^{li} x vj^{s} viij^{d}
j potte w^{g} xv oz iiij^{d} ob qtr q^{r}ter de dd unto Sir G Bowes	Itme iij^{re} Ale pottes wth one Cover Chaced weyeng xlij oz at v^{s} ij^{d} le oz	x^{li} xvij^{s}
To my La North xij pottes j cover w^{g} vxx vij oz q^{r}ter xxvij^{li} xiiij^{s} j^{d} ob	Itme xij Ale pottes Chased on the feete and one other bygger Ale pott wth A Cover weieng togyther v^{xx} xvj oz de at v^{s} ij^{d} le oz	xxx^{li} xxiij^{d}
To the M^{r} of the Rolles	Itme one layer[199] wth a Strawbery on the toppe weieng xj oz iij q^{r}ters de at v^{s} iiij^{d} le oz	xliij^{s} iiij^{d}
	Summa Cl^{li} xx^{d} ob qr partis	

[f.97r]

As yet [the] gilte [plate]

	Itme ij^{o} Crewettes wth ij^{o} covers weieing v oz iij q^{rters} at v^{s} ij^{d} ob le oz	xxix^{s} viij^{d} ob
To my La North as parcell of her legacye	Itme one [grater?] weieng iiij oz at v^{s} ij^{d}	xx^{s} viij^{d}
	Itme one payer of Snuffers weieng iij^{re} oz de at v^{s} le oz	xvij^{s} vj^{d}
	Itme one Spoone wth A harpe on thende weieng ij oz de de qter at v^{s} iiij^{d} le oz	xiiij^{s}
	Itme one lytell square salte wth a Cover having only ij^{o} Crystall feete weieng by est besydes the Crystall x oz at v^{s} le oz	l^{s}
To M^{ris} Ma: Scrope as parte of her legacye dd to Sir Geo: Bowes	Itme one standing Cuppe wth a cover having A man holding A Swoorde weyeng xxij oz q^{r}ter De at v^{s} iiij^{d} le oz	cxix^{s} iiij^{d}
	Itme one neaste of Bowles wth one Cover weyeng lxxj oz at v^{s} ij^{d} le oz	xviij^{li} vj^{s} x^{d}
	Itme ij Rownde Saltes wth one Cover wey^{g} xxj oz at v^{s} ij^{d} le oz	vj^{li} ix^{s} ij^{d}
	Itme one lytell rownde salte wth A cover weyeng iiij oz de q^{r}ter at v^{s} ij^{d} le oz	xxj^{s} iij^{d} ob

196 Intended to resemble the box of ointment from which Mary Magdalene anointed Christ's feet

197 Holy water container and sprinkler, perhaps in the form of a stoup and aspergillum (brush)

198 Presumably, a pouncet box: a container with a perforated lid for perfume

199 Lair: a ewer

Itme one standing Cupp wth a Cover wey^{g} xxxij^{e} oz j q^{r}ter at v^{s} ij^{d} le oz — viij^{li} vj^{s} vij^{d} ob qr

Itme iij^{re} Ale pottes wth one Cover whereof ij^{o} are playne and thother emboste weieng xxxix oz at v^{s} ij^{d} le oz — x^{li} xviij^{d}

Itme one other standing Cuppe wth A Cover weieng xxvj oz at v^{s} iij^{d} le oz — vj^{li} xix^{s} j^{d} ob

To my la: North as parte of her Legacye:

Itme one other standing Cuppe wth A Cover weieng xxiiij oz de j q^{r}ter at v^{s} iiij^{d} le oz — vj^{li} xij^{s}

Itme one other standing Cuppe wth A Cover having a Burre[200] on the toppe weieng xxviij oz iij q^{r}ters at v^{s} ij^{d} le oz — vij^{li} viij^{s} vj^{d} ob

Itme iij^{re} Ale Cuppes wth iij^{re} Covers ij^{o} of one woorke & thother of an other woorke weieng xliij oz j q^{rter} at v^{s} ij^{d} le oz — xj^{li} iij^{s} v^{d} ob

Summa lxxxviij^{li} xix^{s} ix^{d} q^{r} partis

35

[f.97v]

[As yet the] gilte plate

Itme ij^{o} saltes wth one Cover weieng xxvj oz iij q^{ter} at [illeg] ij^{d} le oz — v^{li} ……

Itme one m[illeg] Boxe wth a cover all gylte chaced wth knarres[201] weieng xx^{ti} oz j q^{rter} at v^{s} ij^{d} le oz — Ciiij^{s} vij^{d} ob

Itme viij Stone pottes garnisshed wth Sylver weieng by estimac[i]on xl^{ti} oz at v^{s} le oz — x^{li}

To my L Dyer: Itme one lytell Crystall salte garnysshed wth Sylver all gylte preysed at xiij^{s} iiij^{d} — xiij^{s} iiij^{d}

Summa xxij^{li} xvj^{s} ij^{d} partis

Summa totalis of all the Gylte plate CCCCij^{li} vij^{s} vij^{d} ob de qr

Plate parcell gylte

To M^{ris} Ma: Scrope for parte of her legacye & dd unto Sir Geo Bowes Knight: In primis one Bason and one Ewer wth a Cover weieng iiij^{xx} vj oz de at iiij^{s} xj^{d} le oz — xj^{li} v^{s} iiij^{d} ob

To M^{r} Jo: North: Itme ij^{o} Dosen of Spones wth the appostelles at thendes weieng xlv oz at iiij^{s} viij^{d}

200 Bur: the knob-like base of a deer's horn

201 Meaning uncertain, but possibly referring to knot- or knob-like protuberances

as parte of his Legacye	le oz Itme one Dosen of plates weieng iiij^{xx} x oz de at iiij^{s} x^{d} le oz	xxj^{li} xvij^{s} vj^{d}
To Sir Gyles Alyngton knight[203]	Itme one Tunne[202] cont viij peces wth ij^{o} Saltes and one Cover all gylte weieng iiij^{xx} iij^{re} oz at v^{s} le oz	xx^{li} xv^{s} x^{d}
	Itme ij^{o} Chalyzeis wth ij^{o} patentes weieng xxv oz at iiij^{s} ix^{d} le oz	vj^{li} xiij^{d} ob
To the M^{r} of the Roolles	Itme ij^{o} lavers[204] of Crystall wth Covers all gylte preysed at	liij^{s} iiij^{d}
	Itme one payer of Crewettes weieng vij oz j q^{r}ter at iiij^{s} viij^{d} le oz	xxxiij^{s} x^{d}
	Itme one forke of Crystall wth a pearle at the ende preysed at	v^{s}
	Itme ij paxes the one of mother pearle and thother of Ivorye garnisshed wth sylver	xiiij^{s}
	Summa lxxxv^{li} xv^{s} partis	

[As yet the parcell] gilte plate

[f.99r] [several illegible notes]	.........neaste of......... Cover weieng C.........at iiij^{s} vij^{d} le oz	
	Itme ij^{o} Quarte pottes wthoute covers weieng lxvj oz [preysed?] but at iiij^{s} .... for v^{s} le oz	xvj^{li} x^{s}
	Itme ij^{o} Dosen of Spoones wth thapposte lles weieng xlij oz iij q^{r}ters at iiij^{s} vj^{d} le oz	ix^{li} xix^{s} vj^{d}
	Itme ij^{o} Quarte pottes wth thier Covers weieng lxiiij oz iij q^{r}ters at iiij^{s} x^{d} le oz	xv^{li} xij^{s} xj^{d} ob
	Itme ij^{o} lavers wth their Covers weieng xxij oz at iiij^{s} x^{d} le oz	Cvj^{s} iiij^{d}
	Itme one pepper boxe weieng v oz iij^{re} q^{r}ters at iiij^{s} viij^{d} le oz	xxvj^{s} x^{d}
	Itme ij^{o} Flagens wth Cheynes & Covers weyeng Clxx oz at iiij^{s} viij^{d} le oz	xxxix^{li} xiij^{s} iiij^{d}
To my la North as parte of her Legacye	Itme iij^{re} playne Bowles wthoute A Cover weieng xliiij oz at iiij^{s} ix^{d} le oz	x^{li} xj^{s} iiij^{d} ob
To the M^{r} of the Rolles	Itme one neaste of Gobblettes wth one Cover weieng lxxvj oz de at iiij^{s} x^{d} le oz	xviij^{li} ix^{s} ix^{d}
	Itme one Bason & one Ewer wth a Cover weieng lxxvj oz de at iiij^{s} ix^{d} le oz	xvij^{li} ij^{s}
To my La North as parte of her legacye	Itme one other Bason & one Ewer wth A Starr in the botome weieng C oz de at iiij^{s} ix^{d} le oz	xxiij^{li} xvij^{s} iiij^{d} ob
	Itme ij^{o} pottell pottes wth ij^{o} Covers weyeng iiij^{xx} xj oz at iiij^{s} ix^{d} le oz	xxj^{li} xvij^{s} iij^{d}

202 Tunne (tun) refers here to a chest or box, containing eight wine-cups, dishes or similar vessels ('peces')

203 Sir Giles Alington of Horseheath, Cambridgeshire, a few miles from North's seat at Kirtling. Richard Allington, named in North's will as a member of his staff, was presumably a relation, and perhaps the Richard Allington who married Jane Cordell, sister of North's executor Sir William Cordell, Master of the Rolls

204 Laver: jug or other water container for washing the hands, etc

	Itme ij^{o} pynte pottes wth ij^{o} Covers	x^{li} xiiij^{s} viij^{d}
	weyeng xlvj oz at iiij^{s} viij^{d} le oz	
	Itme ij^{o} Goblettes wth one Cover weieng	xij^{li} vj^{s} ij^{d}
	lij oz ij q^{r}ter at iiij^{s} viij^{d} le oz	
To my L: Dyer	Itm one Dosen of plate Trenchers	xix^{li} xvj^{s} iiij^{d}
vj weyeng x^{li} vij^{d}	weieng iiij^{xx} ij oz at iiij^{s} x^{d} le oz	
xli de oz	Itme one Magdalen Boxe weieng xiij	
	oz j q^{r}ter having a cover wth my L	lxj^{s} x^{d}
	Armes at iiij^{s} viij^{d} le oz	
To M^{ris} Ma Scrope	Itme one Dosen of Spones wth knoppes	
as parte of her	wreythed weieng xiij oz de q^{r}ter at iiij^{s}	lxj^{s} iij^{d}
Legacye & dd unto	viij^{d} le oz	
Sir G Bowes	Summa CClij^{li} xij^{s} j^{d} ob	
	partis	

36

[f.99v]

As yet the parcell gylte plate

	Itme ij^{o} greate Bowles wthoute Covers	
	weieng [lj?] oz iij q^{r}ter at iiij^{s} ix^{d}	xij^{li} x v^{s} iij^{d}
	le oz	
	Itme vj Spones wth mayden heddes	
	weieng vij oz quarter de at iiij^{s} viij^{d}	xxxiiij^{s} v^{d}
	le oz	
	Itme j Standysshe of Sylver wth ij^{o}	
	pennes gylte weieng xviij oz iij q^{r}ters	iiij^{li} vij^{s} vj^{d}
	at iiij^{s} viij^{d} le oz	
To my La North	Itme one Rownde Barbours Bason	xij^{li} ij^{s} viij^{d}
for parte of her/Legacye	weieng lij^{li} oz at iiij^{s} viij^{d} le oz	
	Itme one Dogges Coller prysed at	ij^{s} vj^{d}
	Itme one Spone of mother perle	vj^{d}
	Itme one tosting Forke of [—]	
	preysed at	ij^{s}
	Summa xxxj^{li} iij^{s} x^{d} ob q^{r}	
	partis	
	Summa totalis of All the parcell Gylte plate	CCClxix^{li} xij^{s} qr

Whyte plate

To the M^{r}	Itme vj great Candelstyckes weieng	xxvij^{li} iij^{s} ix^{d}
of the Rolles	Cxij oz de at iiij^{s} x^{d} le oz	
	Itme vj other Candelstyckes weyeng	xix^{li} xix^{s}
	iiij^{xx} iiij^{re} oz at iiij^{s} ix^{d} le oz	
	Itme vj other smaller Candelstyckes	
	weieng lxv oz q^{r}ter at iiij^{s} x^{d} le oz	xv^{li} xv^{s} iiij^{d} ob
To my Lady North	Itme one Ewer wth j Cover weieng	
	xvj oz q^{r}ter at iiij^{s} viij^{d} le oz	lxxv^{s} x^{d}
	Itme one Ewer or laver wthoute a	
	Cover weieng ix oz de at iij^{s} viij^{d}	xliiij^{s} iiij^{d}
	le oz	
	Itme one Jugge wth a Cover weieng	

	xix oz at iij^{s} viij^{d} le oz	iiij^{li} viij^{s} viij^{d}
To my Lady Northe as parte of her legacye	Itme vj Jugges all Covered weieng iiij^{xx} xvj oz at iiij^{s} viij^{d} le oz	xxij^{li} viij^{s}
	~~Summa partis~~ Summa [—] partis	

[f.100r]

	................................plate	
To my Lady North as [part of her] legacie	Itme one greate ....she weieng xliiij oz de at [iiij^{s}?]	x^{li} iij^{s} xj^{d} ob
	Itme one other lesse [chaf?]ing dysshe weieng xxiiij oz at iiij^{s} viij^{d} le oz	Cxij^{s} ....
To my Lady North	Itme ij^{o} hawnce pottes[205] wth ij^{o} Covers weieng xxxvj oz at iiij^{s} viij^{d} le oz	viij^{li} viij^{s}
To M^{r} Jo: North as parte of his legacye	Itme a Barbers bason weieng xxxv oz de q^{r}ter at iiij^{s} viij^{d} le oz	viij^{li} iij^{s} xj^{d}
	Itme iij^{re} lytell Ale pottes wth one Cover weieng xix oz at iiij^{s} viij^{d} le oz	iiij^{li} viij^{s} viij^{d}
.......North as parte of his legacie	Itme one chafing dyshe w^{g} xxxiij^{oz} iij qt^{r} at iiij^{s} vij^{d} le oz	[illeg]^{li} xiiij^{s} viij^{d} qr
	Summa partis [—]	
	Summa totalis of All the whyte plate	Cxl^{li} vj^{s} ij^{d} qr

Summa totalis of all the sayde plate ix^{C} xij^{li} v^{s} x^{d} qr de

Plate morgaged to my L Dyer by the late Lorde North Deceassyd

	In primis one great Cheyne of goolde weieng xli oz cont viij^{xx} iij lynckes and one hooke at [—] le oz	[—]
	Itme one Gyrdell of goolde sett wth a pearle cont xxix peces of goolde weieng [—] at [—] le oz	[—]
	Itme one Byllyment of goolde sett wth pearle cont xxix peces of goolde weieng [—] at [—] le oz	[—]
To my L: Dier j neaste weieng Cxviij oz at v^{s} iiij^{d} xxx^{li} ix^{s} iiij^{d}	Itme ij^{o} neaste of Bowles wth ij^{o} Covers all gylte weieng ~~at~~ CCxxx oz at v^{s} iiij^{d} le oz	lxj^{li} vj^{s} viij^{d}
To my L Dyer	Itme ij^{o} pottell pottes wth thier Covers all gylte weieng iiij^{xx} oz de at v^{s} ~~v~~ij^{d} le oz	xx^{li} xv^{s} xj^{d}
	Itme iij^{re} Goblettes wth A Cover all gylte weieng lxxix oz de at v^{s} ~~v~~ij^{d} le oz	xx^{li} x^{s} ix^{d}
	Itme one Ale Cuppe wth A Cover nutte wyse[206] ~~xx~~ weieng xxvj oz at v^{s} iiij^{d} le oz	vj^{li} xviij^{s} viij^{d}

37

205 Hanse-pot: according to the *OED*, 'An ornamental pot or vase of some kind'. The term probably refers to the shape of the pot, i.e. haunched or hipped

206 Meaning uncertain. Probably referring to a type of lid incorporating or resembling a coconut shell, cups of such construction being referred to as nuts

[f.100v]

As yet [the] plate morgaged to my [Lord Dyer]

	Itme ij^{o} longe .... wth A Cover all gylte	xvj^{li} viij^{s}
To my La North as parte of her Legacye	Itme one great Cuppe wth a Cover having A lyon on the Toppe thereof all gylte weieng lxv oz at v^{s} iiij^{d} le oz	xvij^{li} vj^{s} viij^{d}
To M^{r} Jo: North as parte of his Legacye	Itme one neaste of Bowles wth one Cover all gylte weieng Ciij^{re} oz q^{r}te at v^{s} iiij^{d} le oz	xxvij^{li} xvj^{s} xxvij^{li} xvj^{s}

Parcell gylte plate

	Itme ij^{o} Basons and ij^{o} Ewers weieng Clxvij oz de at iiij^{s} x^{d} le oz	xl^{li} ix^{s} vij^{d}
To my L: Dyer iij goblettes wth a Cover weyeing lxviij oz de	Itme vj iij Goblettes wth ij^{o} Cover weieng ~~Cxxiiij oz de~~ ^lxviij oz^ at iiij^{s} viij^{d} le oz	~~xvj^{li}~~ ~~xix^{li} vij^{s} iiij^{d}~~ xv^{li} xix^{s} viij^{d}
To my La North as parte of her Legacye	Itme ij^{o} longe Saltes wth A Cover weieng ^{xx}iiij iij oz at iiij^{s} viij^{d} le oz	xix^{li} vij^{s} iiij^{d}
	Itme iij goblettes wth one cover weyeng lvj^{li} oz at v^{s} le oz	xiiij^{li}

Jewelles and other thinges fownde in my L Closet and preysed as foloweth

In primis A Flower or Roose set wth v Table Dyamoundes[207] in goolde	~~viij^{li}~~ x^{li}
Itme certeyne Ragged pearle and Beades of Corall	vj^{s} viij^{d}
Itme xviij payer of Rownd Aglettes of goolde xx^{te} payer of Aglettes iij square enamels certeyne peces of goolde taken from A payer of beades weieng togethers v oz iij q^{r}ters preysed at xlv^{s} le oz	xij^{li} xviij^{s} ix^{d}
Itme iij^{re} Rownde Bottons of goolde & enameled j sergeauntes Rynge ij^{o} Jemens[208] of goolde one broken & thother hole weyeng de oz de q^{r}ter at xlv^{s} le oz	xxviij^{s} ij^{d} ob
Itme my L. Signet of goolde weieng one oz wanting de crowne at [—]	l^{s}
Itme xxxvj Badgys or Cognyzaunces of sylver all gylte weieng xxx oz de at iiij^{s} le pece	vij^{li} iiij^{s}
~~Itme one~~ [cheyne?]	

[f.101r]

Itm one ringe of .... great Saphire sett in yt value ....

[inventory of Baines farm, Hoxton, follows]

207 Diamonds cut with a large flat facet on the top and often the bottom too

208 Probably gemews or gemels, i.e. double rings that could be divided into two separate ones

APPENDIX II

Howard House Inventory, 1573

Transcript of Staffordshire Record Office, D(W) 1734/2/7/30. By permission of Staffordshire Record Office

Inventory taken at the Charterhouse, almost certainly in part of Howard House occupied by Thomas, Lord Paget (see page 50), with an associated cleaning list in a different hand. Some entries have been damaged or destroyed as a result of damp. The inventory is dated November (not September) 1573, less than a year and a half after the execution of the fourth Duke of Norfolk.

Endorsement:
Inventory at Charterhowse
of howeshold stuffe
10º IXº 1573

[f.1r]

Thre tables wth ther frames

Hall

A court cupboard[1]
Seven formes
A radel[2] of yron
A folding table
A forme covered wth
grene

Parlor

Seven joynd stoles
Two cupbordes
A paire of awndyrons[4]
A paire of crepers[5]
A fier shovell &
paire of tonges
A chaire of redd cloth
embrodred wth blew
my old lordes picture
Two curtens &
curten rodd for the wyndow
A cownter table[6]
A boarde
~~Seven~~ foure Jugges

[entries lost]

2 A corded bedsted

A matt[3]
A fetherbedd
A bolster
~~Two~~ Thre blanckettes
A coverlet
A table. A stole.
3 A corded bedstead
A matt
A joyned forme

4 A bedstead

[entries damaged]

1 Shelved cupboard or dresser, originally without doors, for displaying plate or earthenware, etc
2 Probably a riddle, for sieving ash and cinder
3 Either a floor mat or an underlay for a bed, typically a piece of coarse sacking used under a featherbed
4 Andirons: decorative stands for supporting burning logs in a fireplace (fire-dogs)
5 Creepers, or small fire-dogs
6 Table for counting money and keeping accounts; also applied to a side table

fyve glasses
foure pewter saltsellers
nyne pewter candlestickes
A bynne wth lock & key
Seven small wooden candlestickes
A basket for bread
A joyned bedsted corded wth
a tester
A matt
A fetherbedd. a bolster.
a paire of blanckettes
A coverlet
An old cupboard
Two latten[7] plates
A bedsted corded
A matt
A fetherbedd
two blanckettes
A coavering of Imagry old
Two old chestes

A fetherbedd
[entry damaged]
A coverlet

5 A truckle bedstead
A mattress & bolster
A fetherbed and
j bolster
Two blanckettes
Two coverlettes
A joyned forme
6 Eight
~~Seven~~ fetherbeds
Eight
~~Seven~~ bolsters
nyne blanckettes

[f.1v]

…..ing tubbe
….. cupboard
….. velvet chaire
….. stoles of caffa[8]
Thre carpettes j of
[illeg] cloth and
Two [turky?] fustion
A grene carpet for
the cupboarde

….chamber

A paire of awndrons
Six counterpointes of
foure curtens and
thre curten rodds
a fier shovell and
paire of tonges
fyve pieces of hanginges
of brauckardes[10]
A field bedstead
A ^seler^[12] tester of scarlet
embrodrie
fyve curtens of
the same
Thre curtens
A matt

fyve peces of old hanginges
of flowers
Two cupboardes

In the study

a lether chaire
A paire of old awndrons
Two curtens j curten rodd

Six counterpointes of
Imagery[9]
A whit rugg & j redd
One fustian blanckett
My lords velvet footecloth
foure coveringes ^q[uarter] lynd^
A grene carpet for a cupboard
Thre lintes[11]
A gonne wth a case
A close stole[13] wth a pann
An arming sword[14]
blade

In the Wardrobe

A rapier and dagger
black wth gyrdel &
scalbardes velvet

7 Latten: brass or similar alloy
8 A rich silk fabric
9 Counterpane
10 Brocades
11 For use as tinder, or wound dressings
12 Celure, or canopy, of a bed
13 Commode
14 Broadsword

My Lords chamber	A mattress A fetherbed & bolster j pillowe A pare of fustion blanckettes A white rugg ….. rugg A chaire of red cloth embrodred with yullow foure pieces of hanginges ij of verder ij brauckard j couterpoint of Imagery A wyndowe cushine of murrey[17] saye[18] embrodred Two curtens & j curtaine rodd A paire of awndrons A fier shovell A lowe stole foure pictures A litle table A close stole wth a pott A mattress A fetherbedd j bolster A paire of blanckettes A redd rugge A skryne
	A course sheat Two old chestes An old press board
In the ynner Dyning chamber	Three pieces of verders[15] A square table & frame A grene carpt to yt A Court cupboarde A grene carpt to yt A cipres[16] chest A chaire of neadle worke Two lowe stoles covered A paire of awndrons vij joyned stoles wrought Thre curtens & ij curten rodds A wainscot chaire Fyve pyctures
In the chamber at the staires head	A bedstead gilt A court cupboard A long table An old chest A joyned cupboard A matt A fether bed. j bolster. A blancket A rugg A redd covering An old cupboard at the staires head

[Separate sheet, f.1r]

	vesselles scoured[19]
	October 1573
	great platt[rs] xlvj
	one odde dishe w[t] a cinqfoile
2	lesser platt[rs] xiiij
3	smale dishes xiij
2	salett[20] dishes ix
	saucers xxj
	saltsellers of tynne iiij
	dishes of plate tynne xx
	plates or trenchers ix
d	ij plates for candles
d	spittes iiij

15 Verdors, or verders: tapestry showing trees or other verdure
16 Cypress-wood
17 Mulberry-coloured
18 Say: a fine, serge-like woollen cloth, sometimes part-silk
19 All or almost all the items are metal. The meaning of the numbers and letters in front of some of the entries is not obvious
20 Salad

d	ij chaffers[21] iiij
d	a colender j
d	a scomm^r[22]
d	an old chafinge dyshe
d	a grater for breade
d	a brasse posstnet[23] j
d	kitchen knyves iij
d	a stone morter & a pestell
d	brasse pottes iij.
d	brasse pannes iiij
L	a kettell j
d	a brasse morter w^t
	an Iron pestell
d	iij drypinge pannes
L	a drypinge panne
	of white plate
d	ij ^paires of^ potte hookes
d	ij grydyrons

[f.1v]

	iij highe tynned
	candelstickes
	iij lower tynned
	candelstickes
	ij have the snuffes[24]
	burned one before
	my L. goinge awey
	the other nowe since
	he com[e]
j	ix tynned plates
j	xx tynned plate
	dishes

21 Chafers or saucepans

22 Scummer: a shallow ladle for skimming

23 Posnet: a small, usually three-footed, cooking pot with a handle

24 Candle-ends, or the exposed wicks (meaning that the candles had been partly used)

APPENDIX III

Howard House Inventory, 1583

Transcript from London Metropolitan Archives, ACC/0446/H/005. By permission of the donor

The inventory from the Paget family archives was taken shortly after the death of Nazareth, Lady Paget (see page 50) and presumably lists the furnishings and other household items in the parts of Howard House which she and her entourage had occupied; many items relate specifically to women. The valuations are all to round pence (unlike the very precise valuations of the 1565 inventory), just a few items apparently considered worthless.

[f.1r]

Charterhouse

The Inventorye taken of alle such goodes & implementes of housholde as were founde there the vth of Maye 1583 and appreysed by William Necton[1] ^gent^ & William Downes ~~gent~~ & William Whittle of London Merchaunt Taylors/ viz.

In the litle chamber at the nether end of the greate chamber

In primis iiij peces of hanginges ^of verdure^ of Cloote[2] Leaves fowles & bestes cont Flemishe Elles at le Elle	vj^{li}
Itm pece of Tappestre of foules & beastes of a coarser making cont elles at le Elle	~~x^{s}~~ viij^{s}
Itm one olde pece of hanging of an olde Imagerye Storie cont elles at le Ell	~~x^{s}~~ viij^{s}
Itm one canapie of Dornix[3] of blewe redd & white wth courteynes rewede[4] for the same	xiij^{s} iiij^{d}
Itm one carpet of tawnye Brode clothe embrodered wth a Border of Flowers Fringed aboute cont in lengthe yardes & in breadthe	xxxiii^{s} iiij^{d}
Itm ij^{o} olde grene carpettes of clothe	v^{s}
Itm iij^{re} lyverye[5] Fethrbeddes wthout Boulsters	liij^{s} iiij^{d}
Itm v Quisshing[6] Stooles of Englisshe Turkey woorke[7]	v^{s}

1 Senior official at Howard House, formerly employed by Lord North

2 Burdock (clote)

3 Dornick: a kind of figured linen originally made at Doornik (Tournai)

4 Probably meaning a set, arranged in order (i.e. by rew) to fit the canopy

5 Livery: for the use of servants or retainers

6 Cushion

7 Woollen material woven on a loom, in imitation of Turkey carpet

Itm one lowe stoole covered wth ^old^ white clothe of Sylver for a wooman	xx^{d}
Itm one Frame of a lowe stoole for a wooman	iiij^{d}
Itm one halfe iij^{re} square Tabls of waynescotte	viii^{d}
Itm one lytell square table of wallnutte tree	ij^{s}
Itm iiij joyned stools of wainescote	ij^{s}
Itm one old cushine stuffed wth fethers wth the Lo: Dacres armes	xij^{d}
Itm one pillowe of downe wth a case of fustian	ij^{s} vj^{d}
Itm one paier of anyrons[8] of yron tipped wth brasse	ij^{s} viij^{d}
Itm too fier shovelles tipped wth brasse	~~ij^{s} viij^{d}~~ xvj^{d}
Itm too paier of tonges	xvj^{d}
Itm too pewter saltes[9]	iiij^{d}
Summa paginae xxiij^{li} xxij^{d}	

[f.1v]

	Itm xiij pewter candelstickes broken & hole	v^{s}
	Itm iij broken candelstickes of Latin[10]	xij^{d}
	Itm one old Bason and Ewer of pewter	ij^{s}
	Itm one chamber pott of Pewter	iiij^{d}
	Itm one chippinge knife & an ^old^ candelplate	iiij^{d}
lynen	Itm vj halle table clothes	~~xij^{s}~~ xiiij^{s}
	Itm [~~illeg~~] ^iiij paier of^ fyne sheetes of canvas at viij^{s} the paier	xxxij^{s} vj^{d}
	Itm vj paier of lyverye ^sheetes^ & one odd sheete at v^{s} the paier	xxxij^{s} vj^{d}
	Itm iij doss & too curse[11] table napkins at iiij^{s} the doss	xii^{s} viij^{d}
	Itm iij cupbord clothes wherof one of dyaper[12]& ij plaine	iiij^{s}
	Itm too wroughte pillowbers[13]	vj^{s}
	Itm iiij plaine pillowbers	iiij^{s}
	Itm too ^old^ dyaper ~~clothes~~ towelles	iij^{s}
	Itm too dyaper towelles milde[14] wth blewe threede	[~~illeg~~] v^{s}
	Itm three old shorte table ^clothes^ of dyaper	vij^{s} vj^{d}
In the grene velvet cheste	In one boxe a paier of sleves begonne to be wroughte wth blacke ~~sleve~~ sylke gold & silver	xx^{s}
	Itm nyne doss of buttons of golde & silver at xviij^{d} a doss	xiij^{s} vj^{d}

8 Andirons: decorative stands for supporting burning logs in a fireplace (fire-dogs)

9 Salt cellars

10 Latten: brass or similar alloy

11 Coarse

12 Diaper: linen cloth textured with a self-coloured ornamental weave in diamond or other pattern

13 Pillowcases

14 Milled

	Itm an old face for a gowen of white satten	
	striped wth golde wth a border to the same	xx^{s}
	Itm in an other boxe ix bodye smockes	
	wthout sleves at vj^{s} the pece	liij^{s}
	Itm a faier cheste for Jewelles of	
	grene velvet wth a casse[15] cheste of lether	xl^{s}
	Itm a coyffe of lawne trimed wth silver	
	wth a forehed clothe to the same	v^{s}
	Itm lawne coyfe of cut worke	ij^{s} vj^{d}
	Itm too paier of blacke drawen woorke cuffes	v^{s}
	Itm a cushine clothe wroughte wth	
	blacke silke & fringed wth golde	xx^{s}
	It a cushine clothe ^of callicoe^ wroughte wth flowers	xx^{s}
	of divers colors	xx^{s}
	Summa	
	paginae xvj^{li} ix^{s} iiij^{d}	
[f.2r]		
In a litle blacke cheste covered wth lether	Itm one very olde cushine clothe wroughte	
	wth grene & redd silke	ij^{s}
	Itm one cushine clothe of hollond begune	
	& not wroughte	ij^{s} vj^{d}
	Itm too cubborde clothes drawne & unroughte	xiij^{s} iiij^{d}
	Itm too ~~yarde~~ ^corner^ kerchers[16] of hollond	ij^{s}
	Itm too yarde kerchers of course hollond	iiij^{s}
	Itm ~~one~~ too curse Rubbers[17]	viij^{d}
	Itm one old night cappe	n^{l}
	Itm v old wornde smockes at ij^{s} vi^{d} the pece	xij^{s} vj^{d}
	Itm one ownce of blacke silke	xvj^{d}
	Itm one plaine cupbord clothe	ij^{s} vj^{d}
	Itm an unroughte cusshine clothe drawne	n^{l}
	Itm a cheine of amber & aggatt wth	
	certayne litle smale silver bedes	xx^{s}
	Itm one blacke cheste covered wth	
	lether	iij^{s}
In a blacke lether chest	Itm an olde dyape table clothe	vj^{s} viij^{d}
	Itm a plaine shorte table clothe	vj^{s}
	of [~~illeg~~] canvas	
	Itm xj plaine ^[~~illeg~~] old table^ napkins of hollond	vj^{s}
	Itm too plaine towelles & on old dyaper	
	towell at ij^{s} vj^{d} the pece	vij^{s} vj^{d}
	Itm xj other plaine table napkins	
	marked wth N	v^{s} vj^{d}
	Itm too yarde kerchers	v^{s}
	Itm too pillowbers	ij^{s}
	Itm a paier of fyne hollond sheetes	xiij^{s} iiij^{d}
	Itm too bondes wherof one white &	
	thether blacke wroughte	viij^{d}

15 Cash

16 Kercher: a kerchief, often for a woman's headdress

17 Rubbing cloths or towels

Itm a blacke cheste covered wth lether	iiij^{s}
Summa vj^{li} vj^{d} paginae	

[f.2v]

The greate chamber

Inprimis a drawinge table of wanskott wth a Frame	xvj^{s}
Itm iiij ^old^ cheyers wherof one covered wth blacke velvet one wth redd tishewe one wth englishe turkye worke & one wth Lether	xiij^{s} iiij^{d}
Itm v hanginges of Tapistrie	vij^{li} x^{s}
Itm three pictures	vij^{s} vj^{d}
Itm a Lyverye cupborde	ij^{s}
Itm an old square table of wainskott	iij^{s}
Itm one old flatt cheste of wainskott	vj^{d}
Itm iiij lyverye ^fether^ beddes wth v boulsters of fethers at xv^{s} the pece	lx^{s}
Itm iiij blancquettes wherof one an old Rugge	iiij^{s}
Itm iiij old tapestrie coverlettes	vj^{s} viij^{d}
Itm ij paier of canvas sheetes at iiij^{s} the paier	viij^{s}

The wthdrawinge chamber

Itm a Table of wainskott wth a Frame of beche	iiij^{s}
Itm a ^square^ carpett of Englyshe turkey worke wth my L armes	lx^{s}
Itm a lyverye cupborde of wainskott	ij^{s} vi^{d}
Itm one other square carpett of englishe turkeye worke wth roses	l^{s}
Itm iiij peces of hanginges wherof	iij^{li}
one wth [illeg] longe one wth cloate leaves & thother three of worse worke	vj^{li}
Itm too lether chayers drawen over wth yealowe taffata & black velvet imbrodered & thother of russett velvett	xiij^{s} iiij^{d}
Itm too cushine stooles of englishe turkey worke	ij^{s} viij^{d}
Itm a lowe stoole for a woman wth a seate of sylver	iiij^{s}
Summa paginae xxvj^{li} vl^{d}	

[f.3r]

Itm a paier of andyron tipped wth Latyn	v^{s}

My Ladyes chamber

Inprimis one bedd of downe wth a bolster of downe to the same	iiij^{li}
Itm a fetherbedd wth a boulster	xl^{s}
Itm iij pillowes of downe	vij^{s} vj^{d}

Itm one wollen blancquett	xvj^{d}
Itm a Russett Rugge	iiij^{s}
Itm a ^old^ Testar & v curteyne of stammelle[18] imbrodered wth blacke velvett	liij^{s} iiij^{d}
Itm a fielde bedsted of walnuttre	xx^{s}
Itm one fether bedd wthout a boulster	xxvj^{s} viij^{d}
Itm a Lyverye fether bedd wth a boulster	xx^{s}
Itm a woole bedd	ij^{s}
Itm a blancquett	ij^{s} vj^{d}
Itm an old coveringe of Tapestrie	ij^{s} vj^{d}
Itm too longe quyshions of yelowe damasse stuffed wth doune	xiij^{s} iiij^{d}
Itm an old curteyne of yealowe & redd Satten a bridges[19]	vj^{s} viij^{d}

The Maydes chamber

Inprimis a lyverye bedstedd of bordes	ij^{s}
Itm a lyverye table	ij^{s}
Itm a lyverye Fetherbedd [~~illeg~~]	xiij^{s} iiij^{d}
Itm a matteras	ij^{s} vj^{d}
Itm a blancquett	xij^{d}
Itm a cheste	iij^{s} iiij^{d}

The entrye

Itm a longe table wthout a frame	ij^{s} vj^{d}
Itm a truckle bedd corded	ij^{s} vj^{d}
Itm a skrene of wycker	xij^{d}
Itm an old curteyne of Saye[20]	xij^{d}

Summa paginae xv^{li} xvj^{s}

[f.3v]

The parlo[u]r

Inprimis a lowe spanishe bedstedd	iiij^{s}
Itm v lyverye fether beddes wth v bolsters	v^{li}
Itm one pillowe of downe covered wth fustian	ij^{s} vi^{d}
Itm too ^old^ fustian blancquettes	iij^{s} iiij^{d}
Itm one white blancquett striped wth redd & blewe	v^{s}
Itm other old blancquett	xij^{d}
Itm A ^old^ matteras	ij^{s} vj^{d}
Itm an old russett rugge	iiij^{s}
Itm a verye old saye quilte	viij^{d}
turky[?] Itm a very old counterpointe[21] peced of old aras	xij^{d}
Itm too ~~old~~ counterpointes of Tapestrey verye old & torne	ij^{s}
Itm a verye old chayer covered wth redd velvet	ij^{s} vj^{d}

18 Stammel: a coarse woollen or linsey-woolsey cloth

19 Bruges

20 Say: a fine, serge-like woollen cloth, sometimes part silk

21 Counterpane

Itm one stoole covered with englishe turkey worke	xij^{s}
Itm one other stoole covered wth a cheveren worke of redd & grene	xij^{d}
Itm too lowe stooles for woman of nedle worke of sundrye colors on redd the other grene	ij^{s}
Itm on litle verye old stoole for a woman covered wth white & blewe englishe turkeye worke	iiij^{d}
Itm one womans stoole wth a backe	ij^{s} vj^{d}
Itm one Lyverye cupborde of wainscott	j^{s}
Itm a lytle square table of wainscotte	ij^{s} vj^{d}
A paier of andyrons tipped wth Latin	iiij^{s}
Itm another ^smale^ andyron	iiij^{d}
Itm a bane Tubb[22]	iiij^{s}
Itm a wicker basskett	iiij^{d}
Itm too verye old curteynes & one curtey[n] rodd	ij^{s}
Itm too rilles[23]	ij^{d}

Summa paginae vij^{li} x^{s} viij^{d}

[f.4r]

The Butterye

Inprimis one old counter table	iiij^{s}
Itm a bine for breade	iij^{s}
Itm a old table	vj^{d}
Itm too joyned stooles	xvj^{d}
Itm a corded bedstedd	ij^{s}
Itm a lyverye fether bedd wth a boulster	xvj^{s}
Itm an old matteras	ij^{s} vj^{d}
Itm an old russett blancquet a coveringe & an old redd blancquet	ij^{s}
Itm A greate stone jugge & iiij other litle pottes of Stone	xij^{d}

The Halle

Inprimis an old table wth a frame	v^{s}
Itm iij wainscott formes	vj^{s}
Itm iij old formes of deale borde	ij^{s} vj^{d}
Itm the hanginges there	v^{s}

The Larder

Inprimis too greate Iron wrackes	xiij^{s} iiij^{d}
Itm viij spittes of yron wherof on a bird spitte	vj^{s} viij^{d}
Itm iij^{re} trevettes	ij^{s} vj^{d}
Itm too verye old gridyrons	xij^{d}

22 Bain tub, i.e. bath-tub

23 Possibly reels, for thread, or pulleys for curtain cord; or rails, cloths worn about the neck by women

[illeg]	Itm one greate paier of pott hookes	iiij^{s}
	Itm too old drippinge pannes	v^{s}
	Itm a large postnett[24] of brasse	ij^{s} ~~ij^{d}~~
	Itm a litle postnett of Laten wth a bile of Iron	vj^{d}
	Itm an old broken scummer[25] of Latyn	xviij^{d}
	Itm on Laten Ladle wth a laten spone	xvj^{d}
	Itm one chopinge knyfe & a clever	viij^{d}
	Itm a brasse morter wthout a pestle	ij^{s} vj^{d}
	Itm a litle Ladle wth a slice of Iron & a bief forke of Iron	viij^{d}
	Itm a motter of alibluster wth a pestle of woode	ij^{s}
	Itm a very old grate	ij^{d}
	Itm a frienge panne	j^{s}
	Summa paginae iij^{li} xv^{s} viij^{d}	

[f.4v]		
	Itm too brasse pottes	xv^{s}
	Itm too yron pottes wherof one broken	ij^{s}
	Itm too brasse pannes	ij^{s}
	Itm a trey wth a treyen[26] dishe	viij^{d}
	Itm too brien Tubbes	iiij^{s}
	Itm one old bucking tube[27]	xij^{d}
	Itm an old boole	n^{l}
	Itm a Runlett wth vergys[28]	vj^{d}
	Itm too Lynen wheeles[29]	ij^{s}
	Itm a woodden peele[30]	ij^{d}
	Itm too joyned Stooles	xvj^{d}
	Itm on old paier of bellowes	ij^{d}
	Itm an old salt tubb	ij^{d}
	Itm an old scuttle	vj^{d}
	Itm a old bedstedd wth Lumber in the seller	xij^{d}
	Itm a old chafing dishe of yron	~~vj^{d}~~ iij^{d}
	Itm too pie plates	~~ij^{d}~~
	Itm three platters of pewter	
	Itm a Pewter colender	
	Itm v fruite dishes	
	Itm iiij sallett[31] dishes	
	Itm a chamber potte	
	Itm a dyshe of pewter molton	
	Itm three saucers	

24 Posnet: a small, usually three-footed, cooking pot with a handle

25 Shallow ladle for skimming

26 Treen, i.e. wooden

27 Bucking-tub: used for washing dirty linen. Typically, the linen was left in the tub to steep in lye, made from ash or other alkali, prior to boiling, or hot water was repeatedly poured through a cloth covered in ash and allowed to drain through the linen in the bucking-tub

28 Runlet: a kind of cask or barrel; verges may refer to the hoops or rims

29 Purpose unknown

30 A small fire-shovel, or a wooden shovel or slice for use in baking

31 Salad

Itm a porrenger of Pewter	
Itm iiij^{re} greate chargers	
Itm vj greate platters	lxvj^{s} viij^{d}
Itm xviij greate platters	
Itm xiiij lesser platters	
Itm too basons & ewers	
Itm xlj smaler dishes	
Itm an old deepe Bason	
Itm [~~f....~~] iiij french dishes	
Itm iij ^old^ saucers	
Itm too old saltes	
Itm ij pie plates	

Summa paginae iiij^{li} xvij^{s} v^{d}

[f.5r]

The wardrope

	Inprimis a gowne of figured velvet laied on wth golde lace fured wth sable	liij^{s} iiij^{d}
	Itm a blacke velvet gowen unlyned	lxvj^{s} viij^{d}
[illeg]	Itm a broad cheste to laye in apparel	x^{s}
	Itm a fore parte of a kertle of clothe of twishewe	liij^{s} iiij^{d}
	Itm a fore parte of a kertle of millyane[32] clothe of silver	xl^{s}
	Itm a stomacher of redd velvet wth gold lace	vj^{s} viij^{d}
	Itm a stomacher of clothe of gold	iij^{s} iiij^{d}
		iiij^{s} iij^{s} iiij^{d}
	Itm a canvas sheete wth a fore parte & a kertle of clothe of Silver	vij^{s} iiij^{d}
	Itm a bedd testor ~~of~~ ^paned^ wth ^ blacke velvett & [~~illeg~~] redd clothe of baudkinge[33] wth Scallopp^{e} shells & dogges heddes wth redd curteynes of Sarsnett[34] to the same	C^{s}
	Itm a counterpointe paned wth blacke velvett & redd redd clothe of tynselle[35] havinge scallope shelles & dogges heddes	v^{li} vj^{s} viij^{d}
	A Longe drawinge cushion of russett velvet edged wth silke & silver	xv^{s}
	Itm a pece of yealowe taffata embrodered of a nelle longe & frenged	iiij^{s}
	A Saddle clothe of of blacke velvett laied one wth golde lace & buttons	Cvj^{s} viij^{d}
	Itm a pece of aras hanginges & ij hanginges of Tapestrey	xxx^{s}
	Itm one Petticote of redd Satten imbrodered	xl^{s}
	Itm the horse harnes of velvet fringed & Laced	vj^{s} viij^{d}

32 Possibly Milan (i.e. milliner's)

33 Baudekin: a rich silk material

34 Sarcenet: very fine, soft silk material

35 Tinsel: cloth such as satin or silk interwoven or brocaded with gold or silver thread, or thinly coated with gold or silver

Itm one cupborde	v^{s}
Itm too dublettes one of ^white^ satten ^xx^{s}^ &	iiij^{s}
thother of striped canvas	xxiiij^{s}
Itm a fether bedd & iij boulsters	xxvj^{s} ~~vj^{s}~~ viij^{d}
Itm a white blancquett	n^{l}
Itm a ^old^ redd rugge	iij^{s} iiij^{d}
Itm ~~field~~ truckle bedsted	ij^{s} vj^{d}
Itm too joyned tables wth fraimes	x^{s}
Itm too old coverlettes	n^{l}
Itm one old coveringe for a stoole of russet velvet	xij^{d}
Summa paginae xxxvj^{li} xij^{s} ij^{d}	

[f.5v]

Itm one square spitte	viij^{d}
Itm a screne	xvj^{d}
Summa partis	ij^{s}

Summa
totalis Cxxxj^{li} vij^{s} j^{d}

per me William Necton

by me Willam Whittell
Wyllym Downes

Dd to me by Richard Ryley 14°
May 1583

One litle trencher salt seller gilt wthout a cover
One sylver spone wth a knobb gilt & Southells
cognisans on yt
An old course napkin
Ther ys in thands off old ~~mas~~[?] Doctor Caldwall[36] here in
london a flower off gold set wth stones, wch was
pawned to his Brother William Caldwall off
Boorto[n][37] for xx^{li} of the rep[…?] L off Richard
Ryley. It was pawnd by xx^{li} for Tomson

36 The physician Richard Caldwall, who was from Staffordshire, where the Pagets had their principal house. Caldwall was associated with Lord Lumley, uncle of Philip Howard, Earl of Arundel, in establishing the Lumleian lecture at the College of Physicians, of which he was elected president in 1570.[1] He may have been the Master Caldewell who visited the Duke of Norfolk at Howard House in 1569 (page 156)

37 Burton-upon-Trent, where William, who had died in 1582, was a clothier, and the two brothers had founded a charity for clothworkers[2]

APPENDIX IV

Howard House Inventory, 1588

Transcript from British Library, Stowe MS 164, ff.33r–54r. By permission of the British Library

This inventory of Howard House is dated in the 30th year of Elizabeth's reign, which ended on 16 November 1588. It was probably made on the order of Lord Burghley after Philip Howard, Earl of Arundel, a prisoner in the Tower since 1585, was accused of having induced a fellow prisoner to celebrate mass in support of the Spanish Armada. Clearly much had already have been removed from the house, though apart from some receipts for wardrobe items, dating from the previous few years, there is no record of what. Among the obvious places excluded from listing are the kitchens and butteries, stores, stables and workshops, the tennis court and the gate-house. The general impression is of a lavishly furnished house, but in places (such as the armoury, f.51v) the contents listed appear to be no more than residue. Among items of particular interest are the hangings detailed in the wardrobe, the paintings in the long gallery, items of costume including some for masques, and other things relating to leisure activities. These include a table, cues and balls for billiards (ff.39v, 40v), an early reference to the game in England.

Headings and marginal notes added in a later hand are italicized.

[f.33r]

Howard house. the Inventorie of suche stuffe and implements of houshold as remayne at Howard house hoc A° Elizabethe Regine xxx^{mo}

1588./ /.

Howard House
Inventory of Furniture etc
1588.

[f.33v blank]
[f.34r]

In the wardrope

A sute of fine hanginges of tapstrye called the sute of the wildernes servinge for the hanginge of the great dyninge chamber of howard house

The first pece havinge in it a Leopard and the wilde boore conteyneth in length be~~g~~inge quarter lyned wth Canvas	iiij yards quarter depth iij yards di di/qr[1]

1 Dimidium (di), i.e. half, and quarterium (qr) are used in combination as follows:
di qr = one eighth
qr di = three-eighths
di di qr = five-eighths
iij qr di = seven-eighths

	The second pece havinge in it a foxe and the birds and hunters quarter lyned wth Canvas conteyneth in lengthe	v yards iij qr Nales[2] depthe as before
7 peces of the wildernesse	The third pece havinge a dragon seisinge uppon an Elephant quarter lyned as the other conteyneth in length	v yards iij qr halfe naile depthe as before
	The fourthe pece havinge an Austriche therin conteyneth in lengthe	v yards one Naile depthe as before
	The fifth pece havinge lyons therin conteynth in lengthe	iiij yards qr di depth as before
	The sixt pece havinge a hind therin conteyneth in length	iiij yards qr depth as before
	The seaventhe pece havinge in it hunters of the beare a broode of ducks and an Owle conteyeth in lenth	~~i~~iij yards di di qr

To hange the bedchamber next the said great dyninge chamber

One pece conteyneth the historie of Jonas[3] cast into the sea conteyneth in lenth	v yards depth iij y iij qr di nale
One pece ymagerie called the historie of Saule and David conteyneth in lenth	~~v~~ iij yards qrt
One pece of the same historie conteyn the ymage of kinge Saule crowned and of Samuell	ij yards iij qr
One pece of the same historie conteyn the ymage of the anoyntinge of kinge Saule and the trumpeters cont in length	iij yards di qr nayle
One other pece of the same historie wth the ymage of Samuell and many othrs conteyninge in lenth	iij yards di
One other pece wth the ymage of a king adoringe the Arke cont in lenth	iij yards di di qr
One other pece of ymagrie of an unknowen historie wch Richard Bedo[4] saith came from Arundell castel conteyninge in lenth	ij yards iij qr di all of one depthe

These vij last hanginges be unlyned

Md my lady drurye hath one pece of ymagrie of the storie of Saule wch is supplied wth the last of the said vij peces

2 Nail = one-sixteenth of a yard, or 2¼ inches

3 Jonah

4 Bedo (or Bedoe) is the servant of the wardrobe of the beds (i.e. the 'high gallerie') named in the 1585 staff list (see page 51)

[f.34v]

To hange the next chamber called the dyninge chamber over the pastrie vj peces of the historie of abraham all unlyned	
The first pece conteyneth in lenth	ij yards iij qr di naile depth iij yard iij qr
The second pece conteyneth in length	v yd di di qr di naile
The third pece conteyneth in length	iij yards di di naile
The forth pece conteyneth in length	v yards & an naile
The fifthe pece conteynth in lenth	iij yards di
The sixt pece conteyneth in lenth	iiij yards di qr
To hange my Ladies Chambe^{r} at the galleries end	all of one depthe viz iij yards iij qrs
One ould lined hanginge of ymagrie of the historie of kinge assuerus and hester[5] wth Englishe meter above and the lo: Mountigues[6] armes conteynnge in lengthe	vj yards di qr depth iiij y di qr
One other pece of the same historie conteyninge in length	viij yards di as before
One other pece of the same historie conteyng in lenth	iij yards qr as before
One pece of the historie of hercules somtyme parte of the hanginge of the great Chamber at keninghall[7]	iiij yards qr di depth v yards qr
One other pece of the same historie Conteyninge in lengthe this is but a pece cute a sunder	ij yards iij qr the dep of all ~~vj~~ v yard ~~di di qr~~
To hange my lo Chamber at the other end of the gallerie iiij peces of the historie of David & Kinge salomon	
The first pece length	v y^{d} di di qr depth
The second pece in lengthe	~~i~~iij y^{d} ~~di di qr~~ iij qr iij yard qr iij naile
The third pece in length	iiij y^{d} di qr
The forth pece conteyneth in length	v ^{yd} iij qr a naile all of one depth
Five hanginges somtyme used for the hanginge of my lo Chamber at the Courte quarter lyned	

[f.35r]

One pece of verdors[8] wth beasts and foules in lenth	iiij yards qr

5 The Persian king Ahasuerus (identified as Xerxes I) and his Jewish queen, Esther

6 Anthony Browne, first Viscount Montagu, was implicated in the plot to bring about the marriage of the fourth Duke of Norfolk to Mary, Queen of Scots

7 Kenninghall palace in Norfolk, the principal seat of the fourth Duke of Norfolk and his grandfather, the third Duke

8 Verdors, or verders: tapestry showing trees or other verdure

	depth iij yd di
One other pece of the same sute in	
lenth	ij yd iij qr
One other pece of the same sute in lenth	iiij yd qr
One other pece of the same sute	
in lenth	iij yd di
One other of the same sute conteyninge	v yd di and a naile
in lenth	all of one depth
Five hanginges retorned From the lo:	
Sheffeild[9] wch did serve to hange	
the Chamber at the Tarris[10] end viz	
One pece of ymagrie the border of	
roses and Frutes the length	ij yd iij qr
One other pece the border of compartementes	
wth Satires[11] and Frutes lenth	iiij yd iij qr
One other pece of the same storie	v yd di depth of all
	iij yd iij qr
One other pece of another sute wth ij	
women therin one horsbake[12] length	ij yd iij qr depth iij y di
One other pece of ymagrie soyled	
wth smoke	ij y and di di qr &
	naile
	depth iij y iij qr
Other hanginges retorned from the	
lo: Sheffeild of sondry sortes wch	
hanged in my lo: william[13] his Chamber	
A hanginge of ould ymagrie wth a	
narrowe border of roses pawnsies	iij yards qr di depth
and Marigouldes cont in length	iiij yardes di
One other of the like border and ymagrie	
cont in length	iij yardes di and naile
	depth as the other
One pece of ould ymagrie of Anthonius	
the emperor the upper border wherof	
is wrought wth ymagrie of Cloth of tissue	vj yards and naile
cont in length	depth iiij yardes
One other pece of tapstrie and roses	
of foliarie and beastes wth a fountaine	v yardes di depth
in the middest cont in lenth	ij yardes iij qr
One pece of tapstrie of parke worke[14] cont	iij yardes di qr
	depth iij yd qr naile
One other pece of the same worke	ij yd di di qr depth
cont in length	iij yard qr naile

[ff.35v, 36r blank]
[f.36v]

9 Baron Sheffield, later first Earl of Mulgrave (1565–1646), was grandson of William Howard, first Baron Howard of Effingham, younger son of the second Duke of Norfolk

10 The Terrace, or Norfolk Cloister

11 Satyrs

12 On horseback

13 Philip Howard's half-brother, later Lord Howard of Naworth

14 Decorated with park-like scenes or subjects

	A ritch bed of whit Cloth of silver	Testor and seler
on the testor the duk armes in the quarter supported wth ij lions and the seler the duk and duchesse ther armes supported wth the lion and red tiger	One testor and seler[15] of Cloth of silver whit wth the armes and supporters of the Duke of Norff and the lady Margaret his wiff A doble valens to the same of the same stuffe fringed wth silke and silver viz iij peces of valence for the owtward parte fringed belowe wth a depe fringe and above wth a narrowe fringe the iij inner peces not fringed above but at the ends and belowe as the other All lyned wth whit Buckram[16] and havinge Claspes for the cominge of them togither	valence
	Five Cortaines of whit taffetie wth the ringles and laces therto wherof ij of one bredth of the taffetie ij of one bredth di and the vth of ij breds depe ij yardes	Curtens v
	A Chaire of the same sute wth a longe quisshion lyned wth whit satten wth the ij buttons or tassels and a lowe stole covered wth the same stuffe over wrought	Chaire and quisshion
	A quilt of purple satten the border wherof is twilted[17] wth silver twist wth the Duke and Duchesse ther armes and supporters in the midest therof	quilt of purple satten
	A testor and seler of Crimsin Cloth of tissue singlie valensed fringed wth a depe Fringe of Crimsin silke and gould	Testor and seler and valens
	Five Curtens of Crimsin taffatie wherof ij of one bredth ij of one and a halfe and one of ij bredths	Curtens v
	One quilt of Crimsin taffatie the border quilted wth gould twist	quilt of Crimsin taffitie
[f.37r]		
	A faire bedsted of walnuttre and enlayed workes wth the Curtene rodes to the same serveth for the said riche bed of Clothe of silver	

15 Celure, or canopy, of a bed

16 Buckram: a fine linen or cotton fabric; also a coarse linen or cotton fabric stiffened with size or gum

17 Quilted

A testor and seler of yelowe cloth of gould braunched wth purple wth a doble valens of the same stuff both depe fringed wherof one is anexed to the seler and the other aparte both lyned wth yelowe bukeram	Tester seler dubble valence
Five Curtens of purple taffetie wth the ringles and lorres[18] therto wherof ij of one bredth twoe of a bredth and halfe and one of ij bredthes	Curtens v
A faire bedsted of walnuttre and of ynlaied worke posted wth the Curtene rodes of yron therto belonginge	
The testor of a Canipie of Crimsin Cloth of gould bordered wth a broad bone lace[19] of gould and Bowed buttons of gould and laid uppon every seme wth a bone lace of gould and fringed wth an uncutt short fringe of Crimsin silke and gould wth thre poyntes of whit silke to tye the same	The Testor of a Canapie
the ij other partes of the same bed in all thinges answerable for the first wthin a Case of wicker lyned wth yelowe cotton the Crowne of the canopie of the same stuffe wth an indented valence wth twelve buttons and tassells to the same all laid over wth smale bone lace of gould wth a gilded glove of gold a Crimsin silke corde and a pulley of lattine[20] to the same	The two Curtens of the same
A quilt of Crimsin taffetie the border twelted wth silver twist	A quilt
A Chaiyre of Crimsin Cloth of gould plaine ~~furnished~~ fringed wth Crimsin silke and gould	the Chaire

[f.37v]

A longe quishion of the same stuff fringed wth a short fringe of Crimsin silke and gould wth three buttons and tassells to the same lyned wth crimsin satten	the longe quishion
A square quishion of the same sute likwise lyned wthought Buttons and tassells	A square quishion

18 Lores, or straps

19 Bone-lace: a type of lace worked on a pattern marked in pins, using bone bobbins

20 Latten: brass or similar alloy

A sparver[21] of purple cloth of gould striped wth gould very large wth the valens anexed fringed wth a depe fringe of purple silke and gould with fower curtens of purple taffetie to the same wth all the furniture of Cords to the same — A sparver

A quilt of purple satine the border twilted wth gould twist — quilt

A Chaire wth fower gilt copper pomels the bake and seat of Crimsin satten imbrodered wth whit cloth of silver and gould twist and fringed wth a crimsin silke and gould fringe — A Chaire

a longe quishion of the same stuffe lyned wth crimsin sattin wth iiij buttons and tassells of crimsin silke and balls of gould — a quishion

A lowe stole wth a backe therto of cloth of silver imbrodered wth a twist of purple and gould twist and crimsin silke — a lowe stole

A longe quishion of the same lyned wth Crimsin branched cloth of silver wth iiij buttons and tassells — a longe quishion

A lowe overworne stole of Crimsine Cloth of gould

One ould chaire of yelowe satten of bridges[22] ymbrodered wth Crimsin velvet

A longe quishion of yellowe velvet one both sydes wth a short fringe of yelowe silke

[f.38r] One ould overworne Chaire of watchet[23] velvet wth the seat and the upper parte of the backe wch remayneth laid one wth iij open bone laces of gould

A longe quishion of the same stuff overworne wth v laces of gould the lyninge all torne

21 Bed (or cradle) canopy

22 Bruges

23 Light blue

A testor and seler of watchet branched
vellet[24] wth bone lace of gould and a
depe fringe of watchet silke and
gould muche ympaired

Md my lo henry[25] hath an ould quilt of purple satten that served this sute

thre overworne curtens of watchet
sarcenett[26]

A testor and seler of blake velvet fringed
wth silke ~~and~~ blake, wch was the cloth
of estat for the duke of Norff morninge
for the seconde duchesse

A tester and seler of Crimsin damaske
old wth the armes of the lo: audley and his
wife[27] and ther supporters uppon the
testor and the lo Audley his armes uppon
the seler wth a single valence anexed
therto fringed wth red silke and gould

A seler of Crimsin velvet and whit satten
in paynes wth a fringed valence to the
same anexed the tester wherof was
by misfortune quit Consumed wth fier

One ould overworne quilt of purple
taffetie

The testor of a bed of purple vellet
and satten in paines the purple vellet
imbrodered wth lyons of silver and the
satten wth open bone lace of gould
and silver cheveron wise wth valence
of the same fringed wth purple silke
gould and silver
thre overworne ould Curtens beinge
blake sarcent windowe curtens
An ould overworne curten of ij bredthes — Seared[28] stuffe
the one yelowe the other russet
An other torne Curten of red and
grenne taffitie of ij paines
An other of whit and red taffitie
all torne

[f.38v]

A faire pece of tapstrie wth the ymage
of Salomon one horsbake used for a — ij yardes ij qr di
Counterpoint[29] cont in length — depth iij yardes iij [qr]

24 Velvet

25 Philip Howard's uncle, Henry Howard, later first Earl of Northampton

26 Very fine, soft silk material

27 Thomas Audley, Lord Audley of Walden (1487/8–1544), Lord Chancellor, whose daughter Margaret was the fourth Duke of Norfolk's second wife

28 Worn-out

29 Counterpane

One ould pece of hanginge unlyned ~~wth~~ of
parke worke wth roses and a fountaine
in the midest used for a counterpoint — iij yardes di di qr
cont in length — depth iiij yard di
An ould counterpaine lyned wth canvas
of tapstrie ymagrie the length — iij yardes di
bredth ij yardes di

A Coveringe of course ymagrie lyned
wth canvas longe iij yardes bredth ij y^{ds}
A Coveringe unlyned ould of tapstrie
parke worke length iij yardes bredth
ij yardes
thre overworne ould lyned coveringes
of course tapstrie past use
seven spanish blankets wherof six
ar striped and one plaine and ould
thre ould blankets of peniston[30] wherof
ij marked with TNK and one wth TN[31]
one other torne and decaied
One ould fustian blanket of iij bredths longe iij yardes
One other of iij bredthes length ij yardes iij qr
One ould torne fustian Blanket of v bredths
~~fower~~ ^iij^ yardes longe
One ould fustian Blanket of the same
content
One other ould fustian Blanket of iiij bredthes
One other ould fustian of iij bredthes ij yardes longe
One other ould fustian of iij bredthes ~~i~~iij yardes longe
Five pillowes of downe wherof iij
^larg^ Marked wth TNK and one marked
wth TN one other lesse marked with AB
Thirten quishions of tapstrie wth the
whit lion in the midest
One other quishion of tapstrie roses
One ould overworne quishion stuft wth
fethers
One ould case of a quishion made of a
pece of an ould windowe cloth past use
xij ould ordnarie smale grenne quishions
of clothe

[f.39r]

A carpet of a yard iij qr square of grenne
damaske fringed wth a short fringe of
grenne silke and gould wth iiij tassells
~~cow~~^cal^led[32] in gould.
A Carpet of one yard naile square of
grenne velvet lyned wth grenne mockadowe[33]
fringed wth grenne silke fower peare
buttons[34] of grenne silke

30 Coarse wool cloth originally made in Penistone, Yorkshire
31 Monograms of Thomas Howard, Duke of Norfolk
32 Probably cowled or cauled (capped) intended
33 Mockado, a woollen imitation velvet, made by Flemish weavers in Norwich (encouraged by the fourth Duke of Norfolk)
34 Pear-shaped ornaments, not pairs of buttons

A Carpet of nedle worke fine crewell[35]
the worke of roses and honisokells &
a border of akorns lyned wth grenne
bocheram fringed wth ~~grene~~ reed silke
length ij yardes qr di bredth j yard qr
A chimney cloth of tapstrie square ij yardes
unlyned
A carpet of tapstrie square j yard iij qrs
and naile unlyned
One ould grenne carpet wth ij lystes[36] theron
longe ij yardes
An other grenne cloth carpet wthought
the lystes longe j yard di
An other grenne cloth carpet wth the
lystes length ij yardes qr di
One ould overworne red carpet length
ij yardes qr naile
A turkye carpet longe ij yardes di di qr
A cubberd carpet of turkey worke[37] j yard iij qr nale overworne
A turkey carpet length ij yardes qr di
An ould overworne carpet of turky worke longe ij yardes qr
An other ould overworne turky carpet length j yards iij qr
An other carpet of turky worke length j yard iij qr
An other turky carpet longe ij yardes
An other turky carpet longe j yard iij qr di
One large turky carpet long iiij yardes di iij nailes broade ijyd
twoe ould windowe clothes of tapstrie parkworke ~~j y di iij naile~~
thre yardes longe a pece overworne
thre ould fouldinge stoles wth seates of red velvet overworne
Twoe perfuminge pannes of brasse
The head of an other
Five ould lattin plates unperfitt
fower ould broken candlstickes of lattin past use

[f.39v]

Five lattin candlstickes
Nyne pewter candlstickes
One broken pewter candlsticke
Chamberpotes viij of pewter
thre close stoles[38] covered wth lether one great the
twoe other of a smaller sort wth thre pannes of tynne
A close chaire covered wth grenne cloth wthout a panne
Thre paire and one Andrions[39] garnished with copper
Flaunders worke
One paire of yron Andyrons
Twoe paire of fier shovells and tonges sutable
to the flaunders andyrons
Twoe paire of lowe Andyrons wherof one paire broken
Twoe smale fier shovels and one paire of tongues
twoe paire of bellowes wherof one carved

35 Crewel: a thin worsted yarn

36 Lists: borders, selvage edges or strips of material

37 Woollen material woven on a loom, in imitation of Turkey carpet; also genuine Turkish tapestry work

38 Commodes

39 Andirons: decorative stands for supporting burning logs in a fireplace (fire-dogs)

A wicker skrenne
halve a dozen of bedstaves
twoe plomets of lead for my lo his exercise of his armes
Thre paier of ould course sheets for kepinge of the beest stuffe aforsaid
a pece of canvas that was partte of the lyninge of an ould coveringe
Thre billyard stickes and one porte[40] and ij balles of yvery
An yron hannakr[41]
A brushe
A longe table of fire[42] deale of iiij yardes longe uppon ij tressells
One square table of yard and qr longe uppon ij tressells
One table of fire deale uppon a joyned frame ij yardes longe
twoe fire deale tables iiij yardes longe a pece uppon thre lowe tressells
A case of leather for a pece of plate
Nyne paier of sheets of hasboroughe cloth[43] of ij bredthes marked wth the matravers knote[44]
Fower pillowbeares[45] of course holland
ij paier of fine canvas sheets of ij bredthes marked wth PA[46]

[f.40r]

Thre paire and one sheete of canvas course of ij bredthes
Twoe paire of ould fine shetes decaied past weringe
Six ould pillowbeares overworne
One ould sheete in the bottome of the chest
An ould fire deale chest wherin this stuff is

one shet lent to Mr Banaster at his goinge downe to trusse his clothes

Bedes in the highe gallerie used for the wardrope

A great pallet fetherbed marked wth TNK wth a boulster marked wth the sammarke
One other large fetherbed wth a boulster marked wth the same marke
One other large pallet fetherbed wth a boulster marked wth the marke aforsaid
One other large pallet fetherbed wth a boulster both marked as before
One other great pallet fetherbed wth a boulster the bed marked TN and the

40 Port: an ivory arch through which the ball was hit in early forms of billiards
41 Hanaper (hamper): a case or chest for valuables
42 Fir
43 Probably a type of cloth originally woven at Happisburgh in Norfolk
44 Maltravers knot: a device based on an interlaced cross and square, used in the Maltravers arms. It came into the Howard family with the Barony of Maltravers, inherited with the Earldom of Arundel
45 Pillowcases
46 Monogram of Philip Howard as Earl of Arundel

boulster wth TNK one other lesse fetherbed
wth a boulster both marked wth TNK
One other large pallet bed wth a boulster
both marked at the corner with TN
One other lesse pallet fetherbed w^th
a boulster marked as this last before
One great pallet bed wth a boulster both
marked wth TNK
One lesse fetherbed wth a boulster
both marked wth PA
Five stocke mattrises of canvas course
Seaven ould straw mattes

Bedsteades in the highe gallerie nowe used for wardrope

A standinge posted bedsted of beache vernished
wth yron rodes and cordes wth all the rest servinge
for the testor and seler of crimsin cloth of
tissue
A bested of ould wanscote wth ij postes and
wth the cordes
Six liverie bedsteds[47] of beache and
wainscote wth iij bedcordes
One lowe beadsted wth turned pillers at the
head servinge for the riche canapie of
yron vises[48]
A little torned coche[49] wch was my younge
ladies
the head and feet of another bedsted the sydes
wherof was burned

[f.40v]

An yron hath[50] uppon fower yron wheels a yard square
wth six ringles to carie the same bye the bottome
therof a little perished
A wrest for to cordes beddes and a ladder of
fire deale of xj staves and a small cord uppon
hookes reatchinge from one end of this gallerie
to the other
A wainscote joyned stole marked PS[51]

In the bedchamber at the end of the halle

A longe foulded table of walnuttrie uppon
a faire frame the posts wherof ar cuninglie
wrought wch table beinge unfoulded and
and length conteyneth vij yardes

47 Beds for servants
48 Probably a canopy carried on or incorporating spiral iron columns
49 Couch or small bed
50 Hearth
51 Monogram of Philip Howard as Earl of Surrey

A large liverie cubberd[52] of wainscote of 2
yardes longe and 3 qr broad wth a bottom
Uppon the wainscote dore of this chamber
cominge ought of the great dyninge chamber
is a springe locke

In the rome over the skrine at the east end of the hall

A billiyard bord covered wth grenne
cloth beinge in length iij yardes di and
breadth j yard qr naile wth a frame of
beache therunto wth fower torned postes
A cloke[53] case of boorde

In the great dyninge chamber

A table of fire deale uppon a frame of
beache wth ix turned pillers longe
iij yardes iij qr and naile bread j yard
wantynge an ynche

the waynscote doores have alle ther
hingles snekes[54] and other yrons
the great dore that partith this chamber
and the last abov said have ij yron
boultes and a great springe plate
locke

[f.41r]

In the utter chamber of my lo his syde

[in a different hand:]
[M]^{d} there be iiij^{or} peeces of arras
[ha]ngins belonging to this chambre
[of] the storie of Masinissa[55] nowe
[re]maninge in the hands of my La:
[D]rewrie, and art at Ortwrie howse

A livery cubber of Beache and fire deale
wth a bottome longe [~~onge~~?] on yard iij qr half
an ell[56] broad

In the bedchamber of y^{t} syde

A livery cubberd of beache and fire wth
a bottome longe j yard halfe and a naile
broad halfe yard halfe qr
One flewed[57] walnuttrie stole
fower wainscote stoles wherof iij wth balls
one the fete the other wth square
fete

52 Livery cupboard: cupboard for storing provisions, especially those for allocation to servants
53 Clock
54 Hinges and snecks (latches)
55 First king of Numidia
56 English ell = 45ins
57 Probably meaning with splayed legs

the head or cner[58] of a waynscote stole
A plaine tressell

In the gallerie

A standynge cubberd wth a curyous carved
Frame of antiques[59] wth divers inlaied
worke and the whit horse uppon the
same wth a chaire of the same worke
framed w^th^in the same wch is decaied
and broken
A large picture of the Quens Matie
in whit wth a braunche of roses in her
left hand
A large picture of the Earle of Surrey
my lo: grandfather wth an yron rode and
a grenne silke curten
A smale picture of the last duke of
Norff my lo: father
A smale picture of the lady Marie
duchesse of Norff my lo: mother
A smale picture in glasse worke
of o^r^ lady wth the picture of Adame
and Eve
A large picture of the bisshop of aquila
in spaine[60]
a smale picture of the ould Erle of
Darby[61] father to my lo: that nowe is
A picture of my lo: of Darby that
nowe is[62]
A smale picture of the late Erle of
Southamoton[63]

[f.41v]

A large picture of S^r^ henrie sidney late
lo: president of wales[64]
A picture of my lo: of Arundell that nowe
is in a sute of grenne
A picture of the lo henrie dudley brother
to my lo: of lycester[65]
a smale picture of Stephen gardner
bishope of winchester[66]
A picture of the lo: Compton[67]
A picture of Sr William Peter[68]

58 Probably knur, perhaps meaning here the top or seat
59 Grotesque or impossibly contorted supporting figures
60 Alvaro de la Quadra, Spanish ambassador in 1559–63
61 Edward Stanley, third Earl of Derby, who married a sister of the third Duke of Norfolk, Philip Howard's great-grandfather
62 Henry Stanley, fourth Earl of Derby
63 Henry Wriothesley, third Earl of Southampton, Shakespeare's supposed patron
64 Sir Henry Sidney (1529–86), Lord Deputy of Ireland
65 Lord Henry Dudley (d.1557), a soldier. His widow, Margaret Audley, had married her cousin the fourth Duke of Norfolk, becoming Philip Howard's stepmother.
66 Gardiner had been a close associate of Philip Howard's great-grandfather, the third Duke of Norfolk
67 Henry Compton of Compton Wynyates, first Baron Compton (1538–89)
68 Sir William Petre (1505/6–72), secretary of state

A picture of the mariage of a duche bowd[69]
A picture of the duke of Norff in his
cote armore of nedle worke wth a
ground of grenne velvet imbrodered
wth silver twist

In the chamber at the galleries end

A posted bedsted wth postes of ~~enlaied~~ ^walnuttre wth the head of
enlaied^ worke ~~in the head~~ wth the laches and
iij curten yron rodes and the corde
A livery cubberd of waynscote wth a bottom
longe one yarde di qr and naile broad
di yard di qr
A foulded wainscote table wth ij leaves
wth a cubberd therin thre joyned stoles
of wainscote wherof ij wth square feete
and one wth a round fotte or ball

In the next utter chamber

A fouldinge frame uppon an yron wth a
table thereuppon of waynscote longe yard
di broad iij qr ij nailes di
A joyned livery cubberd of wainscote w^th
a bottome longe yard qr di broad halfe
an ell
twoe Joyned stoles the fet turned w^th
round balls marked wth PS

In the chamber descoueryes[70] over the landrie

A livery cubberd of waynscote wth a
bottom length ij yardes laking a naile
broad iij qr di naile

In the chamber next therunto

A waynscote joyned presse wth ij dores
wth shelves therin a locke and hespe

[f.42r]

In the chamber over the pasterie called my ladies dyninge chamber

A faire table of walnuttre fouldinge
uppon a frame longe thre yardes beinge
drawne ought a full, and broad
A livery cubberd of waynscote wth turned
pillers and a botome longe j yard di
wantinge a naile bredth iii qr
A walnuttre stole wth square feete

69 Bawd (pander); unless boor (peasant) is intended
70 Reading uncertain. Probably in error for 'descovered', and perhaps meaning 'to be found'

In my lo William chamber

A livery bedsted of beache corded wth a
mate[71]
A livery fetherbed newe and the boulster
marked wth PhA
An ould rugge
An ould coveringe of course tapstrie lyned
marked uppon the canvas wth TN
A downe pillowe marked wth PA
A paire of livery canvas shetes
A livery cubberd beache and waynscote
wth a bottome ij yardes and naile longe
broad iij qr lacking a naile
A walnuttre stole wth square feete
A wainscote stole wth round fet uppon
balls

[f.42v blank]
[f.43r]

In the great sealed[72] chamber below under the chambers at the end of the gallerie

A livery bedsted wth cord and mate
A palled bed marked wth TNK and a
boulster therto wth TN
One plaine ould wollen blancket
An ould ruge
One counterpoint of small verdors and beasts
lyned ~~lyned~~ wth canvas marked wth TN longe
iij yardes and naile broad ij yardes iij qr di
A downe pillowe marked wth TNK
A tester and seler therto anexed of grene
taffatie braunched wth flowers of gould
and whit satten in paines wth a depe fringe
of whit silke and grenne silke in paines
Itm fower ould curtens to the same of
purple sarsnet
Ane ould deale table longe iiij yardes
and yard broad standinge uppon ij great
standinge tressells wth one stalke the
feete uppon a crosse
A great ould joyned forme of waynscote
longe iiij yardes di and halfe a qr
An other ould joyned forme of waynscote
longe iij yardes di qr
An other joyned forme of a newer fashion
wth turned postes and fotstepes longe ij
yardes
Twoe waynscote joyned stoles turned
round at the feete
A joyned table of firre uppon a beachen
turned frame longe ij yardes scarsly
broad yard and naile

71 Mat: an underlay for a bed, typically a piece of coarse sacking used under a featherbed
72 Ceiled, or panelled

[f.43v]

In the ynner chamber

A livery bested wth cord and mate
A livery fetherbed wthought marke
and a large ~~bedsted~~ boulster marked wth TNK
A plaine ~~ould~~ blanket of peniston marked
wth TN
A coverlet of course ymagrie tapstrie unlyned
A waynscote joyned table longe iij yardes
di qr broad iij qr ij nailes uppon ij plaine
tressells
A joyned forme of waynscote wth turned pillers
and fotesteps longe ij yardes wantinge a naile
A joyned stole wth round turned feete

In the other chamber between the said seled chamber and the gate

A table of iij beachinge border put togither
longe iij yardes iij qr broad iij yardes di qr
uppon ij plaine tressells
Item ij shelves on over the other longe ij yardes di qr
A plaine planke forme longe iiij yardes
A pece of tymber of vj ynches square iiij yardes longe

In the laundrie

A table of deale of v yardes di qr longe uppon
ij standinge tressells of one stalke wth crossed
feete
A great yron chest for tresure one yard
di longe depe halfe a yard iij nailes broad
iiij qr wth the boult and the locks and keye
A plaine planke forme longe ij yardes qr
One ould broken forme iiij yardes longe
One washinge stoke[73] iij qr naile square
One other washinge stole uppon 4 foote plaine
A great sistern of lead iij qr depe the length
neare ij yardes wyde one yard somwhat more
A great bathinge tubb of oke full yard depe
one yard and a halfe longe
A stoninge morter grater[74]

In the chamber over the larder

One lyvery bedsted of beache wth the
cord and mate

[f.44r]

A livery cubberd of waynscote the bottome
halfe gone longe j yard di ^di^ qr bredth di Elne[75]

73 Washing-stock: a stand for beating laundry on

74 Probably a stone implement for rubbing laundry on, similar in principle to the nineteenth-century washboard

75 Ell

In the closset

A hanginge round abought the same of ould torne
grene and red saye[76] in paynes
a little square grenne cubberd cloth
the store matted wth strawinge[77] mattes

[f.45r]

Mr Dyx his chamber

Hanginges that did hange over the gathouse at
howard house in Mr Tylney's chamber
One pece of parkworke wth a fountaine in the
midest length iiij y dep iij y di
One pece of the same sute cont in length iiij y dep as befor
One other pece of the same sute cont in ij yardes iij qr depe
length as the other
One pece of ould ymagrie tapstrie wth a iij y iij qr and naile
narrowe border cont in length depth iij yardes di
One great pallet boulster marked at
the Corner wth TN
A spanishe blanket marked wth AC
A peniston blanket marked at the
corner wth TN
One canapie fully furnished of grenne saie
wth an indented valence and gilt knobbes and tassells
One walnuttre stole wth square feete
twoe waynscote stoles wth round feet
One waynscote stole wth square feete
One joyned forme of beache and fire deale
longe ij yardes wantinge a naile
Fier shovell and tonges of flanders worke
twoe paier of hasboroughe sheetes for Mr
Dyx his owne bedd

In the Clossets to his lod[g]inge

A livery bedsted wth mate and corde
A pallet bed wth the boulster marked wth PhA
A spanishe rugge white
A coverlet of course ymagrie lyned wth
canvas marked wth PhA
A pillowe of downe not marked
A close stole covered wth blacke lether
wth a tyne panne
A pewter chamberpott
A livery cubberd of waynscote and wthought
a bottome length j y di qr over halfe an ell
iij paier of canvas sheetes for Mr Dyx his men

[f.45v]

76 Say: a fine, serge-like woollen cloth, sometimes part silk
77 Strawen, made of straw

In the next chamber

A plaine ould borde of fire deale uppon ij
plaine tressells longe ij yards broad ij yard di qr

In the next chamber

1 A livery bedsted wth the mate and cordes
2 A pallet fetherbed wth the boulster marked at
the corner TN
An ould spanishe ruge
An ould coveringe of course ymagrie unlyned
A joyned stole of waynscote wth square feete
twoe plaine tressells

In the chambers aloft

A livery bedsted corded
3 A pallet fetherbed marked wth TN at the corner
the boulster therto marked wth [AC?]
4 A livery bed wth a boulster marked wth TN
thre overworne ould coverlets twoe of ould
course ymagrie the other of course verdors
a joyned stole broken wth square feete
a plaine paier of yron tongues

In another chamber a livery bedsted corded

5 A livery bed ould wthought marke and
wthought a boulster

In Mr Banaster his bedchamber

A counterpoint of tapstrie of verdors
unlyned
twoe waynscote joyned stoles wth round feet
One waynscote joyned stole wth square feete

In the utter chamber

One blanket of peniston marked wth
TN
An ould joyned waysncote stole wth square feete

[f.46r]

In the lowe rome called the auditors hall

A great ould yron baund standerd[78]
ij plaine tressells
a planke forme ould wth the feete broken the length iij yards iij qr

78 Standard: a large packing-case or chest

fower waynscote stoles wth round feete
One waynscote stole wth square feete

In the great hall

A table of fire deale uppon ij tressells longe v yardes
wantynge a naile yard broad
Another short table of fire deale longe iiij yardes broad
one yard
A fayer joyned forme wth turned pillers longe iiij y qr di
An other ould joyned forme of waynscote longe iij y and naile
An other ould joyned forme of Oke uppon thre feete longe
vj yardes & naile di
A plaine planke forme longe ij yardes di a naile di
Another playne plancke forme longe ij y iij qr

In the passage to the Ewrye

A great plaine depe chest of fire deale bound
thynlie wth yron

In the pantry

A plaine waynscote cubberd wth iij severall
ambries[79] therin
A longe waynscote benche wth ij tyles therin
longe iij yard di qr
A plaine planke bord uppon iiij plaine feete
longe j yard iij qr di naile
A plaine plancke forme longe ij yardes j naile
A plaine planke table to fould naprie uppon
joyned to the wall
A great broad binge[80] of iij romes[81]
A walnuttre stole wth square feete

In the chamber wth in that office

A livery bedsted corded wth a mate
A plaine presse of bordes put together
A thicke planke forme
A longe footpace[82] alonge the great binge ther
A hanginge shelfe

In the sellers belowe

A bathinge tub of oke iij qr deepe yard di longe
ij plaine tressells and an old dore
they be furnished wth beare stales[83]

79 Referring here to compartments or pigeonholes
80 Bin
81 Compartments
82 A platform on which to set the feet
83 Beer stalls (stands for casks), referring to the fitting-up of the cellars

[f.46v]

In the Ewrie

An ould standerd bound wth yron wth a hanginge locke
and key therto
Six good hall tableclothes of yard broad eche of them
thre yardes di longe
thre other of the same goodnes and cloth eche of them
vij yardes longe
Twoe ould table clothes overworne of the length of
iiij yardes qr a pece
twoe great livery pottes of pewter
fower great salts[84] of pewter
A little table of ij plaine bordes nailed uppon ij tressells
a short hanginge shelfe
A single quarter of oke ~~i~~iij yardes longe

In the chamber at the tarris end

A plaine joyned waynscote livery cubberd wth a bottome
longe j yard di qr broad halfe an elle
Seaven waynscote bordes to shute the windowes

In the bathinge house under this chamber

A great Sesterne of Tynne

[f.47r]

Mr Buxtons Chamber

A fetherbed and boulster
ij wollen blankets wherof one is a ruge
j coveringe unlyned of hawkinge and huntynge
A pillowe of downe in fustian
Seler and one tester of churchworke[85] fringed
wth crewell fringe red and yelowe
j carpet of parke worke
j payre of crepers[86] in the chymney fire shovell
j paier of tonges
j chamberpott
bedsted of beache wth cord and mattresse
j cubberd of oke
j turned chaire of wode
quishion of tapstrie
table waynscote wth a frame uppon turned pillers

In the yner chamber

j lyvery bed wth boulster
j wollen blanket
j ould pece of hanginge servinge for a coveringe
j livery bedsted of beache wth cord and mate

84 Salt cellars
85 Probably referring to a particularly painstaking sort of embroidery
86 Creepers: small fire-dogs

vj joyned stoles
j latten candlsticke
ij tables uppon tressells

In the corner chamber wher Mr Grene last lay

j posted bedsted of oke wth lathes cord and mate
a square table on a frame
j cubberd of waynscote wth a bottome
j forme joyned of beache
ij stoles joyned

In the ynner chamber

j bedsted of okinge bordes
j plaine table and ij tressells the table longe
j standinge cubberd wth ij leaves and ij bottoms

In the closet of the said chamber wher M^r grene laie

[nothing listed]

[f.47v]

In my lo: henry his chamber over the gate or removed by his lo

iiij peces of hanginges ymagrie unlyned — v peces in ye whole
j pece of hanginge parkworke unlyned
A pallet bed wth boulster
j rugge
j hanginge of Jonas[87] a pece servinge for a counterpoint
j paire of ould fustian blankets
j tester and seler of blacke wrought velvet
paned wth murrey[88] velvet laid on wth stafford
knots[89] and whit lyons
v ould curtens of whit and murrey silke
j close stole wth a pane of tynne j chamber pott
j paier of yron crepers for the chymney
j fier shovell one paier of tonges j turkey carpet
j waynscote cubberd
joyned stoles
j livery bedsted joyned wth cord and mattresse

In the ynner chamber

j livery bed wth boulster
ij blankets
j coveringe of tapstrie lyned
j candlsticke
j livery bedsted wth mat and cord

87 Jonah
88 Mulberry-coloured
89 A decorative device in the form of a loose knot, used as the badge of the Stafford family

j ould cubberd
stolles
j paire of sheets fyne
j paier of canvas sheets

[f.48r]

In Jonne dowdells laundry

j longe talle stoke longe iiij yardes broad j yard
j other iij yardes and qr both joyned togither
iij standinge tressells and one wth iiij feet uppon
wch the said table stands
j other planke table iiij yardes and qr longe and di yard di qr
broad
j other planke table of oke longe iij yard di di qr
bredth di yard di qr
iiij joyned stoles
A plaine bord uppon iiij feet longe j yard di qr
broad ij foote di

In the chamber over the laundresse chamber

An ould joyned waynscote presse wth iij bottomes and ij dores
longe on yard iij qr and naile highe one yard di and a naille
A deale table uppon ij playne tressells longe
ij yardes and a naile broad one yard di qr
A joyned forme of waynscote and beache wth
turned feete longe ij yardes
twoe joyned waynscote stoles wth round feet
In the seled closet within that chamber a waynscote
cubberd joyned to the selinge
A joyned forme of waynscote and beache longe ij yardes

In the chamber next the entry towards the stable

A joyned stole of waynscote

In the chamber called knaves hall

An ould plain longe joyned forme of oke
A square harthe of yron for a charcole fier
A joyned table of oken bord

In the vance roffe[90] called my lo: Thomas his wardrope

A joyned table of waynscote uppon a beachinge frame
wth turned postes longe iij yardes and a naile
bredth j yard and an ynche
ij ould plaine tressells

90 Vance-roof: an East Anglian term for a garret

[f.48v blank]
[f.49r]

In the wardrope of robes

<u>*Robes*</u> *The old Earl of Arundels*	A kirtell for the order of the garter of Crysen vellet lyned wth whit sarsnet wch was the ould erle of Arundells[91] The Robe of purple velvet to the same lyned as the other wth the laces buttons and tassells to the same of purple silke and gould wth the hood of crymsin velvet to the same	the ould Erle of Arundell his Robes for the order of the garter
	A kirtell of crimsin vellet lyned wth ~~wth~~ whit sarsnet A robe of purple velvet wth the huyns[92] laces and tassells as of the other the hoode of crymsin velvet to the same	the late duke of Norff his robes of the garter
the furr wth the Skyner Simond Tuke	A kyrtell of crymsin velvet wth white taffatie ~~lyned~~ unlyned A robe to the same of crimsin velvet likwise lyned the hood and cape to the same	the ould ^Erle^ of Arundells robe of estate
The furr to the same wth the skiner	A kirtell of crimsin vellvet lyned wth white taffatie A robe to the same of crymsin vellet likwise lyned the hoode and cape to the same	the dukes robes of estate
	A kirtell of scarlet edged wth myniver the robe of scarlet to the same faced and bordered wth myniver A hoode to the same of scarlet	the parliament robes of the late Erle of Arundell
	A kirtell of scarlet unlyned The robe of scarlet to the same unlyned the hoode of scarlet to the same	the dukes parliament robes
	A cassoke wth sleves of wrought velvet bound abought wth a partchmentlace[93] of gould lyned wth blake taffitae Another cassoke wth sleves of blacke taffatie cut uppon blacke taffatie laid one and bound abought wth a tufted lace of blake silke and silver and peare buttons of blacke silke and silver A cape of blacke velvet lyned thorowought wth tufted taffatie A paire of bothose[94] of watchet carsey[95] the upper parte of watchet vellet cut and laced and fringed wth watchet silke	

[f.49v]

Another paier of murrey cloth wth the tope or
upper parte of crimsin velvet cut and laced and

91 Henry Fitzalan, twelfth Earl of Arundel, Philip Howard's maternal grandfather
92 Reading uncertain. Possibly a variant of hingle and referring to fastenings or other attachments
93 Parchment lace: a kind of lace in which thread was wound over a core made of parchment
94 Boot-hose
95 Kersey: a coarse wool cloth

fringed wth crimsin silke
Another paier of lynen bothose wth the
toppes of grene vellet cut uppon grene
taffatie and laid one wth silver lace and
fringed wth grene silke and silver
Another payer of lynen bothose wth the toppes of murrey
sattin ymbrodered wth twist of silver and gould and
fringed wth a fringe of murrey silke gould and silver
^the ought syd of^ An ould payer of canyons[96] of purple satten cut
A payer of lynen bothose fringed wth whit silke
and gould
A payer of lynen bothose fringed wth whit silke
and silver
A swet bage[97] of whit taffatie imbrodered wth an hope[98] roses
lyned wth redd sarsnet and tassells wth gould and silke
Another of purple taffatie richlie imbrodered wth gould
silver and grenne silke wth iiij smale tassells of gould
Another of orengtawney taffatie wth a parcement lace of
silver and blake silke
twoe other of cornacion[99] taffatie laced abought wth a
lace of gould and grenne silke
ij little bagges of changeable silke[100] wth one rose
imbrodered on either of them
Another little bagge of cornation changeable silke
A little swet bage of whit sarsnet wth a Cypher of
gould embrodered on either syd therof [TAM?] wth iiij tassells
Another very little bage blake silke striped w^th^
white
Twoe paire of blake silke stockinges ould
one ould paire of silke stockinges
An ould paier of ripped britches of white taffatie
A privie cote of plate[101] lyned and coverd w^th^
fustian wth ij skirtes for the forpart therof
A paire of lyned sleves garded wth male
A paire of lynen hose garded wth male
A trussle[102] of fustian
A sleves wayskote of lynen

[f.50r]

A lyninge of a paier of britches of linen
A skull of plates[103]
A little pillowe wth the beare tydon[104] to laie
uppon the stomacke
A vellet cape w^th^ought a band
iij ould bever hattes
A square mourninge cape

96 Cannions: sets of decorative rolls or fillets to go round the ends of the legs of breeches
97 Sweet-bag: a bag with a fragrant filling, used as a deodorant
98 Reading uncertain. Perhaps hoop or hop
90 Carnation: pink
100 Shot silk
101 A coat of armour designed to wear under ordinary clothes
102 Bundle
103 Helmet
104 With the cover tied on

A night cape of velvet
A night cape of knit silke
A girdle and hangers[105] of crimsin velvet
laid one wth lace of gould
A paier of hangers of watchet velvet
laid one wth silver and watchet
lace
ij paier of hangers of blake vellvet
imbrodered wth blake silke
A rapier and dagger and a skabberd of
velvet therto the rapier and dagger gilt
A rapier and dagger sangwine[106] wth a vellet
skabberd
A turky dagger wth a wodden skabberd
A skabberd of watchet velvet for
an arminge sworde[107]
iij visardes[108] ij therof white one blacke
The banner of St George for the feild
al of damaske fringed wth gren silke and silver
Another of the same of taffatie fringed
wth grenne silke and whit
One other banner of the armes of England
azure and crymsyn taffatie
A Gwydon[109] of crymsin taffatie wth a lyon
of gould and the crose of St george
fringed all wth whit and gren silke
Another Guidon of the same shewe
somwhat lesse all of blewe and crymsin
taffatie fringed wth red and blewe silke
A banner of the armes of England uppon
crymsin and gould taffatie
A banner of crymsin taffatie wth a
whit lyon

[f.50v]

One caparison of bucheram laid one w[th]
whit and watchet fethers wth silver spangells
A rydinge cloke of skye coller[110] cloth laced
wth russet lace wth a hoode to the same
lyned wth watchet bayes[111]
A paier of boses[112] agreeng to the same
A little waynscote boxe wth 19 sortes
of fethers of divers collers proper for
capes
A hatt case
a Javalin
iij ould shets to wrape my lo: hose in

105 Attachments for hanging a sword from
106 Coloured red or purple
107 Broadsword
108 Masks or visors
109 Pennant
110 Sky-colour
111 Baize: woollen fabric with a long nap
112 Presumably bosses

ij other paier of ould sheets to wrape
the forsaid robes another stuffe
ij table presses covered wth yelowe bucheram
j square table or brushinge bord of okinge
bordes put togither uppon a plaine frame
covered wth red bucherame
ij large ^standeret[113] [as?]^ chestes wth lockes and keyes the one
bound wth yron
ij stolles of waynscote wth round feet
ij other stoles of walnuttre
j head of a walnuttre stole
j joyned forme wth turned feet
j buffet forme[114] of waynscote
A liverie bed corded and matted
A fouldinge table of waynscote uppon a
fouldinge frame

In the ij tower chambers

A liverie cubberd wth a bottome one y di longe
j table of oken bordes uppon ij plaine tressells
iij waynscote stoles wth round feet
j joyned fotstep 2 yardes longe under
the windowe
j paier of bellowes

In the closett ther

one waynskote stole broken

[f.51r]

In the brushinge chamber or little wardrope

j table of fire deale uppon ij tressells longe
ij yardes and one yarde broade
ij joyned waynscote stoles
j fotecloth[115] saddell ould of blacke velvet
laid one wth gould twist wth the ould
harnisse to the same
ij lowe presses of oken borde large
one rare coffer of glase di yard longe
wth the case covered of russet blacke vellet
xvij yardes of azure clothe for liveries ynche measure in
j paier of canvas sheets unwhited 3 remnantes
j cradell of crimsin velvet covered
j cover of a booke
j little curten of grenne saie abought di yard
ij little boxes of little value
j round picture of glasse of o^r^ savior Jesus
tryumphinge over death the deavell and hell
wch is in the custodie keper to be redelivered
at eny tyme

[f.51v]

113 Standard: large chest or packing-case
114 Footstool or other low stool
115 Foot-cloth: an ornamental cloth for a horse being ridden, hanging low on each side and adding to the stateliness of equipage

In the armorie

In the Armory

xij calivers[116] wthought eyther flaske or tytcheboxe[117]
iiij cases of letther for dagges[118] wherof ij be complet
wth iiij dagges the stocks ynlayed wth barr flaunders
worke one other case wth blake stokes wth round knobbes
at the end and the forth one dage wth a plaine stocke
One presse of waynskote disjoyned and lyinge all
in peces apart
ij armors of proffe[119] blake and unskowred
wth all the furniture
j ^fore^ plate fore a forfrait[120] for a horse armed
j forniture[121] for a horse of blacke velvet fringed
wth silver tassells whit silke and silver
the number of the tassells ar 21
j forniture for a horse as before of crimsin velvet
laid one wth gould twist and edged wth parchment
lace crymsin silke and gould the tassells ar in
nomber 33 ~~wth tassells~~ of crimsin silke and calls[122]
of gould
j other furniture for a horse of crimsin velvet
plaine fringed wth crimsin silke tassells 24
besyd 4 of the endes of the trappers[123]
ij paier of gilt stirrops
j other furniture for a horse wth hedstalls
pattrell[124] and cruper as ar befor of crymsin
velvet laid one wth studdes silvered
j hedstall and reynes only of blacke velvet
imbrodered wth silver wth 4 tassells of blacke
silke wth calls of silver
ij hedstalls and reynes only of crimsin velvet
wth 2 tassells of red silke and calls of gould
ij furniture for a horse as before wth the
hedstalls the pattrell and crupers but one
pattrell wanteth all is of blacke taffatie
paynted wth silver ij docks[125] to the same
wth one bitt for a great horse whit
wth gilt bosses
j furniture for a horse of watchet velvet
painted   wth studes of copper
j hedstall and reynes of blacke lether wth a
bitt wth rest belonginge to the sadle of
my lo:

[f.52r]

116 Light muskets
117 Touch-box: a box for 'touch-powder' for priming fire arms
118 Dag: heavy pistol or other hand-gun
119 Proof armour: proven impenetrable
120 Perhaps fore-fret. Presumably a piece of horse armour or ornament
121 Furniture: harness and other trappings
122 Cowls or cauls, i.e. caps
123 Decorative or protective coverings for a horse
124 Peytral: piece of horse armour for the breast
125 Covers for docked horse tails

One paier of stirrops of copper wth the stirrops
therto of spanishe lether garded wth vellvet
blacke
ij sadles covered wth blacke taffatie paynted
wth iiij stirrops wantynge the stells[126] to the sadells
ij other sadles covered wth blake vellet lace one wth silver
twist fringed wth One sadle covered wth watchet taffatie
silver wantinge the steels
wth girthes wantinge the stells
ij dockes for a horse of crimsin velvet the
j embrodered wth cloth of gould and pearle
and the other plaine
j worke for a fountaine of allabaster gilt

Maskinge garments ould

Masking Garments

vj Jurkins and hose of blacke cotton drawne
ought wth crymsin and yelowe tinsell[127] worne
vj other Jurkins and hose of red cotton drawne
ought wth yelowe satten of bridges
vj maskinge capes wherof v ar of yelowe and
crymsin cloth of tynsell and one of yelowe and
gren cloth of tynsell wth tassells of red
silke and calls of gould to all except the
said grenne cape
vij ould worne and wast capes of cotton for
maskers
xj visers wth ther stringes to bynd them one
x ould worne curtens of red and gren saye
enterparted[128]
j chest wth gard of yrons
xv scutchens of glasse wth armes of Norff
for glasse windowes wherof some ar
broken
iiij ould rotten cushions
j lyninge of a coveringe of canvas
One picture of M^res Marie Radcliffe[129]
as John Sencler[130] saythe
one sute of yelowe cotton drawne ought
w^th ~~yelowe~~ red satten of bridges

[f.52v]

In the rome next the privie garden comonlie called the sommer parler

iij fild tents wth cordes postes and all other
furniture belonginge to the same
j joyned stole

126 Steels

127 Tinsel: cloth such as satin or silk interwoven or brocaded with gold or silver thread, or thinly coated with gold or silver

128 i.e., some red, some green

129 Mary Fitzalan, Countess of Arundel (d.1557), Philip Howard's step-grandmother. She was formerly married to Robert Radcliffe, Earl of Sussex

130 John Sinclair, keeper of Howard House

ij old dores to serve wth hingells one yron
boult and one locke
j oken table wth tressells fastned into it

In the styllinge rome

vj stilles wth the rest belonginge

[f.53r]

Wardrobe Certen stuffe lent and delivered forth of the wardrope by Richard Bedoe for wch he sheweth certaine bills of the particulers and to whome it was delivered and wher it is as here ensueth and so lent by my lo: commaundment

An Inventorie of all suche houshould stuffe as was delivered by Richard bedo into Ivibridge house[131] and receaved by Edward Kent to the use of his lady M^res the lady Margaret Sacville[132]

Imprimis v peces of hanginges of Salomon
Item on turkey carpett
Item a grenne carpet for a cubberd
Item j walnuttre chaire
Item j table and frame of fire bordes
Item j court cubberd[133] and xij joyned stoles of waynskote
Item one joyned forme
Item vj square quishions of grenne cloth
Item j windowe cloth of parkworke
Item j chaire of crimsin cloth of gould
Item one longe quishion of like stuffe wth iiij gould tassells
Item one square quishion wth the like stuffe
Item iiij peces of hanginges for the passage
between the great chamber and my la:
bedchamber wherof one is of the storie of
Saule parcell of those in my la: bedchamber
Item one ould turky carpet in the windowe
Item ij longe quishions of red wrought velvet
[illeg]ned wth cloth of gould and backed wth red and
yelowe carell[134]
Item v peces of hanginges in my la chamber of the
storie of Saule
Item one bed of downe covered wth fustian the boulster
of tyke[135] and fethers
Item j paier of fustians of iiij bredthes a pece
Item ij spanishe rugges blankets
Item ij pillowes of downe
Item more iij turkey carpets

131 House at Ivy Bridge, in the Strand
132 Philip Howard's half-sister
133 Shelved cupboard or dresser, originally without doors, for displaying plate or earthenware, etc
134 Carrel, a kind of fabric
135 Tick: case of stout linen or cotton material

Item j little square table wth a frame
Item j close stole wth a tyne pane
Item j chamberpot
Item j fire shovle all yron
Item j paire of tonges tyned
Item j paire of bellowes
Item j mattresse of flockes
Item ij peces of hanginges of parkworke and one of flowers

[f.53v]

Item j testure wth the head of the bed of ^red^ cloth of bodkin[136]
paned wth blake silke imbrodered wth red velvet
Item iij fetherbeds wth boulsters wherof ij newe
Item one smale ruge
Item ij wollen blankets
Item iij coveringes of tapstrie wherof ij is newe
Item j pillowe of downe
Item ij liverie bedsteds wth cordes
Item j square quishion of turkey worke wth a whit lion in it
Item j fustian blanket of thre bredthes for M[r]
Mynners bedd
Item iiij livery bedes of fethers wth boulsters
Item iiij blankets
Item iiij coveringes of tapstrie wherof one is lyned
Item ij paire of lockram[137] sheetes
Item iiij paire of canvas sheetes
Item j yrisshe rugge check~~laced~~red
Edward Kent
Receaved of Richard bedoe
delivered to Massiline newname to the use
of my lo: willm howard 22 March 1586
and sent into the north these parce[l]s folowinge

Imprimis vj livery beddes
Item vj blankets to them
Item vj coveringes to them

Receaved of Richard bedoe the 29 of aprill 1587
for the use of my lo: the parcells folowinge

Item v fetherbeds w[th] boulsters
v coveringes
Item vij blankets wherof one ruge
Item vij paire of sheetes wherof ij paire of fine sheetes
Item vj peces of hanginges of broad leaves
Item j fier shovell and a paire of tonges
Item iij bedsteds wth the cordes and mattes
Receaved by me Nicholas Williams

[f.54r]

136 Baudekin: a rich silk material
137 A kind of linen fabric

Received of Richard Bedoe the 24 of maye 1585
for the use of my lo: these parcells followinge

Item ij fetherbeds wth boulsters
Item j rugge
Item ij blankets
Item ij coveringes
Item j matterisse
Item j downe pillowe
and a pillowbeare
Item one paire of ould fine sheetes
Item j ould paire of canvas sheetes
John Ivrie

doctor Martin

I receaved of Richard bedoe 1584 by the comandmt
of my good lo the erle of Arundell these parcells folowinge

twoe fetherbeds ij boulsters ij blankets
ij coveringes lynd j newe a tester paned
wth blewe and red velvet after the ould
fashion wth flowers and crownes of gould
ij strawe mattes

These forsaid iij bills of stuffe delivered to
the la: Margaret sacville my lo: willm
and to Doctor Martyn ar in Richard bedo
his kepinge for his dischardge to be shewed
at all tymes[138]

138 These delivery notes and receipts for wardrobe items are copies in the same hand as the inventory proper, which otherwise ends with the stilling room

References

ABBREVIATIONS

ACA	Arundel Castle Archives
B	*The Builder*
Barber and Thomas	Bruno Barber and Christopher Thomas, *The London Charterhouse, Museum of London Archaeology Service Monograph 10*, 2002
Bearcroft	Philip Bearcroft, *An Historical Account of Thomas Sutton, Esq, and of His Foundation in Charterhouse*, 1737
Benson	Benson Papers, Lambeth Palace Library
BL	British Library
BN	*Building News*
Bodl.	Bodleian Library, Oxford
Bushby	Lady Frances Bushby, *Three Men of the Tudor Time*, 1911
Champneys	Basil Champneys, 'Charterhouse. I. The Monastery', *Architectural Review*, vol.2, Jan–June 1902
CL	*Country Life*
CM	Charterhouse Muniments (archives at Sutton's Hospital in Charterhouse)
Colvin 1982	H. M. Colvin (ed.), *The History of the King's Works: Volume IV 1485–1660 (Part II)*, 1982
Colvin 1996	H. M. Colvin, *Biographical Dictionary of British Architects 1600–1840*, 3rd edn, 1996
CSPD	*Calendar of State Papers, Domestic*
CUL	Cambridge University Library
Davies	Gerald S. Davies, *Charterhouse in London: Monastery, Mansion, Hospital, School*, 1921
DSR	District Surveyors' Returns at London Metropolitan Archives
Edwards	Francis Edwards, *The Marvellous Chance: Thomas Howard Fourth Duke of Norfolk, and the Ridolphi Plot, 1570–1572*, 1968
EH	English Heritage
GEC	G.E.C. (ed.), *The Complete Peerage*, 1910–59
GL	Guildhall Library
Haig Brown	William Haig Brown, *Charterhouse Past and Present*, 1879
Hale 1839	W. H. (William Hale), 'Notes to accompany the plans of the Charterhouse', *The Carthusian, a miscellany in prose and verse*, vol.2, 1839
Hale 1854	William Hale, *Some Account of the Early History and Foundation of the Hospital of King James, founded in Charterhouse*, 1854
Hale 1869	William Hale, 'The Carthusian Monastery of London', *Transactions of the London and Middlesex Archaeological Society*, vol.3, 1869, pp.309–31
Hendriks	Lawrence Hendriks, *The London Charterhouse, its Monks and its Martyrs*, 1889
Highmore	Anthony Highmore, *Pietas Londinensis: The History, Design, and Present State of the Public Charities in and near London*, 1810
HMC	Historical Manuscripts Commission
Hope 1902	William St John Hope, 'The London Charterhouse and its Old Water Supply', *Archaeologia*, vol.58, 1902, pp.293–312
Hope 1925	William St John Hope, *The History of the London Charterhouse from its Foundation until the Suppression of the Monastery*, 1925
IBC	London Borough of Islington, Building Control files
Knowles	David Knowles, *The Religious Orders in England. III: The Tudor Age*, 1959
Knowles and Grimes	David Knowles and W. F. Grimes, *Charterhouse: The Medieval Foundation in the Light of Recent Discoveries*, 1954
KSRL	Kenneth Spencer Research Library, University of Kansas
Lasocki	David Lasocki with Roger Prior, *The Bassanos: Venetian Musicians and Instrument Makers in England, 1531–1665*, 1995
L & P	*Letters & Papers, Foreign and Domestic, Henry VIII*

LM — Loseley MSS, Surrey History Centre

LMA — London Metropolitan Archives

Luxford — Julian M. Luxford (ed.), *Studies in Carthusian Monasticism in the Late Middle Ages* (Medieval Church Studies, vol. 14), Turnhout, Belgium, 2008

MoL — Museum of London

MoLAS — Museum of London Archaeology Service

Morris — Cecil E. Morris, 'The Medical College in the Twentieth Century', in Victor Cornelius Medvei and John L. Thornton (eds), *The Royal Hospital of Saint Bartholomew 1123–1973*, 1974

MTC — Merchant Taylors' Company Court minute books, Guildhall Library

Murdin — William Murdin, *A Collection of State Papers Relating to Affairs in the Reign of Queen Elizabeth from the Year 1571 to 1596*, 1759

NMRC — National Monuments Record Centre

ODNB — *Oxford Dictionary of National Biography*

Patrick — George Patrick, 'The History and Architecture of the Charterhouse', *Journal of the British Archaeological Association*, 2nd series, vol.3, 1897, pp.281–90

Pollen and MacMahon — J. H. Pollen and W. MacMahon, Catholic Record Society, *English Martyrs*, vol.2, *The Venerable Philip Howard, Earl of Arundel 1557–1595*, 1919

Quick — Anthony Quick, *Charterhouse: A History of the School*, 1990

Radclyffe — C. W. Radclyffe, *Memorials of Charterhouse: A Series of Original Views Taken and Drawn on Stone…*, 1844

RCHME — Royal Commission on the Historical Monuments of England

RCHME 1915 — NMRC, record cards relating to the Charterhouse, compiled by A. W. Clapham, 1915

RCHME 1925 — Royal Commission on Historical Monuments (England), *An Inventory of the Historical Monuments in London. Vol. II, West London*, 1925

RO — Record Office

Roper — [William John Duff Roper], *Chronicles of Charter-house, by a Carthusian*, 1847 (also attributed to W. J. D. Ryder)

Salisbury — HMC, *Calendar of Manuscripts of the Marquis Of Salisbury at Hatfield House*

S&P — Seely and Paget Papers, Royal Institute of British Architects

SBH — Archives of St Bartholomew's Hospital

Sewell — Anon., *Charter-house, its Foundation and History: With a Brief Memoir of the Founder, Thomas Sutton, Esq*, pub. M. Sewell, 1849

Smythe — Robert Smythe, *Historical Account of Charter-House; Compiled from the Works of Herne and Bearcroft, Harleian and Cottonian mss.: and from other Authentic Sources*, 1808

SoL — *Survey of London*

SPAB — Society for the Protection of Ancient Buildings

Streitberger 1 — W. R. Streitberger, 'Records of Royal Banqueting Houses and Henry VIII's Timber Lodging, 1543–59', *Journal of the Society of Archivists*, vol.15, no.2, 1994

Streitberger 2 — W. R. Streitberger, *Court Revels, 1485–1559*, 1994

Taylor — William F. Taylor, *The Charterhouse of London: Monastery, Palace, and Thomas Sutton's Foundation*, 1912

Thompson — E. Margaret Thompson, *The Carthusian Order in England*, 1930

TNA — The National Archives

VCH — *The Victoria History of the Counties of England*

Wardle — George Wardle, 'The Ancient Buildings of the Charterhouse', *Archaeological Journal*, vol.43, 1886, pp.231–42

Williams — Neville Williams, *A Tudor Tragedy: Thomas Howard, Fourth Duke of Norfolk*, 1964

Wilmot and Streatfeild — E. P. Eardley Wilmot and E. C. Streatfeild, *Charterhouse Old and New*, 1895

Introduction

pp.3–15

1. Hale 1839, p.496
2. William Makepeace Thackeray, *The Newcomes*, ch. LXXV
3. Davies, p.314
4. See Maurice Howard, *The Building of Elizabethan and Jacobean England*, 2007, p.18
5. Smythe, p.284
6. Hale 1839, p.504
7. *Ibid.*, pp.504,510
8. Radclyffe, largely repeated in Sewell: Roper, pp.143–4,163,165
9. Hale 1869, p.329
10. Wardle, p.236
11. Hendriks, plan between pp.242 and 243
12. Hope 1902, pp.293–4
13. Patrick
14. Champneys
15. Taylor, pp.39,179
16. Hope 1925, pp.ix–xi: The chronicle, or Register, as Hope calls it, is now catalogued as TNA, LR2/61
17. Davies: Taylor, p.vi
18. Knowles and Grimes, p.x
19. Hope, 1902
20. Summary based on account in Knowles and Grimes, the printed form of an address given by Lord Mottistone on 17 April 1957, *The Story of the Restoration of Old Charterhouse…*, and Lord Mottistone and Paul Paget, 'Sequence of Events Leading to the Discovery of the Tomb and Coffin of Sir Walter de Manny…', TS, 20 June 1950, in S&P, box 36
21. Knowles and Grimes, pp.45–6; folding plan at end
22. CM, G/2/19, p.22: MoL, W. F. Grimes archive
23. Taylor, p.35 and plan facing
24. S&P, correspondence in box 36: CM, ECM, G, p.219
25. Arthur Oswald, 'The London Charterhouse Restored', *CL*, 15 Oct 1959: E. E. Harrison, *The History of Charterhouse and its Buildings*, reprinted from *Transactions of the Ancient Monuments Society*, 35, 1991, with revisions. Harrison's account was read to the AMS in the Great Chamber in 1990
26. For a general discussion of recent scholarship on the English Carthusians, see Luxford, pp.5–9. Barber and Thomas; see also M. Barratt and C. Thomas, 'The London Charterhouse', *London Archaeologist*, vol.6, 1991, pp.283–91
27. Nikolaus Pevsner, *London except the Cities of London and Westminster*, 1952, p.121
28. Oswald, p.418: Harrison, p.1
29. Ian Nairn, *Nairn's London*, 1988 edn, p.24
30. Anthony Powell, *Journals 1982–1986*, 1995, p.142
31. The story is not significantly altered in the recent short account by John Clark, 'The London Charterhouse: An Urban Charterhouse and its Dissolution', in *Analecta Carthusiana* 267, Universität Salzburg, 2008
32. For a recent history focusing on the institution itself, see Stephen Porter, *The London Charterhouse*, 2009

CHAPTER I (pp.16–38)

The London Charterhouse

1. Cited in Knowles, p.226
2. See transcripts in Hope 1925, Appendices I and II
3. Barber and Thomas, p.94
4. e.g. Patrick, p.285, 'the extreme harshness of their rigid rule'
5. Thompson, p.185
6. Knowles and Grimes, p.31: *VCH*, *Middlesex*, vol.1, 1969, p.163
7. Thompson, pp.177,185: TNA, SC12/25/55
8. Davies, p.61
9. Nikolaus Pevsner, *Yorkshire: The North Riding*, 1966, p.259
10. Glyn Coppack, *Mount Grace Priory, North Yorkshire*, 1991, p.16
11. Transcript in Davies, pp.323–5: see also Thompson, p.327
12. *ODNB*: Knowles, p.228
13. Davies, p.45. Thompson, pp.327–8: a similar point is made by James Hogg in 'Life in an English Charterhouse in the Fifteenth Century: Discipline and Daily Affairs', in Luxford, pp.36–8
14. See Wines, 'The London Charterhouse in the Later Middle Ages', pp.176,201. Wines concedes that the number of servants 'seems slightly excessive'
15. This figure is from Chauncy, cited in Knowles, p.226
16. Hope 1925, pp.6,8,24: Thompson, p.169: *Cal. Papal Registers, Petitions to the Pope, Volume I, 1342–1419*, p.234: TNA, LR2/61, f.21v
17. John Stow, *The Survey of London*, 1633 edn, p.478a. Duncan Hawkins, 'The Black Death and the New London Cemeteries of 1348', *Antiquity*, vol.64, 1990, pp.637–42: Philip Ziegler, *The Black Death*, 1969, pp.162–4: Richard Britnell, 'The Black Death in English Towns', *Urban History*, vol.21, 1994, pp.198–9
18. Smythe, p.291: Barber and Thomas, p.15
19. *VCH*, *Middlesex*, vol.1, p.160
20. Barber and Thomas, pp.28,70
21. *Cal. Patent Rolls, 1370–74*, p.44: LMA, ACC/1876/D1/1: Hope 1925, pp.24–5
22. Andrew Wines, 'The Founders of the London Charterhouse', in Luxford, pp.61–71
23. Barber and Thomas, pp.7,55
24. BL, Cotton MSS, Claudius E.vi, ff.15r–v,136v–7, 230–v, 233v–4: *L & P*, vol.19, pt 1, pp.278–9: *Cal. Patent Rolls 1547–8*, p.201. See *SoL*, vol.XLVI, ch. X
25. For the exact location, see Colin Bowlt, 'The Great Conduit at the London Charterhouse', *London Archaeologist*, vol.11, 2003, pp.121–3
26. Barber and Thomas, p.36
27. Knowles and Grimes, p.83
28. Hope 1925, pp.129–33
29. *Cal. Papal Registers, 1471–1484*, p.260
30. TNA, SC12/25/55, mm.4–19: Thompson, pp.193–6
31. TNA, SC12/25/55, m.55
32. BL, Cotton MSS, Cleopatra E.iv, f.42: Wines, 'The London Charterhouse in the Later Middle Ages', pp.207–12. He discredits Chauncy's figure of 18 lay brothers, but acknowledges that the priory saw a boom in members—monks, lay brothers, servants, and others—on the eve of the suppression

33. Hope 1925, pp.58,80: For the cell verses, see Michael G. Sargent and Marlene Villalobos Hennessy, 'The Latin Verses over the Cell Doors of London Charterhouse', in Luxford, pp.179–97
34. Thompson, p.180: Barber and Thomas, pp.37,71: Taylor, p.38: Wines, 'The London Charterhouse in the Later Middle Ages', p.201
35. TNA, SC6/HENVIII/2112; SC2/191/60, cited in *VCH*, *Middlesex*, vol.11, 1998, p.62: Champneys, p.181
36. Knowles and Grimes, Figs 6,7
37. *Ibid*., p.83
38. Barber and Thomas, pp.45–9
39. Wardle, p.239: Hope 1925, p.187: Thompson, p.324
40. TNA, SC12/25/55
41. Knowles and Grimes, p.67, Plate VIIID, folding plan at end
42. *Ibid*., p.25
43. Hope 1925, pp.66–7
44. Barber and Thomas, pp.20–4,58–9
45. *Ibid*., pp.19–20,22,36
46. *Ibid*., p.58, The archetypal Carthusian cell-plan, from Clermont, is illustrated by Viollet-le-Duc in his *Dictionnaire raisonné de l'architecture française du XI*[e] *au XVI*[e] *siècle*
47. Barber and Thomas, p.58
48. Davies, pp.35–7
49. Thompson, p.398: Coppack, pp.16–18
50. Hendriks, p.24; details repeated in Champneys, p.175
51. Barber and Thomas, p.58
52. Hope 1925, p.183
53. Memorials described and identified in H. F. Owen Evans, 'Charterhouse, London', *Transactions of the Monumental Brass Society*, vol.9, part 9, Nov 1962, pp.465–75
54. RCHME, Report on Hinton Charterhouse, 1995, p.4: Coppack, p.9
55. Hope 1925, p.98
56. *ODNB*: tomb illustrated in William Dugdale, *The History of St. Paul's Cathedral in London*, 1658: transcript of will in Davies, pp.318–19
57. Davies, p.19: EH, Historians' file, J. H. Harvey to G. H. Chettle, 14 Jan 1944
58. Hope 1925, pp.185–6
59. Knowles and Grimes, pp.62–3, Plate VIIA: Stephen Porter, 'The Martyrs' Memorial', *The Charterhouse Magazine*, 13, 2003
60. Davies, p.81
61. TNA, SC12/25/55, m.55
62. Hope 1925, pp.45,156,159: Davies, who acknowledges Hope's help, gives the same date in his index
63. TNA, LR2/61, f.13: SBH, HA2/1, f.105
64. Hope 1925, pp.51–2,72
65. Knowles and Grimes, pp.32,65: Barber and Thomas, p.33
66. BL, Cotton MSS, Cleopatra E.iv, f.44
67. Thompson, p.311
68. *ODNB*: Hendriks, pp.64–5: TNA, E326/2163: Hope 1925, pp.94,104
69. TNA, SC12/36/26
70. Hope 1925, p.99
71. Thompson, p.180: Taylor, pp.173–4: TNA, SC12/26/60
72. TNA, SC12/36/26
73. Hope 1925, pp.174,183,187
74. TNA, SC12/25/55, m.55: Thompson, p.177
75. TNA, E164/45
76. Barber and Thomas, pp.41–2
77. Hope 1925, pp.45,52,159
78. TNA, LR2/61, f.13: Hope 1925, pp.57,183: Hendriks, folding plan: Knowles and Grimes, p.65: Barber and Thomas, p.33
79. Hope 1925, pp.163,169, plan at end
80. *Ibid*., p.59
81. TNA, E326/2163
82. Chetham's Library, Manchester, Agecroft Collection, F3, box 1, bundle 1, no.300
83. TNA, SC12/25/55; SC6/HENVIII/2112
84. Hale 1839, p.501
85. *L & P*, vol.20, pt 1, p.213
86. Patrick, map; based on one drawn by Carpenter in 1886 (Egypt is by mistake labelled 'Crypt')
87. Hope 1925, pp.45–6,149: St Bartholomew's Medical School & Charterhouse Square, Geophysical Survey, 1997, p.2: MoLAS, *Charterhouse Square: An Archaeological Evaluation*, 1998, p.16
88. TNA, SC12/25/55, m.55
89. LMA, ACC/1876/D1/6
90. J. C. Jeaffreson (ed.), *Middlesex County Records*, vol.1, 1972, pp.149–50
91. TNA, C54/673/51
92. TNA, E164/45: LMA, ACC/1876/AR/1/5/1
93. Barber and Thomas, pp.36–7
94. CM, G/2/19, p.297; correspondence in B/1/7
95. Evans, pp.471–2
96. CM, B/1/7, Letter from Rouse to Lord Mottistone, 25 Nov 1954
97. *L & P*, vol.13, pt 2, 903
98. TNA, E117/12/22
99. Hope 1925, pp.165–92: Davies, pp.106–12,326–35: Hendriks, pp.371–8
100. Knowles and Grimes, pp.74–82
101. Davies, p.112
102. Hope 1925, pp.181,191: Hendriks, p.375: Davies, pp.108–9,333: *OED*
103. Hope 1925, pp.180,178n: *L & P*, vol.21, pt 1, p.775
104. *ODNB*
105. GL, MS 01231: Maurice Chauncy, *Historia aliquot martyrum Anglorum maxime octodecim Cartusianorum*, 1888: Maurice Chauncy, *The History of the Sufferings of Eighteen Carthusians in England*, Burns and Oates Ltd, 1890: *Analecta Bollandiana*, vols 6, pp.36ff (Hague); 14, pp.248–9,268–83 (Vienna); 22, pp.51–78 (Vatican): Maurice Chauncy, *The Passion and Martyrdom of the English Holy Carthusian Fathers. The Short Narration*, ed. by G. W. S. Curtis, SPCK, 1935. See also Thompson, pp.343–52; Knowles, p.226; and *ODNB*, *sub* Chauncy
106. *Short Narration*, 1935, pp.127–9
107. Chauncy, *History of the Sufferings*, p.71: Chauncy, *Historia*, p.120
108. Lasocki, pp.3–11,17–21,93–4
109. Extract from Patent Roll given in Davies, p.338
110. *ODNB*, *sub* Parr: TNA, C4/8/1
111. TNA, C4/8/1
112. Knowles and Grimes, p.75,75n
113. Hope 1925, p.168: Barber and Thomas, pp.39–40
114. TNA, SC12/36/26; transcript in Knowles and Grimes, pp.84–5
115. Hope 1925, p.43
116. Knowles and Grimes, p.79

117. Hope 1925, p.187
118. S&P, correspondence in box 36: MoL, WFG/S/WFG56/Cor2
119. Knowles and Grimes, Figs 4,6,7
120. *Ibid.*, pp.80–2, and folding plan
121. *OED*
122. TNA, SC12/25/55, cited in Thompson, p.195
123. *L & P*, vol.18, pt 1, p.548
124. Streitberger 1 and 2
125. Streitberger 2, pp.18,430–2
126. GEC
127. TNA, C4/8/1
128. Streitberger 2, p.173
129. LM/48: Streitberger 1, p.188
130. Streitberger 1, pp.189–90
131. LM/11
132. LM/8/2; LM/14
133. Streitberger 1, p.189
134. LM/6, calendared in HMC, *7th Report, Appendix*, 1879
135. Streitberger 2, p.174
136. LM/14, f.19
137. LM/14
138. LM/24/1,11
139. Barber and Thomas, pp.56–7
140. TNA, SC12/25/55
141. LM/14
142. LM/8/1; LM/14; LM24/1
143. Streitberger 2, pp.162–3
144. *L & P*, vol.20, pt 1, p.213: Streitberger 2, p.165
145. TNA, C66/752, m.6, calendared in *L & P*, vol.20, pt 1, p.303: LMA, ACC/1876/D1/4
146. LM1

CHAPTER II (pp.39–58)

Howard House

1. *L & P*, vol.20, pt 1, p.303: TNA, C4/8/1: *Returns of Aliens*, vol.3, p.325, cited in Lasocki, p.20: TNA, SC8/332/15738 (undated; probably not the original complaint relating to C4/8/1)
2. TNA, C4/8/1
3. John Gough Nichols (ed.), *Chronicle of the Grey Friars of London*, Camden Society, old series, vol.53, 1852, p.49
4. John Stow, *A Survey of London*, ed. C. L. Kingsford, vol.1, 1908, p.142
5. Barber and Thomas, p.77
6. TNA, LR15/158: *ODNB*
7. *ODNB*: Barrett L. Beer, *Northumberland: The Political Career of John Dudley, Earl of Warwick and Duke of Northumberland*, 1974, ch. VII: TNA, E117/14/78; E154/2/39; LR2/119,120: Davies, p.117
8. Dudley, Lord North, *Some Notes Concerning the Life of Edward, Lord North*, 1658, pp.33–4
9. *VCH*, *Cambridgeshire and the Isle of Ely*, vol.10, 2002, pp.65–6
10. *L & P*, vol.18, pt 1: TNA, SC12/26/60: Davies, p. 115n, identifies the Wilkinson/Leland property as part of what became Rutland House
11. KSRL, SC.MS240A.785
12. TNA, PROB/11/48; C54/673/51; E210/10394,10414, 10431,10445,10496,10518: LMA, ACC/1876/D1/8
13. LMA, ACC/1876/D1/181
14. TNA, SC6/PHIL&MARY/192: for development of this area see *SoL*, vol.XLVI, chs X–XII
15. LMA, ACC/1876/D1/10: TNA, E178/1396
16. Thomas Allen, *The History and Antiquities of the Parish of Lambeth*, 1826, pp.340–1: *SoL*, vol.XXIII, p.137: Bridget Cherry and Nikolaus Pevsner, *London 2: South*, 1983, p.337: TNA, C54/559
17. John Schofield and Richard Lea, *Holy Trinity Priory, Aldgate, City of London: An Archaeological Reconstruction and History*, 2005, pp.164–9: John Schofield, 'Building in Religious Precincts in London at the Dissolution and After', in Roberta Gilchrist and Harold Mytum (eds), *Advances in Monastic Archaeology*, 1993, pp.29,33: John Schofield, *Medieval London Houses*, 1995, pp.155–7: TNA, E41/12
18. For the Norwich palace and the other Howard houses in Norwich, see Ernest A. Kent, 'The Houses of the Dukes of Norfolk in Norwich', *Norfolk Archaeology*, vol.24, 1930, pp.73–87, and Williams
19. Williams, pp.87,90
20. Quoted in Taylor, p.174
21. David Starkey, *Elizabeth: Apprenticeship*, 2000, p.254, and in Susan Doran (ed.), *Elizabeth: The Exhibition at the National Maritime Museum*, 2003, p.6: Williams, p.122
22. TNA, E164/45
23. Williams, pp.116–19: George Dacre's death is described in Cumbria RO, D/LONS/L1/1/4
24. Copy in BL, Cotton, MSS, Titus XIII, f.176
25. Williams, p.222
26. Stephen Alford, *Burghley: William Cecil at the Court of Elizabeth I*, 2008, p.158
27. Williams, pp.120–1
28. BL, Harley MS 787, ff.118–20, as quoted in Pollen and MacMahon, pp.9–10
29. The earliest receiver-general's accounts are in TNA, SC6/ELIZI/3354, and cover the period February 1571 to March 1572; SC6/ELIZI/3355 is a half-year's account for 1574. A set covering 1572–86, with some duplicates, is in ACA, MSS, A/1055–1057, and another set from 1572–9 is in CUL, Dd.13.8. John Blennerhasset was receiver-general until his death in 1573. He was succeeded by William Cantrell and then, from 1583, William Necton
30. Davies, p.313: RCHME 1925, p.24
31. John Martin Robinson, *The Dukes of Norfolk: A Quincentennial History*, 1982, p.56
32. Nikolaus Pevsner, rev. Enid Radcliffe, *Suffolk*, 1975, pp.217–18
33. G. F. Nott (ed.), *The Works of Henry Howard, Earl of Surrey and of Sir Thomas Wyatt the Elder*, 1815, vol.1, pp.lx–lxi: Thomas Kitson Cromwell, *Excursions in the County of Norfolk*, 1818, p.94: Edwin Casady, *Henry Howard, Earl of Surrey*, 1938, p.107: Greg Walker, *Writing under Tyranny: English Literature and the Henrician Reformation*, 2005, p.383: W. A. Sessions, *Henry Howard, the Poet Earl of Surrey: A Life*, 1999, pp.170–2: Jessie Childs, *Henry VIII's Last Victim: The Life and Times of Henry Howard, Earl of Surrey*, 2006, pp.222–3. See also inventories in TNA, LR2/115,117
34. Receiver-general's accounts (see ref. 29)

35. *Salisbury*, Pt 1, 1883, p.570: TNA, E164/16/4
36. Williams, p.196
37. Davies, p.130
38. See Geoffrey Parker, 'The Place of Tudor England in the Messianic Vision of Philip II of Spain', *Transactions of the Royal Historical Society*, 6th series, no.12, 2003, pp.192–3,215–17; Alford, ch.12; Robert Hutchinson, *House of Treason: The Rise and Fall of a Tudor Dynasty*, 2009, ch. 9
39. Davies, p.139: Murdin, p.112
40. Edwards, p.186
41. Murdin, p.121, quoted in Davies, p.137
42. Davies, p.137
43. *Ibid.*, pp.130,138
44. Murdin, p.67
45. Alford, p.173
46. Williams, p.212: Davies, p.140
47. Williams, p.218
48. Murdin, p.89: *Salisbury*, Pt 6, 1895, no.18: Edwards, pp.172,181,202
49. Transcript as in Davies, p.141
50. Murdin, p.107
51. *Ibid.*, p.114
52. BL, Lansdowne MS 45, f.212v: Edwards, pp.200–1
53. TNA, E164/45: Williams, pp.156–7: Davies, p.126
54. *Salisbury*, Pt 1, 1883, p.517
55. Davies, pp.134–5,147: Williams, p.223
56. Quoted in Davies, p.134
57. ACA, MSS, G1/7, 'Fees graunted by letters pattents': receiver-general's accounts (see ref. 29): *Salisbury*, Pt 1, 1883, pp.517,523
58. TNA, E164/45: Davies, p.135
59. BL, Egerton MS 2074, f.42: TNA, LR1/42: ACA, MSS, A1057: Davies, p.152: LMA, ACC/1876/P/1/11
60. TNA, E178/1396
61. Williams, pp.120,122, 215–16
62. Northumberland RO, BMO/D1/Elizabeth/7B: BL, Stowe MS 164
63. *ODNB*: Sessions, p.143
64. e.g. TNA, SP46/39/f.1, letter of 1593 to William Butler 'dwelling in Charterhowse'. The name Butler appears in the priory's churchyard rental list of 1538–9 (TNA, SC12/26/60), and may be the family of Richard Butler, the London grocer whose daughter North married about 1561 (GEC)
65. Davies, p.145n
66. *Ibid.*, pp.153–4,342–3: LMA, ACC/1876/D/1/12: LMA, C54/1751
67. *ODNB*: Pollen and MacMahon, pp.18–19: Sessions, pp.366–8
68. LMA, ACC446/EF/25/11
69. Staffs RO, D(W) 1734/2/7/27
70. *ODNB*: GEC
71. TNA, SP46/34, f.105
72. Davies, p.147: *Calendar of State Papers, Foreign, 1577–1578*, pp.1,68: BL, Cotton MSS, Titus B VII, f.235
73. *CSPD, Edward, Mary and Elizabeth, 1847–80*, 1856, vol.98, p.10, cited in Hendriks, pp.249–50: Davies, pp.147–50
74. *Salisbury*, Pt 4, 1892, p.578
75. BL, Cotton MSS, Titus B VII, f.235
76. J. G. Elzinga, 'Philip Howard', *ODNB*
77. MS at Arundel Castle, cited in Davies, pp.143–4
78. BL, Egerton MS 2074, f.46
79. Pollen and MacMahon, pp.43–5
80. *Ibid.*, p.318
81. *Ibid.*, pp.256,350–1; J. G. Elzinga (*ODNB*) says that he was received into the church by Weston at Arundel Castle
82. BL, Egerton MS 2074, f.22: *ODNB*
83. Martin Marprelate, *Oh Read Over Dr John Bridges: The Epistle*, Oct 1588: *ODNB*: Pollen and MacMahon, p.319, assume that the Marprelate claim referred to a supposed press under the countess's patronage
84. BL, Stowe MS 164, f.46
85. Pollen and MacMahon, pp.18–19
86. *ODNB*: BL, Egerton MS 2074, f.44
87. TNA, E164/45; LR2/107
88. Norfolk RO, 21509/25 (undated, late 1580s)
89. Williams, p.121
90. CUL, Buxton Papers, box 59/14: *ODNB*
91. TNA, E164/45: Richard Newcourt, map of London, 1658: Bodl., MS Tanner 161, f.50
92. *ODNB*
93. BL, Lansdowne MS 45, f.213r
94. Davies, p.151: BL, Lansdowne MS 45, f.196r
95. TNA, PROB11/48/ff.49–55: TNA, C3/485/27
96. Lord Aberdare, *The Willis Faber Book of Tennis and Rackets*, 1980, p.41
97. Williams, p.44: CUL, Dd.13.8, f.16v
98. TNA, E164/45
99. *Ibid.*
100. G. C. Williamson, *George, Third Earl of Cumberland (1558–1605)*, 1920, p.132: Richard T. Spence, *The Privateering Earl*, 1995, p.119
101. Davies, pp.153–4; the letter is quoted more fully in Williamson, p.138
102. See Bushby, p.156, and BL, Lansdowne MS 82/18
103. *Lives of Lady Anne Clifford ... and of her Parents Summarized by Herself. Printed from the Harley MS. 6177*, 1916, p.46: *ODNB*
104. *Salisbury*, Pt 6, 1895, p.257; Pt 13, 1915, p.597: LMA, ACC/1876/D/1/11
105. BL, Lansdowne MS 82, f.40: *Lives of Lady Anne Clifford*, p.20: Spence, p.133
106. Royal College of Physicians, Annals (TS translation from original Latin), 22 Dec 1598, 7 Aug 1600: Francis W. Steer, 'Lord Lumley's Benefaction to the College of Physicians', in *Medical History*, vol.2, 1958, pp.298–305
107. Extract from Land Revenue Enrolments, vol.45, f.B18, Patent Roll no.1564, in Davies, pp.342–3
108. Sarah Williams (ed.), *Letters Written by John Chamberlain During the Reign of Queen Elizabeth*, Camden Society, 1861, p.174
109. Quoted in John Nichols, *The Progresses, Processions, and Magnificent Festivities of King James the First*, 1828, vol.2, p.114: *CSPD, 1603–1610*, p.23: LMA, ACC/1876/D/1/12: TNA, C54/1751
110. Alford, p.251
111. East Kent Archives Centre, NR/CPW/114: Colvin 1996, p.540: Maurice Howard, *The Building of Elizabethan and Jacobean England*, 2007, pp.151–5
112. CM, G/2/1, 10 Dec. 1613, 19 July 1614: LMA, ACC/1876/F/9/30
113. *Salisbury*, Pt 19, 1965, pp.280–1: *ODNB*

114. HMC, *Marquess of Downshire*, vol.3, 1938, pp.271,283,286: *CSPD, 1611–1618*, p.127
115. LMA, ACC/1876/AR/3/9b
116. R. E. Howard et al., 'Tree-ring Analysis of Timbers from the Great Hall of Charterhouse...', University of Nottingham, 1997, copy in Survey of London archive
117. Barber and Thomas, pp.77–8
118. TNA, E164/45
119. LMA, ACC/1876/F/9/30; /F/9/48, bk 9

CHAPTER III (pp.59–85)

Sutton's Hospital

1. *ODNB*: H. R. Trevor-Roper, 'The Bishopric of Durham and the Capitalist Reformation', *Durham Research Review*, vol.18, 1967: Neal R. Shipley, 'Thomas Sutton: Tudor-Stuart Moneylender', *Business History Review*, vol.50, 1976, p.459
2. LMA, ACC/1876/F/6/8–10,12
3. Neal R. Shipley, '"Full Hand and Worthy Purposes": the Foundation of Charterhouse, 1610–1616', *Guildhall Studies in London History*, vol.1, 1975, pp.230–7
4. LMA, ACC/1876/F/3/5/2/54
5. LMA, ACC/1876/D1/13; /G/1/1/1
6. Colvin 1996, p.227
7. LMA, ACC/1876/F/3/2/46; /F/3/5/2/56; /F/9/31
8. Bodl., MS Tanner 161, ff.49v–50: William Le Hardy (ed.), *County of Middlesex: Calendar to the Sessions Records, new series, Volume I 1612–1614*, 1935, p.56
9. BL, Lansdowne MS 1189, ff.14v–15
10. Colvin 1982, pp.772–7: Bearcroft, pp.118–22: Shipley, '"Full Hand and Worthy Purposes"', p.248
11. Danby Pickering, *The Statutes at Large*, vol.7, 1763, pp.43–6: James F. Larkin and Paul L. Hughes (eds), *Stuart Royal Proclamations, Volume I, Royal Proclamations of King James I 1603–1625*, 1973, pp.118–21
12. Quoted in Hale 1854, p.17
13. James Spedding, *The Letters and the Life of Francis Bacon*, vol.4, 1868, pp.249–54. There are copies of Bacon's report in LMA, ACC/1876/G/3/1 and BL, Stowe MS 151. Aileen Reid and Robert Mainura (eds), *Edward Alleyn: Elizabethan Actor, Jacobean Gentleman*, 1994, p.25
14. Larkin and Hughes, p.346
15. Hale 1854, pp.6–7, 11, 16
16. Davies, p.190
17. *SoL*, monograph 7, *East Acton Manor House*, 1921, pp.17,19
18. *Commons Journals, vol.I, 1547–1619*, pp.471,477,685, 736,817,895
19. CM, G/2/1, pp.2,35–8,45
20. Pickering, p.43
21. CM, G/2/1, 28 Dec 1615, 13 Oct 1617: *Charter, Acts of Parliament, and Governors' Statutes for the Foundation and Government of the Charterhouse*, 1832
22. CM, G/2/1, pp.7,14–16,45
23. D. Lupton, *London and the Countrey Carbonadoed and Quatred into Severall Characters*, 1632, p.61
24. CM, G/2/1, pp.9,53,353: *Charter, Acts and Statutes*, p.54
25. Hale 1854, pp.15–16,18
26. CM, AR/1/392; AR/5/18b: LMA, ACC/1876/ AR/1/249–251
27. The painting was destroyed by accident in 1938 during transit. See Lee MacCormick Edwards, *Herkomer: A Victorian Artist*, 1999, p.146; ill. on p.78
28. Davies, p.231: Statutory Instruments, 1983 no.588, *The Charities (Sutton's Hospital in Charterhouse) Order 1983*, p.7
29. *The Works of the Most Reverend Father in God, William Laud, D.D.*, vol.3, 1853, pp.154–5; vol.6, pt 1, 1857, pp.1–4: William B. Bidwell and Maija Jansson (eds), *Proceedings in Parliament 1626, Volume II: House of Commons*, 1992, p.20
30. HMC, *Records of the City of Exeter*, 1916, p.97
31. LMA, ACC/1876/AR/1/22; /F/9/40/1,2,8–13;/G/6/1, ff.279–80; /AR/3/14a,15a,17a,19a
32. LMA, ACC/1876/F/9/29,30
33. CM, G/2/1, p.1
34. LMA, ACC/1876/F/9/48, bk 1
35. LMA, ACC 1876/F/9/47: CM, G/2/1
36. LMA, ACC/1876/F/9/47–52
37. CM, G/2/1, p.28; PS/1/5, f.12
38. Lawrence Stone, 'The Building of Hatfield House', *Archaeological Journal*, vol.112, 1955, p.121: Colvin 1982, pp.33,113,257
39. LMA, ACC/1876/F/9/48, bk 6
40. LMA, ACC/1876/F/9/52
41. LMA, ACC/1876/AR/1/8: Roper, p.166
42. CM, G/2/1, p.135; MP/1/18: LMA, ACC/1876/F/9/48
43. John Newman, 'The Architectural Setting' in Nicholas Tyacke (ed.), *The History of the University of Oxford, Volume IV: Seventeenth-century Oxford*, 1997, p.145
44. LMA, ACC/1876/F/9/53, f.12v
45. LMA, ACC/1876/G/3/3, p.159
46. National Portrait Gallery, NPG D17138
47. LMA, ACC/1876/AR/3/71/4
48. LMA, ACC/1876/AR/7/16/1; /AR/7/17
49. LMA, ACC/1876/M/1/19
50. Bearcroft, p.147
51. SPAB, London, Charterhouse, file ii
52. LMA, ACC/1876/G/2/2, ff.105,111–12; /G/2/3, f.169v; /G/3/4, f.54
53. CM, G/2/3, ff.169v, 176v; G/2/4, p.366; G/2/8, pp.124–5,137–8,200
54. LMA, ACC/1876/G/2/7, p.84; /G/2/8, pp.316–18; /M/1/8
55. LMA, ACC/1876/G/2/6, pp.203–5; /D1/36,36a
56. See *SoL*, vol.XLVI, pp.286–7
57. CM, G/2/8, pp.458–9
58. Smythe, p.292
59. LMA, ACC/1876/AR/3/16a
60. LMA, ACC/1876/G/3/3, pp.41,43,52–3; /G/3/4, ff.59–60
61. Quick, p.25: CM, G/2/2, ff.166,168: LMA, ACC/1876/ G/3/4, ff.34,60
62. CM, G/2/2, ff.174,180,184v: LMA, ACC/1876/G/3/3, p.102
63. LMA, ACC/1876/G/3/3, f.361v: CM, G/2/3, f.108

64. CM, G/2/3, ff.99v–100,105v: LMA, ACC/1876/AR/3/37/1,2
65. LMA, ACC/1876/AR/3/37/3: Rupert Gunnis, *Dictionary of British Sculptors 1660–1851*, revised edn, n.d.
66. LMA, ACC/1876/MP/1/22,27
67. CM, AR/3/465: Radclyffe: Sewell, pp.104–5
68. Smythe, p.270
69. LMA, ACC/1876/AR/4/32, p.275
70. Radclyffe: View by Rudolph Ackermann, 1816
71. A. H. Tod, *Charterhouse*, 1900, p.15: Davies, ch.23: Quick, pp.42–8
72. *BN*, 11 Aug 1876, p.124: Radclyffe
73. Smythe, p.236: LMA, ACC/1876/AR/1/22; AR/3/10a, Lady Day 1629: Maurice Exwood and H. L. Lehmann (eds), *The Journal of William Schellinks' Travels in England, 1661–1663*, 1993, p.71
74. CM, G/2/3, ff.72v–3,84v,93: LMA, ACC/1876/AR/3/41/2; /46/1,4; /48/4; /50/4; /64/1; /65/2
75. *A true Pourtrait with a Brief Description of that Deplorable Fire of London*, 1666
76. LMA, ACC/1876/G/2/3, ff.74,77
77. Illustrated in Stephen Porter and Harriet Richardson, *The Charterhouse: A Guide*, 2000, p.22, and Stephen Porter, *The London Charterhouse*, 2009, Ill. 13
78. KSRL, SC, MS240A.798
79. CM, G/2/3, f.103; G/2/4, p.308: LMA, ACC/1876/G/3/3, p.230
80. Roper, pp.177–8: Davies, p.269: Wilmot and Streatfeild, pp.174–6
81. LMA, ACC/1876/AR/7/21/3; AR/3/464: Davies, p.269: Wilmot and Streatfeild, pp.174–6
82. Smythe, pp.261–2: Roper, p.174: Wilmot and Streatfeild, pp.49–51, plan on p.292
83. Percy M. Young, *A History of British Football*, 1968, pp.100, 101, 115n11, 133n1, 147
84. CM, G/2/10, p.26
85. *Household Words*, 12 June 1852, pp.286–91
86. Hale 1854
87. *Parliamentary Papers*, 1864, xx, 3288
88. CM, G/2/14, pp.228,238,252–3
89. Benson, vol.21, ff.24–5
90. See *SoL*, vol.XLVI, ch. X
91. CM, G/2/15, pp.130,141,400; G/2/16, pp.74–5; ECM, F, p.229: LMA, ACC/1876/AR/1/242,244–5
92. LMA, ACC/1876/G/4/19/1–3: CM, G/2/16, pp.74–6, 85: Benson, vol.21, f.28
93. Benson, vol.21, ff.28–9,30–1: CM, G/2/16, pp.141–2, 150–1,159
94. SPAB, London, Charterhouse, files i,ii: CM, G/2/16, pp.171,175: W. Calvert Watson, *The Charterhouse Bill: The Story of the Charterhouse*, 1886, reprinted from the *Clerkenwell Chronicle*. See also reports in *City Press* and 'The London Charterhouse', *English Illustrated Magazine*, vol.3, Apr 1886, p.497
95. SPAB, London, Charterhouse, file i
96. Hansard, *Commons Debates*, vol.305, 3rd series, 7 May 1886, cc.503,509,516,505
97. CM, G/2/16, pp.190,270,324,346,349,375: LMA, ACC/1876/AR/4/39; /AR/1/244–5,247
98. LMA, ACC/1876/AR/1/247; /6/13: CM, ECM, F, pp.337–8; G/2/17, pp.203,224,229,249,258,268–9,272
99. CM, G/2/17, pp.312,397,446; G/2/18, pp.15,22,67,180
100. CM, G/2/18, pp.289–93; AD/2/8, letter of D. W. H. Kirkaldy, 10 June 1984: S&P, undated TS, in box 36
101. CM, AOB, N, pp.184–5
102. CM, G/2/8, pp.459,484; /9, p.477: LMA, ACC/1876/D1/86; /MP/1/128
103. LMA, ACC/1876/D1/83–5: CM, CS/1/3, p.93
104. LMA/ACC/1876/G/3/5, f.68
105. LMA, ACC/1876/D1/114; /E/1/47
106. CM, G/2/10, pp.110–11; G/2/14, pp.24–5,38,46; ECM, F, p.106: LMA, ACC/1876/AR/4/34, p.532
107. LMA, ACC/1876/G/3/5, ff.68–9
108. CM, G/2/18; ECM, G, pp.168–70: TNA, IR37/102, pt 1
109. CM, AG/6/15–22
110. CM, B/1/2,4
111. CM, B/1/2: TNA, IR37/102, pt 4
112. S&P, correspondence in boxes 37,38,47: TNA, IR37/102, pts 1,3
113. CM, G/2/7, p.216: TNA, IR37/102, pt 2
114. CM, AG/6/23; B/1/5: *The Times*, 8 Dec 1956, pp.8,14: EH, AR/HB/2984
115. CM, G/2/19, pp.120,133–4,151,252; AG/6/24,25,28; B/1/3,10; AD/1/1: S&P, correspondence in box 47
116. CM, B/1/10, report, 4 May 1953: S&P, correspondence in box 29
117. S&P, correspondence in box 43

CHAPTER IV (pp.86–117)

The Chapel and Chapel Cloister Range

1. Knowles and Grimes, pp.43–45,47n5
2. 'The Ancient Buildings of the Charterhouse', *Journal of the London Society*, Dec 1951, pp.101–2: Knowles and Grimes, p.47n6
3. RCHME 1915, p.18: RCHME 1925, p.27
4. See conjectural outline plan of Howard House in Barber and Thomas, pp.74–5
5. Hope 1925, pp.44,58,91,158
6. Information supplied by Margaret Condon
7. Radclyffe
8. Andrew Saint and Richard Lea, 'St Helen Bishopsgate, City of London', EH, London Division, Historians' Report, 1993, par.4.4
9. Knowles and Grimes, p.47
10. CM, G/3/3a, p.174
11. CM, G/2/1, p.25
12. Hope 1925, pp.45,173
13. *Ibid.*, pp.161–2,192: a letter from the bishop himself on the same subject is transcribed in Hendriks, p.365, and Taylor, pp.57–8
14. TNA, E117/12/22; full transcript in Hope 1925, pp.184–92; abbreviated version in Davies, pp.326–9
15. Hale 1839, p.507
16. LMA, ACC/1876/G/3/4, f.60v
17. Colvin 1996, p.227: Malcolm Airs, 'Lawrence Shipway, Freemason', *Architectural History*, vol.27, 1984, pp.368–70
18. LMA, ACC/1876/F/9/48

19. Thomas Allen, *The History and Antiquities of London, Westminster, Southwark, and Parts Adjacent*, vol.4, 1829, pp.420–1
20. LMA, ACC/1876/F/9/48
21. See ch. III, ref. 27
22. LMA, ACC/1876/F/9/48, bk 1; /51, /53; /AR/1/10; /3/12a. The recently restored bell is illustrated in Stephen Porter, *Charterhouse: the official guide*, 2010, p.26
23. LMA, ACC/1876/G3/3
24. LMA, ACC/1876/AR/1/5/1; /7/8, Midsummer 1727: CM, G/2/8, p.33
25. CM, G/2/1, p.26: LMA, ACC/1876/AR/7/16/1
26. LMA, ACC/1876/F/9/53; /AR/1/22: CM, G/2/1, p.190
27. Henry Laverock Phillips, *Annals of the Worshipful Company of Joiners of the City of London*, 1915, p.118
28. LMA, ACC/1876/AR/1/22; /AR/3/7a, 10, 12 Sept, 8 Nov 1626; /AR/3/25; /G/2/2, f.50v; /G/3/2, ff.48v–9
29. John Newman, 'The Architectural Setting', in Nicholas Tyacke (ed.), *The History of the University of Oxford, Volume IV: Seventeenth-century Oxford*, 1997, pp.164–9
30. LMA, ACC/1876/AR/3/17a
31. [John White], *The First Century of Scandalous, Malignant Priests...*,1643, p.5: LMA, ACC/1876/AR/1/44a; /AR/3/25; /G/3/3, p.252
32. Bodl., MS Gough London 11, f.49
33. LMA, ACC/1876/AR/7/8; /G/3/3, p.241
34. CM, G/2/3, f.36: LMA, ACC/1876/AR/3/30/Lady Day 1662: information supplied by David Baldwin: Andrew Ashbee (ed.), *Lists of Payments of the King's Musick in the Reign of Charles II (1660–1685)*, 1981, pp.2,5,6,60
35. Jonathan Keates, *Purcell*, 1995, pp.72–3: Nigel Fortune, 'Purcell: The Domestic Sacred Music', in F. W. Sternfeld, Nigel Fortune and Edward Olleson (eds), *Essays on Opera and English Music*, 1975, pp.63–5: Stephen Porter, 'Composer in Residence: Henry Purcell and the Charterhouse', *Musical Times*, vol.139, 1998, pp.14–17
36. Account based on LMA, ACC/1876/G/2/4, p.264; /G/3/3a, pp.174–5,186–7; /G/3/4, f.115; /AR/7/7,8; /3/90
37. LMA, ACC/1876/G/3/3a, p.174
38. *Ibid.*
39. LMA, ACC/1876/AR/7/15/3: Peter Williams, *A New History of the Organ*, 1980, pp.138–9
40. LMA, ACC/1876/MP/1/23; /AR/7/37; /AG/4/17, p.19: CM, AR/3/465: *Post Office Directory*
41. LMA, ACC/1876/AG/3/10, f.24; /G/2/9, p.328; /AR/7/39/3
42. CM, AR/3/473, pp.192,224: LMA, ACC/1876/AR/7/45/2,3: Davies, p.272
43. CM, G/2/11, p.177: LMA, ACC/1876/AR/7/61; /4/31, p.512
44. LMA, ACC/1876/E/1/50
45. CM, G/2/11, p.176: LMA, ACC/1876/AR/4/31, p.540
46. LMA, ACC/1876/AR/7/61; /AR/4/32, p.44; /E/1/50; /F/9/48
47. Smythe, p.273: LMA, ACC/1876/MP/1/128,132; /E/1/50
48. LMA, ACC/1876/AR/7/61
49. CM, AG/4/23/8
50. MTC, vol.25, p.434: C. H. Reilly, *Scaffolding in the Sky*, 1938, p.21
51. CM, AG/4/8
52. *BN*, 5 Nov 1875, p.519: CM, G/2/15, p.267; AG/4/23/9
53. CM, G/2/20, pp.345,371,375,378,381
54. CM, G/2/11, p.217; Q, p.445; R, p.327; AG/4/3; AG/5/20,21: LMA, ACC/1876/D1/60a; /M/4/4–5: Royal Institute of British Architects, DB/40/1
55. *The Times*, 9 June 1941, p.2a
56. S&P, contract and reports in boxes 45,47: CM, G/2/18, pp.423,434
57. S&P, report and contract in boxes 36,45: Knowles and Grimes, pp.47–8
58. LMA, ACC/1876/F/9/48,51,53; /AG/4/8
59. LMA, ACC/1876/AR/3/17a
60. LMA, ACC/1876/F/9/48,49; /AG/4/8: RCHME 1925, p.28
61. LMA, ACC/1876/AR/3/17a, 28 July 1636. The reredos, its context and possible sources are discussed in Stephen Porter and Adam White, 'John Colt and the Charterhouse Chapel', *Architectural History*, vol.44, 2001, pp.228–36
62. LMA, ACC/1876/AR/3/17a,28c
63. LMA, ACC/1876/AR/3/18a
64. CM, G/2/20
65. LMA, ACC/1876/F/9/48, bks 16,18; /AR/4/32, p.10; /AR/7/59: Radclyffe: information supplied by Dr Michael Kerney
66. Martin Harrison, *Victorian Stained Glass*, 1980, pp.35–6
67. CM, AG/4/22/6; /4/8: Radclyffe: Roper, p.145: *Ecclesiologist*, vol.2, 1846, p.163; vol.5, p.208: LMA, ACC/1876/AG/04/17
68. *Ecclesiologist*, vol.5, new series vol.2, no.10, Apr 1846, pp.163,208
69. Roper, pp.142–3
70. Information supplied by Dr Michael Kerney: LMA, ACC/1876/AG/4/17, pp.31–2: S&P, correspondence in box 39
71. LMA, ACC/1876/G/5/105/2: CM, G/2/5, p.5
72. J. L. Smith-Dampier, *Carthusian Worthies*, 1940, p.22
73. CM, G/2/1, p.211
74. LMA, ACC/1876/E/1/50: Radclyffe
75. LMA, ACC/1876/F/9/1
76. Transcribed in J. P. Malcolm, *Londinium Redivivum*, vol.1, 1802, pp.411–12
77. Smythe, p.222: W. L. Spiers (ed.), *The Notebook and Account Book of Nicholas Stone*, Walpole Society, vol.7, 1919, pp.40–1: LMA, ACC/1876/F/9/1: Davies, p.214, mentions the finding of Stone's original design, showing Sutton in full armour
78. LMA, ACC/1876/F/9/1
79. LMA, ACC/1876/AR/3/77; /AR/7/39/3; /G/2/60/13
80. British Museum, Archer collection, BM 1874-3-14-85: Charles Knight (ed.), *London*, vol.2, 1842, p.131
81. Carol Galvin, 'The Charterhouse, London: The Tomb of Thomas Sutton', 2001 (report for Sutton's Hospital): S&P, correspondence, etc in boxes 33,40,41
82. Spiers, p.40
83. CM, PS/1/5, f.9

84. Stephen Porter, 'Francis Beaumont's Monument in Charterhouse Chapel and Elizabeth, Baroness Cramond as Patroness of Memorials in Early Stuart London', *Transactions of the London & Middlesex Archaeological Society*, vol.54, 2003
85. CM, G/2/6, p.128: LMA, ACC/1876/G/5/105/3
86. Davies, pp.309,350n: LMA, ACC/1876/G/3/4, f.112v; /AR/7/8, Christmas–Lady Day 1728
87. Bridget Cherry and Nikolaus Pevsner, *London 4: North*, 1998, p.619
88. RCHME 1915, p.9: RCHME 1925, pp.29 (plan),30
89. Wardle, p.239: Hendriks, plan between pp.242 and 243
90. *Analecta Bollandiana*, vol.14, p.281
91. Thompson, pp.494–5: Hope 1925, p.59: Knowles and Grimes, p.66; grave sites shown on folding plan at end
92. Wardle, p.237
93. LMA, ACC/1876/F/9/30
94. LMA, ACC/1876/F/9/48, bk 12
95. Hope 1925, p.vi
96. RCHME 1915, marginal annotation by Clapham, p.17: Hendriks, plan between pp.242 and 243
97. Knowles and Grimes, Plate IIB
98. LMA, ACC/1876/E/01/47; /MP/1/99
99. LMA, ACC/1876/AR/7/16/1; /AR/7/17
100. Wilmot and Streatfeild, p.40; sketch plan at end
101. RCHME 1925, p.27
102. CM, G/2/12, p.2: LMA, ACC/1876/AG/4/17; /AR/4/01, pp.329–33
103. *BN*, 25 May 1866, p.349
104. CM, G/3/5; AG/4/22/3: *B*, 19 Nov 1864, p.850: *BN*, 12 Oct 1866, p.685

CHAPTER V (pp.118–125)

Wash-house Court

1. R. E. Howard et al., 'Tree-ring analysis of timbers from Charterhouse, Charterhouse Square, London', University of Nottingham, 1996, copy in Survey of London archive
2. Barber and Thomas, p.34
3. *Ibid.*, pp.34–5
4. BL, Cotton MSS, Cleopatra E.iv, f.42
5. Hope 1925, p.126
6. LMA, ACC/1876/F/9/48
7. Roper, p.167
8. Davies, p.315: RCHME 1925, p.29
9. Wardle, p.240: Hendriks, plan between pp.242 and 243
10. BL, Cotton MSS, Cleopatra E.iv, f.42
11. RCHME 1915, p.6
12. Davies, p.85n
13. LMA, ACC/1876/F/9/48
14. TNA, E164/45
15. LMA, ACC/1876/M2/5; /D1/36a: CM, G/2/8, p.412; AR/3/458, ff.40–1
16. Radclyffe: Davies, p.83: Roper, p.168
17. Roper, p.167
18. e.g. in E. M. Jameson, *Charterhouse*, 1937, p.4
19. See, e.g., C. R. B. Barrett, *Charterhouse 1611–1895 in Pen and Ink*, caption to 'Old Buildings'
20. Roper, p.167
21. Hale 1869, p.328
22. Davies, pp.84–5: Thompson, p.76: Hendriks, p.272: Champneys: Hale 1839, p.510: Knowles and Grimes, p.32n: Barber and Thomas, p.38: James P. S. Thomson, *The Charterhouse Magazine*, 23 Dec 2008
23. Thomson
24. CM, G/2/11, pp.30,178: LMA, ACC/1876/E/01/47; /MP/1/25,27
25. LMA, ACC/1876/AG/4/17: *Architect*, 31 Aug 1872, p.123
26. CM, G/2/16, pp.342,346,349; AG/5/33; Vouchers, Sept 1911–March 1912
27. S&P, boxes 44,45,47
28. CM, Bricklayer's accounts, Aug–Nov 1864; AG/4/22/1
29. S&P, box 28, Seely and Paget to Costains, 18 Aug 1949
30. CM, G/2/19, pp.183,193: S&P, boxes 45, 47
31. LMA, ACC/1876/D1/19; /AR/7/20/1: CM, G/2/6, pp.113–14,185,189
32. S&P, letter of 16 Feb 1950 in box 47

CHAPTER VI (pp.126–152)

Master's Court

1. Knowles and Grimes, pp.32,65
2. LMA, ACC/1876/AR/7/15/1,2; /16/1; /AG/4/2/4
3. LMA, ACC/1876/AR/1/320; /AR/7/17, 1758–9: TNA, IR37/102, pt 3
4. LMA, ACC/1876/AG/04/02/4
5. CM, G/2/8, p.412; AR/3/458, ff.40–1
6. CM, G/2/16, p.375: LMA, ACC/1876/MP/1/74a–b
7. S&P, box 43, 6 May 1953
8. LMA, ACC/1876/F/9/53
9. LMA, ACC/1876/F/9/52
10. LMA, ACC/1876/AR/7/15/3
11. Davies, p.316
12. Thomas Allen, *The History and Antiquities of London, Westminster, Southwark, and Parts Adjacent*, vol.4, 1829, p.424
13. LMA, ACC/1876/AR/3/112
14. RCHME 1925, pp.22,24
15. Haig Brown, p.21
16. CM, AG/4/5, Aug–Sept 1869; AG/4/7, pp.88,92–4
17. CM, G/2/2, ff.105,111–12; C, ff.13,29v: LMA, ACC/1876/G/3/3, p.265; /G/3/4, f.54
18. CM, G/2/4, p.366; E, pp.235–6,255–7; CS/1/3: LMA, ACC/1876/AG/4/2/1,2,5; /AR/7/20/2: Smythe, p.284
19. Information supplied by Dr Claire Gapper. See Claire Gapper, 'Plasterers and Plasterwork in City, Court and Country *c*.1530–*c*.1640', PhD thesis, University of London, 1998, ch.V
20. LMA, ACC/1876/AR/3/9a,12a
21. *Ibid.*
22. Ann Saunders and John Schofield (eds), *Tudor London: A Map and a View*, London Topographical Society Publication No. 159, 2001, pp.39,43–4,Fig. 7
23. *B*, 31 Mar 1906, p.352: Davies, p.313: Knowles and Grimes, p.38, n.33
24. R. E. Howard et al., 'Tree-ring Analysis of Timbers from the Great Hall of Charterhouse...' and 'Tree-ring analysis of timbers from Charterhouse...', University of Nottingham, 1997,1996, copies in Survey of London archive

25. S&P, correspondence in box 36
26. Knowles and Grimes, pp.38n,63n: Davies, pp.163,313: Hendriks, folding plan
27. Knowles and Grimes, p.39n
28. S&P, correspondence in box 36: Knowles and Grimes, p.38, n.33, and Plate VIA
29. LMA, ACC/1876/MP/1/076
30. Knowles and Grimes, folding plan at end
31. Hale 1839, p.510: Hale 1869, p.329
32. E. E. Harrison, *The History of Charterhouse and its Buildings*, reprinted from *Transactions of the Ancient Monuments Society*, vol.35, 1991, with revisions, p.16: Davies, p.313, attributed the oriel to Norfolk
33. Davies, pp.164,313
34. LMA, ACC/1876/AR/3/20a, p.35
35. John Newman, 'The Architectural Setting', in Nicholas Tyacke (ed.), *The History of the University of Oxford, Volume IV: Seventeenth-century Oxford*, 1997, pp.159,163
36. LMA, ACC/1876/AR/3/9a, 3 Apr, 3 June 1628
37. Howard et al., 1997
38. Radclyffe
39. RCHME 1925, plate 43
40. Howard et al., 1997
41. LMA, ACC/1876/F/9/48
42. John Hatcher, *The History of the British Coal Industry. Volume I: Before 1700*, 1993, p.416: TNA, IR37/102, pt 4: CM, undated letter from E. E. Harrison, Master of Charterhouse
43. LMA, ACC/1876/F/9/49
44. LMA, ACC/1876/AR/7/59
45. Davies, pp.163,313
46. LMA, ACC/1876/E/1/50: CM, B/1/7, 'The Roof of the Great Hall, Charterhouse'
47. S&P, contract reports in box 49
48. S&P, correspondence, etc in boxes 37,40,41
49. CM, G/2/19, pp.282–5
50. CM, G/2/19, pp.272–3; B/1/7, 'The Roof of the Great Hall, Charterhouse'; G/2/9, pp.272–4,282–5
51. S&P, Clerk of Works' reports in box 35
52. TNA, IR37/102, pt 1
53. *The Cabinet Maker and Complete House Furnisher*, 9 Aug 1957, p.393
54. CM, B/1/8
55. S&P, correspondence and accounts in boxes 34,37
56. LMA, ACC/1876/F/9/48
57. LMA, ACC/1876/AR/7/14; F/9/48
58. Howard et al., 1996
59. S&P, plan 343 and correspondence in box 34: CM, G/2/20, pp.124–5; AD/1/13
60. Knowles and Grimes, p.46
61. Wilmot and Streatfeild, p.17
62. RCHME 1925, p.25
63. LMA, ACC/1876/AG/04/17
64. S&P, correspondence in box 28
65. S&P, contracts in box 45
66. Davies, p.312
67. S&P, box 44, plans 99,100
68. Lord Mottistone, 'The Ancient Buildings of the London Charterhouse', *The Journal of the London Society*, 1951, pp.104–5
69. William Kent, *The Lost Treasures of London*, 1947, pp.76–7: TNA, IR37/102
70. See Mark Girouard, *Elizabethan Architecture: Its Rise and Fall, 1540–1640*, 2009, pp.371–3
71. LMA, ACC/1876/AR/3/10a
72. LMA, ACC/1876/D3/205,206a
73. Smythe, pp.268,277
74. LMA, ACC/1876/E/1/50
75. *Acts of the Privy Council, 1558–1570*, pp.5–9
76. LMA, ACC/1876/F/9/30,48: CM, G/2/3, f.72v
77. Smythe, p.265
78. LMA, ACC/1876/F/9/30: Bodl., MS Tanner 161, f.50
79. CM, G/2/4, p.345
80. LMA, ACC/1876/F/9/48, bk 14; /F/9/51,53: Smythe, p.265
81. Walter Thornbury, *Old and New London*, vol.2, 1897, p.393
82. LMA, ACC/1876/AR/3/7a, 46/3; /G/3/3, p.159
83. LMA, ACC/1876/AR/7/14/1
84. LMA, ACC/1876/3/21a, p.36
85. CM, G/2/4, pp.333–4: LMA, ACC/1876/AR/7/16/1: Radclyffe
86. CM, G/2/6, p.185: Highmore, p.656: Smythe, pp.264–5
87. Roper, pp.161–2: LMA, ACC/1876/E/1/47
88. LMA, ACC/1876/AR/7/57; /4/31, p.502: CM, G/2/11, p.177
89. LMA, ACC/1876/E/1/50; /AR/7/58
90. CM, G/2/8, p.171
91. S&P, reports and correspondence in boxes 29,33,35, 37,39,42
92. S&P, reports and correspondence in boxes 33,37
93. S&P, reports and correspondence in boxes 33,42
94. LMA, ACC/1876/F/9/30
95. CUL, Dd.13.8, f.16r: information from Dr Claire Gapper
96. Information supplied by T. Woodcock, Norroy and Ulster King of Arms. *ODNB* repeats the garbled version
97. S&P, correspondence in box 39
98. LMA, ACC/1876/AR/3/7a
99. Haig Brown, p.19: Smythe, p.265
100. Smythe, p.265: E. W. Brayley, *Londiniana; or, Reminiscences of the British Metropolis*, vol.2, 1829, p.218: Haig Brown, p.19: Wilmot and Streatfeild, p.289: RCHME 1925, p.26
101. RCHME 1925, p.26
102. Edward Croft-Murray, *Decorative Painting in England 1537–1837*, vol.1, 1962, pp.32–3,194–5: Lawrence Stone, 'The Building of Hatfield House', *Archaeological Journal*, vol.112, 1955, pp.119,122
103. Haig Brown, p.19

CHAPTER VII (pp.153–162)

The Norfolk Cloister and Old Schoolhouse

1. *Salisbury*, Pt 15, 1930, pp.318–19
2. For the development of galleries, and their typology, see Colvin 1982, pp.17–21; Mark Girouard, *Life in the English Country House: A Social and Architectural History*, 1978, pp.100–1; Rosalys Coope, 'The Gallery in England: Names and Meanings' and 'The "Long Gallery": Its Origins, Development, Use and Decoration', *Architectural History*, vols 27, 1984, pp.446–55; 29, 1986, pp.43–84: M. Howard, *The Early Tudor Country House: Architecture and Politics 1490–1550*, pp.88–95,116–18

3. Simon Thurley, *Hampton Court: A Social and Architectural History*, 2003, p.95
4. John Schofield, *Medieval London Houses*, 1994, pp.210–11: Coope 1986, p.57
5. Tim Tatton-Brown, *Lambeth Palace. A History of the Archbishops of Canterbury and their Houses*, 2000, pp.62,64–5,69
6. Coope 1986, p.56
7. Champneys, p.175n
8. See plan in R. W. Pilkington, *A Letter to the … Governors of the Charter-house, in Reply to Certain Allegations*, 1834
9. Hope 1925, pp.41–2,49: see also reconstructions in Barber and Thomas, pp.56–7
10. Knowles and Grimes, pp.65,67, Plate VIIID, folding plan at end
11. CUL, Dd.3.86(2); spelling modernized: see Williams, p.161, for another version of how the news came to him
12. CUL, Dd.13.8
13. TNA, E164/45: CM, G/2/3, ff.92,174,177; G/2/4, p.103: LMA, ACC/1876/AR/3/47/1; /AR/3/49/3; /AR/3/70/4
14. TNA, E164/45: LMA, ACC/1876/AR/1/12
15. TNA, E164/45: LMA, ACC/1876/F/9/48: Hale 1839, p.499: *BN*, 4 Mar 1870, p.177
16. LMA, ACC/1876/F/9/48
17. TNA, E164/45
18. Williams, p.44
19. TNA, HLG 126/1115
20. Roper, pp.171–2
21. LMA, ACC/1876/AR/7/14/3
22. Hale 1839, p.511: Davies, p.166
23. LMA, ACC/1876/MP/1/28a
24. LMA, ACC/1876/MP/1/20/A
25. *Ibid.*: Highmore, p.654: NMRC, AA67/1302
26. CM, G/2/1, p.109: LMA, ACC/1876/AR/1/12
27. CM, G/2/2, f.37v: LMA, ACC/1876/AR/3/22, Lady Day, pp.32,34–5,39; Midsummer, p.36; /G/3/2, f.40v
28. Davies, pp.269,294–6: Wilmot and Streatfeild, pp.74–6,96–8: Radclyffe
29. LMA, ACC/1876/AR/7/14/3: CM, AR/3/455; G/2/8, p.9
30. TNA, E164/45
31. LMA, ACC/1876/AR/7/76; /MP/1/25,32
32. LMA, ACC/1876/MP/1/68a: CM, G/2/10, pp.11,26; G/3/3a, p.208
33. LMA, ACC/1876/MP/1/28a
34. LMA, ACC/1876/E/1/56
35. LMA, ACC/1876/MP/1/20
36. Davies, pp.71,207–8,207n
37. Roper, p.171
38. CM, G/2/12, pp.13,22
39. MTC, vol.29, pp.114,116
40. *B*, 17 Apr 1875, p.354
41. MTC, vol.31, pp.159,165
42. CM, G/2/17, p.125
43. TNA, HLG126/1115/39: CM, G/3/8, pp.385–6
44. CM, G/2/20, pp.19,34,46
45. Williams, pp.45,91,159
46. TNA, LR1/42; E164/45: BL, Stowe MS 164, f.99r
47. LMA, ACC/1876/F/9/48
48. Davies, p.208
49. LMA, ACC/1876/F/9/48
50. LMA, ACC/1876/G/2/60/37: Davies, p.208
51. LMA, ACC/1876/G/2/60/28
52. Smythe, p.263
53. LMA, ACC/1876/AR/1/320; /MP/1/20/A; /MP/1/22h; /AG/4/2/3,4; /AG/4/6: CM, G/2/5, pp.293–4, 308,365: Smythe, pp.262–3
54. Illustrated in Quick, p.59
55. LMA, ACC/1876/MP/1/106,107
56. CM, G/2/13, pp.348,353–4,366–7; /14, pp.4,38: *B*, 21 June 1873, p.478
57. LMA, ACC/1876/AR/4/32, p.275; /07/61: Roper, p.170
58. *BN*, 11 Aug. 1876, p.124: Davies, p.209n

CHAPTER VIII (pp.163–168)

The Gatehouse and 17 Charterhouse Square

1. Maurice Chauncy, *The History of the Sufferings of Eighteen Carthusians in England*, 1890, p.59: GL, MS 01231
2. Hope 1925, pp.42–3: SBH, HA2/1, f.105
3. W. H. Bliss and J. A. Twemlow (eds), *Calendar of Papal Registers Relating to Great Britain and Ireland*, vol.5, 1904, p.256
4. Davies, p.61
5. Hope 1925, p.44
6. Knowles and Grimes, p.64
7. CM, G/2/19, pp.420–1
8. Davies, p.308
9. TNA, SC12/25/55, m.55
10. LM/8/1, etc: Staffs RO, D(W) 1734/2/7/27: TNA, E164/45
11. LMA, ACC/1876/F/9/48; /MP/1/48: CM G/2/1, pp.34,93,135
12. CM, G/2/1, pp.185,192,225–6,252,285–6: LMA, ACC/1876/AR/5, pp.1–2
13. LMA, ACC/1876/MP/1/48; /E/1/57: CM, G/2/12, pp.60,96
14. CM, AR/3/470
15. CM, G/3/4, ff.102v–103; G/2/4, pp.145–6,161,163; G/3/3a, pp.55,103–5: LMA, ACC/1876/D/1/23a
16. GL, MS 8674/6, p.290. GL, MS 8674/6, policy 32,090
17. Hendriks, p.269n: Davies, p.308
18. CM, CS/1/3: Radclyffe: Smythe, p.284
19. CM, ECM, G, pp.279–80; B/1/5
20. CM, G/2/17, p.121; Vouchers, 1907–8
21. LMA, ACC/1876/AR/7/15/1
22. CM, AR/3/473, p.450
23. Evidence of several plans: *The Pavior*, Dec 2009. The annexe is oddly absent from the block plan of 1835 (LMA, ACC/1876/MP01/32), but appears on the general plan published in *The Carthusian* in 1839, and there is nothing in its appearance to indicate that it is other than contemporary with the house. The corridor was in place by the time of George Perry's 1863 block plan (LMA, ACC/1876/MP/01/60)

CHAPTER IX (pp.169–176)

Pensioners' Court and Preacher's Court

1. J. L. Smith-Dampier, *Carthusian Worthies*, 1940, p.114
2. LMA, ACC/1876/AR/7/50
3. Hale 1854, p.17
4. CM, G3/3a, p.204: LMA, ACC/1876/MP/1/25b
5. LMA, ACC/1876/AR/7/45/3
6. CM, G/2/10, pp.91–2: LMA, ACC/1876/MP/1/28a: R. W. Pilkington, *A Letter to the ... Governors of the Charter-house, in Reply to Certain Allegations*, 1834
7. LMA, ACC/1876/MP/1/60
8. CM, AR/3/473
9. LMA, ACC/1876/AR/7/76: CM, G/2/10, pp.118,125
10. LMA, ACC/1876/AR/4/31, p.327
11. Colvin 1996, p.755
12. Roper, p.169
13. LMA, ACC/1876/AG/4/17, p.43: CM, Office files
14. CM, AR/3/473, p.302
15. CM, G/2/11, p.377: LMA, ACC/1876/AG/4/17, p.33
16. CM, G/2/10, p.522
17. LMA, ACC/1876/AR/7/76: CM, G/2/10, p.177
18. LMA, ACC/1876/AR/7/50
19. CM, G/2/10, pp.512–13
20. Pilkington
21. CM, G/2/10, p.268; AR/3/474, p.89, ECM, D, p.61
22. CM, ECM, D, p.213
23. CM, G/2/11, pp.30,109
24. Radclyffe
25. CM, G/2/11, pp.125–6,178–9
26. CM, G/2/11, pp.178–9; /12, p.375: LMA, ACC/1876/AG/4/17, p.26
27. LMA, ACC/1876/AG/4/17
28. CM, G/2/16, p.357; /17, pp.233,366,372
29. CM, G/2/18, p.382
30. CM, G/2/19, p.261; B/1/5,6,10
31. CM, G/2/19, pp.167–8,185,365–6,394; B/1/4,6: Tony Venison, 'A Garden in the Barbican', *CL*, 13 Sept 1979
32. CM, B/1/10
33. CM, ECM, G, pp.303–4; B/1/10
34. S&P, plans 299–306,312–17,337
35. S&P, boxes 34,42: CM, B/1/5
36. CM, B/1/10

CHAPTER X (pp.177–179)

Rutland House

1. Bushby, p.13
2. Richard Flecknoe's *Ariadne* (1654) is now more generally considered the first
3. L. W.[Lawrence Weaver], 'The Charterhouse, the residence of the Master & the Brethren', *CL*, 14 Sept 1912 (citing unidentified 'contemporary leases')
4. LMA, ACC/1876/D1/19
5. *Archaeologia*, vol.19, 1821, pp.286–7: Bushby, pp.77–8. The originals are in BL, Stowe MS 774
6. GEC: TNA, PROB11/97/6
7. Dudley North, *A Forest of Varieties/Exonerations*, 1645, p.118: Dale B. J. Randall, *Gentle Flame: The Life and Verse of Dudley, Fourth Lord North (1602–1677)*, 1983, p.14
8. North, p.121
9. *ODNB*: BL MSS, Add. 61,873, ff.15,16: HMC, *The Manuscripts of His Grace the Duke of Rutland*, vol.1, 1888, p.385, vol.4, 1901, pp.436,444,451,452,458,499: Belvoir Castle Muniments, Acc.513,795
10. Randall, p.14: CM, 'The Inventory of Charterhouse', 1608
11. KSRL, SC.MS240A.798
12. *Ibid.*: TNA, PROB11/163/6: Mary Anne Everett Green (ed.), *Calendar, of Committee for Compounding*, Pt 4, 1892, pp.2189,2735: LMA, ACC/1876/G/3/3, p.61
13. North, p.2
14. Belvoir Castle Muniments, Acc.69
15. LMA, ACC/1876/D1/64; MDR 1741/3/455
16. Smythe, p.290
17. BL, Lansdown MS 1171, illustrated in John Orrell, *The Theatres of Inigo Jones and John Webb*, 1985, p.70
18. TNA, C10/99/21; C33/217, f.137v; SP18/128/108: Curtis Price, 'The Siege of Rhodes' in Stanley Sadie, ed., *The New Grove Dictionary of Opera*, vol.4, 1992, pp.336–7: W. G. Keith, 'The Designs for the First Movable Scenery on the English Stage', *Burlington Magazine*, vol.25, 1915, p.32: Orrell, p.71
19. See *SoL*, vol.XLVI, pp.278–9
20. GL, MS 15,818, f.6: TNA, C10/235/22; PROB/11/459/7, f.55: *ODNB*
21. See *SoL*, vol.XLVI, pp.257–8

CHAPTER XI (pp.180–187)

Merchant Taylors' School

1. *Parliamentary Papers*, 1864 XX 3288, 15 Feb 1864
2. MTC, vols 25, pp.418–20; 26, p.403
3. MTC, vol.27, pp.34,95,173–4
4. *SoL*, vol.XLVI, p.390
5. MTC, vol.28, pp.32ff
6. *Ibid.*, pp.121–3
7. *The Times*, 7 Apr 1875, p.14a: MTC, vols 29, pp.141–9,188; 30, pp.3–5; 31, p.55: *B*, 21 June 1873, pp.478–9
8. *BN*, 9 Apr 1875, p.393
9. MTC, vol.31, p.71
10. MTC, vols 31, p.218; 40, pp.346–7
11. MTC, vols 31, pp.160,169; 32, p.54; 33, pp.252,264
12. *BN*, 9 Apr 1875, p.393
13. MTC, vol.33, pp.213–16,235,252
14. MTC, vols 32, pp.156–7; 33, p.110; 37, p.148
15. C. H. Reilly, *Scaffolding in the Sky*, 1938, pp.20–1
16. MTC, vol.34, pp.332,341
17. MTC, vol.35, pp.262,331–2,355,412
18. MTC, vols 35, p.335; 36, p.11; 37, pp.448,472; 38, p.167; 42, pp.200,237: DSR
19. MTC, vol.39, pp.20,30–1,80–2,96
20. MTC, vols 39, p.410; 46, p.477
21. MTC, vol.43, p.126
22. See *SoL*, vol.XLVI, pp.275–7

23. MTC, vols 46, pp.170,196,336,383,434,476; 47, p.215: DSR
24. MTC, vols 47, p.412; 49, p.5. Corporation of London RO, City Schools Committee Minute Book, vol. 2, pp.108–9,113: MTC, vol. 48, p.167

CHAPTER XII (pp.188–195)

Medical College of St Bartholomew's Hospital

1. Morris, pp.78,82,84–5: SBH, Dean's File 1: MTC, vol.48, pp.338,417–20
2. SBH, Dean's File 1; MS 20/1937–8, p.12: *St Bartholomew's Hospital Journal*, vol.43, Nov 1935, p.28: IBC
3. *St Bartholomew's Hospital Journal*, vol.43, p.30: information from Mr Nick Davie, Queen Mary and Westfield College
4. Morris, p.85: *St Bartholomew's Hospital Journal*, vol.43, pp.28,30,36: IBC
5. Morris, p.86: SBH, MS 30/1, pp.236,255; correspondence in Dean's File 32
6. SBH, MS 30/1, p.302; MS 30/2, pp.1–2,9–10, 16–19,22,40–2,89
7. SBH, MS 30/2, p.141; Dean's Files 31, 32: Morris, p.89
8. Morris, p.88: SBH, MS 30/2, pp.262–3,266,287–8: information supplied by Prof. James Malpas
9. SBH, MS 30/3, ff.6,25,31,196: IBC
10. SBH, MS 30/3, ff.48,53,68,75,121,226,269; 30/4, p.543: *Architect and Building News*, 29 May 1952, pp.620–9: Morris, p.91
11. SBH, MS 27/3, pp.26,162; MS 27/4, p.3
12. Knowles and Grimes, p.67
13. S&P, correspondence in box 40: CM, G/2/19, p.150: Royal Fine Art Commission, file 501: SBH, MS 30/3, ff.116,179
14. CM, account of Daniel Watney etc., 13 Feb 1952; Conveyance, 4 Apr 1952: SBH, MS 30/3, ff.111,225, 302,321,338,378. For Foresters' Hall and Foresters' Hall Place, see *SoL*, vol.XLVI, pp.390–2
15. SBH, MS 30/3, ff.245,283; MS 27/3, p.26; MS 20/1952–3, p.9
16. SBH, MS 27/3, pp.67,113,162; MS 30/4, p.868; MS 20/1964–5, p.11: IBC, NE 888
17. Alec Forshaw, *20th Century Buildings in Islington*, 2001, p.34
18. IBC: SBH, MS 27/5
19. SBH, MS 27/4, pp.26,77,92; MS 27/5: Morris, p.97
20. SBH, Medical College *Annual Reports*
21. SBH, MS 27/5: IBC: thornsettgroup.com: *Barts and The London Chronicle*, Spring 2006, pp.20–1: information from Mr Steve Wiles
22. *The Times*, 12 June 1868, p.9f; 27 July 1883, p.5g; Charles Boutell, *The Arts and the Artistic Manufactures of Denmark*, 1874, pp.41–2: information supplied by Anna Schram Vejlby of Ny Carlsberg Glyptotek, Copenhagen
23. SBH, SBHX8/2037/1
24. 'The Panther Hunter', in Peter Nørgaard Larsen and Sven Bjerkof (eds), *SMK Highlight*, Statens Museum for Kunst, Copenhagen, 2005: catalogue of Ny Carlsberg Glyptotek
25. Antoninus Liberalis, 'Collection of Metamorphoses', trans. in Stephen Trzaskoma, R. Scott Smith, Stephen Brunet and Thomas G. Palaima (eds), *Anthology of Classical Myth: Primary Sources in Translation*, Indianapolis, 2004, p.11

APPENDIX III (pp.256–264)

Howard House Inventory, 1583

1. *ODNB*
2. *VCH*, *Stafford*, vol.9, 2003, p.160

Index

Where subjects have multiple references, major references are in bold type